TOBIT

WISDOM COMMENTARY

Volume 15

Tobit

Michele Murray

Amy-Jill Levine
Volume Editor

Barbara E. Reid, OP
General Editor

A Michael Glazier Book

LITURGICAL PRESS

Collegeville, Minnesota

www.litpress.org

A Michael Glazier Book published by Liturgical Press

1   2   3   4   5   6   7   8   9

Library of Congress Cataloging-in-Publication Data

Names: Murray, Michele, author. | Levine, Amy-Jill, 1956– editor. | Reid, Barbara E., editor.
Title: Tobit / Michele Murray ; Amy-Jill Levine, volume editor ; Barbara E. Reid, OP, general editor.
Description: Collegeville, Minnesota : Liturgical Press, 2023. | Series: Wisdom commentary; volume 15 | Includes bibliographical references and index. | Summary: "This commentary on the book of Tobit provides a feminist interpretation of Scripture in serious, scholarly engagement with the whole text, not only those texts that explicitly mention women. It addresses not only issues of gender but also those of power, authority, ethnicity, racism, and classism"— Provided by publisher.
Identifiers: LCCN 2022054399 (print) | LCCN 2022054400 (ebook) | ISBN 9780814681145 (hardcover) | ISBN 9780814681398 (epub) | ISBN 9780814681398 (pdf) | ISBN 9780814669495 (pdf)
Subjects: LCSH: Bible. Tobit—Feminist criticism. | Bible. Tobit—Criticism, interpretation, etc.
Classification: LCC BS1725.52 .M87 2023 (print) | LCC BS1725.52 (ebook) | DDC 229/.22—dc23/eng/20230320
LC record available at https://lccn.loc.gov/2022054399
LC ebook record available at https://lccn.loc.gov/2022054400

To my mother, Lorie Murray, and my mother-in-law, Ruth Miller,
two of the most inspiring women I know.

Contents

Acknowledgments   ix

List of Abbreviations   xi

List of Contributors   xiii

Foreword: *"Tell It on the Mountain"*—or, *"And You Shall Tell Your Daughter [as Well]"*   xv
  Athalya Brenner-Idan

Editor's Introduction to Wisdom Commentary: *"She Is a Breath of the Power of God" (Wis 7:25)*   xix
  Barbara E. Reid, OP

Authors' Introduction: Setting the Scene   xxxix

Tobit 1–2   When Bad Things Happen to Good People   1

Tobit 3   When Your Husbands Keep Dying   55

Tobit 4   Living a Good Life   87

Tobit 5–6   How to Hire an Angel   107

Tobit 7–9   Ridding Your Life of a Demon in One Simple Step   131

Tobit 10   The Good Mother   171

Tobit 11   Sarah Arrives at Her New Home   183

Tobit 12   An Angel Is Revealed (to the Men)   195

Tobit 13–14   Restoration   207

Conclusion: Feminist Commentaries Are Not for the Faint
    of Heart   229

Works Cited   231

Index of Scripture References and Other Ancient Writings   257

Index of Subjects   265

Acknowledgments

Sometimes it takes a village to write a book. I am grateful to so many for their support:

- Bishop's University, in particular Principal Michael Goldbloom, for enabling me to take a year's leave while I was dean, during which I could truly focus on writing;

- Amy-Jill Levine, who drew from me work of which I am so proud;

- Miles Turnbull, for his support and friendship (over sips of port);

- The inspiring sisterhood of deans (and an associate vice-principal academic) with whom I've had the honor of working over the years at Bishop's University: Reena Atanasiadis, Marie-Josée Berger, Julie Desjardins, Claire Grogan, Corinne Haigh, Kerry Hull, and Francine Turmel.

- Justina Browne, for protecting my blocked one-day-per-week writing schedule over the years and holding down the dean's office so well;

- Monetta Gallichon, whose skillful administrative support has helped to see this project over the finish line;

- Laurel Thomson, for being a steadfast source of friendship, laughter, and wisdom;

- My beloved sister, Roz, five provinces away but close to my heart;

- Austen Metcalfe, my research assistant *par excellence* from the very beginning of this project;

- Linda Chaput, for being one of my most trusted soft places to fall;

- Anne-Christine Gervais, for her sage advice;

- Lisa Beckman and Obie, the best walking buddies ever;

- Marley, for his canine companionship and our contemplative walks, during which I thought a lot about Tobit;

and, most of all, my husband Daniel for being a feminist, and for loving me so well.

Abbreviations

ABD	*The Anchor Bible Dictionary*
AJSR	*Association for Jewish Studies Review*
AMD	Ancient Magic and Divination
AYBRL	Anchor Yale Bible Reference Library
BAR	*Biblical Archaeology Review*
Bib	*Biblica*
BibInt	Biblical Interpretation Series
BRev	*Bible Review*
CBQ	*Catholic Biblical Quarterly*
ChrCent	*The Christian Century*
ClAnt	*Classical Antiquity*
CIJ	*Corpus Inscriptionum Judaicarum*
DJD	Discoveries in the Judean Desert
DSD	*Dead Sea Discoveries*
EvT	*Evangelische Theologie*
FAT	Forschungen zum Alten Testament
FCB	Feminist Companion to the Bible
GBS	Guides to Biblical Scholarship
HTR	*Harvard Theological Review*
HTS	Harvard Theological Studies

HuffPost	*Huffington Post*
IFT	Introductions in Feminist Theology
JBL	*Journal of Biblical Literature*
JFSR	*Journal of Feminist Studies in Religion*
JPS	Jewish Publication Society
JQR	*Jewish Quarterly Review*
JR	*Journal of Religion*
JSem	*Journal for Semitics*
JSNT	*Journal for the Study of the New Testament*
JSOT	*Journal for the Study of the Old Testament*
JSOTSup	Journal for the Study of the Old Testament Supplement series
JSP	*Journal for the Study of the Pseudepigrapha*
LCL	Loeb Classical Library
LHBOTS	Library of Hebrew Bible/Old Testament Studies
NOAB	New Oxford Annotated Bible: New Revised Standard Version
NRSV	New Revised Standard Version
OBT	Overtures to Biblical Theology
PL	Patrologia Latina
RB	*Revue biblique*
RHPR	*Revue D'Histoire Et de Philosophie Religieuses*
SBL	Society of Biblical Literature
SymS	Symposium Series
TWOT	*Theological Wordbook of the Old Testament*. Edited by R. Laird Harris, Gleason L. Archer Jr., and Bruce K. Waltke. 2 vols. Chicago: Moody Press, 1980.
VAB	Vorderasiatische Bibliothek
VC	*Vigiliae christianae*
WCS	Wisdom Commentary series
ZPE	*Zeitschrift für Papyrologie und Epigra*
ZWT	*Zeitschrift für Wissenschaftliche Theologie*

Contributors

Elisabeth Cunningham works full time in the helping profession in Canada. A mother of three, she has developed a profound empathy for women navigating bereavement after being widowed in her forties.

EunHee Kang is a Korean feminist professor of Hebrew Bible who earned her doctorate from the Graduate Theological Union. She currently teaches in South Korea.

Gabriel Kwenga is originally from Kumba, Cameroon, and is an ordained minister in the Anglican Church of Canada. He studied religion at Bishop's University and is currently completing graduate studies at Atlantic School of Theology in Halifax, Nova Scotia, Canada.

Jse-Che Lam is a Chinese Canadian teacher of secondary school English and history based in Toronto. Her interests include origin stories, Canadian-produced documentaries, and teaching her niece and nephew the art of negotiating.

Francis Macatangay is adjunct professor of Sacred Scripture and theology at the University of St. Thomas School of Theology at St. Mary's Seminary in Houston, Texas. He also serves as pastor of St. Cecilia Catholic Church in Houston.

Tatum Tricarico is an American blind disability justice advocate, author, and speaker who is completing her Master of Divinity at Duke Divinity School. She can be found organizing and advocating on Instagram at @blind_person_in_area, and she works with organizations such as YO (youth organizing) Disabled and Proud and L'arche North Carolina to explore the connection between the disability justice movement and theology.

Foreword

"Tell It on the Mountain"—or, "And You Shall Tell Your Daughter [as Well]"

Athalya Brenner-Idan

Universiteit van Amsterdam/Tel Aviv University

What can Wisdom Commentary do to help, and for whom?
The commentary genre has always been privileged in biblical studies. Traditionally acclaimed commentary series, such as the International Critical Commentary, Old Testament and New Testament Library, Hermeneia, Anchor Bible, Eerdmans, and Word—to name but several—enjoy nearly automatic prestige, and the number of women authors who participate in those is relatively small by comparison to their growing number in the scholarly guild. There certainly are some volumes written by women in them, especially in recent decades. At this time, however, this does not reflect the situation on the ground. Further, size matters. In that sense, the sheer size of the Wisdom Commentary is essential. This also represents a considerable investment and the possibility of reaching a wider audience than those already "converted."

Expecting women scholars to deal especially or only with what are considered strictly "female" matters seems unwarranted. According to Audre Lorde, "The master's tools will never dismantle the master's house."[1] But this maxim is not relevant to our case. The point of this commentary is not to destroy but to attain greater participation in the interpretive dialogue about biblical texts. Women scholars may bring additional questions to the readerly agenda as well as fresh angles to existing issues. To assume that their questions are designed only to topple a certain male hegemony is not convincing.

At first I did ask myself: is this commentary series an addition to calm raw nerves, an embellishment to make upholding the old hierarchy palatable? Or is it indeed about becoming the Master? On second and third thoughts, however, I understood that becoming the Master is not what this is about. Knowledge is power. Since Foucault at the very least, this cannot be in dispute. Writing commentaries for biblical texts by feminist women and men for women and for men, of confessional as well as non-confessional convictions, will sabotage (hopefully) the established hierarchy but will not topple it. This is about an attempt to integrate more fully, to introduce another viewpoint, to become. What excites me about the Wisdom Commentary is that it is not offered as just an alternative supplanting or substituting for the dominant discourse.

These commentaries on biblical books will retain nonauthoritative, pluralistic viewpoints. And yes, once again, the weight of a dedicated series, to distinguish from collections of stand-alone volumes, will prove weightier.

That such an approach is especially important in the case of the Hebrew Bible/Old Testament is beyond doubt. Women of Judaism, Christianity, and also Islam have struggled to make it their own for centuries, even more than they have fought for the New Testament and the Qur'an. Every Hebrew Bible/Old Testament volume in this project is evidence that the day has arrived: it is now possible to read *all* the Jewish canonical books as a collection, for a collection they are, with guidance conceived of with the needs of women readers (not only men) as an integral inspiration and part thereof.

In my Jewish tradition, the main motivation for reciting the Haggadah, the ritual text recited yearly on Passover, the festival of liberation from

---

1. Audre Lorde, "The Master's Tools Will Never Dismantle the Master's House," in *Sister Outsider: Essays and Speeches* (Berkeley, CA: Crossing Press, 1984, 2007), 110–14. First delivered in the Second Sex Conference in New York, 1979.

bondage, is given as "And you shall tell your son" (from Exod 13:8). The knowledge and experience of past generations is thus transferred to the next, for constructing the present and the future. The ancient maxim is, literally, limited to a male audience. This series remolds the maxim into a new inclusive shape, which is of the utmost consequence: "And you shall tell your son" is extended to "And you shall tell your daughter [as well as your son]." Or, if you want, "Tell it on the mountain," for all to hear.

This is what it's all about.

Editor's Introduction to Wisdom Commentary

"She Is a Breath of the Power of God" (Wis 7:25)

Barbara E. Reid, OP

General Editor

Wisdom Commentary is the first series to offer detailed feminist interpretation of every book of the Bible. The fruit of collaborative work by an ecumenical and interreligious team of scholars, the volumes provide serious, scholarly engagement with the whole biblical text, not only those texts that explicitly mention women. The series is intended for clergy, teachers, ministers, and all serious students of the Bible. Designed to be both accessible and informed by the various approaches of biblical scholarship, it pays particular attention to the world in front of the text, that is, how the text is heard and appropriated. At the same time, this series aims to be faithful to the ancient text and its earliest audiences; thus the volumes also explicate the worlds behind the text and within it. While issues of gender are primary in this project, the volumes also address the intersecting issues of power, authority, ethnicity, race, class, and religious belief and practice. The fifty-eight volumes include the books regarded as canonical by Jews (i.e., the Tanakh); Protestants (the "Hebrew Bible" and the New Testament); and Roman Catholic, Anglican, and Eastern

Orthodox Communions (i.e., Tobit, Judith, 1 and 2 Maccabees, Wisdom of Solomon, Sirach/Ecclesiasticus, Baruch, including the Letter of Jeremiah, the additions to Esther, and Susanna and Bel and the Dragon in Daniel).

A Symphony of Diverse Voices

Included in the Wisdom Commentary series are voices from scholars of many different religious traditions, of diverse ages, differing sexual identities, and varying cultural, racial, ethnic, and social contexts. Some have been pioneers in feminist biblical interpretation; others are newer contributors from a younger generation. A further distinctive feature of this series is that each volume incorporates voices other than that of the lead author(s). These voices appear alongside the commentary of the lead author(s), in the grayscale inserts. At times, a contributor may offer an alternative interpretation or a critique of the position taken by the lead author(s). At other times, they may offer a complementary interpretation from a different cultural context or subject position. Occasionally, portions of previously published material bring in other views. The diverse voices are not intended to be contestants in a debate or a cacophony of discordant notes. The multiple voices reflect that there is no single definitive feminist interpretation of a text. In addition, they show the importance of subject position in the process of interpretation. In this regard, the Wisdom Commentary series takes inspiration from the Talmud and from *The Torah: A Women's Commentary* (ed. Tamara Cohn Eskenazi and Andrea L. Weiss; New York: URJ Press and Women of Reform Judaism, The Federation of Temple Sisterhoods, 2008), in which many voices, even conflicting ones, are included and not harmonized.

Contributors include biblical scholars, theologians, and readers of Scripture from outside the scholarly and religious guilds. At times, their comments pertain to a particular text. In some instances they address a theme or topic that arises from the text.

Another feature that highlights the collaborative nature of feminist biblical interpretation is that a number of the volumes have two lead authors who have worked in tandem from the inception of the project and whose voices interweave throughout the commentary.

Woman Wisdom

The title, Wisdom Commentary, reflects both the importance to feminists of the figure of Woman Wisdom in the Scriptures and the distinct wisdom that feminist women and men bring to the interpretive process. In the Scriptures, Woman Wisdom appears as "a breath of the power of God, and a pure emanation of the glory of the Almighty" (Wis 7:25), who was present and active in fashioning all that exists (Prov 8:22-31; Wis 8:6). She is a spirit who pervades and penetrates all things (Wis 7:22-23), and she provides guidance and nourishment at her all-inclusive table (Prov 9:1-5). In both postexilic biblical and nonbiblical Jewish sources, Woman Wisdom is often equated with Torah, e.g., Sirach 24:23-34; Baruch 3:9–4:4; 38:2; 46:4-5; 2 Baruch 48:33, 36; 4 Ezra 5:9-10; 13:55; 14:40; 1 Enoch 42.

The New Testament frequently portrays Jesus as Wisdom incarnate. He invites his followers, "take my yoke upon you and learn from me" (Matt 11:29), just as Ben Sira advises, "put your neck under her [Wisdom's] yoke and let your souls receive instruction" (Sir 51:26). Just as Wisdom experiences rejection (Prov 1:23-25; Sir 15:7-8; Wis 10:3; Bar 3:12), so too does Jesus (Mark 8:31; John 1:10-11). Only some accept his invitation to his all-inclusive banquet (Matt 22:1-14; Luke 14:15-24; compare Prov 1:20-21; 9:3-5). Yet, "wisdom is vindicated by her deeds" (Matt 11:19, speaking of Jesus and John the Baptist; in the Lukan parallel at 7:35 they are called "wisdom's children"). There are numerous parallels between what is said of Wisdom and of the *Logos* in the Prologue of the Fourth Gospel (John 1:1-18). These are only a few of many examples. This female embodiment of divine presence and power is an apt image to guide the work of this series.

Feminism

There are many different understandings of the term "feminism." The various meanings, aims, and methods have developed exponentially in recent decades. Feminism is a perspective and a movement that springs from a recognition of inequities toward women, and it advocates for changes in whatever structures prevent full flourishing of human beings and all creation. Three waves of feminism in the United States are commonly recognized. The first, arising in the mid-nineteenth century and lasting into the early twentieth, was sparked by women's efforts to be involved in the public sphere and to win the right to vote. In the 1960s and 1970s, the second wave focused on civil rights and equality for women. With the third wave, from the 1980s forward, came global feminism and the emphasis on the contextual nature of interpretation. Now a fourth wave is emerging, with a stronger emphasis on the intersectionality of women's concerns with those of other marginalized groups and the increased use of the internet as a platform for discussion and activism.[1] As feminism has matured, it has recognized that inequities based on gender are interwoven with power imbalances based on race, class, ethnicity, religion, sexual identity, physical ability, and a host of other social markers.

Feminist Women and Men

Men as well as nonbinary people who choose to identify with and partner with feminist women in the work of deconstructing systems of domination and building structures of equality are rightly regarded as feminists. Some men readily identify with experiences of women who are discriminated against on the basis of sex/gender, having themselves had comparable experiences; others who may not have faced direct discrimination or stereotyping recognize that inequity and problematic characterization still occur, and they seek correction. This series is pleased to include feminist men both as lead authors and as contributing voices.

Feminist Biblical Interpretation

Women interpreting the Bible from the lenses of their own experience is nothing new. Throughout the ages women have recounted the biblical stories, teaching them to their children and others, all the while interpreting them afresh for their time and circumstances.[2] Following is a very brief sketch of select foremothers who laid the groundwork for contemporary feminist biblical interpretation.

One of the earliest known Christian women who challenged patriarchal interpretations of Scripture was a consecrated virgin named Helie, who lived in the second century CE. When she refused to marry, her

---

1. See Martha Rampton, "Four Waves of Feminism" (October 25, 2015), at https://www.pacificu.edu/magazine/four-waves-feminism; and Ealasaid Munro, "Feminism: A Fourth Wave?," *Political Insight* (September 2013), https://journals.sagepub.com/doi/pdf/10.1111/2041-9066.12021.

2. For fuller treatments of this history, see chap. 7, "One Thousand Years of Feminist Bible Criticism," in Gerda Lerner, *Creation of Feminist Consciousness: From the Middle Ages to Eighteen-Seventy* (New York: Oxford University Press, 1993), 138–66; Susanne Scholz, "From the 'Woman's Bible' to the 'Women's Bible,' The History of Feminist Approaches to the Hebrew Bible," in *Introducing the Women's Hebrew Bible*, IFT 13 (New York: T&T Clark, 2007), 12–32; Marion Ann Taylor and Agnes Choi, eds., *Handbook of Women Biblical Interpreters: A Historical and Biographical Guide* (Grand Rapids: Baker Academic, 2012).

parents brought her before a judge, who quoted to her Paul's admonition, "It is better to marry than to be aflame with passion" (1 Cor 7:9). In response, Helie first acknowledges that this is what Scripture says, but then she retorts, "but not for everyone, that is, not for holy virgins."[3] She is one of the first to question the notion that a text has one meaning that is applicable in all situations.

A Jewish woman who also lived in the second century CE, Beruriah, is said to have had "profound knowledge of biblical exegesis and outstanding intelligence."[4] One story preserved in the Talmud (b. Ber. 10a) tells of how she challenged her husband, Rabbi Meir, when he prayed for the destruction of a sinner. Proffering an alternate interpretation, she argued that Psalm 104:35 advocated praying for the destruction of sin, not the sinner.

In medieval times the first written commentaries on Scripture from a critical feminist point of view emerge. While others may have been produced and passed on orally, they are for the most part lost to us now. Among the earliest preserved feminist writings are those of Hildegard of Bingen (1098–1179), German writer, mystic, and abbess of a Benedictine monastery. She reinterpreted the Genesis narratives in a way that presented women and men as complementary and interdependent. She frequently wrote about the Divine as feminine.[5] Along with other women mystics of the time, such as Julian of Norwich (1342–ca. 1416), she spoke authoritatively from her personal experiences of God's revelation in prayer.

In this era, women were also among the scribes who copied biblical manuscripts. Notable among them is Paula Dei Mansi of Verona, from a distinguished family of Jewish scribes. In 1288, she translated from Hebrew into Italian a collection of Bible commentaries written by her father and added her own explanations.[6]

Another pioneer, Christine de Pizan (1365–ca. 1430), was a French court writer and prolific poet. She used allegory and common sense

3. Madrid, Escorial MS, a II 9, f. 90 v., as cited in Lerner, *Feminist Consciousness*, 140.

4. See Judith R. Baskin, "Women and Post-Biblical Commentary," in *The Torah: A Women's Commentary*, ed. Tamara Cohn Eskenazi and Andrea L. Weiss (New York: URJ Press and Women of Reform Judaism, The Federation of Temple Sisterhoods, 2008), xlix–lv, at lii.

5. Hildegard of Bingen, *De Operatione Dei*, 1.4.100; PL 197:885bc, as cited in Lerner, *Feminist Consciousness*, 142–43. See also Barbara Newman, *Sister of Wisdom: St. Hildegard's Theology of the Feminine* (Berkeley: University of California Press, 1987).

6. Emily Taitz, Sondra Henry, Cheryl Tallan, eds., *JPS Guide to Jewish Women 600 B.C.E.–1900 C.E.* (Philadelphia: JPS, 2003), 110–11.

to subvert misogynist readings of Scripture and celebrated the accomplishments of female biblical figures to argue for women's active roles in building society.[7]

By the seventeenth century, there were women who asserted that the biblical text needs to be understood and interpreted in its historical context. For example, Rachel Speght (1597–ca. 1630), a Calvinist English poet, elaborates on the historical situation in first-century Corinth that prompted Paul to say, "It is well for a man not to touch a woman" (1 Cor 7:1). Her aim was to show that the biblical texts should not be applied in a literal fashion to all times and circumstances. Similarly, Margaret Fell (1614–1702), one of the founders of the Religious Society of Friends (Quakers) in Britain, addressed the Pauline prohibitions against women speaking in church by insisting that they do not have universal validity. Rather, they need to be understood in their historical context, as addressed to a local church in particular time-bound circumstances.[8]

Along with analyzing the historical context of the biblical writings, women in the eighteenth and nineteenth centuries began to attend to misogynistic interpretations based on faulty translations. One of the first to do so was British feminist Mary Astell (1666–1731).[9] In the United States, the Grimké sisters, Sarah (1792–1873) and Angelina (1805–1879), Quaker women from a slaveholding family in South Carolina, learned biblical Greek and Hebrew so that they could interpret the Bible for themselves. They were prompted to do so after men sought to silence them from speaking out against slavery and for women's rights by claiming that the Bible (e.g., 1 Cor 14:34) prevented women from speaking in public.[10] Another prominent abolitionist, Isabella Baumfree, was a former slave who adopted the name Sojourner Truth (ca. 1797–1883); she quoted the Bible liberally in her speeches[11] and in so doing challenged cultural assumptions and biblical interpretations that undergird gender inequities.

---

7. See further Taylor and Choi, *Handbook of Women Biblical Interpreters*, 127–32.

8. Her major work, *Women's Speaking Justified, Proved and Allowed by the Scriptures*, published in London in 1667, gave a systematic feminist reading of all biblical texts pertaining to women.

9. Mary Astell, *Some Reflections upon Marriage* (New York: Source Book Press, 1970, reprint of the 1730 edition; earliest edition of this work is 1700), 103–4.

10. See further Sarah Grimké, *Letters on the Equality of the Sexes and the Condition of Woman* (Boston: Isaac Knapp, 1838).

11. See, for example, her most famous speech, "Ain't I a Woman?," delivered in 1851 at the Ohio Women's Rights Convention in Akron, OH; Modern History Sourcebook, https://sourcebooks.fordham.edu/mod/sojtruth-woman.asp.

Another monumental work that emerged in nineteenth-century England was that of Jewish theologian Grace Aguilar (1816–1847), *The Women of Israel*,[12] published in 1845. Aguilar's approach was to make connections between the biblical women and contemporary Jewish women's concerns. She aimed to counter the widespread notion that women were degraded in Jewish law and that only in Christianity were women's dignity and value upheld. Her intent was to help Jewish women find strength and encouragement by seeing the evidence of God's compassionate love in the history of every woman in the Bible. While not a full commentary on the Bible, Aguilar's work stands out for its comprehensive treatment of every female biblical character, including even the most obscure references.[13]

The first person to produce a full-blown feminist commentary on the Bible was Elizabeth Cady Stanton (1815–1902). A leading proponent in the United States for women's right to vote, she found that whenever women tried to make inroads into politics, education, or the work world, the Bible was quoted against them. Along with a team of like-minded women, she produced her own commentary on every text of the Bible that concerned women. Her pioneering two-volume project, *The Woman's Bible*, published in 1895 and 1898, urges women to recognize that texts that degrade women come from the men who wrote the texts, not from God, and to use their common sense to rethink what has been presented to them as sacred.

Nearly a century later, *The Women's Bible Commentary*, edited by Carol A. Newsom and Sharon H. Ringe (Louisville: Westminster John Knox, 1992), appeared. This one-volume commentary features North American feminist scholarship on each book of the Protestant canon. Like Cady Stanton's commentary, it does not contain comments on every section of the biblical text but only on those passages deemed relevant to women. It was revised and expanded in 1998 to include the Apocrypha/Deuterocanonical books, and the contributors to this new volume reflect the global face of contemporary feminist scholarship. The revisions made in the third edition, which appeared in 2012, represent the profound advances in feminist biblical scholarship and include newer voices (with Jacqueline E. Lapsley as an additional editor). In both the second and third editions, *The* has been dropped from the title.

12. The full title is *The Women of Israel or Characters and Sketches from the Holy Scriptures and Jewish History Illustrative of the Past History, Present Duty, and Future Destiny of the Hebrew Females, as Based on the Word of God.*

13. See further Eskenazi and Weiss, *The Torah: A Women's Commentary*, xxxviii; Taylor and Choi, *Handbook of Women Biblical Interpreters*, 31–37.

Also appearing at the centennial of Cady Stanton's *The Woman's Bible* were two volumes edited by Elisabeth Schüssler Fiorenza with the assistance of Shelly Matthews. The first, *Searching the Scriptures: A Feminist Introduction* (New York: Crossroad, 1993), charts a comprehensive approach to feminist interpretation from ecumenical, interreligious, and multicultural perspectives. The second volume, published in 1994, provides critical feminist commentary on each book of the New Testament as well as on three books of Jewish Pseudepigrapha and eleven other early Christian writings.

In Europe, similar endeavors have been undertaken, such as the one-volume *Kompendium Feministische Bibelauslegung*, edited by Luise Schottroff and Marie-Theres Wacker (Gütersloh: Gütersloher Verlagshaus, 2007), featuring German feminist biblical interpretation of each book of the Bible, along with Deuterocanonical apocryphal books, and several extrabiblical writings. This work, now in its third edition, was translated into English.[14] A multivolume project, The Bible and Women: An Encyclopaedia of Exegesis and Cultural History, edited by Mary Ann Beavis, Irmtraud Fischer, Mercedes Navarro Puerto, and Adriana Valerio, is currently in production. This project presents a history of the reception of the Bible as embedded in Western cultural history and focuses particularly on gender-relevant biblical themes, biblical female characters, and women recipients of the Bible. The volumes are published in English, Spanish, Italian, and German.[15]

---

14. *Feminist Biblical Interpretation: A Compendium of Critical Commentary on the Books of the Bible and Related Literature*, trans. Lisa E. Dahill, Everett R. Kalin, Nancy Lukens, Linda M. Maloney, Barbara Rumscheidt, Martin Rumscheidt, and Tina Steiner (Grand Rapids: Eerdmans, 2012). Another notable collection is the three volumes edited by Susanne Scholz, *Feminist Interpretation of the Hebrew Bible in Retrospect*, Recent Research in Biblical Studies 7, 8, 9 (Sheffield: Sheffield Phoenix, 2013, 2014, 2016).

15. The first volume, on the Torah, appeared in Spanish in 2009, in German and Italian in 2010, and in English in 2011 (Atlanta: SBL). The other available volumes are as follows: *Feminist Biblical Studies in the Twentieth Century*, ed. Elisabeth Schüssler Fiorenza (2014); *The Writings and Later Wisdom Books*, ed. Christl M. Maier and Nuria Calduch-Benages (2014); *Gospels: Narrative and History*, ed. Mercedes Navarro Puerto and Marinella Perroni; Amy-Jill Levine, English ed. (2015); *The High Middle Ages*, ed. Kari Elisabeth Børresen and Adriana Valerio (2015); *Early Jewish Writings*, ed. Eileen Schuller and Marie-Theres Wacker (2017); *Faith and Feminism in Nineteenth-Century Religious Communities*, ed. Michaela Sohn-Kronthaler and Ruth Albrecht (2019); *The Early Middle Ages*, ed. Franca Ela Consolino and Judith Herrin (2020); *Prophecy and Gender in the Hebrew Bible*, ed. L. Juliana Claassens and Irmtraud Fischer (2021); and *Rabbinic Literature*, ed. Tal Ilan, Lorena Miralles-Maciá, and Ronit Nikolsky (2022). For further information, see https://www.bibleandwomen.org.

Another groundbreaking work is the collection The Feminist Companion to the Bible Series, edited by Athalya Brenner (Sheffield: Sheffield Academic, 1993–2015), which comprises twenty volumes of commentaries on the Old Testament. The parallel series, Feminist Companion to the New Testament and Early Christian Writings, edited by Amy-Jill Levine with Marianne Blickenstaff and Maria Mayo Robbins (Sheffield: Sheffield Academic, 2001–2010), contains thirteen volumes. These two series are not full commentaries on the biblical books but comprise collected essays on discrete biblical texts.

Works by individual feminist biblical scholars in all parts of the world abound, and they are now too numerous to list in this introduction. Feminist biblical interpretation has reached a level of maturity that now makes possible a commentary series on every book of the Bible. In recent decades, women have had greater access to formal theological education, have been able to learn critical analytical tools, have put their own interpretations into writing, and have developed new methods of biblical interpretation. Until recent decades the work of feminist biblical interpreters was largely unknown, both to other women and to their brothers in the synagogue, church, and academy. Feminists now have taken their place in the professional world of biblical scholars, where they build on the work of their foremothers and connect with one another across the globe in ways not previously possible. In a few short decades, feminist biblical criticism has become an integral part of the academy.

Methodologies

Feminist biblical scholars use a variety of methods and often employ a number of them together.[16] In the Wisdom Commentary series, the authors will explain their understanding of feminism and the feminist reading strategies used in their commentary. Each volume treats the biblical text in blocks of material, not an analysis verse by verse. The entire text is considered, not only those passages that feature female characters or that speak specifically about women. When women are not apparent in the narrative, feminist lenses are used to analyze the dynamics in the text between male characters, the models of power, binary ways of thinking, and the dynamics of imperialism. Attention is given to how the whole

16. See the seventeen essays in Caroline Vander Stichele and Todd Penner, eds., *Her Master's Tools? Feminist and Postcolonial Engagements of Historical-Critical Discourse* (Atlanta: SBL, 2005), which show the complementarity of various approaches.

text functions and how it was and is heard, both in its original context and today. Issues of particular concern to women—e.g., poverty, food, health, the environment, water—come to the fore.

One of the approaches used by early feminists and still popular today is to lift up the overlooked and forgotten stories of women in the Bible. Studies of women in each of the Testaments have been done, and there are also studies on women in particular biblical books.[17] Feminists recognize that the examples of biblical characters can be both empowering and problematic. The point of the feminist enterprise is not to serve as an apologetic for women; it is rather, in part, to recover women's history and literary roles in all their complexity and to learn from that recovery.

Retrieving the submerged history of biblical women is a crucial step for constructing the story of the past so as to lead to liberative possibilities for the present and future. There are, however, some pitfalls to this approach. Sometimes depictions of biblical women have been naïve and romantic. Some commentators exalt the virtues of both biblical and contemporary women and paint women as superior to men. Such reverse discrimination inhibits movement toward equality for all. In addition, some feminists challenge the idea that one can "pluck positive images out of an admittedly androcentric text, separating literary characterizations from the androcentric interests they were created to serve."[18] Still other feminists find these images to have enormous value.

One other danger with seeking the submerged history of women is the tendency for Christian feminists to paint Jesus and even Paul as liberators of women in a way that demonizes Judaism.[19] Wisdom Commentary

---

17. See, e.g., Alice Bach, ed., *Women in the Hebrew Bible: A Reader* (New York: Routledge, 1999); Tikva Frymer-Kensky, *Reading the Women of the Bible* (New York: Schocken Books, 2002); Carol Meyers, Toni Craven, and Ross S. Kraemer, eds., *Women in Scripture* (Grand Rapids: Eerdmans, 2001); Irene Nowell, *Women in the Old Testament* (Collegeville, MN: Liturgical Press, 1997); Katharine Doob Sakenfeld, *Just Wives? Stories of Power and Survival in the Old Testament and Today* (Louisville: Westminster John Knox, 2003); Mary Ann Getty-Sullivan, *Women in the New Testament* (Collegeville, MN: Liturgical Press, 2001); Bonnie Thurston, *Women in the New Testament: Questions and Commentary*, Companions to the New Testament (New York: Crossroad, 1998).

18. J. Cheryl Exum, "Second Thoughts about Secondary Characters: Women in Exodus 1.8–2.10," in *A Feminist Companion to Exodus to Deuteronomy*, FCB 6, ed. Athalya Brenner (Sheffield: Sheffield Academic, 1994), 75–97, at 76.

19. See Judith Plaskow, "Anti-Judaism in Feminist Christian Interpretation," in *Searching the Scriptures: A Feminist Introduction*, vol. 1, ed. Elisabeth Schüssler Fiorenza with Shelly Matthews (New York: Crossroad, 1993), 117–29; Amy-Jill Levine, "The

aims to enhance understanding of Jesus as well as Paul as Jews of their day and to forge solidarity among Jewish and Christian feminists.

Feminist scholars who use historical-critical methods analyze the world behind the text; they seek to understand the historical context from which the text emerged and the circumstances of the communities to whom it was addressed. In bringing feminist lenses to this approach, the aim is not to impose modern expectations on ancient cultures but to unmask the ways that ideologically problematic mind-sets that produced the ancient texts are still promulgated through the text. Feminist biblical scholars aim not only to deconstruct but also to reclaim and reconstruct biblical history as women's history, in which women were central and active agents in creating religious heritage.[20] A further step is to construct meaning for contemporary women and men in a liberative movement toward transformation of social, political, economic, and religious structures.[21] In recent years, some feminists have embraced new historicism, which accents the creative role of the interpreter in any construction of history and exposes the power struggles to which the text witnesses.[22]

Literary critics analyze the world of the text: its form, language patterns, and rhetorical function.[23] They do not attempt to separate layers

---

New Testament and Anti-Judaism," in *The Misunderstood Jew: The Church and the Scandal of the Jewish Jesus* (San Francisco: HarperSanFrancisco, 2006), 87–117.

20. See, for example, Phyllis A. Bird, *Missing Persons and Mistaken Identities: Women and Gender in Ancient Israel* (Minneapolis: Fortress, 1997); Elisabeth Schüssler Fiorenza, *In Memory of Her: A Feminist Theological Reconstruction of Christian Origins* (New York: Crossroad, 1994); Ross Shepard Kraemer and Mary Rose D'Angelo, eds., *Women and Christian Origins* (New York: Oxford University Press, 1999).

21. See, e.g., Sandra M. Schneiders, *The Revelatory Text: Interpreting the New Testament as Sacred Scripture*, rev. ed. (Collegeville, MN: Liturgical Press, 1999), whose aim is to engage in biblical interpretation not only for intellectual enlightenment but, even more important, for personal and communal transformation. Elisabeth Schüssler Fiorenza (*Wisdom Ways: Introducing Feminist Biblical Interpretation* [Maryknoll, NY: Orbis Books, 2001]) envisions the work of feminist biblical interpretation as a dance of Wisdom that consists of seven steps that interweave in spiral movements toward liberation, the final one being transformative action for change.

22. See Gina Hens-Piazza, *The New Historicism*, GBS, Old Testament Series (Minneapolis: Fortress, 2002).

23. Phyllis Trible was among the first to employ this method with texts from Genesis and Ruth in her groundbreaking book *God and the Rhetoric of Sexuality*, OBT (Philadelphia: Fortress, 1978). Another pioneer in feminist literary criticism is Mieke Bal (*Lethal Love: Feminist Literary Readings of Biblical Love Stories* [Bloomington: Indiana University

of tradition and redaction but focus on the text holistically, as it is in its present form. They examine how meaning is created in the interaction between the text and its reader in multiple contexts. Within the arena of literary approaches are reader-oriented approaches, narrative, rhetorical, structuralist, post-structuralist, deconstructive, ideological, autobiographical, and performance criticism.[24] Narrative critics study the interrelation among author, text, and audience through investigation of settings, both spatial and temporal; characters; plot; and narrative techniques (e.g., irony, parody, intertextual allusions). Reader-response critics attend to the impact that the text has on the reader or hearer. They recognize that when a text is detrimental toward women there is the choice either to affirm the text or to read against the grain toward a liberative end. Rhetorical criticism analyzes the style of argumentation and attends to how the author is attempting to shape the thinking or actions of the hearer. Structuralist critics analyze the complex patterns of binary oppositions in the text to derive its meaning.[25] Post-structuralist approaches challenge the notion that there are fixed meanings to any biblical text or that there is one universal truth. They engage in close readings of the text and often engage in intertextual analysis.[26] Within this approach is deconstructionist criticism, which views the text as a site of conflict, with competing narratives. The interpreter aims to expose the fault lines and overturn and reconfigure binaries by elevating the underling of a pair and foregrounding it.[27] Feminists also use other

---

Press, 1987]). For surveys of recent developments in literary methods, see Terry Eagleton, *Literary Theory: An Introduction*, 3rd ed. (Minneapolis: University of Minnesota Press, 2008); Janice Capel Anderson and Stephen D. Moore, eds., *Mark and Method: New Approaches in Biblical Studies*, 2nd ed. (Minneapolis: Fortress, 2008); Michal Beth Dinkler, *Literary Theory and the New Testament*, AYBRL (New Haven: Yale University Press, 2019).

24. See, e.g., J. Cheryl Exum and David J. A. Clines, eds., *The New Literary Criticism and the Hebrew Bible* (Valley Forge, PA: Trinity Press International, 1993); Edgar V. McKnight and Elizabeth Struthers Malbon, eds., *The New Literary Criticism and the New Testament* (Valley Forge, PA: Trinity Press International, 1994).

25. See, e.g., David Jobling, *The Sense of Biblical Narrative: Three Structural Analyses in the Old Testament*, JSOTSup 7 (Sheffield: University of Sheffield Press, 1978).

26. See, e.g., Stephen D. Moore, *Poststructuralism and the New Testament: Derrida and Foucault at the Foot of the Cross* (Minneapolis: Fortress, 1994); *The Bible in Theory: Critical and Postcritical Essays* (Atlanta: SBL, 2010); Yvonne Sherwood, *A Biblical Text and Its Afterlives: The Survival of Jonah in Western Culture* (Cambridge: Cambridge University Press, 2000).

27. David Penchansky, "Deconstruction," in *The Oxford Encyclopedia of Biblical Interpretation*, ed. Steven McKenzie (New York: Oxford University Press, 2013), 196–205.

postmodern approaches, such as ideological and autobiographical criticism. The former analyzes the system of ideas that underlies the power and values concealed in the text as well as that of the interpreter.[28] The latter involves deliberate self-disclosure while reading the text as a critical exegete.[29] Performance criticism attends to how the text was passed on orally, usually in communal settings, and to the verbal and nonverbal interactions between the performer and the audience.[30]

From the beginning, feminists have understood that interpreting the Bible is an act of power. In recent decades, feminist biblical scholars have developed hermeneutical theories of the ethics and politics of biblical interpretation to challenge the claims to value neutrality of most academic biblical scholarship. Feminist biblical scholars have also turned their attention to how some biblical writings were shaped by the power of empire and how this still shapes readers' self-understandings today. They have developed hermeneutical approaches that reveal, critique, and evaluate the interactions depicted in the text against the context of empire, and they consider implications for contemporary contexts.[31] Feminists also analyze the dynamics of colonization and the mentalities of colonized peoples in the exercise of biblical interpretation. As Kwok Pui-lan explains, "A postcolonial feminist interpretation of the Bible needs to investigate the deployment of gender in the narration of identity, the negotiation of power differentials between the colonizers and

---

See, for example, Danna Nolan Fewell and David M. Gunn, *Gender, Power, and Promise: The Subject of the Bible's First Story* (Nashville: Abingdon, 1993); David Rutledge, *Reading Marginally: Feminism, Deconstruction and the Bible*, BibInt 21 (Leiden: Brill, 1996).

28. See David Jobling and Tina Pippin, eds., *Semeia 59: Ideological Criticism of Biblical Texts* (Atlanta: Scholars Press, 1992); Terry Eagleton, *Ideology: An Introduction* (London: Verso, 2007).

29. See, e.g., Ingrid Rosa Kitzberger, ed., *Autobiographical Biblical Interpretation: Between Text and Self* (Leiden: Deo, 2002); P. J. W. Schutte, "When *They*, *We*, and the Passive Become *I*—Introducing Autobiographical Biblical Criticism," *HTS Teologiese Studies / Theological Studies* 61 (2005): 401–16.

30. See, e.g., Holly E. Hearon and Philip Ruge-Jones, eds., *The Bible in Ancient and Modern Media: Story and Performance* (Eugene, OR: Cascade, 2009).

31. E.g., Gale Yee, ed., *Judges and Method: New Approaches in Biblical Studies* (Minneapolis: Fortress, 1995); Warren Carter, *The Gospel of Matthew in Its Roman Imperial Context* (London: T&T Clark, 2005); *The Roman Empire and the New Testament: An Essential Guide* (Nashville: Abingdon, 2006); Elisabeth Schüssler Fiorenza, *The Power of the Word: Scripture and the Rhetoric of Empire* (Minneapolis: Fortress, 2007); Judith E. McKinlay, *Reframing Her: Biblical Women in Postcolonial Focus* (Sheffield: Sheffield Phoenix, 2004).

the colonized, and the reinforcement of patriarchal control over spheres where these elites could exercise control."[32] Methods and models from sociology and cultural anthropology are used by feminists to investigate women's everyday lives, their experiences of marriage, childrearing, labor, money, illness, etc.[33]

As feminists have examined the construction of gender from varying cultural perspectives, they have become ever more cognizant that the way gender roles are defined within differing cultures varies radically. As Mary Ann Tolbert observes, "Attempts to isolate some universal role that cross-culturally defines 'woman' have run into contradictory evidence at every turn."[34] Some women have coined new terms to highlight the particularities of their socio-cultural context. Many African American feminists, for example, call themselves *womanists* to draw attention to the double oppression of racism and sexism they experience.[35] Similarly, many US Hispanic feminists speak of themselves as *mujeristas* (*mujer* is Spanish for "woman").[36] Others prefer to be called "Latina feminists."[37] As a gender-neutral or nonbinary alternative, many today use Latinx or

32. Kwok Pui-lan, *Postcolonial Imagination and Feminist Theology* (Louisville: Westminster John Knox, 2005), 9. See also Musa W. Dube, ed., *Postcolonial Feminist Interpretation of the Bible* (St. Louis: Chalice, 2000); Cristl M. Maier and Carolyn J. Sharp, *Prophecy and Power: Jeremiah in Feminist and Postcolonial Perspective* (London: Bloomsbury, 2013); L. Juliana Claassens and Carolyn J. Sharp, eds., *Feminist Frameworks and the Bible: Power, Ambiguity, and Intersectionality*, LHBOTS 630 (London: Bloomsbury T&T Clark, 2017).

33. See, for example, Carol Meyers, *Discovering Eve: Ancient Israelite Women in Context* (New York: Oxford University Press, 1991); Luise Schottroff, *Lydia's Impatient Sisters: A Feminist Social History of Early Christianity*, trans. Barbara and Martin Rumscheidt (Louisville: Westminster John Knox, 1995); Susan Niditch, *"My Brother Esau Is a Hairy Man": Hair and Identity in Ancient Israel* (Oxford: Oxford University Press, 2008).

34. Mary Ann Tolbert, "Social, Sociological, and Anthropological Methods," in *Searching the Scriptures*, 1:255–71, at 265.

35. Alice Walker coined the term (*In Search of Our Mothers' Gardens: Womanist Prose* [New York: Harcourt Brace Jovanovich, 1967, 1983]). See also Katie G. Cannon, "The Emergence of Black Feminist Consciousness," in *Feminist Interpretation of the Bible*, ed. Letty M. Russell (Philadelphia: Westminster, 1985), 30–40; Renita J. Weems, *Just a Sister Away: A Womanist Vision of Women's Relationships in the Bible* (San Diego: Lura Media, 1988); Nyasha Junior, *An Introduction to Womanist Biblical Interpretation* (Louisville: Westminster John Knox, 2015).

36. Ada María Isasi-Díaz (*Mujerista Theology: A Theology for the Twenty-First Century* [Maryknoll, NY: Orbis Books, 1996]) is credited with coining the term.

37. E.g., María Pilar Aquino, Daisy L. Machado, and Jeanette Rodríguez, eds., *A Reader in Latina Feminist Theology* (Austin: University of Texas Press, 2002).

Latine. *Mujeristas*, Latina and Latine feminists emphasize that the context for their theologizing is *mestizaje* and *mulatez* (racial and cultural mixture), done *en conjunto* (in community), with *lo cotidiano* (everyday lived experience) of Latina women as starting points for theological reflection and the encounter with the divine. Intercultural analysis has become an indispensable tool for working toward justice for women at the global level.[38]

Some feminists are among those who have developed lesbian, gay, bisexual, and transgender (LGBT+) interpretation. This approach focuses on issues of sexual identity and uses various reading strategies. Some point out the ways in which categories that emerged in recent centuries are applied anachronistically to biblical texts to make modern-day judgments. Others show how the Bible is silent on contemporary issues about sexual identity. Still others examine same-sex relationships in the Bible by figures such as Ruth and Naomi or David and Jonathan. In recent years, queer theory has emerged; it emphasizes the blurriness of boundaries not just of sexual identity but also of gender roles. Queer critics often focus on texts in which figures transgress what is traditionally considered proper gender behavior.[39]

Feminists have also been engaged in studying the reception history of the text[40] and have engaged in studies in the emerging fields of disability theory and of children in the Bible.

---

38. See, e.g., María Pilar Aquino and María José Rosado-Nunes, eds., *Feminist Intercultural Theology: Latina Explorations for a Just World*, Studies in Latino/a Catholicism (Maryknoll, NY: Orbis Books, 2007). See also Michelle A. Gonzalez, "Latina Feminist Theology: Past, Present, and Future," *JFSR* 25 (2009): 150–55. See also Elisabeth Schüssler Fiorenza, ed., *Feminist Biblical Studies in the Twentieth Century: Scholarship and Movement*, The Bible and Women 9.1 (Atlanta: SBL Press, 2014), who charts feminist studies around the globe as well as emerging feminist methodologies.

39. See, e.g., Bernadette J. Brooten, *Love Between Women: Early Christian Responses to Female Homoeroticism* (Chicago: University of Chicago Press, 1996); Mary Rose D'Angelo, "Women Partners in the New Testament," *JFSR* 6 (1990): 65–86; Deirdre J. Good, "Reading Strategies for Biblical Passages on Same-Sex Relations," *Theology and Sexuality* 7 (1997): 70–82; Deryn Guest, *When Deborah Met Jael: Lesbian Feminist Hermeneutics* (London: SCM, 2005); Teresa Hornsby and Ken Stone, eds., *Bible Trouble: Queer Readings at the Boundaries of Biblical Scholarship* (Atlanta: SBL, 2011); Joseph A. Marchal, "Queer Studies and Critical Masculinity Studies in Feminist Biblical Studies," in *Feminist Biblical Studies in the Twentieth Century*, ed. Schüssler Fiorenza, 261–80.

40. See Sharon H. Ringe, "When Women Interpret the Bible," in *Women's Bible Commentary*, ed. Carol A. Newsom, Sharon H. Ringe, and Jacqueline E. Lapsley, 3rd ed. (Louisville: Westminster John Knox, 2012), 5; Taylor and Choi, *Handbook of Women Biblical Interpreters*; Yvonne Sherwood, "Introduction," in *The Bible and Feminism: Remapping the Field* (New York: Oxford University Press, 2017).

Feminists also recognize that the struggle for women's equality and dignity is intimately connected with the struggle for respect for Earth and for the whole of the cosmos. Ecofeminists interpret Scripture in ways that highlight the link between human domination of nature and male subjugation of women. They show how anthropocentric ways of interpreting the Bible have overlooked or dismissed Earth and Earth community. They invite readers to identify not only with human characters in the biblical narrative but also with other Earth creatures and domains of nature, especially those that are the object of injustice. Some use creative imagination to retrieve the interests of Earth implicit in the narrative and enable Earth to speak.[41]

Biblical Authority

By the late nineteenth century, some feminists, such as Elizabeth Cady Stanton, began to question openly whether the Bible could continue to be regarded as authoritative for women. They viewed the Bible itself as the source of women's oppression, and some rejected its sacred origin and saving claims. Some decided that the Bible and the religious traditions that enshrine it are too thoroughly saturated with androcentrism and patriarchy to be redeemable.[42]

In the Wisdom Commentary series, questions such as these may be raised, but the aim of this series is not to lead readers to reject the authority of the biblical text. Rather, the aim is to promote better understanding of the contexts from which the text arose and of the rhetorical effects it has on people in contemporary contexts. Such understanding can lead to a deepening of faith, with the Bible serving as an aid to bring flourishing of life.

Language for God

Because of the ways in which the term "God" has been used to symbolize the divine in predominantly male, patriarchal, and monarchical modes, feminists have designed new ways of speaking of the divine. Some have called attention to the inadequacy of the term *God* by trying to visually destabilize our ways of thinking and speaking of the divine.

41. E.g., Norman C. Habel and Peter Trudinger, *Exploring Ecological Hermeneutics*, SymS 46 (Atlanta: SBL, 2008); Mary Judith Ress, *Ecofeminism in Latin America*, Women from the Margins (Maryknoll, NY: Orbis Books, 2006).

42. E.g., Mary Daly, *Beyond God the Father: A Philosophy of Women's Liberation* (Boston: Beacon, 1973).

Rosemary Radford Ruether proposed *God/ess*, as an unpronounceable term pointing to the unnameable understanding of the divine that transcends patriarchal limitations.[43] Some have followed traditional Jewish practice, writing *G-d*. Elisabeth Schüssler Fiorenza has adopted *G*d*.[44] Others draw on the biblical tradition to mine female and non-gender-specific metaphors and symbols.[45] In Wisdom Commentary, there is not one standard way of expressing the divine; each author will use her or his preferred ways. The one exception is that when the tetragrammaton, YHWH, the name revealed to Moses in Exodus 3:14, is used, it will be without vowels, respecting the Jewish custom of avoiding pronouncing the divine name out of reverence.

Nomenclature for the Two Testaments

In recent decades, some biblical scholars have begun to call the two Testaments of the Bible by names other than the traditional nomenclature: Old and New Testament. Some regard "Old" as derogatory, implying that it is no longer relevant or that it has been superseded. Consequently, terms like Hebrew Bible, First Testament, and Jewish Scriptures and, correspondingly, Christian Scriptures or Second Testament have come into use. There are a number of difficulties with these designations. The term "Hebrew Bible" does not take into account that parts of the Old Testament are written not in Hebrew but in Aramaic.[46] Moreover, for Roman Catholics and Eastern Orthodox believers, the Old Testament includes books written in Greek—the Deuterocanonical books, considered Apocrypha by Protestants.[47] The term "Jewish Scriptures" is inadequate because these books are also sacred to Christians. Conversely, "Christian Scriptures"

43. Rosemary Radford Ruether, *Sexism and God-Talk: Toward a Feminist Theology* (Boston: Beacon, 1993).

44. Elisabeth Schüssler Fiorenza, *Jesus: Miriam's Child, Sophia's Prophet; Critical Issues in Feminist Christology* (New York: Continuum, 1994), 191n3.

45. E.g., Sallie McFague, *Models of God: Theology for an Ecological, Nuclear Age* (Philadelphia: Fortress, 1987); Catherine Mowry LaCugna, *God for Us: The Trinity and Christian Life* (San Francisco: HarperCollins, 1991); Elizabeth A. Johnson, *She Who Is: The Mystery of God in Feminist Theological Discourse* (New York: Crossroad, 1992). See further Elizabeth A. Johnson, "God," in *Dictionary of Feminist Theologies*, ed. Letty M. Russell and J. Shannon Clarkson (Louisville: Westminster John Knox, 1996), 128–30.

46. Gen 31:47; Jer 10:11; Ezra 4:7–6:18; 7:12-26; Dan 2:4–7:28.

47. Representing the *via media* between Catholic and reformed, Anglicans generally consider the Apocrypha to be profitable, if not canonical, and utilize select Wisdom texts liturgically.

is not an accurate designation for the New Testament, since the Old Testament is also part of the Christian Scriptures. Using "First and Second Testament" also has difficulties, in that it can imply a hierarchy and a value judgment.[48] Jews generally use the term Tanakh, an acronym for Torah (Pentateuch), Nevi'im (Prophets), and Ketuvim (Writings).

In Wisdom Commentary, if authors choose to use a designation other than Tanakh, Old Testament, and New Testament, they will explain how they mean the term.

Translation

Modern feminist scholars recognize the complexities connected with biblical translation, as they have delved into questions about philosophy of language, how meanings are produced, and how they are culturally situated. Today it is evident that simply translating into gender-neutral formulations cannot address all the challenges presented by androcentric texts. Efforts at feminist translation must also deal with issues around authority and canonicity.[49]

Because of these complexities, the editors of the Wisdom Commentary series have chosen to use an existing translation, the New Revised Standard Version (NRSV), which is provided for easy reference at the top of each page of commentary. The NRSV was produced by a team of ecumenical and interreligious scholars, is a fairly literal translation, and uses inclusive language for human beings. Brief discussions about problematic translations appear in the inserts labeled "Translation Matters." When more detailed discussions are available, these will be indicated in footnotes. In the commentary, wherever Hebrew or Greek words are used, English translation is provided. In cases where a wordplay is involved, transliteration is provided to enable understanding.

Art and Poetry

Artistic expression in poetry, music, sculpture, painting, and various other modes is very important to feminist interpretation. Where possible, art and poetry are included in the print volumes of the series. In a number of instances, these are original works created for this project.

48. See Levine, *The Misunderstood Jew*, 193–99.
49. Elizabeth Castelli, "*Les Belles Infidèles*/Fidelity or Feminism? The Meanings of Feminist Biblical Translation," in *Searching the Scriptures*, 1:189–204, here 190.

Regrettably, copyright and production costs prohibit the inclusion of color photographs and other artistic work.

Glossary

Because there are a number of excellent readily available resources that provide definitions and concise explanations of terms used in feminist theological and biblical studies, this series will not include a glossary. We refer you to works such as *Dictionary of Feminist Theologies*, edited by Letty M. Russell and J. Shannon Clarkson, and volume 1 of *Searching the Scriptures*, edited by Elisabeth Schüssler Fiorenza with the assistance of Shelly Matthews. Individual authors in the Wisdom Commentary series will define the way they are using terms that may be unfamiliar.

A Concluding Word

In just a few short decades, feminist biblical studies has grown exponentially, both in the methods that have been developed and in the number of scholars who have embraced it. We realize that this series is limited and will soon need to be revised and updated. It is our hope that Wisdom Commentary, by making the best of current feminist biblical scholarship available in an accessible format to ministers, preachers, teachers, scholars, and students, will aid all readers in their advancement toward God's vision of dignity, equality, and justice for all.

Acknowledgments

There are a great many people who have made this series possible: first, Peter Dwyer, retired director of Liturgical Press, and Hans Christoffersen, editorial director of Liturgical Press, who have believed in this project and have shepherded it since it was conceived in 2008. I am grateful to Therese L. Ratliff, the Press's new director and CEO, who is now championing this project. Editorial consultants Athalya Brenner-Idan and Elisabeth Schüssler Fiorenza have not only been an inspiration with their pioneering work but have encouraged us all along the way with their personal involvement. Volume editors Mary Ann Beavis, Carol J. Dempsey, Amy-Jill Levine, Linda M. Maloney, Song-Mi Suzie Park, Ahida Pilarski, Sarah Tanzer, and Lauress Wilkins Lawrence have lent their extraordinary wisdom to the shaping of the series, have used their extensive networks of relationships to secure authors and contributors, and have worked tirelessly to guide their work to completion. Others who have contributed greatly to the shaping of the project are Linda M. Day, Gina Hens-Piazza, Mignon Jacobs, Seung Ai Yang, and Barbara E. Bowe of blessed memory (d. 2010). Editorial and research assistant Susan M. Hickman provided invaluable support with administrative details and arrangements at the outset of the project. I am grateful to Brian Eisenschenk and Christine Henderson who assisted Susan Hickman with the Wiki. I am especially thankful to Lauren L. Murphy and Justin Howell for their work in copyediting; and to the staff at Liturgical Press, especially Colleen Stiller, retired production manager; Angie Steffens, production manager; Stephanie Lancour, production editor; Julie Surma, desktop publisher; and Tara Durheim, marketing director.

Author's Introduction:
Setting the Scene

When Barbara Reid invited me to participate in the Wisdom Commentary series by doing a feminist commentary on the book of Tobit (Tobit hereafter), I enthusiastically said yes. Who could resist engaging with a narrative featuring feisty females; a Jewish, male Antigone; a deadly demon; an aggressive fish; and a bird who defecates in the eyes of the titular character and causes him to lose his sight? Plus, there is a dog in Tobit, and I love dogs. Surely such a rich text would yield much material for feminist analysis.

And it does: theodicy, the suffering of innocent people, disability, gender constructions, minority status, anger, gossip, slavery, trust, childlessness, mother-daughter relationships, marriage, magic, healing, death, suicide, women's labor, treatment of corpses, honor and shame, domestic abuse, the slaughter of animals for food—and more. In applying a feminist lens to Tobit, I discuss the original writer's context and perspective and try to gain deeper insight into our text by juxtaposing it with pieces of other ancient literature; I question assumptions, tease out Tobit's implications for women and for other people not at the center of power at the time, and challenge the text when these implications are negative; I offer alternative ways of understanding what the author of Tobit writes and make connections with contemporary issues.

This has been the most challenging writing project in which I've engaged. My scholarly training taught me to approach texts dispassionately, keeping my personal feelings and experience bracketed. I was to engage with the evidence (i.e., words in a text, archaeological data, contextual history, and culture) in as objective a manner as possible. What this project asked of me was to engage with the evidence of the text and the time in which it was composed but also to bring my lived experience, as a human being who identifies as female, to the text. This was difficult and stretched me beyond my comfort zone. My patient editor, Amy-Jill Levine, had to remind me multiple times to let the reader know *my* thoughts and feelings about what I was reading. Eventually, it got easier. Over and over, I discovered ways of personally connecting with aspects of the narrative and added this dimension to the commentary.

The Story

Tobit recounts the story of two Israelite families, both from the tribe of Naphtali, living in exile. The setting is the expulsion of Israelites from the Northern Kingdom of Israel by the Neo-Assyrians in the eighth century BCE. A member of each family—Tobit (the Greek form of the Hebrew טובי [*tobi*], "my good") is the patriarch of one, and Sarah (whose name, שרה [*sarah*], means "princess" in Hebrew) is the only daughter of the other—undergoes a crisis so devastating that each seeks escape by praying to God for death.

The narrative invites its readers as observers into the lives of these two diaspora families in the Neo-Assyrian capital of Nineveh (in modern Iraq) and in Ecbatana, Media (present-day Iran), under the Neo-Assyrian kings. Tobit works as a purchaser for the royal household of King Shalmaneser. The king chooses to show his disdain for Israelites not only by killing many of them but also by leaving their dead bodies exposed to the elements. One way Tobit expresses his devotion to the Torah is by burying the corpses of his people. For these acts of piety, the king seeks to kill him, so Tobit flees and leaves behind his wife Anna and his son Tobias (whose name also reflects the Hebrew word for "good") and all of his possessions. He tumbles from his high-profile position in the government and loses his secure income. When the king's brother takes over, Tobit's standing seems to stabilize; no longer is his life in danger, so he returns to Nineveh. One evening, Tobit sends Tobias to invite a needy Israelite to join the family for dinner. Instead of returning with a guest, Tobias arrives back home with word that another Israelite's body has been found exposed. Tobit abandons the impending dinner and goes to bury the body. When he comes home much later, he sleeps outside. As Tobit sleeps, a bird proves treacherous: its excrement falls into his eyes and Tobit becomes blind. No longer can he continue in the work he was doing, which means that he no longer can provide for his wife and son. Anna becomes the sole financial sustainer of the family, which leads to marital tension. Tobit prays for death.

Meanwhile, in Ecbatana, Sarah, the only daughter of Edna and Raguel, is experiencing her own predicament. The demon Asmodeus has killed each of her prospective husbands on the night of the marriage, seven times over. Raguel engages in his own burial activities by disposing of the bodies quietly, under the cover of darkness, in hopes of keeping this family tragedy hidden. Sarah, taunted by the enslaved women in her household, prays for death.

God hears their prayers and decides to restore them to healing and happiness through the mediation of the angel Raphael, whose name, appropriately, means "God heals."

Tobit, seeking to safeguard his son's future, sends him to retrieve a sum of money left with a relative in Medea. Before Tobias departs, Tobit shares with him ancestral wisdom, such as the importance of following Torah and of marrying a woman from his own tribe. Tobit also hires Azariah (who is actually the angel Raphael in disguise) as a guide for the expedition. Raphael accompanies Tobias on an event-filled voyage that leads him to meet his relative Sarah. They eventually marry. Tobias drives away Asmodeus and successfully reclaims his father's money. Upon returning home, Tobias heals his elderly father, again thanks to Raphael's advice. Raphael reveals his true identity and disappears. The story ends with Tobit's offering thanksgiving for what has transpired and with an expression of hope, both for the rebuilding of Jerusalem and its temple and for the restoration of exiles to their homeland.

My Story

Becoming a professor of ancient Mediterranean religion was not on my radar as a girl growing up in western Canada. Neither of my parents had the opportunity to attend university, and because of this they stressed to my younger sister and me the importance of higher education. I loved old things from a young age—at around nine or ten years old I "rescued" a set of yellowed school notes that an elderly neighbor had thrown in her garbage. I was fascinated, and, to my mother's chagrin, this "find" motivated me to look through other neighborhood garbage for additional valuable artifacts (I never found any). Flash forward a few decades and I was digging through truly ancient garbage by participating in archaeological excavations, two in Jordan (at Wadi ath-Thamad) and one in Israel (at Yodefat). I suppose the ancient focus of my work is consistent with that early manifestation of interest in history. But the "religion" part would have surprised me as well as my family. I grew up in a nominally Protestant family—nominally, since we only went to church a few times at Christmas to sing carols, and I had been baptized as a baby.

I surprised my parents when, at the age of fifteen, I invited them to come to church to see me be baptized (again). I had begun to attend a local Pentecostal church. At the start of that year I experienced my first break-up with a serious boyfriend, and I found myself asking the big questions—about what love is, what living a meaningful life was, etc. My search led me to the Bible and I began reading it, starting with Genesis. I furthermore asked a friend who had recently identified herself as a born-again Christian if I could attend church with her. By the end of that summer, I too had given my heart to Jesus.

But I had questions. I recall seeing the movie *Gandhi* and asking how such an exemplary person would be going to hell because he didn't accept Jesus as Lord. I did not receive a satisfactory answer, but I learned to keep my questions to myself. Questioning my new faith apparently meant that I lacked it. My discomfort grew.

I now recognize that many other Christian churches would have provided space for asking questions and expressing doubt. At a time when I was looking for a clear framework of meaning for my life, the fundamentalist community fulfilled that need. It also brought me into contact with many kind and wonderful people, and I am still grateful for that. As my life and worldview changed, however, I came to feel like an imposter continuing to go to church. When, in my mid-twenties, I stated aloud to a friend that I was no longer a Christian, I felt a weight lift from my shoulders.

At the age of eighteen, in the summer after my first year at university, I went on a study tour: one week in Egypt; one week in Israel. It was my first venture outside of North America, and it changed my life. Exploring the rich archaeological sites firsthand made a deep impression on me. It was also the first time I came face-to-face with extreme poverty. As I looked down from the rooftop pool of a Cairo hotel, I noticed children playing around their houses made of cardboard and tin. I remember asking myself: "Why are they down there and I'm up here? What is the difference between us? Am I more deserving than they?" I recall the stark realization that our positions could have been reversed and that it was the luck of birth that gave me the privileged position. This moment of self-awareness in Egypt helped to shift and broaden my worldview.

I enjoyed visiting Egypt, but I fell in love with Israel. At the time I was blissfully unaware of its political problems. What I loved was how you could walk down a bustling modern street and casually encounter a two-thousand-year-old wall. I loved how within two hours you could travel from rolling hills of desert to lush farming lands. I even loved the smell of the air. There was a vibrancy to life in Israel that made me feel so alive. After I returned to Canada, all I could think about was how to get back. My opportunity came during my junior year when I enrolled in the Rothberg One-Year Program at the Hebrew University of Jerusalem. During that year I took a course with Prof. Isaiah Gafni on Jewish-Christian relations in the rabbinic period—and I was hooked. After I returned to Canada for a final year and graduated with a bachelor's degree in history, I entered the Hebrew University's master's degree program in Second Temple period Jewish history. I had to become fluent in Modern Hebrew, so I spent the spring and summer leading up to my first year in intensive Ulpan (language school) courses in Jerusalem. I passed the required exam, but it took several months before I could truly understand the lectures. Many of my professors were new immigrants to Israel themselves, so they could relate to my struggles, and they were patient when I attended their office hours to ask questions.

One summer while back in Canada, I had the chance to take a half-hour exploratory flight in a single-engine Cessna 150. I loved it. Between shifts working at McDonalds, I began taking flying lessons. I earned my private pilot's license before I had to return to Jerusalem. That next year in Israel, I kept thinking about how practical flying was in contrast to my graduate studies. I was not certain where the academics were leading me; being a university professor was not in my sights. Many of my high school friends were getting full-time jobs, and I too wanted this. Flying struck me as more likely to lead to a real job. After much thought, I decided that that year would be my last in Israel. One of the best pieces of advice I received during that time was this: Finish your courses off well, Michele, because you never know if you will want to pick up your studies again. When I returned to Canada, I got a job and began working on my commercial pilot's license. Airlines were particularly interested in female pilots. My plan was to build my flight hours by becoming a flight instructor and then eventually I would apply to the airlines. One of the lessons drummed into me was how even one bird caught in an aircraft engine can be deadly—especially for a light aircraft. I became aware of the presence of birds on airstrips and while flying and to avoid them. Like Tobit, I learned that birds can be dangerous.

By the end of that year, I earned the commercial pilot's license. But I missed the academics. With flying, it was possible to learn all that I needed to know in order to be a pilot. With history, there was always more to study—and I realized that I most enjoyed never reaching the "end" of learning.

My (incredible) parents supported my decision to return to Israel to complete my master's degree. Friends in Jerusalem had given me going-away parties the year before, so it was embarrassing for me to go back. But I returned with a new sense of direction. My academic focus morphed from Second Temple Jewish history to Jewish-Christian relations in antiquity and eventually to a doctorate in religion.[1]

Living in Israel afforded me the opportunity to become friends with Jews and Muslims, and I learned more about both Judaism and Islam. I became increasingly attracted to Judaism, especially its history and its focus on family and community. While completing my PhD at the University of Toronto, I started to attend sabbath services at a Reform synagogue. After a few years, I made my Jewish identity official and underwent the conversion process.

That was over twenty years ago. I identify as Jewish, though neither my husband (who was raised in a Secular Humanist Jewish family) nor I is particularly observant. Every so often we hold a Passover seder, to which we invite Jewish and non-Jewish friends. And as a result of the stress I felt due to the COVID-19 pandemic, I found myself needing to carve out time for rest. I began lighting Sabbath candles on Friday evenings concretely to mark the end of the work week.

I was the first woman, and first Jew, hired as a full-time professor in the Department of Religion (now the Department of Religion, Society, and Culture) at Bishop's University, in Sherbrooke, Quebec. Bishop's is a relatively small (about 2,800 students) liberal arts university. It is an anglophone university in a very francophone region. The same year that I said yes to working on this Tobit commentary, I became dean of arts and science and am now dean of arts—the first woman to hold these positions. Taking on administrative jobs and this project at the same time meant a considerable delay in the writing process.

I feel as if Tobit, Anna, Sarah, Edna, Raguel, and Raphael have been my companions along this path. I already understood that power dynamics

---

1. My dissertation was published as *Playing a Jewish Game: Gentile Christian Judaizing in the First and Second Centuries CE*, Studies in Christianity and Judaism 13 (Waterloo, ON: Wilfrid Laurier University Press, 2004).

in a classroom or a meeting influence whose opinion dominates, but this project has made me much more cognizant of those who do not speak up. I find myself reflecting more than I did before on what I can do to create an environment in which all participants feel comfortable voicing their perspectives. As Bishop's faculty and staff work to increase diversity on campus so that students of all backgrounds—especially those from traditionally marginalized communities—can feel more welcome by seeing themselves reflected within the university, I have found synergy between working on this commentary and my work as dean and professor in trying to identify and dismantle systemic racism in our environment. It has been an extraordinary learning process. We turn now to the story of Tobit.

Date of Writing of Tobit

Although set in the eighth century BCE, Tobit was written much later. References to the Torah (e.g., "the book of Moses" in 1:8) and quotations from prophetic writings (2:6; "the prophets of Israel" in 14:4) as authoritative mean that the text cannot have been written earlier than the fourth century BCE. That the text reflects no knowledge of either the persecutions of Jews under Seleucid ruler Antiochus IV Epiphanes (c. 175–164 BCE) or the Maccabean Revolt (c. 167–164 BCE) means it was likely written prior to these events. Five fragmentary copies of Tobit—four in Aramaic and one in Hebrew—recovered from the caves at Qumran, the earliest extant manuscripts of the text, set the latest possible date of writing at around 100 or 50 BCE. The consensus date is approximately 250 BCE. Tobit joins a number of other early Jewish writings, such as Ezekiel, Lamentations, the book of Esther, and the book of Daniel, that grapple with Jewish life in the diaspora.

Genre

Tobit, part of a long Jewish tradition of teaching through storytelling, is a work of humorous fiction written to entertain but also to critique and instruct. It contains farcical elements: blindness by bird excrement, a murderous love-sick demon, a father with the corpses of his sons-in-law in the backyard. There's also a magical fish. We can laugh at these ideas and, for a moment, feel better about what is occurring in our own lives. But we cannot laugh too hard: we also sympathize with the sincere intentions of the characters and their struggles to understand God's plan for their lives. More, the story expresses the fact that living piously does not mean a life without hardship. The tale also provides instruction: about the exclusive legitimacy of the Jerusalem temple (1:4-8; 13:9-15); that righteousness means risking political persecution by burying exposed bodies, giving alms, and marrying within one's own tribe (1:9; 7:1-11); and that—to put it bluntly—while "shit happens," pressing onward means not only survival but a chance to thrive.

Language

Greek manuscripts are used for English translations of Tobit, but Hebrew was most likely the original language. The Qumran fragments are in Hebrew (4Q200) and Aramaic (4Q196-199).[2] Jerome, the fourth-century CE church father best known for his translation of the Bible into Latin (the Vulgate, Latin for "common or colloquial speech"), says that he translated Tobit into Latin from an Aramaic version. Since Aramaic was more popularly used than Hebrew, it is more probable that Tobit was translated from a Hebrew original into Aramaic than the reverse. Thus, Tobit was originally written in Hebrew, translated into Aramaic, and then into Greek and Latin. The languages in which the texts are written matter for a feminist reading, since meanings of words are shaped by the cultures in which they are written. An original meaning can be altered or lost by changing its language, in particular if the text is translated into the dominant languages of ruling peoples. Consequently, at certain points I take time to explore the Semitic and Greek meanings of words.

Two versions of Tobit are extant in Greek: a shorter version in Codex Vaticanus and Codex Alexandrinus (G1), and a longer one in Codex Sinaiticus (G2), discovered in 1844 in the library of St. Catherine in the Sinai. G2 is more similar to the Qumran Aramaic and Hebrew fragments, and most scholars consider it to correspond most accurately to the original form of Tobit.[3] The New Revised Standard Version translation is based on the text of G2, and I use it for this commentary. Tobit's popularity in the late antique world was attested by its availability in Coptic,

---

2. Joseph A. Fitzmyer, "The Aramaic and Hebrew Fragments of Tobit from Cave 4m," *CBQ* 57 (1995): 655–75; DJD 19, *Qumran Cave 4.XIV*, Parabiblical Texts, part 2, ed. Magen Brochi, Esther Eshel, Joseph A. Fitzmyer (Oxford: Clarendon Press, 1995).

3. Alexander A. Di Lella, "Tobit," in *A New English Translation of the Septuagint*, ed. Albert Pietersma and Benjamin G. Wright (Oxford: Oxford University Press, 2007), 456.

Syriac, Ethiopic, Sahidic, Armenian, and Arabic languages.[4] Christians were responsible for several of these translations into different languages. They used Tobit and Tobias as examples of how to live ethically with respect to parent-child relationships, prayer, burial, caring for one's community through almsgiving, as well as how to grapple honorably with suffering.[5] It is also a humorous story, and this contributed to its popularity through the centuries as well.

Location

Amy-Jill Levine notes that "[t]he book of Tobit is . . . replete with information concerning family life, travel, burial and eating customs, gender roles, and medicine. These matters testify to the author's interest in providing guidance for life in the diaspora."[6] But *where* precisely its author wrote is not certain. For the first half of the twentieth century, most scholars argued that the document was composed in Egypt, in large part because the "Tale of Ahikar," which the author of Tobit apparently knew (Tobit's nephew is named Ahikar), was thought to be Egyptian in origin. Today, many scholars propose a composition either in the eastern diaspora (Syria or Mesopotamia) or even in Judea. That the demon Asmodeus has an Iranian name (Ashmedai) in my view tips the scale slightly in favor of Syria or Judea. The use of a non-Semitic name was a means of communicating that this monster was "other" and, consequently, dangerous.

Tobit is one of about twenty Jewish documents classified by Protestants as comprising the Apocrypha (literally "hidden things") and by Catholics as deuterocanonical (i.e., the second canon). Many of these books, including Tobit, were accepted into the Septuagint—the translation of the Hebrew Scriptures into Greek around 200 BCE; they found their way into the early Christian canons, but they are not part of the Jewish canon, the Tanakh (an acronym from the beginning letters of the three

4. Robert J. Littman, *Tobit: The Book of Tobit in Codex Sinaiticus*, Septuagint Commentary Series (Leiden: Brill, 2008), xix, n. 2.

5. Chris L. De Wet, "The Book of Tobit in Early Christianity: Greek and Latin Interpretations from the 2nd to the 5th Century CE," *HTS Teologiese Studies/Theological Studies* [online] 76 (2020): 13 pages.

6. Amy-Jill Levine, "Tobit," in *The New Oxford Annotated Bible with Apocrypha: New Revised Standard Version*, ed. Michael D. Coogan, 4th ed. (Oxford: Oxford University Press, 2010), 168.

divisions of the Hebrew Bible: Torah, Nevi'im, Ketuvim used by Jews).[7] Protestants consider Tobit to be extracanonical and thus not counted among authoritative Scriptures. The term "canon," from the ancient Greek *kanon*, refers to a straight rod—a ruler or standard. Writings in a sacred canon, such as the Tanakh, the Old Testament, and the New Testament, have influence; they have moral and ethical force. Canons contain writings considered most important—but those who make the assessment typically are the people with the most power and influence in a society. Feminists, therefore, are critical of canons since they tend to reinforce the worldviews of the most powerful and to disparage, obscure, or ignore those of others. Roman Catholics; Greek and Eastern Orthodox; Armenian, Syrian, and Coptic Orthodox Christians consider Tobit an authoritative text.[8] For me, Tobit is a meaningful document irrespective of its canonical status. It is worthy of reading because it provides fascinating—and entertaining—glimpses into Jewish history.

This Commentary

Of the many commentaries on Tobit,[9] feminist issues are particularly addressed by those of Eileen M. Schuller, Amy-Jill Levine, and Naomi

7. The first division, Torah, means "teaching, instruction" in Hebrew and refers to the Pentateuch or five books of Moses (Genesis through Deuteronomy), considered the most sacred texts of the Bible by Jews; Nevi'im means "Prophets" and is the second division of the Hebrew Scriptures, and Ketuvim is "Writings" and refers to the third section.

8. It was at the Council of Trent (1545–1563) that the Apocrypha, except for 1 and 2 Esdras and the Prayer of Manasseh, was accepted.

9. F. Zimmermann, *The Book of Tobit* (New York: Harper and Brothers, 1958); Paul Deselaers, *Das Buch Tobit: Studien zu seiner Entstehung, Komposition und Theologie* (Freiburg, Switzerland/Göttingen, Germany: Universitätsverlag, Vandenhoeck & Ruprecht, 1982); George W. E. Nickelsburg, "Tobit," in *Harper's Bible Commentary*, ed. James L. Mays (New York: Harper and Row, 1988), 791–803; Carey A. Moore, *Tobit: A New Translation with Introduction and Commentary* (New York: Doubleday, 1996); Amy-Jill Levine, "Tobit," 11–31; Benedikt Otzen, *Tobit and Judith* (London: Sheffield Academic, 2002); Joseph A. Fitzmyer, *Tobit* (New York: de Gruyter, 2003); Robert J. Littman, *Tobit: The Book of Tobit in Codex Sinaiticus*; Naomi S.S. Jacobs, "Book of Tobit," in *Eerdmans Dictionary of Early Judaism*, ed. John J. Collins and Daniel C. Harlow (Grand Rapids: Eerdmans, 2010), 1314–15; Eileen M. Schuller, "Tobit," in *Women's Bible Commentary*, ed. Carol A. Newsom, Sharon H. Ringe, and Jacqueline E. Lapsley, 3rd ed. (Louisville: Westminster John Knox, 2012), 376–82; Naomi S. S. Jacobs, *Delicious Prose: Reading the Tale of Tobit with Food and Drink: A Commentary* (Leiden: Brill, 2018);

Jacobs. This commentary stands on the shoulders of the work of these scholars. As the first full commentary to look at Tobit through feminist lenses, however, this volume is unique.

A goal of a feminist commentary is to challenge the text and provide different ways of reading it. I assess equity issues both within the text's historical context and within our current world. Systems in antiquity benefitted some people and disadvantaged others, and it is the same today. I discuss the many issues pertaining to justice and equity that arise in Tobit, as well as the implications of these issues for modern readers. I pay careful attention to how gender, economics, and social status constructed power in Tobit's day and in ours. Tobit can inform modern reflections about what constitutes justice in dialogue with the realities of gender and racial discrimination and the marginalization of various groups of people around the globe. Feminist analysis shows how Tobit can help in the quest to establish societies built on relationships of mutual dignity and respect among people in our day and age.

Gender and Historical Context

As Elisabeth Schüssler Fiorenza states, "Gender relations are neither natural nor divinely ordained but linguistically and socially constructed in the interest of patriarchal power relations."[10] Tobit reflects the prevailing perspectives of its historical context, which means that gender was defined by biological characteristics and was understood to be split into the binary designations of male and female. Gender status was conceptualized as hierarchical; males held the superior position to the female: "Males are subjects, females are objects; males act, females react; males are mobile, females are stationary."[11] Tobit was shaped by the historical context in which the document was written, but there are examples of women in the narrative exercising agency typically reserved for men: a paternal grandmother educates her son (1:8), a wife is the breadwinner for her husband and son (2:11-14), and a daughter-in-law's wealth brings the family's finances back from the brink. Each of these provides

---

Naomi S.S. Jacobs, "Tobit," in *The Jewish Annotated Apocrypha*, ed. Jonathan Klawans and Lawrence M. Wills (Oxford: Oxford University Press, 2020), 149–75.

10. Elisabeth Schüssler Fiorenza, "Feminist Hermeneutics," in *ABD*, ed. David Noel Freedman (New York: Doubleday, 1992), 2:785.

11. Shira L. Lander, "Gender," in Klawans and Wills, *The Jewish Annotated Apocrypha*, 637.

fodder for feminist analysis. Reconstructing the lives of Anna, Sarah, and Edna from Tobit, a text that is manifestly fictional, is tricky. In fact, I think it is not possible to do so with certainty. The closest we can get is informed speculation.

Jewish history in the third century BCE was a time of cultural change. Alexander of Macedon, known as "the Great" in the West, was tutored as a youth by the eminent philosopher Aristotle, and he became enamored of Greek culture. Through a series of military campaigns beginning in 331 BCE and ending with his death thirteen years later, in 323 BCE, Alexander conquered parts of Europe as well as Syria, Egypt, Mesopotamia, and all of the Persian Empire. As a result, Judah, which had been part of the Persian Transeuphratine satrapy (province), passed into the control of Alexander's generals. The Ptolemaic house ruled Judea in the third century BCE, and in the second, that of the Seleucids. Greek thought and Greek language (known as *koine* Greek, literally "common Greek") dominated. Scholars coined the term "Hellenism" (from "Hellas," the Greek name for Greece) to denote the fusion of Indigenous cultures with the Greek-Macedonian worldview Alexander encouraged. Some Jews embraced Hellenistic culture while others rejected it, and still others attempted to combine the two.

At Tobit's time of writing, ancient Israelite society had given way to the initial stages of early Judaism. The eighth-century BCE setting of the document means that the term "Judaism" is not found, and the characters are appropriately referred to as "Israelites" or "sons/descendants of Israel" (1:8; 5:9; 13:3; 14:7)—though the author uses the term "Jews" (Ἰουδαῖοι) once in reference to their living in Nineveh (11:17). That term, which derives from the Hebrew name of the southern kingdom of Judah or, in Hebrew, "Yehudah" (יהודה), is typically not used until the late sixth century BCE and so is anachronistic for a document set, as Tobit is, in the eighth century BCE. The writer's choice to set the story at the time of the Neo-Assyrian invasion, rather than the exile created by the Babylonian invasion of the Southern Kingdom of Judah in the sixth century BCE, is strategic. In Tobit's third-century BCE context, the majority of Jews (who hailed from the Southern Kingdom of Judah)—and the editors of the Tanakh—did not consider the Israelite population affected by the Neo-Assyrian conquest properly Jewish. The biblical writers portray Israel in a much more negative light than they do Judah; Israel is described as unceasingly apostate from legitimate Yahwistic worship, which in the view of the biblical writers—most of whom were from Judah—was to be centered in Jerusalem, in Judah. Our author depicts

Tobit as one of the many inhabitants of the Northern Kingdom of Israel deported by the Neo-Assyrians to Nineveh. Yet as a northerner Tobit's devotion to the Jerusalem temple would have made him an outlier in the eighth-century BCE setting of the tale, as the northern tribes would have worshiped at shrines built by King Jeroboam I at Bethel and at Dan (1 Kgs 12:29) rather than at Jerusalem. The author presents Tobit's practices—which are widely embraced by Jews living at the time of the writing of Tobit—as the ones to be observed by all Jews wishing to live piously outside of Israel.[12]

Community Voices

This commentary benefits from perspectives different from my own. Gabriel Kwenga reflects on Tobit through his experience growing up among strong women in postcolonial Cameroon. EunHee Kang writes about the exchange between Sarah and her enslaved woman from a Korean societal point of view. Francis Macatangay, a professor and pastor, has provided two pieces, one on the argument between Anna and Tobit, and another on Sarah. Elisabeth Cunningham, a Canadian mother and social worker who was widowed at the age of thirty-six, reflects on the similarities and differences between her experience as a widow and that of Sarah. Chinese Canadian high-school teacher Jse-Che Lam considers the issue of not having children from her cultural point of view, and Tatum Tricarico, a blind activist and biblical scholar, provides her perspective on Tobit.

12. Devorah Dimant, "Tobit in Galilee," in *From Enoch to Tobit: Collected Studies in Ancient Jewish Literature* (Tübingen: Mohr Siebeck, 2017), 217–18.

Tobit 1–2

When Bad Things Happen to Good People

Tobit's two first chapters establish the plot and introduce a number of central characters. They also introduce a wide array of issues inviting feminist analysis, including women's labor, violence against women, civil disobedience, disability, being a member of a marginalized group, and burial practices.

Tobit and His Context (1:1-2)

The first two sentences introduce the titular character in terms of genealogy, geography, and geopolitics. They also establish an omniscient but unidentified narrator who presents what appears to be a historical account. But the guise of an objective report can mask numerous points of feminist inquiry, including how to assess the narrator, what meaning names have, and how to understand the setting of the story.

Literally, our story opens with the title "the book of the words of Tobit [βίβλος λόγων Τωβιθ]." This is the Greek equivalent of the Hebrew ספר דברי שלמה found in 1 Kings 11:41, used as a title for "The book of the 'words' of Solomon," an otherwise unknown text. For the earlier author, appeal to the "book of the words of Solomon" suggests that everything recorded in 1 Kings is accurate and based on legitimate sources. But we do not have these annals. A similar title is also found in the Greek Testament

Tob 1:1-2

^{1:1}This book tells the story of Tobit son of Tobiel son of Hananiel son of Aduel son of Gabael son of Raphael of the descendants of Asiel, of the tribe of Naphtali, ²who in the days of King Shalmaneser of the Assyrians was taken into captivity from Thisbe, which is to the south of Kedesh Naphtali in Upper Galilee, above Asher toward the west, and north of Phogor.

of Job, a first-century BCE or CE document that expands on the biblical book of Job.[1] With this start, Tobit's narrator is signaling that our book is objective history, but this very signal suggests special pleading. This ought to give readers pause. The need to apply critical thinking when reading ancient or modern narratives—or, for that matter, when reading or hearing the current news—is crucial. The title leads from the third-person narrator to Tobit's first-person account, or testament, in 1:1–2:6.

"Tobit" is the short form of "Tobiel" or "Tobias," which is also the name of Tobit's father. "Tobiel" means "God is my good," and "Tobias" is "The Lord is my good." The two names share the same Hebrew root, טוב (*tov*, "good"), with Tobiel incorporating "El," a common Hebrew word for "God," and Tobias incorporating "Yah," a curtailed form of the divine name YHWH (Yahweh).[2] "Tobit" is the Greek form of the Hebrew טובי (*tobi*), "my good." "Tova" is a woman's version of the name. Soon we meet Tobit's son, Tobias, a member of the family's third generation who shares this connection with טוב. Names matter in early Jewish literature; as Karla Bohmback notes, "To know the name is to know something of the fundamental traits, nature, or destiny of the name's bearer."[3] The overwhelming manifestations of the word "good" in the names of this family convey the message that Tobit and family are good people—or at least the narrator wants to suggest that they are. One of the principal questions Tobit grapples with is "Why do bad things happen to good people?" Names, however, can be ironic: given the tragedies that Tobit and his family will encounter, we may have to search for the good.

---

1. Richard C. Steiner, "The Heading of the 'Book of the Words of Noah' on a Fragment of the Genesis Apocryphon: New Light on a 'Lost' Work," *DSD* 2 (1995): 67.

2. Karla G. Bohmbach, "Names and Naming in the Biblical World," in *Women in Scripture: A Dictionary of Named and Unnamed Women in the Hebrew Bible, The Apocryphal/Deuterocanonical Books, and the New Testament*, ed. Carol Meyers, Toni Craven, and Ross S. Kraemer (Grand Rapids: Eerdmans, 2000), 35.

3. Bohmbach, "Names and Naming in the Biblical World," 33.

Naomi, the older heroine of the book of Ruth, insists that her name, which means "pleasant," be changed to Mara, which means "bitterness," because her husband and sons have died (Ruth 1:20). Tobit will similarly despair, but he holds on to his name and to his faith in his goodness.

The listing of Tobit's ancestors is not unusual in early Jewish writings; such genealogies appear regularly in biblical texts (e.g., Gen 5:1-32; 1 Chr 1–9). Even in a fictional story, a genealogy anchors a character to a particular family and context. The lists need not be accurate, and some, such as the list in Judith 8:1, are invented. The Gospels of Matthew and Luke have two for Jesus, and the listings do not agree. Inventing or enhancing genealogies, like padding resumes, was not in antiquity nor today uncommon. The list indicates both the importance of family, a theme that will continue in his son Tobias's search for a bride, and that Tobit had a solid Israelite pedigree. The genealogy also raises the feminist questions: To what extent are we who we are because of our past? To what extent are we judged on the basis of our family? Whose names do we carry, and how do we honor those names?

Biblical genealogies are also typically androcentric, as males are mostly listed. Tobit's genealogy mentions only men, and all of their names are theophoric, in that they each end with "El," Hebrew for "God" (i.e., Tobiel, Hananiel, Aduel, Gabael, Raphael, Asiel). Not only does this detail convey that Tobit was from godly stock, but the names will repeat: Hananiel (Tobit's grandfather) foreshadows the name of his brother (mentioned in 1:21); Gabael, Tobit's great-great-grandfather, shares a name with the man to whom Tobit entrusts his money (4:1); Raphael, the name of Tobit's great-great-great-grandfather, shares the name of the book's angel-in-disguise (and appears elsewhere only in 1 Chr 26:7); Tobit's great-great-great-great-grandfather shares the name of Sarah's father, Tobias's future father-in-law, Raguel, whose name means "friend of God" in Hebrew. Genealogies establish chains of authority and imply that the past shapes the present, so the message here is that just as God's presence imbued Tobit's history, through the names of his male relatives, so too was God guiding Tobit's present—though he doesn't know it yet.

Because biblical and other ancient genealogies customarily traced patrilineal descent, women's names go missing. The Greek of Tobit 1:1 literally reads "of the seed [ἐκ τοῦ σπέρματος] of Asiel," as if no female participation were involved. Patrilineal descent understood males (fathers, brothers, and sons) to be the primary means through which a lineage continued, and in this way both established and sustained the patriarchal idea that men were better, and more important, than women. Christine Mitchell states with regard to genealogies in 1 and 2 Chronicles, "The mothers are all effaced and silenced. In a fantasy of masculine performativity, men replicate themselves, bypassing their women altogether."[4]

Yet the Bible does on occasion mention women in genealogical lists, and there are hints of matrilineage, in which lineage is based on the mother, not the father. For example, the family of Abraham traces its descent through Sarah, not Hagar. In Genesis 17:16, God informs Abraham that he will bless *Sarah* with a son, "I will bless her so that she shall give rise to nations; rulers of people shall issue from her." Isaac's genealogy begins in Genesis 25:19 and is cut short in verse 20 by pivoting to his marriage with Rebekah. Rebekah's lineage is then provided, with the implication that it is her family background that is more important. Jacob's sons are presented not in order of birth but according to their matrilineal order (Gen 35:22-26; 46:8-26). The practice of polygynous marriages required the inclusion of women to verify which of the mothers gave birth to the featured son.[5]

The identity of the wife (or wives) that a son selected could also determine the line of succession. Esau had the "right" mother, but he married the "wrong" wives: his genealogical narrative in Genesis 36 stresses his intermarriage with foreigners (e.g., "Esau took his wives from the Canaanites" in verse 2). While Sarah Shectman asserts, "Women are an important building block in the developing nation of Israel, particularly as mothers and wives who validate specific lineages, but they are little more than that,"[6] the building blocks are much stronger than she suggests. Ingeborg Löwisch's recent work on the genealogies in Chronicles underlines how, "in the strongly male-gendered genealogy genre, female-gendered fragments hold potential for deviation" by complicating and subverting principal rules of succession lineage.[7]

In the apocryphal book of Judith, Judith's kinship information takes precedence over that of Manasseh, her husband. Manasseh receives

4. Christine Mitchell, "1 and 2 Chronicles," in *Women's Bible Commentary*, ed. Carol A. Newsom, Sharon H. Ringe, and Jacqueline E. Lapsley, 3rd ed. (Louisville: Westminster John Knox, 2012), 186.

5. Polygyny (multiple wives) is found more frequently than polyandry (multiple husbands) because of issues of paternity. A husband with multiple wives could be certain, as long as the women were faithful to him, about his children's lineage. A woman with multiple sexual partners could not be certain about who fathered the child.

6. Sarah Shectman, "Women in the Priestly Narrative," *Strata: Bulletin of the Anglo-Israel Archaeological Society* 27 (2009): 184.

7. Ingeborg Löwisch, "Miriam Ben Amram, or How to Make Sense of the Absence of Women in the Genealogies of Levi (1 Chronicles 5:27–6:66)," in *The Bible and Feminism*, ed. Yvonne Sherwood (Oxford: Oxford University Press, 2017), 356.

only cursory reference: "Her husband Manasseh, who belonged to her tribe and family, had died during the barley harvest" (8:2). Remarkably, Manasseh's identity stems from Judith, whereas conventionally, the husband gives his wife identity.[8] Amy-Jill Levine observes that "it is Judith herself who confers value, meaning and legitimacy to those whom she represents."[9]

The names of four women interrupt an otherwise patriarchal genealogy for Jesus in the Gospel of Matthew 1:1-17: Tamar, a Canaanite or Aramean who has sexual relations with her father-in-law (Gen 38); Rahab, a Canaanite prostitute who helped Joshua's spies escape (Judg 2–6); Ruth, a Moabite who asserts herself with Boaz (Ruth 3); and "the wife of Uriah," Bathsheba, with whom David commits adultery (2 Sam 11–12; 1 Kgs 15). The women, three of whom are gentiles, were involved in unusual sexual relations but are praised in later Jewish tradition as instrumental for the continuation of the Davidic line (Pseudo-Philo 3:14; Avot of Rabbi Natan 45 b; Pesiq. Rab. 40:3-4). Their inclusion anticipates Jesus's atypical conception as well as Joseph's hesitancy to marry his pregnant fiancée, and it also foreshadows the invitation to "all the Gentiles" (Matt 28:19) to follow Jesus.

Tobit is from the tribe of Naphtali, and various women associated with this tribe find resonances in the narrative, and, like Sarah in Tobit, they endure struggles. When Rachel, Jacob's preferred wife, is unable to bear children, she gives Bilhah, her slave, to Jacob; Bilhah's children will serve as Rachel's children (Gen 30:4-8). Bilhah's first son is Dan and the second is Naphtali (30:6).[10] Naming each infant, Rachel announces her authority over the children as if she bore them. Naphtali means "a contest of God": Rachel chooses this name because she has won "a fateful contest" with her sister, Leah (30:8). Thus Genesis 35:25 calls Dan and Naphtali "the sons of Bilhah, Rachel's maid." The NRSV has "maid," but the original Greek is παιδίσκης, a word more accurately translated as "slave," not maid.

---

8. Jan Willem van Henten, "Judith as Alternative Leader: A Rereading of Judith 7–13," in *A Feminist Companion to Esther, Judith and Susanna*, ed. Athalya Brenner, FCB 7 (London: T&T Clark, 1995), 249, notes that the reference to Manasseh "almost seems to be a joke." But Manasseh's death is not funny; the poor man dies of sunstroke, as a result of overseeing binders of barley sheaves (Jdt 8:3).

9. Amy-Jill Levine, "Sacrifice and Salvation: Otherness and Domestication in the Book of Judith," in Brenner, *A Feminist Companion to Esther, Judith and Susanna*, 214–15.

10. Similarly, the infertile Sarah gave Hagar to Abraham (Gen 16:2-4).

The story of Bilhah continues. Jacob, facing what he thinks will be a tense confrontation with his brother, Esau, places the "two 'maids' and their children" at the front of his household, Leah and her children next, and Rachel and Joseph in the (protected) rear (Gen 33:1-3).[11] Jacob is willing to sacrifice Bilhah and the sons she bore him, before he is willing to lose Rachel and Joseph, the son she eventually bore. When the danger passes, the narrator again refers to Bilhah as one of Jacob's women (γυναικῶν, 37.2). When Jacob is away, his first-born son, Reuben, has sex with Bilhah—identified as his father's concubine (παλλακῆς)—and "Israel found out" (35:22). Reuben is later cursed for this act (Gen 49:3-4), since a son's sleeping with his father's concubine was deemed dishonoring to the father. We do not hear Bilhah's perspective on this episode—that is, whether it was consensual or not. In Margaret Atwood's *The Handmaid's Tale*, handmaids are used as surrogates for the infertile wives of high-ranking men. The impregnation ceremony is based on Genesis 30:3, where the infertile Rachel says to Jacob, "Here is my maid Bilhah; go in to her, that she may bear upon my knees and that I too may have children through her."[12]

The land of Naphtali is highlighted in the biblical account of the Assyrian conquest of the Northern Kingdom of Israel (2 Kgs 15:29), as we shall discuss below. Kedesh-Naphtali was the hometown of Barak, commander of the army involved in the defeat of the Canaanites (Judg 4–5), a victory lauded in the Song of Deborah (Judg 5:18). Devorah Dimant rightly points out that "this episode renders notable the tribe of Naphtali in the early biblical history of the northern tribes and therefore had additional appeal for the author of Tobit."[13] This history is reflected in a later verse, as we shall see (Tob 1:8).

11. Tikva Frymer-Kensky, "Bilhah," in Meyers, Craven, and Kraemer, *Women in Scripture*, 62.

12. Margaret Atwood, *The Handmaid's Tale* (Toronto: McClelland and Stewart, 1985).

13. Devorah Dimant, "Tobit in Galilee," in *From Enoch to Tobit: Collected Studies in Ancient Jewish Literature* (Tübingen: Mohr Siebeck, 2017), 216. Dimant points out that Tobit's author associates the Galilean Kedesh, which was destroyed by the Neo-Assyrians, with the hometown of Barak, as if they were one and the same location. There are two distinct cities with two different sites: one in the lower Galilee, near Mount Tabor and the Kishon river, where the battle with the Canaanites took place, and one in the Upper Galilee. See Yohanan Aharoni and Miriam Tadmor, "Kedesh (in Upper Galilee)," 855–56, and Ephraim Stern, "Kedesh, Tel (in Jezreel Valley)," 860, in *The New Encyclopedia of Archaeological Excavations in the Holy Land*, ed. E. Stern, vol. 3 (Jerusalem: Israel Exploration Society, 1993).

The second verse sets the (fictional) context by providing the name of the ruling king, "Shalmaneser." His name in both Greek versions of Tobit is *Enemessaros* (Ενεμεσσαρος), which appears only here in verse 2, later in verses 13, 15, and 16, and in no other text. Carey Moore allows that *Enemessaros* is either a distorted rendering of the name Shalmaneser or, perhaps, another name for him.[14] The later Old Latin and the Vulgate read *Salmanassar*. Even were the reference to the historical Shalmaneser, a problem nonetheless remains: Sargon II (722–705 BCE), the *brother* of Shalmaneser V (721–722 BCE), took the tribe of Naphtali into captivity.[15] This historical inaccuracy and others (for example, 1:15 incorrectly identifies Shalmaneser V as the father of King Sennacherib; the reference should be to Sargon II) suggest an author at the very least not concerned about accuracy. The author probably made these mistakes deliberately in order to signal to readers the text's fictional nature, an approach that marks the book of Judith.

The inaccuracies might indicate, furthermore, a form of resistance: the author sees these ancient Neo-Assyrians as interchangeable, as unimportant on their own. While the opening details the names of Tobit's ancestors, the text shows a disrespect toward the names of the Neo-Assyrian rulers. The otherwise unknown *Enemessaros* could be like the foolish king Ahasueros of Esther. While possibly a reference to Xerxes II of Persia, Esther's king is masked behind an unknown name.

Having the narrative's central character be a member of one of the northern tribes (1:2) is highly unusual in Jewish literature. The biblical story depicts the division of a supposed united monarchy under kings David and Solomon into two kingdoms: the Northern Kingdom of Israel and the Southern Kingdom of Judah (1 Kgs 12:12-19).[16] The town of Thisbe is not known outside of this document, but Kedesh Naphtali, a city in the Upper Galilee near to which Thisbe supposedly was located, *is* well known. Second Kings 15:29 describes how "the entire region of Naphtali" was conquered by the Neo-Assyrian king Tiglath-Pileser III and that the people of Kedesh and "the entire region of Naphtali" were deported to Neo-Assyria. As Dimant correctly notes, "Tobit's religious

---

14. Carey A. Moore, *Tobit: A New Translation with Introduction and Commentary* (New Haven: Yale University Press, 1996), 101.

15. Moore, *Tobit*, 95–96.

16. There is inscriptional attestation for the existence of the two political entities of Israel and Judah; such incontestable evidence is lacking for the existence of the United Kingdom. See J. Maxwell Miller and John H. Hayes, *A History of Ancient Israel and Judah*, 2nd ed. (London: Westminster John Knox, 2006).

practice and attitude are defined in terms of the Judaite faith: loyalty to the Jerusalem temple and furnishing it with the cultic gifts of produce, in compliance with the Torah directives (Tob. 1:6-9)," as are those of the other characters in the narrative, despite their northern Israel origins.[17] In this way, the author presents Tobit's practices—which are those widely embraced by Jews living at the time of the writing of Tobit—as the correct ones to be observed by all Jews living outside of Israel.[18] Tobit, then, is depicted as one of the many inhabitants of the Northern Kingdom of Israel deported by Neo-Assyria to Nineveh.

Neo-Assyria ruthlessly defeated the Northern Kingdom of Israel, relegating it to the status of a province. They moved peoples of other provinces into the new province while expelling in particular elite Israelites and others.[19] This displacement and mixing of populations was meant, as J. Maxwell Miller and John H. Hayes state, "primarily to reduce moves towards nationalistic resurgence."[20] The exilic context of Tobit reverberates throughout the narrative.

Tobit Boasts of His Piety (1:3-9)

The narrative shifts to the first person as Tobit boasts of his pious acts and faithful endurance. The use of the first person as narrator serves as a form of literary protection: the narrator of the story is responsible for any mistakes, not the author.[21] Furthermore, such a strategy gives the impression that the author, like the readers of the story, is observing how Tobit behaves as the plot advances, and he might not be a reliable narrator. The story unfolds bearing two different points of view: one from the perspective of the characters, and the another from the perspective of the readers or hearers.

Before the exile, Tobit was generous to the needy, especially to orphans and widows, practiced tithing, did not eat "the food of the Gentiles" (v. 10), and celebrated the festivals in Jerusalem. He also practiced en-

---

17. Dimant, "Tobit in Galilee," 217–18.

18. Dimant, "Tobit in Galilee," 218.

19. Miller and Hayes, *A History of Ancient Israel and Judah*, 368.

20. Miller and Hayes, *A History of Ancient Israel and Judah*, 368.

21. Moore, *Tobit*, 105, states that the first-person account "was often used by authors for stories of questionable authenticity or veracity"; Joseph A. Fitzmyer, *Tobit* (Berlin: de Gruyter, 2003), 101, says that it indicates that the author "does not guarantee what he recounts."

³I, Tobit, walked in the ways of truth and righteousness all the days of my life. I performed many acts of charity for my kindred and my people who had gone with me in exile to Nineveh in the land of the Assyrians. ⁴When I was in my own country, in the land of Israel, while I was still a young man, the whole tribe of my ancestor Naphtali deserted the house of David and Jerusalem. This city had been chosen from among all the tribes of Israel, where all the tribes of Israel should offer sacrifice and where the temple, the dwelling of God, had been consecrated and established for all generations forever.

⁵All my kindred and our ancestral house of Naphtali sacrificed to the calf that King Jeroboam of Israel had erected in Dan and on all the mountains of Galilee. ⁶But I alone went often to Jerusalem for the festivals, as it is prescribed for all Israel by an everlasting decree. I would hurry off to Jerusalem with the first fruits of the crops and the firstlings of the flock, the tithes of the cattle, and the first shearings of the sheep. ⁷I would give these to the priests,

dogamy by marrying a woman from among his own kinsfolk. Tobit says he worshiped and tithed in Jerusalem (in accordance with Deut 14:23), rather than at the shrine at Dan, near his own home. Tobit's focus on the Judahite center of worship, Jerusalem, challenges the stereotype that northern Israelites (1:4) did not care about the temple in Jerusalem.

Even though it was located within the traditional borders of the tribe of Judah, Jerusalem initially was a Jebusite city (the Jebusites were a subgroup of Canaanites) until David conquered it (2 Sam 5), thereby uniting the tribe of Judah and the northern tribes of Israel under his rule. When David made Jerusalem his capital, it came to be known as the "city of David." When David subsequently brought the ark of the covenant to Jerusalem (2 Sam 6), the city became not only his administrative center but a religious hub as well, a holy "city of God."²² David's son and

22. Observant Jews to this day pray in the direction of Jerusalem, and the final line in the Passover Haggadah is "Next year in Jerusalem" (or, "Next year in Jerusalem, the rebuilt," for Jews living in Israel). This articulates the traditional longing for Jerusalem felt by diaspora Jews, just as the lament of Jews exiled to Babylon in Psalm 137 expresses, "If I forget you, O Jerusalem, let my right hand wither." The city later became holy within Christianity: according to the canonical Gospels, Jesus, a Jew, went to Jerusalem to celebrate Passover and it was there, during Passover, that he was arrested, executed, buried, and miraculously raised from the dead. For Muslims Jerusalem is holy because Muhammad was miraculously transported from Mecca to Jerusalem, and from Jerusalem to heaven to speak with God; Jerusalem is

Tob 1:3-9 (cont.)

the sons of Aaron, at the altar; likewise the tenth of the grain, wine, olive oil, pomegranates, figs, and the rest of the fruits to the sons of Levi who ministered at Jerusalem. Also, for six years I would save up a second tenth in money and go and distribute it in Jerusalem. ⁸A third tenth I would give to the orphans and widows and to the converts who had attached themselves to Israel. I would bring it and give it to them in the third year, and we would eat it according to the ordinance decreed concerning it in the law of Moses and according to the instructions of Deborah, the mother of my father Tobiel, for my father had died and left me an orphan. ⁹When I became a man I married a woman, a member of our own family, and by her I became the father of a son whom I named Tobias.

successor, Solomon, built the temple in Jerusalem as a place of worship for all Israelites, as Tobit 1:4 states. The Babylonian army destroyed the temple in 586 BCE, but Judeans repatriated from Babylon by the Persian emperor Cyrus rebuilt it in the late sixth century BCE. Herod the Great renovated it with a new splendor in the late first century BCE. The second temple was destroyed in 70 CE; all that remains is the massive platform on which the temple stood and part of the western retaining wall around this platform, known as the Western Wall or Kotel. Tobit 1:4 notes that Naphtali was one of the ten northern tribes that rebelled against Davidic rule in 928 BCE and instead supported Jeroboam as king (1 Kgs 12:19-20).

Tobit's family was divided in terms of their religious practice: the other members of his family followed the rest of the Naphtali tribe and worshiped the image of a calf erected by King Jeroboam (1 Kgs 12:28-29). Whether Tobit's family chose out of convenience (Dan was only about eleven miles away from the family home, whereas Jerusalem was much farther) or conviction, the potential is there for Tobit's having experienced intrafamily tension or feelings of alienation from his family members, though he does not discuss this. Perhaps he has exaggerated his singular religiosity, so did not face opposition. I felt less tension in my family when I converted to Judaism than when I became a Christian—and I understand why. Proselytizing was considered an important part of

---

considered Islam's third holiest city after Mecca and Medina and is called *al-Quds* ("the Holy [city]"). The status of this city remains one of the most contentious issues in the Israeli-Palestinian conflict.

the Christian identity I embraced, so I endeavored to persuade family members to be saved. No doubt my zeal was annoying. In contrast, my conversion to Judaism took place when I was older, and wiser, and there is no impetus to proselytize in Judaism. (The Lubavitcher movement seeks to convince Jews to be more observant, but non-Jews are not targeted for conversion.) My family was not taken by surprise when I decided to make my Jewish identity official, and they were supportive. My mom even flew from Vancouver to Toronto to attend the conversion ceremony and celebratory meal afterward. I was—and am—so grateful for this support. I knew others who, because of their decision to convert, faced opposition, even to the point of being cut off from family members. In certain cases, non-Jewish family members were unhappy about the conversion to Judaism. In others, if the person who was converting was doing so because they were marrying an observant Jewish partner, conversion through the Reform synagogue was not always considered sufficiently stringent (an Orthodox conversion was preferred).

Tobit demonstrates his commitment to the Jerusalem temple by making the three prescribed pilgrimages (Deut 16:16-17) to the city for Passover (Pesach), Weeks (Shavuot or Pentecost), and Booths (Sukkot) and expresses his thanks to God for his bounty by giving the sons of Aaron, who presided over the altar, an amount from each of his crops and animals (1:7) and to the sons of Levi a tenth of the additional grains, wine, oil, and fruit from his land. The descendants of Aaron and Levi were consecrated to the priesthood (Lev 8; Deut 18:1), and a level of purity had to be maintained by these members because they were working in the temple, though the wives and daughters of priests could eat the sacrificed meat.[23]

Tobit furthermore highlights his generosity to "orphans and widows and to the converts" (1:8). The Torah consistently stresses care for the people most vulnerable in society, including the poor, orphans, widows, and the stranger (e.g., Exod 22:21-23; Deut 27:19; Ps 68:6; Jer 22:3). One of the ways that individuals could show their piety was to give charity. Providing loans and not charging interest to other people in the community was a moral obligation (Exod 22:24).

The Torah's legal code suggests that widows, like orphans and strangers, were vulnerable to poverty and, by extension, potential exploitation.

---

23. One tradition, exemplified by the book of Leviticus, holds that only Aaron and his sons are priests while the Levites are assistants and therefore subordinate to them (e.g., Num 18:2).

Ancient society (and parts of today's world as well) did not favor women living independently of men, and singleness could disadvantage them. A woman lacking a husband might struggle financially—particularly if there were children to feed and extended family members were not nearby. Inheritance was typically patrimonial, through the father or husband.

Yet plenty of evidence shows that not all widows were helpless. Exceptions to the inheritance tradition occurred (e.g., Jdt 16:23-24), and widows frequently proved to be among the strongest and most resilient of individuals. Levine points out that "biblical widows are the most unconventional of conventional figures: expected to be weak, they move mountains; expected to be poor, they prove savvy stewards; expected to be exploited, they take advantage where they find it," as widows such as Tamar (Gen 28:11), Naomi, Ruth, Orpah, Abigail (1 Sam 27:3; 30:5; 2 Sam 2:2; 3:3), the woman of Tekoa (2 Sam 14:5), the widow of Zarephath (1 Kgs 17), and Judith manifest.[24] The widow in Tobit, Sarah, endures the loss of seven husbands (3:8) but goes on to successfully marry an eighth time, to Tobias (7:12-13). She, the daughter of a wealthy family, contributes to the eventual financial stability of Tobit's family.

In addition to having their dowry to help them, widows would also receive communal support, as mandated by Jewish law (Deut 24:17-22). The Mishnah and later rabbinic texts list various ways widows were protected. For example, m. Ketub. 4.12 states that even if a marriage contract (*ketubah*) lacked the clause "You will dwell in my house and derive support from my property so long as you are a widow in my house," a widow could maintain herself from her deceased husband's estate. There was a certain freedom in widowhood: women could decide for themselves how to spend their money and use their time.

The Bible defines an orphan as someone whose father had died, whether his or her mother was alive or not. Such was the perceived importance of men's protective role. Tobit, therefore, was an orphan (1:8): his father had died, and we hear nothing about whether his mother was alive or not. Orphans frequently were identified along with widows as among the poor needing assistance. Just as the God of Israel exercised power by protecting the disadvantaged—he was the "father of orphans and protector of widows" (Ps 68:5)—so Israelites were to "seek justice, rescue the oppressed, defend the orphan, plead for the widow" (Isa 1:17). The New Testament expresses the same concern: "Religion that is

24. Amy-Jill Levine, " 'This Widow Keeps Bothering Me' (Luke 18:5)," in *Finding a Woman's Place: Essays in Honor of Carolyn Osiek*, ed. David L Balch and Jason T. Lamoreaux (Eugene: Wipf and Stock, 2011), 124.

pure and undefiled before God, the Father, is this: to care for orphans and widows in their distress" (Jas 1:27).

Tobit's generosity extends to "the converts [προσηλύτοις] who had attached themselves to Israel" (1:8). The Greek term προσηλύτος appears first in the Septuagint (the 200 BCE translation of the Hebrew Bible into Greek) as a translation of the biblical Hebrew word גר, which referred to a gentile "stranger" or "resident alien" living among Israelites. In the Tanakh, there is no procedure for religious conversion of gentiles to Israelites; if a gentile married an Israelite, or lived among the Israelites for generations, they were considered Israelites.[25] The Torah granted resident aliens protective rights without the expectation of their religious conformity, though different biblical books reflect variable attitudes toward them. In the Second Temple period (during which Tobit was written), the meaning of גר came to be understood as "convert," and, later, an official procedure for conversion was created that included male circumcision and immersion and the offering of a sacrifice for both females and males. In the rabbinic period, גר takes on the meaning of "proselyte."[26] The second-century BCE book of Judith describes the voluntary circumcision of Achior, the Ammonite general (Jdt 14:10); this is an early example of conversion to Judaism. Tobit shows an ethical concern for non-Jews: they were recipients of his charity. Yet his repeated instructions to his son Tobias to marry "from among the descendants of your ancestors" (Tob 4:12) indicate a preference for endogamy. Gentiles were to be respected and supported but rejected as spouses likely out of concern that they would encourage the abandonment of the worship of the God of Israel (as is expressed about marrying Canaanites in Exod 34:16: "their daughters who prostitute themselves to their gods will make your sons also prostitute themselves to their gods").

Tobit states that he engaged in all of these virtuous acts in fulfillment of "the law of Moses" and in accordance with "the instructions of Deborah, the mother of my father Tobiel, for my father had died and left me an orphan" (1:8). Deborah is the first woman Tobit names. She plays a role that typically is thought to belong to a man. This example, however, subverts that conventional understanding. Mothers and grandmothers taught their children. Plato, in book 2 of the *Republic*, refers to mothers and nurses telling stories to children. Beverly Bow and George Nickelsburg

---

25. Jeffrey H. Tigay, "Exodus," in *The Jewish Study Bible*, ed. Adele Berlin and Marc Z. Brettler, 2nd ed. (New York: Oxford University Press, 2014), 123.

26. Tigay, "Exodus," 123.

refer to this and other elements of Tobit as a "patriarchal twist."[27] Yet perhaps it is our conventional understandings that are twisted and that sell short the historical actions in which women engaged.

The presence of Deborah's name, and especially the mention of her contribution to Tobit's development, disrupts the all-male genealogy that opens the book. We hear nothing about whether Tobit's male ancestors—theophoric names notwithstanding—shaped his faith, whereas Deborah, his grandmother, established its foundation. Deborah shares her name with two other biblical women. Rebekah's wet nurse (Gen 24:59; 35:8) is referred to as Deborah when she dies. Wet nurses are rarely mentioned in the Tanakh, let alone named in ancient literature. Deborah's death gives the etymology for the name of a landmark known as "the oak of the weeping" (35:8). The association of her death with weeping indicates that her loss was grieved—probably by the women she supported—and that she had a close relationship with Rebekah. It serves as a reminder of nonbiological mothers who care for children, in ancient society and our own. A tree is a beautiful representation of the contribution of wet nurses to communities of women and children and how, through such support, families grew and flourished, deepening their roots and spreading their limbs.

Another biblical Deborah was the judge and prophet associated with Tobit's tribe of Naphtali. She summons Barak, son of Abinoam "of Kedesh in Naphtali," and tells him that God has called him to "Go, march up to Mount Tabor, and take with you ten thousand men of Naphtali and Zebulun" (Judg 4:6) to defeat the army of King Jabin, the Canaanite ruler who had long oppressed the Israelites. Her victory hymn, referred to as the "Song of Deborah" (Judg 5:2-31), engages in self-praise: "The peasantry prospered in Israel, they grew fat on plunder, because you arose, Deborah, arose as a mother in Israel" (5:7). Here motherhood is not biological but protective.

Deborah's Hebrew name דבורה means "bee." Beehives are matriarchal social structures in which the queen bee rules the hive.[28] Today "queen bee" is an idiom for a powerful female who squashes competition. Not all

27. Beverly Bow and George W. E. Nickelsburg, "Patriarchy with a Twist: Men and Women in Tobit," in *"Women Like This": New Perspectives on Jewish Women in the Greco-Roman World*, ed. Amy-Jill Levine (Atlanta: Scholars Press, 1991), 127–44.

28. Thomas D. Seeley, *Honeybee Ecology: A Study of Adaptation in Social Life* (Princeton: Princeton University Press, 1985), 20, explains that the social structure of honeybee colonies "is that of a matriarchal family. At the heart of each colony lies one long-lived female, the queen, who is the mother of the thirty thousand or so members of a typical colony." I thank my student Audrey Marcil for this reference.

women help other women up the corporate, or academic, ladder. Given the importance of names in Hebrew literature, Tobit's grandmother Deborah can be seen as a matriarch who took over the task usually fulfilled by a male. If so, she anticipates Anna, Tobit's wife, who will become the family's wage earner.

I agree with Bow that Tobit evinces no shame in conveying this information about his education, but I cannot concur that this was a "casual remark."[29] The detail about Deborah is not necessary to the plot, so we may ask why the author included it. One answer may concern the diasporic setting. In exile or in colonized contexts, preservation of tradition is exceptionally important. Women, for Tobit, are trusted authorities, and they have the requisite knowledge to pass along instruction. By foregrounding women characters such as Judith, the LXX Esther, and the martyred Maccabean mother, Jewish Hellenistic stories recognized (described) as well as encouraged (prescribed) women's education and authority. But this authority is circumscribed: its activation—or at least notice of it—comes in the absence of capable men. The message is more than "having a woman teach Torah is better than having a son be ignorant." It turns out positively: as Carey Moore states, Tobit's "paternal grandmother, of necessity, did it—and did a splendid job of it."[30] For this society, both women and men provide instruction, and we should have expected Tobit to learn from both his grandmother Deborah and his father (who himself would have learned from Deborah). That a man educates his offspring does not mean that a woman cannot or does not.

The reference to Tobit's grandmother teaching him recollects the wise woman tradition, expressed with particular saliency in the biblical book of Proverbs. The author personifies wisdom as a wife, prophet, and teacher; those who adhere to her will experience "fruit . . . better than gold, even fine gold" (8:19) while those who do not, she will "mock when panic strikes you, when panic strikes you like a storm, and your calamity comes like a whirlwind" (1:26). The final chapter of Proverbs (31), a teaching called "the words of Lemuel," is composed by his mother. There she advises her son not to waste his energies on wine or women, and then she describes the אשת חיל, the "woman of courage," a wise, strong woman much like herself (31:10-31). Jewish men traditionally recite the

---

29. Bow, "Deborah 3," in *Women in Scripture: A Dictionary of Named and Unnamed Women in the Hebrew Bible, the Apocryphal/Deuterocanonical Books, and the New Testament*, ed. Carol Meyers, Toni Craven, and Ross S. Kraemer (Grand Rapids: Eerdmans, 2000), 68.

30. Moore, *Tobit*, 110.

poem to their wives on sabbath evenings, and it is also sometimes read at weddings or at the funerals of women. That each line begins with a sequential letter of the Hebrew alphabet (an alphabetic acrostic) invites such usage.

Naomi Seidman traces the fascinating translation history into English of חיל אשת and how its philological understanding was affected by cultural realities, from the earliest King James Version's "virtuous woman" in 1611, to the earliest Jewish Publication Society's (JPS) "woman of valour" in 1917, to the JPS's current "capable woman" dating to 1985.[31] Seidman notes that "virtue" of the King James translation may have stemmed from the Latin *vir* ("man") and so intended to convey strength. But by the twentieth century, the term "virtue," when applied to a woman, conveyed "sexual faithfulness," which was not on the author's long list of positive qualities.[32] The Septuagint's Greek for חיל אשת is Γυναῖκα ἀνδρείαν (literally "manly" or "courageous" woman). My preferred translation of Proverbs 31:10, therefore, is "Who can find a courageous wife?" since "courageous" best fits the meaning of חיל, meaning "soldier" (it is the word used for "soldier" in Modern Hebrew). When the term is applied to males, it conveys power, courage, and strength—and ought to do so when applied to females as well.

In 1:9, Tobit mentions his wife but does not provide her a name. He simply states: "I married a woman." He adds that she was "a member of [literally, 'from the seed of'] our own family, and by her I became the father of a son whom I named Tobias." The naming of the son, following the naming of Deborah, makes the absence of the wife and mother's name even more striking. In introducing this woman, *his wife*, who will prove the family lifesaver, Tobit reduces her to relational roles: kinswoman and son's mother. Tobit does not accord her any characterization of her own. As we shall see, he will continue to deny her autonomy. Whether he ever comes to appreciate his wife remains a matter of speculation; we readers may find ourselves more in sympathy with this woman than is her own husband. We might even sense that his treatment of her requires our critique, and in critiquing a man who fails to recognize his wife's worth, we also critique others who do the same. Perhaps Tobit is not as "good" as he seems.

---

31. Naomi Seidman, " 'A New Garb for the Jewish Soul': The JPS Bible in the Light of the King James," in *The King James Version at 400: Assessing Its Genius as Bible Translation and Its Literary Influence*, ed. D. G. Burke, J. F. Kutsko, and P. H. Towner (Atlanta: SBL, 2013), 487.

32. Seidman, " 'A New Garb for the Jewish Soul,' " 491.

Tobit repeats the theme of endogamy, the practice of marrying within one's family group: in 4:12 and 13, Tobit urges his son to do likewise, as does the angel-in-disguise Raphael in 6:12, 13, 16. The application of mirror reading is useful here. In mirror reading, we determine the target audience from the words of the text. For example, when an author makes an assertion, mirror reading suggests that the author thought some readers were in danger of overlooking or neglecting what the author has stipulated.[33] The recurring calls for endogamous marriage in Tobit may reflect the author's awareness of intermarriage between Jews and gentiles and his desire to persuade readers not to do this.[34] Intermarriage was and is a reality for diasporic populations, and as Toni Craven states, "Endogamy . . . was important for preserving national and religious identity."[35] While endogamy is foregrounded in the ancestral tales (e.g., Gen 24:15), Israel's Scriptures also attest exogamous marriages. For example, Abraham's slave wife is Hagar, the Egyptian; Joseph marries Aseneth, an Egyptian (Gen 41:45); Moses marries a Midianite/Cushite (Num 12:1); Samson marries a Philistine woman (Judg 14); David's wife Maacah is from Geshur, an Aramean kingdom (2 Sam 3:3; 1 Chr 3:2); Bathsheba's first husband was Uriah the Hittite; and Boaz's wife, Ruth, was a Moabite. Samson's marriage to the unnamed Philistine woman did not end well, and the biblical narrator criticizes Solomon for his marriages with foreign women (1 Kgs 11:1-43). Yet other intermarriages are condoned: indeed, the son of Ruth and Boaz, Obed, becomes King David's paternal grandfather. As Carol Meyers points out, since "religion was not a discrete aspect of Israelite society, but rather an integral part of its political, economic, social, as well as cultic identity, the anxiety about intermarriage and the worship of foreign deities actually expresses a broader concern about cultural boundaries."[36] One strategy biblical writers used to condemn intermarriage was portraying foreign women as dangerous temptresses. While the Tanakh rules out Israelite intermarriage only with the seven Canaanite nations (Hittites, Girgashites, Amorites, Canaanites, Perizzites, Hivites, and Jebusites [Exod 34:11-16;

33. John Barclay, "Mirror Reading a Polemical Letter: Galatians as a Test Case," *JSNT* 31 (1987): 73–93.

34. See Will Soll, "The Book of Tobit as a Window on the Hellenistic Jewish Family," in *Passion, Vitality, and Foment: The Dynamics of Second Temple Judaism*, ed. Lamontte M. Luke (Harrisburg, PA: Trinity Press International, 2001), 242–74.

35. Toni Craven, "Kinship Wife," in Meyers, Craven, and Kraemer, *Women in Scripture*, 358.

36. Carol Meyers, "Daughter of the Inhabitants of the Land as Marriage Partners," in Meyers, Craven, and Kraemer, *Women in Scripture*, 200.

Deut 7:1]), the book of Proverbs is replete with the trope of the dangerous foreign woman, such as Proverbs 5:3-5:

> For the lips of a loose woman drip honey, and her speech is smoother
> than oil;
> but in the end she is bitter as wormwood, sharp as a two-edged sword.
> Her feet go down to death; her steps follow the path to Sheol.

What is at stake here is nothing less than survival; thus, Meyers continues, "the notion of Israelite cultural exclusivity or ethnic purity as reasons for endogamy should be questioned."[37] The environment in which
Israelites lived—both within the land of Israel and outside of it—was
challenging, and shared cultural customs and traditions increased the
chances of the family's success.[38] Losing land through marriage to out-
siders was a possibility, and so was losing Israelite identity.

Most of the Tanakh's intermarriages are between Israelite men and
foreign women, but Deuteronomy 7:3 addresses both possibilities: "You
shall not give your daughter to their son, nor take their daughter for your
son." Bathsheba is (possibly) an Israelite women married to a foreign
man (Uriah, a Hittite), and David arranges his murder so that he can
marry the pregnant Bathsheba. Another is Esther, who becomes the wife
of Persian King Ahasuerus and uses her position as queen of the Persian
Empire to save her people from genocide. Craven astutely observes
that when Tobit tells his son, "Our ancestors of old, *all* took wives from
among their kindred" (4:12), he was "overstat[ing] the case."[39] Thus the
narrator drives home the point that intermarriage was not to be an option for Tobit's readers.

Captive of Neo-Assyria but Preserving Israelite Identity (1:10-15)

In 1:10-11 Tobit boasts about how, in contrast to his fellow Israelites living in Nineveh, he avoided the "food" (literally, the "bread") of gentiles
(τῶν ἄρτων τῶν ἐθνῶν). In 1825, the French lawyer, politician, and gour-
mand Jean Anthelme Brillat-Savarin wrote, "Dis-moi ce que tu mange,
je te dirai ce que tu es" ("Tell me what you eat, I will tell you what you
are"); he recognized that the eating of food was deeply connected with
culture and identity. German philosopher Ludwig Feuerbach in 1850

---

37. Meyers, "Daughter of the Inhabitants of the Land as Marriage Partners," 201.
38. Meyers, "Daughter of the Inhabitants of the Land as Marriage Partners," 201.
39. Craven, "Kinship Wife," 358, emphasis in original.

¹⁰After I was carried away captive to Assyria and came as a captive to Nineveh, everyone of my kindred and my people ate the food of the Gentiles, ¹¹but I kept myself from eating the food of the Gentiles. ¹²Because I was mindful of God with all my heart, ¹³the Most High gave me favor and good standing with Shalmaneser, and I used to buy everything he needed. ¹⁴Until his death I used to go into Media, and buy for him there. While in the country of Media I left bags of silver worth ten talents in trust with Gabael, the brother of Gabri. ¹⁵But when Shalmaneser died, and his son Sennacherib reigned in his place, the highways into Media became unsafe and I could no longer go there.

wrote, "Der Mensch ist, was er ißt" ("What one eats, one is").⁴⁰ The eating of certain foods, and the avoiding of others, indicates our group membership and distinguishes our group from an "other"; groups of people characterize themselves, or are mocked by others, based on what they classify as acceptable to eat. Indeed, food is "central to our sense of identity."⁴¹ The food Tobit rejects is not identified as "impure": it is "Gentile." Daniel, during his experience in Babylonian exile, likewise refuses to eat of "the royal rations of food and wine" (Dan 1:8); there is no suggestion that his rejection of the king's food is based on its ingredients (in contrast to Hos 9:3; Ezek 4:13).⁴² Nor is there indication that Daniel is concerned about the impurity of the gentile preparers of the food—if that were the case, he would not have accepted to eat the legumes and water instead (Dan 1:11-16). Christine Hayes and Jonathan Klawans have persuasively argued that the circumstantial impurity of gentiles is not a worry reflected in either biblical or Hellenistic texts.⁴³ Tobit refuses to eat the "food of gentiles" not because of the food itself, but *because it was prepared by gentiles*, and his actions reflect his being "mindful of

---

40. Ludwig Feuerbach, *Sämmtliche Werke*, vol. 10, ed. Wilhelm Bolin und Friedrich Jodl (Stuttgart, 1911), 5.

41. Claude Fischler, "Food, Self, and Identity," *Social Science Information* 27 (1988): 275.

42. David M. Freidenreich, *Their Food: Constructing Otherness in Jewish, Christian, and Islamic Law* (Berkeley: University of California Press, 2011), 35.

43. Christine Hayes, *Gentile Impurities and Jewish Identities: Intermarriage and Conversion from the Bible to the Talmud* (Oxford: Oxford University Press, 2002), 19–22, 47–54; Jonathan Klawans, "Notions of Gentile Impurity in Ancient Judaism," *AJSR* 20 (1995): 285–312.

God" with all his heart (1:11). Tobit understands his high position in the courts of Shalmaneser to be a reward for this mindfulness. Other texts written in the Hellenistic period reflect a similar concern for food (Jdt 10:5; 12:1-2; 1 Macc 1:62-63; 2 Macc 5:27). Women are in control of this crucial element of identity, since food preparation traditionally falls to them. Tobit explains that he will not eat food prepared by gentiles, but he never describes where the food he *does* eat comes from, nor does he mention the woman who prepares it (which is probably Anna, his wife). The whole family likely ate the same food, but we learn nothing from Tobit about Anna and Tobias in this regard.

Tobit's association with the king brings him high status. Several of his identities intersect: his association with power elevates his status, as does being a male. Yet the fact that he is an Israelite—a member of a minority ethnic community—made him vulnerable. Minority groups can particularly be in danger during regime changes, as we see with Pharoah who "knew not Joseph" and so oppressed Joseph's people, a minority group in Egypt (Exod 1:8). The same problem arises in Esther, where Haman speaks of "a certain people scattered and separated among the peoples in all the provinces of your kingdom; their laws are different from those of every other people, and they do not keep the king's laws, so that it is not appropriate for the king to tolerate them" (Esth 3:8); ironically, the same description fits Haman's own people, Amalekites living in Persia.

Tobit's job as a purchaser for the king puts him in a privileged position despite his being a member of a minority group. Such a position can be risky. We sometimes see this danger on display in our day when members of minority groups and/or immigrants attain power or success. For example, in late nineteenth-century Germany Jews experienced significant social mobility and had attained positions of power in business, academia, and culture. German-born historian Götz Aly persuasively argues that the Nazis used the envy and greed on the part of lower-middle-class Christian Germans who felt their own social and economic status was threatened as building blocks toward the Shoah.[44] Female politicians still face misogynist backlash from those who feel "threatened" by women in power. Catherine McKenna was Canada's minister of the environment (2015–2019) and experienced sexism for years: her Ottawa campaign office was desecrated by a misogynistic word painted on its windows, she was derisively nicknamed "climate

---

44. Götz Aly, *Why the Germans? Why the Jews? Envy, Race Hatred, and the Prehistory of the Holocaust* (New York: Metropolitan Books, 2014).

Barbie," and she received threats of such serious nature that she required a security detail.[45] "Incel"—short for "involuntary celibate"—is the label used by men online who belong to a misogynist community that blames women for denying them their right to sex.[46] Minutes before driving his van down a busy Toronto sidewalk in April 2018, killing ten and injuring sixteen people (mostly women), the perpetrator posted a tribute to another incel member who had killed six people in the United States and proclaimed, "The Incel Rebellion has already begun!"[47]

It is possible that Tobit received his position precisely because he was a member of a minority community. The king could trust—and control—a more precariously placed person than a native Ninevite. That Tobit leaves bags of silver with a relative indicates that he understood his position to be uncertain: should something untoward happen to him in Nineveh, his money stored in Media would be safe.

The reference to the highways becoming "unsafe" following the regime change suggests an increase in banditry. As Lincoln Blumell notes from his survey of material from the later Roman Empire, "Bandits posed escalating dangers to the traveler that ranged from highway robbery, which was usually accompanied by violence, to abduction if the bandits felt that the abducted might fetch a reasonable ransom or could serve as a slave, or in a worst-case scenario to robbery accompanied by murder."[48] The well-known parable of the Good Samaritan in Luke 10:25-37, tells the story of a traveler who is robbed and battered by bandits as he made his way from Jerusalem to Jericho.

Traveling in groups and avoiding night journeys mitigated danger on the roads. Lionel Casson suggests that "only exiles, refugees or the like travelled alone."[49] But exiles to Neo-Assyria and Babylon would

45. Anne Kingston, "The 2019 Election Revealed that Sexism Is Status Quo," *Maclean's*, November 5, 2019, https://www.macleans.ca/opinion/the-2019-election-revealed-that-sexism-is-status-quo/.

46. Niraj Chokshi, "What Is an Incel? A Term Used by the Toronto Van Attack Suspect, Explained," *New York Times*, April 24, 2018, https://www.nytimes.com/2018/04/24/world/canada/incel-reddit-meaning-rebellion.html?action=click&module=RelatedLinks&pgtype=Article.

47. Catherine Porter, "Toronto Van Attacker Found Guilty in City's Worst Mass Killing," *New York Times*, March 3, 2021, https://www.nytimes.com/2021/03/03/world/canada/toronto-van-alek-minassian.html.

48. Lincoln Blumell, "Beware of Bandits! Banditry and Land Travel in the Roman Empire," *Journeys: The International Journal of Travel and Travel Writing* 8 (2007): 7.

49. Lionel Casson, *Travel in the Ancient World*, 2nd ed. (Baltimore: Johns Hopkins University, 1994), 76.

have travelled in groups, and Tobias, who is neither exile nor refugee, would have journeyed alone. Women, generally speaking, had less autonomy to travel. As Catherine Hezser asserts, women were "not as free as their husbands and sons to roam the neighborhoods, not to mention any independent travel to more distant locations."[50] If they did travel, they did so with their husbands or other "male relatives or guardians," since there were fears of women becoming "enslaved, raped, and sold into prostitution."[51] Men were vulnerable to such malevolence as well and had to be very careful.

Lack of safety in travel remains a concern for women today. The Thomson Reuters Foundation 2018 poll on the world's most dangerous countries for women named India the most dangerous country for women traveling alone. The 2012 gang rape and murder of a twenty-three-year-old physiotherapy intern, Jyoti Singh Pandey, who was travelling on a bus with a male friend in New Delhi, received national and international media exposure. Public demonstrations occurred throughout India, and women charged state and central governments for not providing adequate security. Alas, little has changed in the years since the 2012 attack.[52] Women travelling by themselves face gender-based dangers that solo male travelers do not throughout the globe. Despite the challenges, increasing numbers of women are travelling alone, according to survey results from 2021.[53] Underlying gender stereotypes and social conventions influence the types of dangers women might encounter. The need to be vigilant, to watch our backs, both when alone and in public areas, is required. Black women traveling alone are exposed to additional dangers. Jessica Nabongo, a frequent solo traveler, states, "In many European cities that I've been in—like Barcelona, Madrid, Rome, Milano—women of color are in more danger because a lot of people think we are prostitutes. . . . My fear is always that if something happens to me in a European city, no one will care. I could be running down the

50. Catherine Hezser, *Jewish Travel in Antiquity* (Tübingen: Mohr Siebeck, 2011), 390.

51. Hezser, *Jewish Travel in Antiquity*, 394.

52. Gethin Chamberlain and Soudhriti Bhabani, "Five Years after the Gang-Rape and Murder of Jyoti Singh, What Has Changed for Women in India?," *The Guardian*, December 3, 2017, https://www.theguardian.com/society/2017/dec/03/five-years-after-gang-murder-jyoti-singh-how-has-delhi-changed.

53. "Solo Female Travel Trends and Statistics," *Solo Female Travelers Club*, https://www.solofemaletravelers.club/solo-female-travel-stats/.

street screaming in Italy and onlookers won't care because I'm black."[54] Dianelle Rivers-Mitchell founded Black Girls Travel Too,[55] a site that offers travel tips and organizes group travel. Guidebooks and apps such as Chirpey, RedZone, MayDay, Tripwhistle, and Noonlight provide additional support for women traveling solo; they let women warn about incidents and areas of danger, and they facilitate contact with local law enforcement.

Tobit, an Israelite Antigone (1:16-20)

In Israelite culture, treating a corpse with respect meant rapid burial. Even executed criminals were to be buried by the end of day (Deut 21:22-23). Jews view the body as holy; it is a gift from God (Deut 10:14; Ps 24:1). It is to be carefully maintained so as to preserve health during life; indeed, rabbinic literature indicates that a Jew was not to live in a community in which a doctor did not reside (y. Qidd. 66d; cf. b. Sanh. 17b).[56] And after death, though the spirit or life force has departed, the body is to be treated with honor (כבוד המת "honoring the dead"). In the ancient world, quickly burying the body prevented it from becoming carrion (2 Sam 21:10), and this is perhaps one of the motivations for Tobit's actions. One of the worst punishments for disobeying the covenant was to be left an unburied corpse (Deut 28:26). Jeremiah condemns King Jehoiakim by calling for his humiliating burial: "With the burial of a donkey he shall be buried—dragged off and thrown out beyond the gates of Jerusalem" (Jer 22:19 cf. 7:33).

Caring for the dead was—and is—not particular to Israelites or the Jewish tradition. The ancient Egyptians were careful to bury their dead, and Mesopotamian peoples too feared the thought of lying exposed. Non-burial could be weaponized. Neo-Assyrian kings punished particularly loathed enemies by refusing to bury their dead: Esarhaddon is depicted as saying, "The corpses of his warriors I did not bury but fed to

---

54. Megan Specia and Tariro Mzezewa, "Adventurous. Alone. Attacked," *New York Times*, March 25, 2019, https://www.nytimes.com/2019/03/25/travel/solo-female-travel.html.

55. https://www.blackgirlstraveltoo.com.

56. Elliot N. Dorff, "Jewish Perspectives on Death and Dying," in *Religion, Death, and Dying*, vol. 1: *Perspectives on Dying and Death*, ed. Lucy Bregman (Santa Barbara: Praeger Perspectives, 2010), 91.

Tob 1:16-20

[16]In the days of Shalmaneser I performed many acts of charity to my kindred, those of my tribe. [17]I would give my food to the hungry and my clothing to the naked; and if I saw the dead body of any of my people thrown out behind the wall of Nineveh, I would bury it. [18]I also buried any whom King Sennacherib put to death when he came fleeing from Judea in those days of judgment that the king of heaven executed upon him because of his blasphemies. For in his anger he put to death many Israelites; but I would secretly remove the bodies and bury them. So when Sennacherib looked for them he could not find them. [19]Then one of the Ninevites went and informed the king about me, that I was burying them; so I hid myself. But when I realized that the king knew about me and that I was being searched for to be put to death, I was afraid and ran away. [20]Then all my property was confiscated; nothing was left to me that was not taken into the royal treasury except my wife Anna and my son Tobias.

vultures," and a curse repeatedly found in Mesopotamian texts is "May the earth not receive your corpses."[57]

Ancient Greek culture considered the burial of the dead to have repercussions in the afterlife. The plot of *Antigone*, the fifth-century BCE tragedy by Sophocles, revolves around civic disobedience in the name of honoring the dead. Brothers Eteocles and Polynices died fighting on opposite sides of Thebes's civil war. Creon, ruler of Thebes, resolves that Eteocles will be buried in honor but that the body of Polyneices, who rebelled against the city, will endure public shame by lying unburied and being picked over by carrion. Antigone, their sister, finds Creon's edict immoral, since in her view burial rites ought to be provided to every individual, no matter how they behaved in life. The Greeks believed that the souls of the dead would travel safely through the underworld only if provided the appropriate burial rituals. Antigone defies Creon by burying Polyneices, and she pays for this rebellious act when he kills her by burying her alive in a cave. She has been called "one of the first great heroines of civil disobedience and the inspiration of resistance movements against tyranny" and "the prototype of alterity in her resistance to the law."[58]

57. Tzvi Abusch, *Mesopotamian Witchcraft: Toward a History and Understanding of Babylonian Witchcraft Beliefs and Literature*, AMD 5 (Leiden: Brill, 2002), 231.

58. Susan W. Tiefenbrun, "On Civil Disobedience, Jurisprudence, Feminism and the Law in the Antigones of Sophocles and Anouilh," *Law & Literature* 11 (1999): 35.

Tobit's engagement in *k'vod hamet* by burying Israelite corpses emerges strongly in these early chapters (1:18-20; 2:3-8; 4:3-4; 6:15; 14:10-13).[59] Rabbinic Judaism later will refer to *met mitzvah* (מת מצוה): the obligation on the part of a Jew to drop everything to bury a corpse that would otherwise remain uncared for (b. B. Kam. 81a). The first-century CE Jewish historian Flavius Josephus likewise states that it is forbidden to let a corpse lie unburied (*Ag. Ap.* 2.211). Thus, Jewish hearers of the parable of the good Samaritan would have been appalled that a priest and Levite left the injured man, "half dead" (Luke 10:38) and so appearing like a corpse, by the side of the road.[60]

Jewish law requires not only that the body be buried as soon as possible after death, preferably within twenty-four hours, but also that the corpse be attended by family or community members prior to burial. The reasoning is that we do not enter the world alone, and therefore we ought not to depart it alone. In modern times, male and female voluntary members of the local burial society (the *Chevra Kadisha*, literally "holy society") serve in this role.[61] In the ancient world, both women and men prepared bodies for burial (washed and dried them, treated them with herbs).[62]

How we treat corpses speaks to how we regard the human body. The person no longer exists, yet in antiquity and today as well, what we do with the bodies of our dead has deep meaning for us. In her *Advice for Future Corpses—And Those Who Love Them*, Sally Tisdale writes: "Whether we cling to it or flee it, what happens to the emptied body feels momentous. As long as we will continue to live, we will remember what happened to the body of the one who died."[63] She approvingly quotes philosopher Daniel Dennett's suggestion for why it matters so much: "If we start treating corpses as garbage, for instance, it might change the

59. Moore, *Tobit*, 121, notes that Tobit in the Middle Ages was the "patron saint of gravediggers."

60. Amy-Jill Levine, *Short Stories by Jesus: The Enigmatic Parables of a Controversial Rabbi* (New York: HarperOne, 2014), 71–106.

61. Rebecca Alpert, "Grief and the Rituals Surrounding Death: A Jewish Approach," in *Religion, Death, and Dying*, vol. 3: *Bereavement and Death Rituals*, ed. Lucy Bregman (Santa Barbara: Praeger Perspectives, 2010), 29. Members of the Chevra Kadisha are never paid, since what they are doing fulfills a commandment from God and thus needs no financial reward.

62. Nicola Denzey, Review of Kathleen E. Corley, *Maranatha: Women's Funerary Rituals and Christian Origins* (Philadelphia: Fortress, 2010) in *CBQ* 74 (2012): 594–96.

63. Sally Tisdale, *Advice for Future Corpses—And Those Who Love Them* (New York: Simon & Schuster, 2018), 149.

way we treat near-corpses—those of us who are still alive but dying."[64] In Tobit, dead Israelites are being treated like garbage.

Such contemptuous treatment of Israelite dead speaks to power—or the lack thereof—on the part of Israelites. Concerning dishonoring the dead, "there can be no mistaking the aggression implicit in the act."[65] Tossing of Israelite corpses outside the city wall, typically where garbage was dumped, indicated their powerlessness in the society to which they had been exiled. More, it indicated that the king, and others who supported the king's policy, regarded them as garbage. Dishonoring of corpses targeted less the dead than the society left behind. Leaving the dead to be picked over by scavengers was "the ultimate insult."[66] Such acts conveyed not only the message "You are not welcome here" but also the view "You are rotting garbage." We might think of the ashes of those "unwanted people"—Jews, members of LGBTQ2 communities, the Roma and Sinti, people who are mentally disabled—that the Nazis killed. We might think of bodies of Africans on the Middle Passage, dumped overboard if the food ran out. We might think of bodies of immigrants today, stuffed into airless trucks or hiding in the wheel well (the landing gear compartment) of an aircraft.

We can also look at the public violence Tobit describes from a gender perspective. Gina Rippon, professor of cognitive neuroimaging, studies the idea of essential gender-based differences in the newborn brain.[67] Rippon finds minimal evidence for brain sex differences in newborns; instead, the gendered world shapes the human brain, including such "gender clues" as toys, sports, and clothing. "Gender reveal" parties— a trendy celebration in which expectant parents cut into a cake, break open a piñata, or release balloons in a particular color (typically pink or blue) to reveal their baby's sex—can impact parents' expectations of and behavior toward their babies, even before they are born. Given recent evidence of brain plasticity, even in adults, Rippon's argument that any observed differences in male and female brains might be the result of gendered experiences in an individual's life is compelling.

---

64. Tisdale, *Advice for Future Corpses*, 149. The quote is from Daniel C. Dennett, *Consciousness Explained* (New York: Little, Brown and Company, 1992), 37.

65. Bruce Lincoln, *Discourse and the Construction of Society: Comparative Studies of Myth, Ritual, and Classification* (New York: Oxford University Press, 1989), 117.

66. Moore, *Tobit*, 120.

67. Gina Rippon, *Gender and Our Brains: How New Neuroscience Explodes the Myths of the Male and Female Minds* (New York: Pantheon, 2019).

Behavior expectations associated with particular genders differ among societies, but in every society (past and present), power relations are a part of the equation. As Catia Confortini notes, "Feminists see gender as a way of organizing the world into sets of distinct, mutually exclusive, categories. These categories are in a relationship of super/subordination one to the other and they both reflect and reproduce the gender order."[68] The feminine categories are less esteemed than the masculine ones in patriarchal societies. Included among the dichotomies may be "activity versus passivity, rationality versus emotion, and strength versus weakness" and violence versus peace, with the former term typically linked with masculinity and allotted more respect than the latter term.[69]

Gender is a practice that is both created by and reliant on a hierarchy topped by hegemonic masculinity—a masculinity that idealizes stereotypical (or "macho") male traits, such as "being (to at least some extent) assertive and aggressive, courageous, almost invulnerable to threats and problems, and stoic in the face of adversity."[70] This masculinity, in turn, "is always constructed in relation to various subordinated masculinities as well as in relation to women."[71] In this hierarchy, subordinated masculinities include openly gay men, or marginalized men—often men of color or with disabilities. In the rules of ancient masculinity, a man was manly when he controlled himself and others. The top male inflicts control on subordinate males and females; subordinate males inflict control on males and females lower in the hierarchy than they. The king of Nineveh, at the top of the hierarchy, is the supreme male figure who maintains his position by inflicting violence on males such as Tobit—who, as an Israelite exile, is in a subordinate, more female, position.

To reclaim some control, and thereby the masculine role, Tobit might have tried to prevent the killings. But when he was working within the king's administration, was his position too precarious to do so? Did he feel hopeless? Did he seek the opportunity to demonstrate his fidelity and manifest his courage? Esther is also in a vulnerable position, but she

68. Catia C. Confortini, "Galtung, Violence, and Gender: The Case for a Peace Studies/Feminism Alliance," *Peace & Change: A Journal of Peace Research* 31 (July 2006): 345.

69. Confortini, "Galtung, Violence, and Gender," 345.

70. Chris McVittie, Julie Hepworth, Karen Goodall, "Masculinities and Health: Whose Identities, Whose Constructions?," in *The Psychology of Gender and Health*, ed. M. Pilar Sánchez-López, Rosa M. Limiñana-Gras (Cambridge, MA: Academic Press, 2017), 123.

71. Confortini, "Galtung, Violence, and Gender," 353, cites Robert W. Connell, *Gender and Power: Society, the Person and Sexual Politics* (Stanford: Stanford University Press, 1987), 183.

directly challenges the king, and she decides, "If I perish, I perish": she is willing to sacrifice herself to save her people (Esth 4:16).

Tobit does not show Esther's resourcefulness or courage. Instead, he responds to the public humiliation of Israelite bodies by burying them, an act that was believed to restore dignity to the dead.

Verse 18 tells us that through divine intervention Sennacherib experiences defeat and is forced to withdraw his troops from Jerusalem (2 Kgs 19:35-36), but in his angry retreat the king kills "many Israelites." Tobit says that life was more secure under Shalmaneser than under his son Sennacherib, yet when Shalmaneser was ruling, *he* was the problem. Danger came from the streets—but it also came from the throne. Tobit buries his countrymen and women, whom he understands were killed because of God's meddling. Tobit is critical; he does not yet know that God remains faithful to his nation.

Verse 19 states that an informant from Nineveh reports Tobit's actions to the king. Such informing would be an effective way for an envious Ninevite to topple Tobit from a powerful position that he was perceived not to deserve. Now Tobit's life is threatened for burying the king's victims, echoing what happens in Sophocles's *Antigone*.

Sennacherib seeks to kill Tobit, and the political danger prompts Tobit to flee. The king then confiscates his property. As Joseph Fitzmyer states, "The irony is that despite all the good that he has been doing, misery comes into Tobit's life: he loses all his possessions."[72] Tobit is similar to Job in enduring suffering despite personal fidelity, but there are distinct differences in their responses to the suffering. Job consistently asserts his innocence and that he does not deserve the suffering God gives him. He wishes for death or nonexistence rather than the life of suffering he has (e.g., Job 3:11-22; 7:16, 21; 10:18). Tobit does good by burying the dead, but in the process of that loses his property (1:18-19) and becomes blind (2:9-10), a condition that consequently evoked pity and dependency on others (2:11). In contrast to Job, Tobit sees his condition as God's legitimate punishment for his sins, his "unwitting offences," and those sins that his "ancestors committed before you" (Tob 3:3, 4, 5). JiSeong James Kwon notes that "Tobit neither challenges God's order over the world nor summons God into the court to give him an answer (Tob 3:2-6), as Job desperately does (Job 9:17-35; 10:1-22)."[73] Like Job, Tobit seeks death

---

72. Fitzmyer, *Tobit*, 120.
73. JiSeong James Kwon, "Meaning and Context in Job and Tobit," *JSOT* 43 (2019): 629.

(Tob 3:6). But as we shall see, he seeks death because he wishes to escape what he refers to as "undeserved insults" from his wife. Readers of Tobit, in contrast to those of Job, know from the start that all will work out okay for him by the end of the story. What they don't know is *how* that will be achieved.

Finally, in 1:20, Tobit gives names to his immediate family. In 1:20, he states, "Nothing was left to me that was not taken into the royal treasury except my wife Anna and my son Tobias." In 2:1, however, he states that Anna and Tobias "were restored to me." Both sentences present the wife and child as forms of property—property about which he is being intentionally vague, since he either left Anna and Tobias when he fled or he did not. Both Anna and Tobias will prove much more than property: they emerge as independent figures with distinct personalities.

"Anna" is the Hellenized (or Grecianized) form of the Hebrew "Hannah," which means "grace."[74] It is also the name of the eighty-four-year-old prophet mentioned in Luke's Gospel (2:36-38). That Anna is identified as being of the tribe of Asher, whose geographical location is contiguous to Tobit's tribe of Naphtali. The author of the Gospel of Luke might have been familiar with Tobit and known of this earlier Anna, and so Tobit's wife and the elderly widow provide an intertextual reading. Luke describes Anna as a widow whose husband died only seven years after their marriage, and then Luke makes the unrealistic comment that she "never left the temple but worshiped there with fasting and prayer night and day" (2:37). Anna identifies Jesus as the one who will redeem Jerusalem, and she proceeds to proclaim this to all seeking the redemption of the city (Luke 2:38), although we never hear her voice. Despite the loss of a husband in one case and the loss of a husband's income in the other, both Annas are stalwart, resilient women who can be depended on.

The second-century apocryphal Gospel (or Protoevangelium, "pre-Gospel") of James names another Anna, this one mother of Mary and so Jesus's grandmother. The elderly Anna and her husband Joachim are yet another infertile Jewish couple, but in this case the miraculous and wanted child is a baby girl.

The primary connection between Tobit's Anna and another biblical figure is with Hannah, the once-infertile mother of Samuel. Both Anna the wife of Tobit and Hannah the mother of Samuel share more than a name. Both women face false accusations by men in authority: Tobit

---

74. Bohmbach, "Names and Naming in the Biblical World," 34.

accuses Anna of stealing a goat that had in fact been given to her (2:13-14), and Eli the priest accuses Hannah of being drunk when in reality she was praying to God (1 Sam 1:13-17). Both women defend themselves with clarity and fortitude.

Both are also matched with husbands who do not understand them, and this lack of understanding leads to poignant descriptions of each woman's isolation. Hannah's polygynous husband Elkanah does not understand why she weeps at the annual pilgrimage to Shiloh. "On the day when Elkanah sacrificed, he would give portions to his wife Peninnah [Hannah's fertile rival] and to all her sons and daughters; but to Hannah he gave a double portion, because he loved her, though the LORD had closed her womb" (1 Sam 1:4-5). Elkanah's gesture was well intentioned, but it only served to highlight Hannah's reality: she had no children. Peninnah, each year, "used to provoke her severely, to irritate her, because the LORD had closed her womb" (1 Sam 1:6). When Hannah cried and refused to eat the sacrifice (1 Sam 1:7), Elkanah did not understand why (1:8). When he asks her, "Hannah, why do you weep? Why do you not eat? Why is your heart sad? Am I not more to you than ten sons?" (1:8), he does not realize that the answer is "No, you are not." He does not understand her desire for a child. And "So it went on year by year" (1:7).

Desiring a child and not being able to have one is a difficult situation for men and women but can be particularly painful for women. In a study of two hundred American couples successively attending a fertility clinic, half of the women and 15 percent of the men indicated that infertility "was the most upsetting experience of their lives,"[75] and in another study, women with infertility issues felt "as anxious or depressed as those diagnosed with cancer, hypertension, or recovering from a heart attack."[76] Similar results were found in a study of one hundred Tunisian couples: infertility affected women's self-esteem more than their male partners, and they experienced higher levels of anxiety and depression.[77] Both my

75. L. H. Burnes, "Psychiatric Aspects of Infertility and Infertility Treatments," *Psychiatric Clinics of North America* 30 (December 2007): 693.

76. T. M. Cousineau and A. D. Domar, "Psychological Impact of Infertility," *Best Practice and Research: Clinical Obstetrics and Gynaecology* 30 (April 2007): 295.

77. Yousri El Kissi, Asma Ben Romdhane, Samir Hidar, Souhail Bannour, Khadija Ayoubi Idrissi, Hedi Khairi, Bechir Ben Hadj Ali, "General Psychopathology, Anxiety, Depression and Self-Esteem in Couples Undergoing Infertility Treatment: A Comparative Study between Men and Women," *European Journal of Obstetrics and Gynecology and Reproductive Biology* 167 (2012): 185–89.

husband and I were devastated by our miscarriage, but in alignment with these studies, the effects on me were deeper and longer lasting—I'll say more about this later.

Tobit's lack of concern for his wife disturbs me. He engages in the right practice by attending to corpses, but he does not consider how his actions would impact his wife and son. Challenging injustice through civil disobedience, as Tobit does, can put in danger not only the one involved, but also family members and friends. Doing the right thing is easier if there is no collateral damage. Thus Tobit forces readers to make a choice: do I put my family at risk in order to do what is morally right? Tobit, on the one hand, was generous in his almsgiving to the poor, the orphan, the widow, and the stranger; he benefited his community (Tob 2:1-8; 4:7, 11, 15). But on the other, his neglect for his wife points to a piety that is defective, contradictory, and self-centered. We might also consider how many male heroes and martyrs we celebrate without knowing who else was impacted by their actions: Abraham Lincoln, Mahatma Gandhi, Albert Einstein, Jackie Robinson, to name just a few. Were there any "Annas" among their partners and family members?

Tobit's Reprieve and Return to Nineveh (1:21-22)

Tobit's nephew Ahikar helps him reestablish himself (also in 2:10; 11:18; 14:10). The *Story of Ahikar*, an account of a high-status Neo-Assyrian statesman in Esarhaddon's court, was found among the papyri of the fifth-century BCE Jewish community in Elephantine, Egypt, near the Aswan damn; the name also appears on a fourth-century BCE tablet from Uruk. The story recounts how Ahikar raised his nephew Nadin[78] as if he were his own son, including providing him with sage advice, and wished for him to succeed him at court. But Nadin betrayed his uncle by making false accusations against him. As a result, Ahikar faced jail and death; he escaped and was hidden by a royal officer. When Esarhaddon later needed Ahikar's wisdom, he recovered him from his hiding place and gave him back his old job; it is Nadin who is then put to death.[79] This story was so popular that Tobit's author knew his readers would understand the allusion.[80] Jonas Greenfield argues that Tobit's author was

---

78. In Tobit the nephew's name is Nadab (11:18; 14:10).
79. Benedikt Otzen, *Tobit and Judith* (London: Sheffield Academic, 2002), 24–25.
80. Otzen, *Tobit and Judith*, 25.

[21]But not forty days passed before two of Sennacherib's sons killed him, and they fled to the mountains of Ararat, and his son Esar-haddon reigned after him. He appointed Ahikar, the son of my brother Hanael over all the accounts of his kingdom, and he had authority over the entire administration. [22]Ahikar interceded for me, and I returned to Nineveh. Now Ahikar was chief cupbearer, keeper of the signet, and in charge of administration of the accounts under King Sennacherib of Assyria; so Esar-haddon reappointed him. He was my nephew and so a close relative.

engaging in name-dropping to boost his protagonist's social standing.[81] This intertextual connection likely has deeper implications.

Tobit does more than name-drop: he suggests that he is Ahikar's uncle and thus turns Ahikar into an Israelite.[82] Members of minority groups— throughout history—will seek to claim the power they lack. We can draw two lessons from this point. First, when a member of a minority group achieves a position of power, that achievement can have a positive impact on members of that group, both individually and collectively. This is why it is so important that members of marginalized groups (women, visible minorities, members of the LGBTQ2 communities, and differently abled individuals) are represented in leadership positions, be it in government, in educational institutions, or in businesses. Such representation can disrupt the creation and perpetuation of negative stereotypes, and it can positively impact the aspirations of youth. According to the Inter-Parliamentary Union, as of 2022, only 26.4 percent of national parliamentarians were women; this is up from 11.3 percent in 1995, but much more work is needed.[83]

At the same time, the prominence of a person from a marginalized group can create problems for other members of the group; were the prominent member to fail, or to be blamed for a failure, negative repercussions for the group emerge (this situation sets the plot for the book

---

81. Cited by James C. VanderKam, "Ahikar/Ahiqar," in *ABD*, ed. David Noel Freedman, vol. 1 (New York: Doubleday, 1992), 113–15.

82. In Judith, the sage "leader of all the Ammonites" (5:5) who eventually converts to Judaism (14:6-10) and is named Achior may also be based on Ahikar.

83. Every month, the Inter-Parliamentary Union publishes rankings of the percentage of women in national parliaments, https://data.ipu.org/women-ranking ?month=1&year=2022.

of Esther). If the minoritized group is already negatively stereotyped—which is likely to be the case—then the person in prominence will face scrutiny to which the majority in authority will not. Women in power, for example, former German Chancellor Angela Merkle or former Australian Prime Minister Julia Guilland, face criticism for what they wear and are subject to gender stereotyping that male politicians are not.[84]

A Good Deed and Its Negative Repercussions (2:1-6)

In 2:1-10, Tobit the narrator trumpets his hospitality and his fidelity to the Feast of Weeks (Hebrew: *Shavuot*; Greek: *Pentecost*). Speaking of "a good dinner" that "was prepared for me" and "an abundance of food [that was] placed before me," he makes no mention of who prepared the food. Unless Tobit had servants or slaves whom he also ignored, Anna would have been the responsible one. Nor does Tobit mention her presence at the feast. Her lack of mention corresponds with other biblical descriptions of meals where only males are noted (e.g., Gen 18:8-9; 19:3; 24:54). Women—as we saw with Hannah—did participate in pilgrimage festivals, however, and the absence of reference is not indicative of an absence of presence. Susan Ackerman points out, "The male-dominated culture that gave us the Bible . . . tended not to include significant information concerning women's religious activities."[85]

Tobit states that Anna and Tobias "were restored to me." The Greek ἀπεδόθη is in the passive form, possibly conveying that divine intervention brought Tobit's family back to him. On the other hand, Ahikar could have facilitated this restoration. We can choose to see divine presence, and divine intervention is not mutually exclusive with human action. In either case, Tobit—who tends to keep the focus on himself—does not mention how this restoration occurred. Nor does he mention how Anna and Tobias might have suffered during his absence, nor where he fled, nor for how long. Again, we are reminded, if we read between the lines, how families can suffer when one member, in the effort to do the

---

84. Julia Guillard's 2012 "misogyny speech" was voted the most unforgettable Australian TV moment: https://www.youtube.com/watch?v=fCNuPcf8L00; Judith Mischke, "Merkel: Clothing Criticism Reveals Double Standards," *Politico*, January 23, 2019, https://www.politico.eu/article/german-chancellor-angela-merkel-clothing-criticism-reveals-double-standards/.

85. Susan Ackerman, "The Queen Mother and the Cult in Ancient Israel," *JBL* 112 (1993): 385–401, esp. 388.

Tob 2:1-6

²:¹Then during the reign of Esarhaddon I returned home, and my wife Anna and my son Tobias were restored to me. At our festival of Pentecost, which is the sacred festival of weeks, a good dinner was prepared for me and I reclined to eat. ²When the table was set for me and an abundance of food placed before me, I said to my son Tobias, "Go, my child, and bring whatever poor person you may find of our people among the exiles in Nineveh, who is wholeheartedly mindful of God, and he shall eat together with me. I will wait for you, until you come back." ³So Tobias went to look for some poor person of our people. When he had returned he said, "Father!" And I replied, "Here I am, my child." Then he went on

right thing, is sentenced to prison, forced to flee, or becomes a martyr. Raif Badawi, a Saudi Arabian condemned in 2014 to ten years in prison, one thousand lashes, and a $266,000 fine, ran a blog that critiqued the Saudi government and promoted free speech and secularism.[86] His wife, Ensaf Haidar, fled Saudi Arabia with their three children and now lives in Sherbrooke, Quebec. They were granted Canadian citizenship in 2018; the Canadian government continues to advocate for Badawi's release.

In like manner, Tobit mentions only himself and his son, Tobias, in relation to extending the generous dinner invitation to a struggling fellow Israelite. He instructs Tobias to invite "whatever poor person" (2:2), *as long as that person is faithful*. Tobit is already at the table and the food has already "been prepared" (probably, by Anna): it's a bit late to be inviting others even though he states that he will not start the feast until his command is fulfilled. Tobit's piety appears suspect. While his gesture of inviting a poor Israelite "among the exiles" seems generous and pious, there is a condition. The poor person is to be "wholeheartedly mindful of God" (2:2). Tobit frequently contrasts his own devotion to other Israelites; we might wonder if he really expected his son to find someone to invite.

Rather than bring home a guest, Tobias returns with horrific news: another Israelite murdered and body desecrated. Tobias's calling out, "Father!" and Tobit's response of "Here I am, my child" is reminiscent of Isaac's calling out, "Father," to Abraham, and Abraham's response of "Yes, my son" (Gen 22:7) in the account of God's test by asking him to sacrifice his beloved and much-longed-for son, Isaac. The closest English translation for the Hebrew *hineni* is "here I am," but this is not precise.

---

86. Mireille Vachon, "Des Nouvelles de Raif Badawi," *La Tribune*, June 17, 2020.

to say, "Look, father, one of our own people has been murdered and thrown into the market-place, and now he lies there strangled." ⁴Then I sprang up, left the dinner before even tasting it, and removed the body from the square and laid it in one of the rooms until sunset when I might bury it. ⁵When I returned, I washed myself and ate my food in sorrow. ⁶Then I remembered the prophecy of Amos, how he said against Bethel,

> "Your festivals shall be turned into
> mourning,
> and all your songs into
> lamentation."

And I wept.

The term "indicates readiness, alertness, attentiveness, receptivity, and responsiveness to instructions,"[87] and Abraham uses it in Genesis 22:1 in response to God, in 22:7 to Isaac, and in 22:11 to the angel who stops him from sacrificing his son. This response sets the events of Tobit 2 as a "test": again faced with the corpse of a fellow Israelite, what will Tobit do? He has already faced punishment for burying the dead.

We also realize that Tobias has a different reaction from that of his father. Seeing the body, he does not bury it; instead, he mentions it to Tobit. Is he asking for advice? Is he suggesting that burying corpses, and so facing possible political repercussions, is his father's job? Is he looking for his father to give him courage or help? When we see an injustice, is our better move to step in and fix it or to consult with our elders as to the best response? Given the original Ahikar story, could he be hoping that his father will both bury the corpse and face exile? Tobias does not mention the corpse to his mother; we can only guess what her response would have been. Given the intertextual notes with Antigone, it is possible she would have attended to the corpse herself.

Just as Abraham does not tell Sarah that he is setting out for Mount Moriah to sacrifice Isaac, so Tobit does not tell Anna why he is leaving the dinner. According to G2, Tobit "removed the body from the square and laid it in one of the rooms [ἓν τῶν οἰκιδίων] until sunset when I might bury it" (2:4). The literal translation of οἰκιδίων is "small house" or "outbuilding" rather than "rooms"; the implication is that Tobit brings the body to a smaller building, not into the rooms of his

---

87. Jon D. Levenson, "Genesis," in *The Jewish Study Bible*, ed. Adele Berlin and Marc Zvi Brettler, 2nd ed. (New York: Oxford University Press, 2014), 42.

own home.[88] If it were in his own residence, the presence of a dead body would render "his entire home unclean for seven days" (Num 19:11-22), as Carey Moore points out.[89] But it is not clear why Tobit or his family would need to be in a state of ritual purity. Tobit does not explain why he sleeps in the courtyard. Perhaps to avoid waking up members of his family, he opts to sleep outside; it is warm, so perhaps he would enjoy a breeze. Had Tobit opted to sleep inside the house with his wife Anna, he would have been safe from the outside danger, whereas in the chapters to come, Tobias's opting to sleep inside the home with his wife, Sarah, puts him at risk.

In having Tobit wait until after sunset to bury the body (2:4), the author suggests that deed was to be done under darkness for self-protection. Tobit also washes himself. No extant law would require his avoiding his house to prevent spreading of impurity. Sometimes, dirt is simply dirt.

Tobit's act extends the danger to his wife Anna and his child Tobias, yet he shows no consideration for his family. Nor does he mention them when he says he ate his food "in sorrow" (2:5). He does manage to eat, despite the corpse in the next room. There is no indication that Anna and Tobit ate at all.

The author's quotation of part of Amos 8:10 likely derives from *metalepsis*, the implied knowledge of a verse, located near the cited text, that provides the connection. The second half of Amos 8:3 reads,

> The dead bodies shall be many,
> cast out in every place.
> Be silent!

The author presumes some among the readers will make the connection. The move is clever; it is also indicative of an aware and elite reader, sharing connections that not all readers can make.

In the subsequent verses (4-7) Amos decries how the Israelites worshiping at the sanctuary of Bethel are anxious for holidays to be over so that they can return to their work, through which they may take advantage of the poor. Because of this behavior, the Lord says in verse 10: "I will turn your feasts into mourning, and all your songs into lamentation"

---

88. "οἰκιδίων," in J. Lust, E. Eynikel, and K. Hauspie, *Greek-English Lexicon of the Septuagint*, rev. ed. (Stuttgart: Deutsche Bibelgesellschaft, 2003), 429. The GI version has εἴς τι οἴκημα, "in a room, chamber," in Lust, Eynikel, and Hauspie, *Greek-English Lexicon*, 429.

89. Moore, *Tobit*, 128.

(Amos 8:10; cf. Tob 2:6). Tobit changes the verb to a passive, which, as Fitzmyer observes, "thereby eliminat[es] God's action as the source of the reversal."[90] Given that Tobit has just attempted to invite a poor person to join him for a meal—the opposite of what Amos describes—the quotation of this verse seems out of place, even ironic.[91]

But maybe not. Tobit invites "whatever poor person you may find of our people," but, as already noted, he adds a condition, "who is wholeheartedly mindful of God." Throughout the narrative Tobit has emphasized that only he is "wholeheartedly mindful of God." Perhaps the author, in quoting Amos, is leveling a judgment of Tobit's empty invitation. Perhaps Tobit's hypocrisy, his inability to see that others also are faithful, including his family, provides some narrative justification for what will befall him.

Yet a feminist lens resists this narrative satisfaction, since nothing justifies suffering. Nothing justifies physical torture. Schadenfreude—feeling pleasure at the downfall of others—might be a natural human emotion, but it is one that ought to be rejected if we want to live honorable lives. Allowing ourselves to indulge in schadenfreude diminishes us.

Another Burial and Tobit's Blindness (2:7-10)

Tobit's "neighbors laughed" (2:8) at him for returning to the activity that already compromised his relationship with the king. The neighbors probably were fellow Israelites, incredulous at Tobit's persistence in behavior that twice led to punishment. Perhaps the neighbors speak for Anna and Tobias: Why does their husband/father keep putting himself (and them) in danger? Were the neighbors worried that Tobit would put them all in danger with the authorities? Or maybe their laughter was a defensive reaction to their own feelings of guilt, since they did not have the courage to do what Tobit was doing. Tobit waited until dark to bury the body yet did not seem to care if he was seen by his neighbors. Nor did he respond to these taunts. Given that Tobit describes his piety as surpassing that of his peers (Tob 1:4-5, 6, 10), he likely did not concern

---

90. Fitzmyer, *Tobit*, 135. Fitzmyer suggests that the quotation is "to support his [Tobit's] concern for the poor dead even on Pentecost."

91. Moore, *Tobit*, 129, notes, "The appearance of this passage from Amos is quite ironic. After all, the passage in Amos referred to Bethel's Israelites who *had* exploited the poor (cf. Amos 8:4-6). The soon-to-be-blind Tobit had the exact opposite" (italics are in original).

⁷When the sun had set, I went and dug a grave and buried him. ⁸And my neighbors laughed and said, "Is he still not afraid? He has already been hunted down to be put to death for doing this, and he ran away; yet here he is again burying the dead!" ⁹That same night I washed myself and went into my courtyard and slept by the wall of the courtyard; and my face was uncovered because of the heat. ¹⁰I did not know that there were sparrows on the wall; their fresh droppings fell into my eyes and produced white films. I went to physicians to be healed, but the more they treated me with ointments the more my vision was obscured by the white films, until I became completely blind. For four years I remained unable to see. All my kindred were sorry for me, and Ahikar took care of me for two years before he went to Elymais.

himself with what they thought about him; maybe he even thought it beneath him to respond.

Tobit's "reward" for burying the corpse of a fellow Israelite is bird excrement falling into his eyes. This bizarre event moves the story into farce. Had we not seen Tobit as buffoonish or a caricature earlier, it is hard now to escape this conclusion. I might laugh at the ridiculousness of what befalls Tobit and feel better about the struggles I am undergoing in my own life. At the same time, this farce expresses critique: Tobit boasted about his piety and now he is brought low, firmly to ground, by that which flies high. Yet I cannot laugh too much at Tobit; I relate too much with his good intentions and his struggle to understand God's plan for his life. Additionally, I have the advantage of knowing that all will work out, but Tobit does not. I may root for him as the underdog, even if he is somewhat of a buffoon.

Tobit's multiple visits to doctors yield only increasing blindness—his statement amounts to a gentle critique of physicians. Skepticism toward doctors surfaces also in the Gospels' story of the woman with a twelve-year hemorrhage (Mark 5:25-34; cf. Matt 9:20-22; Luke 8:43-48). She, like Tobit, sought help from multiple physicians, but her only return is financial ruin. Though not explicitly stated, the cost of seeing the doctors and not getting better might be behind Tobit's frustration. Finances—better, the lack thereof—become central to Tobit's story.

The idea that Tobit, blinded, would not have been able to contribute to the sustaining of his family is extreme. Tobit does not state that he did not work. While blind people in antiquity are sometimes portrayed as beggars (Luke 18:35; Mark 10:46, named "Bartimaeus son of Timaeus"; Matt

20:30), this was not their only option. Both historical and mythological literature depict blind people as prophets, poets, and musicians (Homer, *Od.* 8.62–70; Dio Chrysostom, *Or.* 36.10–11; Pausanias, *Descr.* 7.5.7).[92] Apollodorus describes the blind Theban seer, Teiresias, as walking with the aid of a staff "like those who see" (3.6.7).[93] In Sophocles, *Antigone* 910–11, Teiresias's slave guides him.[94] No reference to guide dogs has been found, but, "the lack of reference does not indicate an absence of guide dogs."[95] From Homer, thought to be blind (*To Apollo* 170–72), to Didymus the Blind of the fourth century CE, we find the description of the sightless who have insight and memory. Nor is there any "practical reason why a blind person would have been banned a priori from most occupations,"[96] including agricultural work.[97] Blind biblical characters include Isaac (Gen 27:1), Eli (1 Sam 3:2), and Ahijah (1 Kgs 14:4); instructions on treating them suggest that blind people were active participants within the community (Lev 19:14, "You shall not . . . put a stumbling block before the blind"; Deut 27:18, "Cursed be anyone who misleads a blind person on the road"). Jesus's comment about the blind leading the blind and that "both will fall into a pit" (Matt 15:14; Luke 6:39) is inaccurate and reflective of the conventional view that blind people cannot navigate. Disability studies alerts the sighted person to our stereotypes about the blind. Tobit's being newly blind (rather than from birth) would have required a difficult, but not insurmountable, adjustment.

Tobit acknowledges Ahikar's two years of assistance. He also acknowledges that his family members were sorry for him. This latter comment might be a dig: if all they did was pity him, Tobit is saying they ought to have done more. The next chapter demonstrates that Anna contributes to the family's survival by working, but Tobit makes no acknowledgment of this contribution. Tobit seems to take for granted Anna's role as nurturer and caregiver. Such attitudes are sometimes seen in our day

---

92. Nicole Kelley, "Deformity and Disability in Greece and Rome," in *This Abled Body: Rethinking Disabilities in Biblical Studies*, ed. Hector Avalos, Sarah J. Melcher, and Jeremy Schipper (Atlanta: SBL, 2007), 41.

93. Apollodorus, *The Library*, trans. Sir James George Frazer, 2 vols. (London, William Heinemann Ltd., 1921).

94. Martha L. Rose, *The Staff of Oedipus: Transforming Disability in Ancient Greece* (Ann Arbor: University of Michigan Press, 2003), 88.

95. Rose, *The Staff of Oedipus*, 90.

96. Rose, *The Staff of Oedipus*, 91.

97. Rose, *The Staff of Oedipus*, 91. Polyphemus, in *Odyssey* 9.440-60, keeps watch over his sheep and knows them by running his hands over their backs.

too when daughters more so than sons are expected to care for aging parents. According to the statistics from 2017 and 2018, among the 40.4 million eldercare providers in the United States—that is, those who provide unpaid care to someone age sixty-five or older needing help because of a condition related to aging—the majority (58 percent) are women.[98] It is, however, true that women live longer than men and so it is older women (widows) who might be doing more of the elder care simply because there are more widows.

Eye ailments and problems with vision are listed in medical books and other ancient sources. The fifth-century BCE physician Hippocrates refers to cataracts (*On Vision* 9.4-5) as does Galen (10.990), a Greek physician and surgeon in the Roman Empire during the second and third centuries CE. A fourth-century CE papyrus counsels a person with "white eyes" (*leukeumatiôn*) to travel to the nearest city for treatment (*P. Oxy.* 31.2601).[99] Clay models of eyes, and a high number of representations of eyes in inscriptions, have been found at the Athenian temple of the god of healing, Asclepius. Dated to between the middle of the fourth and third centuries BCE, these texts and artifacts "may represent preventative measures against eye disease or pleas or thanks for cures of eye disease."[100] Given the higher prominence of visually impaired people in ancient Rome, Martha L. Rose asserts that "sighted people knew blind and sight-impaired people well enough to understand the abilities and limitations of failing vision."[101] For the wealthy, loss of sight likely was manageable; for the poor, it would have been a much more challenging situation with which to deal.[102]

Annie Attia notes that "bird droppings were often used as medication in the Mesopotamian recipes" to cure eye ailments, including blindness.[103] She also astutely observes: "It is striking that a key product of Mesopotamian ocular therapeutics became the cause of Tobit's blindness. . . . We have here a disguised criticism or caricature of Neo-Assyrian medicine,

98. https://www.bls.gov/news.release/pdf/elcare.pdf.

99. Cited in Rose, *The Staff of Oedipus*, 84.

100. Rose, *The Staff of Oedipus*, 84.

101. Rose, *The Staff of Oedipus*, 93.

102. Lisa Trentin, "Exploring Visual Impairment in Ancient Rome," in *Disabilities in Roman Antiquity*, ed. Martha L. Rose, C. F. Goodey, Christian Laes (Boston: Brill, 2013), 111.

103. Annie Attia, "Disease and Healing in the Book of Tobit and in Mesopotamian Medicine," in *Mesopotamian Medicine and Magic: Studies in Honor of Markham J. Geller*, ed. Strahil V. Panayotov and Ludek Vacín (Leiden: Brill, 2018), 62.

which must have been understood by the readers and the audience of this narrative."[104] In the ancient world, medicine was practiced but the lack of antibiotics and vaccinations made dealing with illnesses and disabilities challenging. Tobit's multiple, and unfruitful, visits to doctors suggest that his eye problems were severe.

Disability studies, a relatively recent field of study, does not focus on an individual's imperfection or deficiency; disability theorists define disability as a discrepancy in power.[105] For example, in communities in which staircases are the predominant means of entering restaurants, a person in a wheelchair is at a disadvantage. Clearly no one on the planning committee of such a community had awareness of and sensitivity to the reality of the variety of mobility needs. Giving voice, agency, and power to those with disabilities means that they will be on city planning committees, and ramps as well as stairs will be built to enter restaurants. A feminist perspective understands disability to be "a cultural interpretation of human variation rather than an inherent inferiority, a pathology to cure, or an undesirable trait to eliminate" and seeks to question assumptions about disability in the same way it challenges patriarchal assumptions about gender.[106] Using our earlier example, access to buildings constructed only for those capable of climbing stairs privileges people who can walk and represents a limited view of human mobility and of who needs to enter buildings. Just as social markers such as race, social class, and sexuality influence how gender is performed, these markers shape how disabled people see themselves (and perform their identities) and how they live in their communities.[107] Tobit's blindness is presented as an "undesirable trait to eliminate," reinforcing negative stereotypes associated with vision impairment.

Perceptions of disability are contingent, both in the ancient world and in ours, on the cultural ideas about what constitutes "normal" male and female lives. In antiquity, the paradigm of human perfection was the able-bodied adult male. As Brittany E. Wilson notes, "Manly men were

---

104. Annie Attia, "Disease and Healing in the Book of Tobit and in Mesopotamian Medicine," in *Mesopotamian Medicine and Magic: Studies in Honor of Markham J. Geller*, ed. Strahil V. Panayotov and Ludek Vacin (Leiden: Brill, 2018), 64.

105. Nandini Ghosh, *Impaired Bodies, Gendered Lives* (New Delhi: Primus Books, 2016), 7.

106. Rosemarie Garland-Thomson, "Feminist Disability Studies," *Signs* 30 (Winter 2005): 1557, 1559.

107. Ghosh, *Impaired Bodies, Gendered Lives*, 8.

to exercise self-control and to safeguard the boundaries of their bodies from outside invasion or penetration."[108] These same ideals are associated with masculinity in modern societies, where images of disabled men undermine cultural definitions of masculinity. Nandini Ghosh points out that one of the central reasons that the paralysis of the American president (from 1933 to 1945) Franklin Delano Roosevelt was kept from the public was because his using a wheelchair would have been understood to be a "symbol of dependency and lack of autonomy."[109] Today, disabled politicians are more visible than they were seventy years ago (e.g., Texas governor Greg Abbott is partially paralyzed and uses a wheelchair; US senator from Illinois, Tammy Duckworth, is a double amputee who uses prosthetics and sometimes a wheelchair), but a recent study shows that people with disabilities continue to be underrepresented in US politics.[110]

When the adult male body does not match "the expected natural capacities of a 'young, non-disabled, ideally-shaped, healthy adult male,'" including "the ability to earn wages . . . being able to walk, hear and see, well," a man is perceived to be disabled and lesser-than.[111] Indeed, the disabled male "is aligned with the 'feminine' realm, assumed to be devoid of self-mastery and control, social independence, physical and interactive competence and social productivity."[112] Aristotle considered females to be a "maimed" or "deformed" (πεπηρωμένον) male (*Gen. An.* 737a. 28). Tobit's inability to see would have been judged against what his society considered to be ideal male qualities, including strength, control of self, honor, independence, and authority (control of others). The fact that his blindness would have diminished his independence, and his ability to control himself and others, meant that he was perceived as feminized. He tries to hang on to his masculine privilege by scolding and commanding Anna (in 2:11-14).

Ancient texts sometimes associate illness and disability with sin. In John 9:2, for example, Jesus's disciples see a blind man and ask Jesus,

---

108. Brittany E. Wilson, "The Blinding of Paul and the Power of God: Masculinity, Sight, and Self-Control in Acts 9," *JBL* 133 (2014): 370.

109. Ghosh, *Impaired Bodies, Gendered Lives*, 28.

110. Lisa Schur and Douglas Kruse, "Fact Sheet: Elected Officials with Disabilities," 2019, Rutgers School of Management and Labor Relations, https://smlr.rutgers.edu/.

111. Cassandra Loeser, Vicki Crowley, and Barbara Pini, "Introductory Essay: Disability and Masculinities," in *Disability and Masculinities: Corporeality, Pedagogy, and the Critique of Otherness*, ed. Cassandra Loeser, Vicki Crowley, and Barbara Pini (London: Palgrave Macmillan, 2017), xxx.

112. Loeser, Crowley, and Pini, "Introductory Essay," xxxi.

"Rabbi, who sinned, this man or his parents, that he was born blind?" The association between sin and divine retribution via illness is made in the Tanakh: for example, Miriam is stricken with a skin condition by God because she (and her brother Aaron) spoke negatively about (or perhaps on behalf of) Moses's Cushite wife and his leadership (Num 12:10); the house of Joab is to pay for Joab's killing Abner by never being free of "a discharge or an eruption," which probably referred to a venereal disease and a skin disease, respectively (2 Sam 3:29). But this is not a strong biblical theme, since illness and disability occur without any causal relationship to sin (e.g., Isaac goes blind simply because he is old in Gen 27:1).

In the Tanakh, the human body is used as a metaphor for social values.[113] Instructing judges, for example, Exodus 23:8 states, "You shall take no bribe, for a bribe blinds the officials, and subverts the cause of those who are in the right." Vision—being able to see clearly—conveyed that the individual possessed understanding and knowledge. Blindness could indicate lack of these qualities. In the Bible, "moral disability is equated with physical disability. Israel is conceived of as a body, a person; and her immorality is symbolized by various physical disabilities."[114] Isaiah decries the current state of Israel as spiritually dimwitted by depicting a suffering servant—which, in Isaiah, is Israel—as blind and deaf: "Listen, you that are deaf; and you that are blind, look up and see! Who is blind but my servant, or deaf like my messenger whom I send? Who is blind like my dedicated one, or blind like the servant of the LORD? He sees many things, but does not observe them; his ears are open, but he does not hear" (Isa 42:18-20). Sight, in Isaiah, represents spiritual discernment; the people of Israel are blind—spiritually obtuse—due to their willful disloyalty to their God.

Words associated with sight are inexorably linked with knowledge: having insight, having vision as a leader, being perspicacious, being clearsighted. People who are blind have the same access as sighted people to knowledge and understanding. Being sensitive to the use of words is a feminist issue. Surely it is possible to more creatively express intellectual or moral knowledge than using words associated with sight.

Becoming aware of, and removing, barriers that inhibit differently abled individuals from full access to standard human rights is also a feminist

---

113. Judith Z. Abrams, *Judaism and Disability: Portrayals in Ancient Texts from the Tanach through the Bavli* (Washington, DC: Gallaudet University Press, 1998), 75.

114. Abrams, *Judaism and Disability*, 76.

concern. Haben Girma is blind, and while she attended Lewis & Clark College, each day the cafeteria menu was posted outside the entrance so that students could read it and know which food station to go to in order to eat the meal of their choice. When Girma told the cafeteria manager that she was not able to read the menu because she was blind, the manager offered to have a staff member read the menu to her. But that suggestion did not solve the problem because Girma is also deaf. What was agreed upon was that the menu would be sent electronically to Girma in advance. This way, Girma's computer could convert the menu to braille, and she would then know which food station to go to in order to eat food she liked. But the manager often forgot to send her the menu in advance, so she often would be forced to choose a food station randomly and hope that she liked what was served. When Girma complained, she was told to be grateful that they gave her a menu in advance at all, since the cafeteria workers were very busy. After experiencing several unpleasant meal surprises, Girma decided to fight for her right to have a choice about what she ate at the cafeteria, like other students. She reminded the college of the Americans with Disabilities Act, a civil rights law that passed in 1990. This law prohibits discrimination against individuals with disabilities in the public sphere. The cafeteria manager, fearing a lawsuit, made sure thereafter to send the menu consistently in advance. This experience of advocating for her own—and for other blind peoples'—rights began her life's path of activism on behalf of people with disabilities. In 2013, Girma was the first deaf-blind person to graduate from Harvard Law School. She currently is a civil rights attorney in Berkeley and has given a TED talk, has been named one of Forbes's 30 under 30, and was honored by President Obama as a White House Champion of Change. In 2019, she published a book about her life so far.[115]

Anna's Work and Tobit's False Accusation (2:11-14)

Anna supplements the household income by earning money through what Tobit calls "women's work" (τοῖς γυναικείοις, 2:11). Reference to "a piece she had woven" (2:12) suggests that Anna was a weaver, and she would sell her handiwork or perhaps repair textiles. Eileen Schuller suggests that "the male is reduced to dependence on what the female

---

115. Haben Girma, *Haben: The Deafblind Woman Who Conquered Harvard Law* (New York: Twelve, 2019).

[11]At that time, also, my wife Anna earned money at women's work. [12]She used to send what she made to the owners and they would pay wages to her. One day, the seventh of Dystrus, when she cut off a piece she had woven and sent it to the owners, they paid her full wages and also gave her a kid for a meal. [13]When she returned to me, the kid began to bleat. So I called her and said, "Where did you get this kid? It is surely not stolen, is it? Return it to the owners; for we have no right to eat anything stolen." [14]But she said to me, "It was given to me as a gift in addition to my wages." But I did not believe her, and told her to return it to the owners. I became flushed with anger against her over this. Then she replied to me, "Where are your acts of charity? Where are your righteous deeds? These things are known about you!"

can earn."[116] In fact, the text does not explicitly state that Anna began to work *because* Tobit was blind; it says "at that time" (v. 11) Anna was engaging in women's work.

Women *did* engage in work in the Hellenistic period, but it was often determined by gender. Weaving was done in the home and then sold outside of it. The edited late Persian or Hellenistic period book of Proverbs attests to women's working in textiles: "She seeks wool and flax, and works with willing hands" (31:13) and "She makes linen garments and sells them; she supplies the merchant with sashes" (31:24). Miriam Peskowitz has shown how women's spinning wool was not just acceptable; it also formed part of the gender ideology establishing proper female behavior. For example, associating a man with such work was effectively calling him effeminate. Later rabbinic literature states that independent women (adult unmarried daughters, divorcées, and non-levirate widows) could keep what they made from weaving and could buy and sell without hindrance (m. Nid. 5:7; m. B. Mes. 1:5).[117]

Anna is working for τοῖς κυρίοις: literally "lords," suggesting that her employers were wealthy, of high societal status, and probably gentiles. One day, they not only paid Anna "her wages" but "also gave her a young goat for a meal." Maybe they were particularly pleased with

116. Eileen M. Schuller, "Tobit," in *Women's Bible Commentary*, ed. Carol A. Newsom, Sharon H. Ringe, and Jacqueline E. Lapsley, 3rd ed. (Louisville: Westminster John Knox, 2012), 378–79.

117. Miriam B. Peskowitz, *Spinning Fantasies: Rabbis, Gender, and History* (Berkeley: University of California Press, 1997).

Anna's work, or maybe they understood the difficult circumstances in which her family was living. A goat would have been a welcome gift. In addition to being eaten, goats could be milked, and their hair could be woven into cloth or for stuffing pillows. Today goat's hair is still the material of choice for shepherds and goat-keepers for their winter cloaks.[118] The givers of the goat might have intended Anna to use it "for a meal" but she could have chosen to do what she wished with it; for example, she might have opted to use it for either milk or hair, or both.

Upon hearing the goat bleat (he would not have been able to see it), Tobit responds by accusing Anna of stealing it (2:13). The charge has no justification. We are left to determine if Anna had a history of kleptomania, if she had been stealing in order to provide the family more money, or if Tobit accuses her of stealing in order to dishonor her and so to provide himself the honor he lost. I prefer to see Tobit as reflecting his frustration at his personal situation: he is blind and perceives himself as unable to support his family. He was used to giving out charity to others, and now he is in the position of receiving it. That he has to rely on his wife for financial support may have been particularly painful for him. He has ceded the man's role as protector and provider to a woman.

Anna explains—and for the first time we hear her voice—"it was given to me as a gift in addition to my wages" (2:14). But Tobit again insists, with increasing anger, that she stole the goat. As Tobit accuses her of stealing (taking something without permission), she asks: "Where are your acts of charity? Where are your righteous deeds? These things are known about you!" (2:14). Interpretations of Anna's last comment range from "Look where they got you!"[119] to "You seem to know everything"[120] (see "Translation Matters" for more on this). She echoes frustrated responses of Job's wife to his afflictions, "Do you still persist in your integrity? Curse God, and die!" (Job 2:9). The Hebrew word translated as "curse" in the New Revised Standard Version actually is "bless" (ברך). Job's wife's advice, "Bless God and die," is antagonistic since it aligns with the goal of the Satan (or the Adversary) (1:11; 2:5). Tobit's wife is antagonistic as well (2:14). Anna calls Tobit a hypocrite: he is known for his devotion and righteousness, but where are these qualities now, in his own home? In accusing Anna, his piety is nowhere to be seen.

---

118. Y. Hatziminaoglou and J. Boyazoglu, "The Goat in Ancient Civilizations: From the Fertile Crescent to the Aegean Sea," *Small Ruminant Research* 51 (2004): 128.

119. Moore, *Tobit*, 134.

120. Revised Standard Version.

TRANSLATION MATTERS

Anna's final comment to Tobit in their argument about the goat (Tob 2:14b) has been translated in several different ways. The Greek version considered to be more accurately the original form (G2) is as follows: ποῦ εἰσιν αἱ δικαιοσύναι σου; ἰδὲ ταῦτα μετὰ σοῦ γνωστά ἐστιν (literally: "Where are your acts of righteousness? See, these things with you are known!"). The meaning of the Greek is challenging and has been translated in different ways:

RSV: "Where are your charities and your righteous deeds? You seem to know everything!"

NAB: "Where are your charitable deeds now? Where are your righteous acts? Look! All that has happened to you is well known!"

NRSV: "Where are your acts of charity? Where are your righteous deeds? These things are known about you!"

My interpretation is that Anna is calling Tobit out on his current behavior toward her and contrasting it with his reputation as a righteous man. Her message is that he is not being righteous by labeling her a thief, and the statement, "These things with you are known!" hints that she is sarcastically questioning his reputation as a righteous man.

As Helen Schüngel-Straumann notes, commentators "seize on this mockery, which apparently represents a model in the postexilic period: the suffering of the righteous is magnified by the lack of understanding he receives from his wife!"[121] An early example is Cyprian, a third-century CE bishop of Carthage (located in what is now Tunisia), who was an important early Christian writer. He states the following (calling "Tobit" in error "Tobias"): "And Tobias, after his excellent works, after the many and glorious illustrations of his merciful spirit, having suffered the loss of his sight, fearing and blessing God in his adversity, by his very bodily affliction increased in praise; and even him also his wife tried to pervert, saying, 'Where are thy righteousnesses? Behold what thou sufferest!' But he, steadfast and firm in respect of the fear of God, and armed by the faith of his religion to all endurance of suffering, yielded not to the temptation of his weak wife in his trouble" (Treatise 7, *On the Mortality* 10).[122]

---

121. Helen Schüngel-Straumann, "Tobit: A Lesson on Marriage and Family in the Diaspora," in *Feminist Biblical Interpretation: A Compendium of Critical Commentary on the Books of the Bible and Related Literature,* ed. Luise Schottroff and Marie-Theres Wacker (Grand Rapids: Eerdmans, 2012), 506.

122. Cyprian, "Mortality," *Treatises,* trans. Roy J. Deferrari, The Fathers of the Church 36 (Washington, DC: The Catholic University of America Press, 1958), 206–7.

Schüngel-Straumann points out how the much later commentary by Athanasius Miller (published in 1940–1941) suggests that Tobit 2:14 "is altogether a repetition of the scene in Job (2:9-10): the *agitated woman, whom the devil loves to lead astray and uses to tempt the righteous,* but in doing so only increases his virtue and fame, *in contrast to the calm and objectively-judging righteous man.*"[123] In his 1987 commentary on Tobit, Heinrich Gross uses the subtitle "Tobit Is Mocked by His Wife" and does not make mention in the discussion of Anna's being accused of stealing by her husband.[124] Gross blames Anna alone, puzzlingly adding that she "is in no way equal to her husband in mental power and greatness."[125] This "misogynistic history of reception" has been "very powerful," as Schüngel-Straumann observes. In a popular textbook used in university courses on the Old Testament, the author's take is that "Tobit's wife Anna was forced to work, *and she reproached him for his piety.*"[126] This is an inaccurate understanding of the text. Anna is not reproaching Tobit for his acts of righteousness, as such, but for his being a hypocrite: his righteousness benefits his community but not his family—more specifically, his suspicions about Anna and his accusations of her are not righteous.

In my view, Tobit's *dependency* on Anna created the problem. The book of Sirach, written around the same time as Tobit, observes: "There is wrath and impudence and great disgrace when a wife supports her husband" (Sir 25:22). In Tobit's world, the expectation was that males ruled in the public sphere and so they attained social honor. Men's influence was in the forum, at the gates of a city, in business, in the military. But Tobit presents himself as restricted to the home. The place he once fled has now become in effect his self-imposed prison. And in allowing his wife to support the family, he has lost all honor.

Women were expected to be subservient to their fathers and then husbands, and their sphere of influence was the home. They were in charge of domestic matters such as preparing food, bearing and raising children, and managing household finances. We might imagine Anna

---

123. Athanasius Miller, *Das Buch Tobias übersetzt und erklärt.* Die Heilige Schrift des Alten Testamentes, vol. 4.3 (Bonn, 1940–1941), quoted in Schüngel-Straumann, "Tobit: A Lesson on Marriage," 506, italics added.

124. Schüngel-Straumann, "Tobit: A Lesson on Marriage," 506; the commentary is that of Heinrich Gross, *Tobit, Judit,* Neue Echter Bibel (Würzburg: Echter-Verlag, 1987), 20.

125. Gross, *Tobit, Judit,* 21.

126. Michael D. Coogan, *The Old Testament: A Historical and Literary Introduction to the Hebrew Scriptures,* 3rd ed. (Oxford: Oxford University Press, 2014), 528, my emphasis.

to have been a decade or so younger than her husband; first marriages in Jewish communities in antiquity took place between girls in their early-to-late-teen years and men in their thirties or even older, without concern as to whether affection existed between the individuals.[127] As Ross Kraemer notes, a successful marriage was one in which the wife produced children, conducted herself with modesty, and submitted to her husband's authority and judgment.[128]

Anna and God's Limitless Generosity

Commentators often claim that Anna is the character who raises the critical question in the book of Tobit: Does it really pay to do good? Does God care for the righteous? Does God reward the performance of good deeds? In a heated argument over a goat, Anna seems to have shut Tobit up with her sharp remark: "these things are known about you." This retort is often taken to mean that Tobit's many acts of charity have brought him nothing but misfortunes. If Tobit's righteousness were to matter at all, he would be enjoying blessings instead.

To get to the heart of what might be going on in this episode, it is good to look at what started the spousal quarrel (2:11-14). Due to Tobit's inability to work, Anna finds a job as a weaver of cloth. After finishing and delivering the woven cloth to her employers, she receives her usual wages and a goat as a bonus. Tobit hears the goat bleating and assumes that the goat was stolen. Even after Anna's assurance that the goat is a bonus given to her on top of her usual wages, Tobit does not believe her. He actually gets angry with his wife.

One wonders what kind of mindset Tobit must have to doubt that the goat Anna received as a bonus was stolen. How is it that Tobit's initial reaction to the bleating of the goat was to suspect that his wife would steal a goat for a meal? Perhaps, in Tobit's mind, a bonus is not something that can exist in his circumstances; a bonus is not something that can ever be expected or earned. Such suspicion, then, can enter his mind only if he adheres to the view that proper work deserves reward and payment—the employer pays a worker his wages according to the work rendered. In Tobit's

---

127. Ross Shepard Kraemer, "Jewish Family Life in the First Century CE," in *The Jewish Annotated New Testament*, ed. Amy-Jill Levine and Marc Zvi Brettler, 2nd ed. (Oxford: Oxford University Press, 2017), 606.

128. Kraemer, "Jewish Family Life in the First Century CE," 607.

way of thinking, Anna certainly deserves her wages for her work but for her to receive a bonus boggles Tobit's mind. Since Tobit has not entertained this possibility, Tobit searches for a way to explain Anna's bonus away. Tobit hides his confusion under the suspicious charge that the goat was stolen. The goat makes him angry because this is not how it is supposed to work. Tobit is hard pressed to imagine that an employer can offer something good not entirely because of the work done but because of the generous nature of the employer. This episode shows that Tobit would need to rearrange his theological furniture in order to accommodate the idea of a bonus in the calculus of work rendered and payment, which functions as a metaphor for deeds and divine rewards.

And so, Anna's response to Tobit, cutting though her series of questions may seem, can in fact be an invitation for reflection on what it means for Tobit himself to provide mercy. Mercy and good deeds are central themes in the narrative. Tobit performs acts of mercy for his exiled co-religionists, and he hopes that God will return the favor with mercy. Tobit presents himself as one who performs acts of mercy not because the recipient merits the good deed but because of who Tobit is, one who is righteous and faithful to the law. And yet, Anna's question, "Where are your righteous deeds?" certainly goes

to the heart of Tobit's claims. Anna seems to be asking, "Did you perform acts of charity because they deserve it? If you believe that they deserve it, then it is likely not an act of charity. But if you perform a good deed for them without waiting for anything in return, then it is truly an act of mercy." In her bonus, Anna experienced what it means to receive mercy. Tobit has yet to see how mercy works.

This programmatic episode of husband-wife disagreement questions the often-posited link between act and consequence, good deed and reward. The narrative seems to have set this expectation up early on and seems to be heading toward affirming this theological tenet until Anna comes along and throws it into doubt. By employing a metaphor borrowed from the world of business, the story views Anna's bonus as an experience of mercy, a kind favor and gift that is not entirely dependent on her finished work but on the nature of her employer. This has, of course, clear implications on the character of God, the Supreme Employer of all, whom the narrative describes as merciful (cf. 3:2; 8:17; 11:15; 13:5).

The rewards that Tobit and his household receive at the end of the story are not necessarily rewards for his performance of charity. God's benevolent reach toward Tobit is not inevitably or automatically tied to Tobit's good works. Rather, they affirm the mercy that resides in God, one who gives his people blessings not because they deserve or earn them in exchange for the righteous work that they do in his service but because of God's merciful character. What God offers is more than what one deserves, like bonuses, like gifts, like grace. It is no narrative accident that the character that brings this up is Anna, whose name literally means "grace."

Francis M. Macatangay

Anna is a strong woman. She is a successful wage earner and perhaps entrepreneur; she is also a forceful interlocutor. Tobit, the unreliable narrator, does not highlight her piety—nor would he, since he presents himself as the only righteous Israelite in exile—but it is not an overstatement to observe that, at this juncture, Anna saves her family. The author would not have included these details were they not credible to his readers. The author likely knew of women—mothers, wives, sisters, and/or daughters—who supported their families. Perhaps the author also knew of disabled, or incapacitated, men who felt that they were failing in their responsibilities when others took care of them.

Today women still face a number of barriers when it comes to wage earning globally. All women earned only $0.82 for every dollar that all men made in 2022.[129] Looking specifically at women of color shows how the intersection of race and gender produces larger pay gaps for them: for example, American Indian and Native Alaskan women make $0.71 for every dollar white men make.[130] The United Nations Development Programme has made ending discrimination against women and girls a central goal; it "is not only a basic human right, it's crucial for sustainable future; it's proven that empowering women and girls helps economic growth and development."[131] Gender roles still remain in place. In Kenya, for example, "Women are seen as responsible for domestic and care work, while men are considered the primary breadwinners."[132]

---

129. Payscale, "2022 State of the Gender Pay Gap Report," https://www.payscale.com/data/gender-pay-gap.

130. Payscale, "2022 State of the Gender Pay Gap Report."

131. https://www.undp.org/content/undp/en/home/sustainable-development-goals.html.

132. Lauren Shields, Lucia Flores Guevara, and Margaux Yost, "Financial Inclusion for Workers: Including a Gender Lens," December 2018; https://www.idhsustainabletrade.com/uploaded/2018/12/Financial-Inclusion-for-Workers-Including-a-Gender-Lens-IDH-HERfinance.pdf.

Sometimes, when women start to work, tension arises in the household. A 2018 report reveals survey results in which Kenyan men "expressed feeling threatened by women's participation in the workforce" and "were opposed to their spouses earning more than them."[133] Some respondents understood women working outside the home to be a challenge to traditional gender roles and saw married women in the workforce as reflecting a lack of respect for their husbands.[134]

The Universal Declaration of Human Rights, written and adopted by the UN General Assembly on December 10, 1948, proclaims that all people are "equal 'without distinction of any kind such as race, colour, sex, language . . . or other status'" and led to the establishment of international programs and goals to "advance the status of women worldwide."[135] Yet, it took time for women to experience change. New York–born Sheila Barshay Goldbloom, a pioneer in the development of curricula related to community organization and faculty member of the McGill School of Social Work in Montreal, states in her recent memoir that in the 1950s, "Big companies like the Morgan's department store would not even interview a woman for a job if she was married."[136] I was surprised to learn from Goldbloom, furthermore, of the existence of a law in my home province of Quebec, Canada, "requiring a mother, in the absence of the father caused by any reason from business travel to hospitalization, to secure a letter signed by the father, giving the mother 'permission' to make decisions concerning their children."[137] Thus in the 1950s—a time period when caring for children was considered to be *the* role for women—women were not to be trusted and so were infantilized themselves. We have come far when we think of the existence of such laws. But there is more to do; in Canada, among workers aged twenty-five to fifty-four, the gender wage gap from 1998 to 2021 decreased 7.7 percentage points to 11.1 percent so in 2021 female employees "in this age group earned $0.89 for every dollar earned by men."[138]

133. Shields, Guevara, and Yost, "Financial Inclusion for Workers," 9.

134. Shields, Guevara, and Yost, "Financial Inclusion for Workers," 9.

135. Sally Armstrong, *Ascent of Women: A New Age Is Dawning for Every Mother's Daughter* (Toronto: Random House Canada, 2013), 96.

136. Sheila Barshay Goldbloom, *Opening Doors* (Montreal: John Aylen Books, 2019), 106.

137. Goldbloom, *Opening Doors*, 106.

138. "Quality of Employment in Canada: Pay Gap, 1998 to 2021," Statistics Canada, May 30, 2022, https://www150.statcan.gc.ca/n1/pub/14-28-0001/2020001/article/00003-eng.htm.

Tobit's world is falling apart by the end of chapter 2. His prayer in chapter 3 demonstrates the depth to which he has plummeted—but he is not alone in his despair. Readers are introduced to another of Tobit's female characters. Sarah is her name—and she has a prayer as well.

Tobit 3

When Your Husbands Keep Dying

In chapter 3 we meet another female character, Sarah, daughter of Raguel and Edna, and find several issues worthy of investigation from a feminist perspective: slavery, domestic violence, suicide, intergenerational suffering, infertility, honor and shame, demons who fall in love with women; we also address questions of dealing with unwarranted disappointment and sorrowful events.

Tobit's Prayer for Death (3:1-6)

Despite repeatedly touting his righteousness in chapters 1 and 2, in his prayer Tobit seems to admit that he is not as pious as he earlier presented himself to be. Yes, Tobit admits to sinning, but he initially describes his offences as "unwitting" or "out of ignorance" (ἀγνοήμασίν) and thereby reduces his responsibility (3:3): he did not intend to transgress, nor was he aware that he did. He grants no such nuance to his ancestors, whom he declares "sinned against you and disobeyed your commandments" (3:3b, 4). Tobit blames them for the present difficulties of all exiled Israelites: "plunder, exile, and death"; being "the talk, the byword, and an object of reproach among all the nations" (3:4). Yet he also blames God. Despite his opening and conventional words of praise, and his equally conventional attribution of hardship to punishment for sin, he states,

Tob 3:1-6

³:¹Then with much grief and anguish of
heart I wept, and with groaning began
to pray:
  ²"You are righteous, O Lord,
      and all your deeds are just
    all your ways are mercy and truth;
      you judge the world.
  ³And now, O Lord, remember me
      and look favorably upon me.
    Do not punish me for my sins
      and for my unwitting offenses
      and those that my ancestors
          committed before you.
    They sinned against you,

⁴and disobeyed your
    commandments.
So you gave us over to plunder,
    exile, and death,
  to become the talk, the
    byword, and an object of
    reproach,
  among all the nations among
    whom you have
    dispersed us.
⁵And now your many judgments
    are true
  in exacting penalty from me for
    my sins.

"*You* gave us over." Tobit insists, repeatedly, that God is just and righteous. A more cynical reader would wonder if Tobit, like Job, did not "sin with his lips" (Job 2:10b) but did have thoughts condemning God. Tobit might have thought that the punishment did not fit the crime. Despite the humor of the volume and the occasionally bombastic pronouncements of its titular character, Tobit raises issues that require assessment.

Should the present generation suffer for the sins of the past? There seems to be no alternative: decisions made in the past inevitably have repercussions on the present. We can look for examples to the new generations of Germans who must grapple with the burden of their nation's history during World War II, even though they were not alive to participate in it, and to the United States, where current conversations about race relations are profoundly shaped by the country's history of slavery. In the Canadian context, past racist treatment—for example, the forcing of Indigenous children into residential schools and forbidding practice of their own cultures and speaking their own languages—continues to affect the lives of First Nation, Inuit, and Métis people. The Commission of Truth and Reconciliation calls on all currently living Canadians to participate in the ninety-four calls to action.[1] And when it comes to climate change, across the planet younger generations have

---

1. "Truth and Reconciliation Commission of Canada: Calls to Action," 2015, www
.trc.ca.

For we have not kept your
commandments
and have not walked in
accordance with truth
before you.
⁶So now deal with me as you will;
command my spirit to be taken
from me,
so that I may be released from
the face of the earth and
become dust.
For it is better for me to die than
to live,

because I have had to listen to
undeserved insults,
and great is the sorrow within me.
Command, O Lord, that I be
released from this distress;
release me to go to the eternal
home,
and do not, O Lord, turn your
face away from me.
For it is better for me to die
than to see so much distress
in my life
and to listen to insults."

been actively pushing politicians to make more environmentally sound decisions; they recognize that they will disproportionately experience the negative consequences of environmental damage created by past generations.

Psychologists have shown how traumatic events of the past can manifest themselves in subsequent generations through mental and physical illnesses. Studies of the children of Holocaust survivors, African American descendants of enslaved individuals, descendants of the people who survived America's bombing of the Japanese cities of Hiroshima and Nagasaki, the children of those who survived the slaughter of 800,000 members of the Tutsi community by ethnic Hutu extremists in Rwanda, the children of parents who survived the Twin Towers attack by nineteen Islamist terrorists from al-Qaeda on September 11, 2001, have shown this to be the case.[2]

In verse 5, "For we have not kept your commandments and have not walked in accordance with truth before you," Tobit binds himself to his ancestors—and so seems prepared to accept God's judgment. Carey Moore points out that this recognition of national responsibility is one of the "characteristic features of postexilic piety (cf. Isa 59:12, Ezra

2. Pam Weintraub, "Haunted by History: War, Famine and Persecution Inflict Profound Changes on Bodies and Brains; Could These Changes Persist over Generations?," *Aeon*, April 16, 2018, https://aeon.co/essays/how-the-sufferings-of-one-generation-are-passed-on-to-the-next.

9:6-7; Neh 1:6; Dan 9:4-19; and Bar 1-3)."[3] One of the key messages of the book is that Tobit's story is not a story of a mere individual. Tobit is connected to the past, and at the same time, he and all in his generation are connected to the future. How we assess our past, and what we leave to the future, matters. One of the leading experts in transgenerational trauma is Maria Yellow Horse Brave Heart, a clinical social work researcher at the University of New Mexico and member of the Lakota tribe. Brave Heart asserts that trauma experienced by Native Americans (and other peoples) in the past reverberates through the hearts and minds of survivors and their descendants, resulting in "unresolved grief." This manifests in emotional and psychological illnesses, such as depression, self-harming behavior, resentment and anger, and higher mortality rates from suicide and cardiovascular diseases.[4] Such unresolved grief must be confronted through a balance of culturally grounded traditions and behavioral-health interventions. Native women, in particular, have been at the forefront of confronting the legacies of the past and leading in the healing interventions: women traditionally have been the culture-carriers, nurturers, and caregivers of the community, and they also bear the highest risks of suffering interpersonal violence.[5]

By declaring that God's "judgments are true" and connecting these judgments to sin, Tobit seeks to resolve the dissonance that arises when bad things happen to people who perceive themselves faithful. Deep and painful questions about suffering have been asked over the centuries. Assurbanipal, the seventh-century BCE king of Neo-Assyria, the country that destroyed Tobit's home, asks:

> I made arrangements for the funerary offerings and libations for the ghosts of my royal predecessors, which had fallen into abeyance; I did

---

3. Carey A. Moore, *Tobit: A New Translation with Introduction and Commentary* (New Haven: Yale University Press, 1996), 139.

4. Weintraub, "Haunted by History." Maria Yellow Horse Brave Heart, "The Historical Trauma Response among Natives and Its Relationship with Substance Abuse: A Lakota Illustration," *Journal of Psychoactive Drugs* 35 (2003): 11, states, "Lakota mortality rates for heart disease are, to this day, almost twice the rate for the general United States population; suicide rates are more than double the national average." Poverty, racism, and lack of access to education and health care also contribute to these statistics.

5. Maria Yellow Horse Brave Heart, Josephine Chase, Jennifer Elkins, Jennifer Martin, Jennifer S. Nanez, and Jennifer J. Mootz, "Women Finding the Way: American Indian Women Leading Intervention Research in Native Communities," *American Indian and Alaska Native Mental Health Research* 23 (2016): 28.

good to god and man, to dead and living. Why are sickness, sorrow, loss and expense always connected with me?[6]

Job raises the same question:

> How many are my iniquities and my sins?
> Make me know my transgression and my sin.
> Why do you hide your face,
> And count me as your enemy? (13:23-24)

If Tobit's God is sovereign, then God placed the hardships in Tobit's life. If God is righteous, there must be justification for the hardships, and hence Tobit suffers because he is being punished not so much for his own failings but for the transgressions of his Israelite ancestors. Random human suffering renders belief in a caring, compassionate deity challenging. In the midst of Job's misery, his friend Eliphaz tells him, "How happy is the one whom God reproves; therefore do not despise the discipline of the Almighty" (Job 5:17), suggesting that suffering is divine discipline—so Job is undergoing punishment from God because he has sinned, and he should feel blessed because of this. But Job does not feel blessed—he protests that he was innocent—and by the end of the book, Job is vindicated: God agrees with him. Job's suffering does come from God, but not as punishment for sin, so his friends were incorrect.

Theodicy, from the Greek for "God's justice," raises the question of divine justice in the face of experiences that seem to suggest the deity's lack of concern or even hostility toward righteous people. There is no such thing as "random" suffering: there is suffering on behalf of others or suffering as a test. From a feminist perspective, attempting to justify suffering and violence is problematic, since frequently it is the least powerful in society who suffer the most. Violence against women is normalized in societies in which women are not respected and valued as equal to men. As the 1993 UN Declaration on the Elimination of Violence against Women states, "Violence against women is a manifestation of historically unequal power relations between men and women," and such violence "is one of the crucial social mechanisms by which women are forced into a subordinate position compared with men."[7] Using God as a model, those with power—historically, that has been men—have justified their

---

6. M. Streck, VAB 7, 250 11.1-5 quoted in footnote 61 on p. 123 in Miranda Bayliss "The Cult of Dead Kin in Assyria and Babylonia," *Iraq* 35 (1973).

7. "Declaration on the Elimination of Violence against Women," United Nations Documents, December 20, 1993, http://www.un-documents.net/a48r104.htm.

violence by framing it as "instructive" for those less powerful than they. Killings in the name of honor, for example, usually involve the murder of a woman or girl by male family members because they believe that the victim has brought dishonor or shame upon the family, and a message is sent to other females in the family about proper behavior. In the summer of 2009, three daughters—Zainab, nineteen; Sahar, seventeen; and Geeti, thirteen—and their mother, Rona Mohammad Amir, were murdered in Kingston, Ontario, Canada. Their father, their brother, and their father's second wife were convicted of first-degree murder; the jury heard recordings of the father referring to his daughters, after he'd killed them, as "whores" because of the way they dressed. The judge concluded that the murders were motivated by a "notion of honour that is founded upon the domination and control of women, a sick notion of honour that has absolutely no place in any civilized society."[8]

Tobit's prayer justifies the pain of exile by blaming his ancestors'—and his—sins. But he does not ask God for death because he is overwhelmed by guilt. It is because he cannot deal any more with the "undeserved insults" (3:6) that Tobit ironically commands God, "command my spirit to be taken from me. . . . Command, O Lord, that I be released from this distress." Thus, worse than exile are Anna's words in chapter 2. Tobit's prayer is motivated by self-pity.[9] He expresses no concern for how his wife or his son suffers, nor how his blindness has increased their struggles. It is not an attractive portrayal.

In Tobit's prayer he addresses God—but the message was truly to Anna. He says that he accepts God's "exacting penalty from me for my sins" (3:5), but he does not behave as if this acceptance is genuine. He is angry, and he directs this anger toward Anna in two ways. The accusation of thievery is made directly to her—he doesn't *really* think she's stolen the goat: he's angry and frustrated, and hearing the bleating of the goat is a concrete confirmation of his lack of control (what is a goat doing in his home?) and of his wife's increased control (she received the goat as a gift for her work, she brought it home). He wanted Anna

---

8. Colin Harris, "Mother Convicted in Shafia Daughters' Canal Killings Granted 5-Hour Escorted Absence from Prison," CBC News, https://www.cbc.ca/news/canada/montreal/shafia-honour-killings-tooba-yahya-parole-board-1.5396177.

9. Beverly Bow and George W. E. Nickelsburg identify the tone of the prayer to be "self-centered and whining," in "Patriarchy with a Twist: Men and Women in Tobit," in *"Women Like This": New Perspectives on Jewish Women in the Greco-Roman World*, ed. Amy-Jill Levine (Atlanta: Scholars Press, 1991), 130.

to hear his prayer. In it, he identifies her "undeserved insults" as that which drives his death wish. Instead of expressing his fear and anger about his blindness directly to God, he channels it toward Anna. This is Tobit's passive-aggressive way of undercutting his wife and trying to gain back the control that he feels he has lost. Being on the receiving end of passive-aggressive behavior is unbalancing and infuriating. Such behavior is, by its very nature, indirect and leaves a person subject to it feeling hurt and confused.

Sarah's Enslaved Person Insults Her (3:7-9)

"Sarah" (שרה) is a Hebrew name meaning "princess." The name evokes Sarah, Abraham's wife, who accompanied her husband from Ur to Haran to Canaan, then to Egypt, and then to Canaan. A second connection between the Sarah of Genesis and the Sarah of Tobit is an initial inability to conceive and bear a child. The first Sarah, recognizing her infertile condition, commanded her husband Abraham to have sexual relations with her Egyptian enslaved person, Hagar, so that, as she states, "It may be that I shall obtain children by her" (Gen 16:2). When Hagar conceives, Sarah "becomes light"—both in terms of relative weight and in terms of honor—in her eyes. Hagar's disrespect leads Sarah to abuse her (Gen 16:6).

Tobit's Sarah presents variations on these themes. When we first meet her, she is not (yet) a mother, despite her multiple marriages. In her case, the problem is not infertility but a jealous demon who slaughters her husbands, apparently on their wedding night. Young women in the ancient world—both Israelites and non-Israelites—tended to marry for the first time between the ages of twelve and twenty.[10] When we meet Sarah, she has already married seven men, so her age is probably closer to twenty than twelve. Her situation can be taken as tragic, as would be the case with infertility, but the absurdity of the plot to this point, coupled with

---

10. Ross S. Kraemer, "Typical and Atypical Jewish Family Dynamics: The Cases of Babatha and Berenice," in *Early Christian Families in Context: An Interdisciplinary Dialogue*, ed. David L. Balch and Carolyn Osiek (Grand Rapids: Eerdmans, 2003), 140; "Jewish Family Life in the First Century CE," in *The Jewish Annotated New Testament*, ed. Amy-Jill Levine and Marc Zvi Brettler, 2nd ed. (Oxford: Oxford University Press, 2017), 605; Adiel Schremer, *Male and Female He Created Them: Jewish Marriage in the Late Second Temple, Mishnah, and Talmud Periods* [Hebrew] (Jerusalem: Zalman Shazar Center, 2003), esp. 121–25.

Tob 3:7-9

⁷On the same day, at Ecbatana in Media, it also happened that Sarah, the daughter of Raguel, was reproached by one of her father's female slaves. ⁸For she had been married to seven husbands, and the wicked demon Asmodeus had killed each of them before they had been with her as is customary for wives. So the maid said to her, "You are the one who kills your husbands! See, you have already been married to seven husbands and have not borne the name of a single one of them. ⁹Why do you beat us? Because your husbands are dead? Go with them! May we never see a son or daughter of yours!"

the logical but unstated question of why husbands two through seven would have gone through with the marriage, makes it more laughable.

More problematic, especially from a feminist perspective, is how slavery and abuse are connected to infertility. One of her "father's maids" reproaches Sarah (3:7), but the Greek word that the NRSV translates here as "maids," παιδισκῶν (the form is genitive plural), and also in verse 8 (παιδίσκη, in nominative singular form), actually designates a female slave. The English "maid" or "servant girl" veils the fact that slaves are present.[11] Hagar treats her mistress—her owner—with contempt (Gen 16:1-4), and one of the slaves owned by Tobit's Sarah accuses Sarah of murder: "You are the one who kills your husbands!" (3:8). More, she impugns Sarah's fertility by noting that not a single one of her seven marriages has yielded a child. The original Sarah "dealt harshly" with Hagar; our Sarah beat her slaves (3:8). Although Sarah's motives are not stated, the slave implies that the beatings come not from disrespect but from frustration—it is "because your husbands are dead." Consequently, her slave wishes upon her barrenness and death (3:8).

Like Anna, who is falsely accused of stealing by a person (her husband) typically perceived to have more authority, Sarah too is falsely accused (of murdering her husbands). But she is denounced by a person (her slave) who has less authority than she. The two accusers, Tobit and the slave, are in the same structural position. Such a parallel highlights Tobit's diminished power and control, his enslavement to his frustration and anger. The parallel also underlines the similarities between Sarah and Anna: one, a woman grappling with the memory of seven dead husbands, and the other, with a husband who *wishes* he were dead.

11. In Tobit 10:10, the NRSV translation more accurately provides the English word "slaves" for the same Greek word (παιδίσκας, in accusative plural).

Double Bind: Sarah, Victimizing and Victimized

Tobit 3 introduces Sarah as a bride of misfortune. She was married to seven men, all of whom died before the culmination of their marriages. Overcoming suicidal impulse, Sarah yields herself to God's providence. Sarah's prayer highlights two issues: her virginity is intact, and she wants to protect the honor of her father. Her prayer is answered. Sarah and Tobias are arranged as meant-to-be spouses for each other. On one level, this story presents Sarah as a model daughter and pious woman: a well-behaved woman finally gets the blessing of God. Seen from a feminist perspective, independent from the author's intention, Sarah's story shows the dilemma of women in a patriarchal system.

In Tobit 3:7-9, Sarah and a maid attack each other using a patriarchal value system that very often devalues women themselves. Sarah hears insults from one of her father's maids. The maid accuses Sarah of the deaths of her husbands. The narrator explains the reason for their death: Asmodeus, the wicked demon. From the text, however, it is not clear if the maid knew about the existence of the demon. Whether or not the maid knew, she denounces Sarah for the ill fate. Whatever it is, it is woman who is to blame: this is typical misogyny.

Women have often been considered the bearers of bad luck in some cultures, and the case in Korea is not an exception. Until not so long ago, women used to be unwelcomed as the first customer of a day in stores or taxis, especially in conservative rural areas. If some unusually bad thing happened in a house, a woman was often considered as the source of that evil luck: if the husband dies, the wife is to blame. Interestingly, when the wife dies, never is the husband blamed. Being familiar with this kind of culture, a modern reader might well sense misogyny in Tobit 3:8: women are responsible for the ill fate. And here, this misogynic insult comes out of a woman's mouth.

How about Sarah, then? Her prayer presents Sarah as a victim: a poor bride who worries about the honor of her father and of the house over her own life (3:14-15). She is not, however, an innocent victim. Her maid criticizes Sarah for her violence. What instigated her violence? Was she punishing the maid for insulting her? Or was Sarah simply venting her anger, which provoked the insult from the maid? It is not clear from the text, but the maid's retort insinuates Sarah's action was unfair. How could Sarah exercise physical violence over the maid? Not because she was physically dominant, but because it was a given: she is the daughter of the father's house. She exercises the hierarchical power of the patriarchal system in which she is incorporated.

> Sarah's violence and the defiance of the maid show how women unconsciously internalize patriarchal power and value systems. Both women attack each other with the very system that is unfavorable to themselves. The system is thus reinforced, leaving both of them victimizer and victims in a patriarchal system.
>
> *EunHee Kang*

Slavery in the Ancient World and Our Own

Slavery was a deeply entrenched component of life from biblical times and beyond.[12] Like Tobit, other Hellenistic-Jewish writings such as Judith and the works of Philo and Josephus, along with the New Testament Gospels and letters of Paul and Peter, "reveal a strong presence of slaves within every facet of society. In particular slaves populated the lives of the upper classes, working on their lands and in their homes."[13] Indeed, slave ownership was a sign of status in Mediterranean antiquity.[14] Most of the writings give the name of the slave owner, not that of the slave; this is a bias most ancient texts share.[15] But there are stories that enrich the understanding of the slave's life and challenge the stereotypes of slaves as uneducated and unskilled. First-century Rabbi Gamliel owned a slave called Tabi, with whom he was close (m. Sukkah 2:1; m. Ber. 2:7). When Tabi died, Gamliel accepted condolences in the same manner as for a family member, reflecting the establishment of friendship between the two.

Modern societies are not free of the scourge of slavery. Human trafficking—the forced exploitation of people in the commercial sex trade or other forms of labor through intimidation or violence—often is referred to as "modern-day slavery." Given the clandestine nature of the operation, there are no official numbers, but it is estimated that hundreds of thousands of victims in the United States are working in the sex, hospitality, beauty salon, and agricultural industries, with between eighteen thousand and twenty thousand victims introduced every year.[16] The United

---

12. Catherine Hezser, *Jewish Slavery in Antiquity* (Oxford: Oxford University Press, 2005), 320.

13. Hezser, *Jewish Slavery*, 320.

14. Hezser, *Jewish Slavery*, 174.

15. Jennifer A. Glancy, "The Mistress-Slave Dialectic: Paradoxes of Slavery in Three LXX Narratives," *JSOT* 72 (1996): 71.

16. Jason Pasley, "20 Staggering Facts about Human Trafficking in the US," *Business Insider*, December 13, 2019, https://www.businessinsider.com/human-trafficking -in-the-us-facts-statistics-2019-7.

States, Mexico, and the Philippines were the countries with the highest presence of human trafficking in 2018.[17] According to the 2017 report "Global Estimates of Modern Slavery," women and girls represent 99 percent of victims in the commercial sex industry and 58 percent in other sectors.[18] Children are more likely to be targets for recruitment than adults, particularly those raised in foster care, especially those who were not given the opportunity to be with foster families with whom they could develop safe and healthy relationships. Native American (or First Nations) women are especially at risk because they are subjected to systemic discrimination and disenfranchisement.[19]

Human trafficking is so widespread that the UN Office on Drugs and Crime asked airlines to train flight attendants to spot signs that a person is being trafficked, such as if the person is not in control of their own boarding pass or money[20] or if a child is with an adult and there is no evidence of any emotional connection between them.[21] In 2011, Air Alaskan flight attendant Shelia Fedrick saw "a disheveled girl sitting beside an older, well-dressed man on her flight," and this worried her; when the man refused to let Fedrick speak to the girl, she left a note for the girl in the toilet of the aircraft. This allowed the girl to explain that she needed help, and the man with whom she was travelling was arrested for participating in human trafficking.[22] As Bible readers, we ought to remember the story of the exodus, and then, in reading Tobit, recall that the ancestors of Tobit and Sarah (and their families) were slaves. Biblical texts use the history of Israelite slavery to call descendants of these slaves to exercise kindness to the stranger, to the incarcerated, and to the slave. For example, Jeremiah 22:3 states, "do no wrong or violence to the alien, the orphan, and the widow"; and a prophet's declaration in Isaiah 61:1 is to "bring good news to the oppressed, to bind up the brokenhearted, to proclaim liberty to the captives, and release the prisoners." There is a special responsibility on those who once were slaves to put a stop to slavery.

---

17. Pasley, "20 Staggering Facts.".

18. "Global Estimates of Modern Slavery: Forced Labour and Forced Marriage," International Labour Organization, 2017, https://www.ilo.org/global/publications/books/WCMS_575479/lang--en/index.htm.

19. Pasley, "20 Staggering Facts."

20. Pasley, "20 Staggering Facts."

21. Rebecca Ratcliffe, "Airlines urged to train staff to help spot victims of trafficking," *The Guardian*, June 12, 2017.

22. "Flight Attendant Shares Story of Saving Trafficking Victim," BBC News, February 6, 2017, https://www.bbc.com/news/world-us-canada-38880612.

While slave owners would have held out the possibility of manumission as motivation for reliable service,[23] Catherine Hezser's study on Jewish slavery in the ancient world shows that, while slavery was taken for granted and deemed a regular and indispensable part of the fabric of society, Jewish writers sometimes encouraged "mild treatment of slaves and tried to protect slaves from the overt cruelty of their masters," in accordance with biblical laws.[24] Such biblical laws include the stipulation that slaves were to rest, like their masters, from work on the sabbath (Exod 20:10); that Israelite slaves were to be freed after six years unless they chose to remain with their owners (Exod 20:2, 5-6); that if an Israelite had to sell himself or herself into slavery to another Israelite, such a person was not to be treated as a slave but instead as a temporary paid laborer (Lev 25:39-41) and not to be treated poorly (Lev 25:43); that manumitted Israelite slaves were not to be sent away empty handed (Deut 15:13-14); and that escaped slaves were not to be returned to their masters (since presumably they were being ill-treated, Deut 23:16-17). Such laws were informed and shaped by the Israelite nation's experience of being slaves themselves in Egypt. Regarding the Hellenistic period, when Tobit was composed, Hezser questions whether the manumission of Israelite slaves after six years of service mentioned in the Torah (Exod 21:2-11; Deut 15:12-18) was practiced.[25]

Tobit's Sarah does not respond to the slave's accusation: she does not defend herself or protest her innocence. It is not surprising that she says not a word about beating her slaves, not even in her subsequent prayer. We are left with the impression that the slave's reproach concerning the beatings is *not* false.[26] We modern readers of Tobit should be morally challenged by these details. On the one hand, we may feel sympathy for Sarah, a woman who is deprived, through no fault of her own, of

---

23. Hezser, *Jewish Slavery*, 387.

24. Hezser, *Jewish Slavery*, 385.

25. Hezser, *Jewish Slavery*, 387; she states further that "[a]lready in biblical times the manumission of Israelite slaves in the seventh or Jubilee year seems to have been an ideal rather than reality."

26. Toni Craven states: "She is likely not innocent of the charge of physical abuse, even if she does not deserve the servant's wish that she will be barren"; see her essay "Female (and Male) Servants," in *Women in Scripture: A Dictionary of Named and Un-named Women in the Hebrew Bible, the Apocryphal/Deuterocanonical Books, and the New Testament*, ed. Carol Meyers, Toni Craven, and Ross S. Kraemer (Grand Rapids: Eerdmans, 2000), 359. In contrast, see Bow and Nickelsburg, "Patriarchy with a Twist," 139, who highlight Sarah's passivity and make it sound as though her slave's accusation of abuse is false. See Glancy, "Mistress-Slave Dialectic," 81–82.

a normal marriage seven times. On the other hand, by taking out her frustrations through physically abusing those more vulnerable than she, she is committing domestic violence.

Sarah engages in soul-searching that determines her decision not to kill herself, but, as Jennifer Glancy notes, her "self-examination does not extend to her capricious beating of her slaves."[27] Her behavior might be understood to be a classic example of the defense mechanism called displacement: the act of reallocating stress—in this case, the pain, anger, and feelings of helplessness stemming from the deaths of seven husbands—to an outlet where the stakes are lower, in accordance with the "kick the dog" idiom (i.e., higher-ranked persons take out their frustrations by mistreating a lower-ranked person, who in turn abuses someone lower on the social ladder than they; in this scenario dogs are considered low-ranked and can be subject to abuse).[28] Sarah takes out her frustration on her slaves. She physically does to them what she perceives life, or fate, to be doing to her. Given that Asmodeus is the source of her own pain, she has become metaphorically demonic.

Ancient readers would not have considered the beating of an enslaved person to signal a character flaw or a lack of morality. But we must consider this slave within her context too. She was vulnerable to the physical and sexual abuse of her owners, yet she stands up for herself by confronting Sarah. In Tobit she is nameless, as is the slave in Judith, but she is not without power and her words matter. Judith's defeat of Holofernes would not have been possible without the aid of her slave (10:10, 17; 12:15; 13:3, 9, 10), who, like Judith, risks her life to save the people of Israel. As Glancy notes, "Like most slaves . . . Judith's maid is bereft of the personal identity conferred by family connections."[29] In Tobit, no one comes to the slave's defense: she alone stands up for herself. She bravely confronts her abuser and so exercises power. The risk here, as for all victims of domestic violence, is that she could face more abuse as punishment for asserting herself.[30] But assert herself she did.

---

27. Glancy, "Mistress-Slave Dialectic," 81.

28. R. F. Baumeister, K. Dale, K. L. Sommer, "Freudian Defense Mechanisms and Empirical Findings in Modern Social Psychology: Reaction Formation, Projection, Displacement, Undoing, Isolation, Sublimation, and Denial," *Journal of Personality* 66 (1998): 1081–1124.

29. Glancy, "Mistress-Slave Dialectic," 83.

30. "Domestic Violence against Women: Recognize Patterns, Seek Help," Mayo Clinic, April 14, 2022, https://www.mayoclinic.org/healthy-lifestyle/adult-health/in-depth/domestic-violence/art-20048397.

Infertility and Childless Women in the Ancient World and Our Own

Her slave wishes two things upon Sarah: death and childlessness. Infertility was equivalent to death for a woman. Biblical verses equate a fertile wife with happiness (Ps 128:3) and the miscarrying womb with divine anger (Hos 9:14). The social standing of a wife who did not bear children could be precarious: for example, her husband could divorce her for it, since biblical law allows for rather broad-ranging reasons (such as "she fails to please him"). Childless women like the poor (Ps 113:7, 9) and widows (Job 24: 21) were vulnerable. The rabbis stipulated that a man must divorce a wife who, after ten years, did not bear a child (t. Yebam. 8:5), or, if he did not wish to divorce her, he could marry a second wife (b. Yebam. 65a). There is acknowledgment that the lack of children might not be the woman's fault, however, as t. Yebamot 8:6 states, the divorced woman could marry again and try to have children through that husband. In b. Yebamot 65b–66a, a majority of rabbis affirm that the obligation to procreate is limited to men. For the rabbis, procreation is a masculine expression of potency quite different from the feminine role of bearing and giving birth to the fruit of male seed.

But there are alternative ways of understanding infertility in the Bible. In their monograph on the topic, Candida R. Moss and Joel S. Baden show that childlessness is not always negative, nor is it "the hallmark of impiety, immorality, divine abandonment, or divine punishment" in the Bible.[31] Indeed, while a married Jewish woman who bore no children could be perceived negatively by her community, there are plenty of biblical examples of women (such as Sarah, Rebekah, Rachel, the unnamed mother of Samson, Hannah the mother of Samuel, the woman of Shunem who is Elisha's patron) who were childless and not pronounced "sinful" or "guilty."[32] In the Bible there are prominent women who never had children (Dinah, Miriam, Deborah, Huldah), as well as in the Apocrypha (Judith). Such examples belie the notion that infertility was considered a curse.

Even in the twenty-first century, women who do not have children sometimes are characterized as egocentric, resentful, and lacking in maternal instincts. In some cultures, this characterization is reflected in language; for example, the word for an infertile woman in Japan and Korea translates as "a woman made of stone."[33]

---

31. Candida R. Moss and Joel S. Baden, *Reconceiving Infertility: Biblical Perspectives on Procreation and Childlessness* (Princeton: Princeton University Press, 2015), 17.

32. Moss and Baden, *Reconceiving Infertility*, 67.

33. Moss and Baden, *Reconceiving Infertility*, 8.

Being a woman means much more than motherhood. But gender stereotypes persist, and sometimes these are internalized. Writer Katy Lindemann expresses her frustration at how her inability to have a child makes her feel: "As a 21st-century feminist, of course I don't believe a woman's worth is determined by her ability to reproduce. . . . Yet I feel like a failure as a woman because I can't have children. My own sense of self-worth is inextricably intertwined with my inability to get or stay pregnant."[34]

I can empathize with Lindemann. I had said since I was a little girl that I did not want to have children. But at thirty-eight years old, with a wonderful long-term life partner and a stable job, I began to reconsider. I loved my life, so it was not that I felt that something was missing. But I began thinking that having a child would add another dimension of meaning to life, and I wondered if, on my deathbed, I would regret not having a child. My husband was open to the idea, and I got pregnant within weeks of making the decision. I was overjoyed: I couldn't believe how happy I was. I told everyone I was pregnant: no waiting for me! The miscarriage happened in the twelfth week. It was devastating. Friends and family were so supportive; in particular, I was touched by how many of my female friends revealed that they had experienced miscarriages too—some of them multiple times. We don't speak very much about miscarriages, though that is changing. I remember one offhand comment made to me that was not meant to be as hurtful as it was: that maybe I needed time to work on being a woman. I had a hard time brushing this off because part of me *did* feel like a failure as a woman. That both surprised and infuriated me. Like Lindemann, I knew it was ridiculous, yet my emotions suggested otherwise, and it took a while to sort through that. My doctor encouraged my husband and me to try again, but I never got to the point of wanting to; I reverted to my earlier attitude of not wanting a child. I know that, in choosing not to become a parent, I will have missed out on many beautiful aspects of life, but I am at peace with my decision. I have a life that is meaningful in a multitude of ways, and I am grateful that I can enjoy my friends' children without feeling envy or regret. What I came to realize was that I would experience a mix of joy and pain either way (with having children and with not having children); there wasn't *one* right path for me.

34. Katy Lindemann, "I'm a Feminist: So Why Does Infertility Make Me Feel Like a Failure?," *The Guardian*, November 2, 2018, https://www.theguardian.com/commentisfree/2018/nov/02/feminist-infertility-failure-child-mother.

It's been suggested that humans experience true, unselfish love only by having children. I disagree. Ashley Brown, author of *Letters to the Daughter I'll Never Have*, makes the following wise observation: "[T]here is not one universally grand and ultimate way to experience love. For some, parenting may awaken in them some new kind of love, something beautiful and transformative. For others, that love is alive and well whether or not they reproduce or adopt human children of their own."[35]

Chinese-Canadian Perspective on Not Having Children

I am a daughter, an aunt, and an educator.

The one role that I have never played is that of a parent. Not having my own children was never about not wanting children. It has never been about a refusal to raise them in a world that is tumultuous and unpredictable. Life choices, circumstances, and timing have factored into this more than anything else. Being an aunt is an honor and not at all a consolation prize for not having my own kids.

When my niece was born, I was already projecting our future together at film festivals, live theater, and concerts. I started to accumulate books and toys for her even though she was only a few days old and most certainly not quite ready for the wood block sushi set that I ordered online.

What I remember best about my niece's birth was my brother's reaction. Unlike our ancestors, my brother embraced the fact that his firstborn would be a strong-willed, vocal girl. While this may seem unremarkable to most people, some cultural context and family history may illuminate why this is so significant.

The Chinese have traditionally valued patrilineal inheritance and filial piety. Sons carry on the bloodline. They are expected to look after their aging parents. When the Communist Party of China enacted the One Child Policy in the 1980s, families either abandoned their infant daughters or committed infanticide. The consequences of this family planning policy continue to plague China and nearby countries today.

If our paternal grandparents had lived to see how committed we are to making sure that we cut through gender lines, they would be aghast. They hoped for a firstborn grandson, something that fate and biology did not

35. Ashley Brown, *Letters to the Daughter I'll Never Have* (Norman, OK: Mezcalita Press, 2018); the quote is from Brown's article, "No, I'm Not Missing Out on the 'Ultimate Love' Because I Chose Not to Be a Mom," *HuffPost Personal*, October 28, 2019, https://www.huffpost.com/entry/no-child-ultimate-love_n_5db1c1b4e4b0131fa99b0095.

oblige when I was born. I love both of my brother's children equally, but my bond with my niece is unique because of birth order and gender. I am relieved that she will never have to deal with the ingrained family prejudices that characterized my childhood.

My brother's parenting philosophy toward his children marks a critical break with old ways that were oppressive and punitive toward women.

As a dad, he wants his kids to grow up with confidence. To not feel that gender should be a burden. If this means that my niece will stand on chairs to deliver speeches about why we need to listen to her, so be it. If she sings arias about how annoying her little brother is, bring it on. As hard as it may be to guide and mentor a strong-willed child, the caring adults in her life want her to grow up to be the best person she can be.

I am relieved that my niece, former Baby Ninja and future Rebel Girl, will grow up to be a Woman Warrior. May all girls be as fortunate as she to have people who are committed to smashing patriarchy for good.

Jse-Che Lam

As for Anna and Tobit, perhaps they have fertility problems. That they have only one child is unusual in early Jewish narratives, though it is not unheard of: Sarah has only Isaac (Gen 21:2-3); the widow of Nain has only one child (Luke 7:11-17); and in Tobit Edna and Raguel, Sarah's parents, join Anna and Tobit in having only one child. Such only children were deeply cherished. Jeremiah uses the mourning for the death of an only child as an example of grief, since such children are so deeply loved: "O my poor people, put on sackcloth, and roll in ashes; make mourning as for only child" (Jer 6:26). Amos 8:10, the first half of which is quoted in Tobit 2:6, likewise highlights how precious is an only child.

Interpreting Sarah's Situation

Sarah's slave introduces the cross-cultural trope of the "killer wife," also known as the "black widow" (after the spider that kills its mate). Having a sexual relationship with such a woman could prove fatal, and killer wives are directly responsible for the deaths of their husbands.[36] The trope is an expression of male fears of female sexuality, and it can be

---

36. Beate Ego, "A Self-Response to 'Textual Variants,'" in *A Feminist Companion to Tobit and Judith*, ed. Athalya Brenner and Helen Efthimiadis-Keith (London: Bloomsbury, 2015), 75.

found in various cultures. In Hinduism, for example, up until the middle of the twentieth century widows were held responsible by Indian society for the deaths of their husbands and were not allowed to remarry even after one marriage.[37]

Tal Ilan suggests that one plausible reason why the early second-century CE widow Babatha was not paid what she was owed according to her *ketubah* (marriage contract), and so had to engage in litigation to receive it, was because her late husband's family considered her to be a killer wife.[38] According to documents found in a cave in the Judean desert, Babatha had been married to two men (one named Jesus, and the other Judah) who died within six years of each another. Ilan argues that a woman in such a situation "would have been viewed as being directly responsible for the death of her husbands," since there is convincing evidence for the existence of the belief in the killer-wife trope in ancient Jewish society.[39] Ilan suggests that "the discussion of the killer-wife motif in Jewish tradition should begin with the Book of Tobit," as she sees the marriage of Sarah to seven grooms who are killed by the demon Asmodeus on the night of their marriage as affirmation of "the belief in the very real existence of women to whom it is deadly to be married, *even when they are not entirely at fault*" among Jews during the Greco-Roman period.[40]

The killer-wife motif, which Finnish folklorist Ante Aarne labeled "The Monster in the Bridal Chamber," is indeed present in Jewish literature of late antiquity.[41] The Talmud mentions the *qatlanit* (literally: "killer/fatal wife") and depicts rabbis strategizing about how to limit the number of husbands such a woman could have. According to Rabbi Yehuda HaNasi, if a woman has already experienced the deaths of two

---

37. Mitra Sharafi, "How the Taboo on Hindu Widow Remarriage Led to Liberal Abortion Norms in Colonial India," Scroll.in, August 10, 2020, https://scroll.in/article/963935/how-the-taboo-on-hindu-widow-remarriage-led-to-liberal-abortion-norms-in-colonial-india.

38. Tal Ilan, "Babatha the Killer-Wife: Literature, Folk Religion and Documentary Papyri," in *Law and Narrative in the Bible and in Neighbouring Ancient Cultures*, ed. Klaus-Peter Adam, Friedrich Avemarie, and Nili Wazana, FAT 2.54 (Tübingen: Mohr Siebeck 2012), 266–67. Also H. M. Cotton and J. C. Greenfield, "Babatha's Property and the Law of Succession in the Babatha Archive," *ZPE* 104 (1994): 211–21.

39. Ilan, "Babatha the Killer-Wife," 266–67.

40. Ilan, "Babatha the Killer-Wife," 267, emphasis added.

41. Ilan, "Babatha the Killer-Wife," 267.

husbands, she ought not to be able to marry a third. Rabban Shimon ben Gamliel, more compassionate toward the widow, says that she may marry a third but not a fourth husband (b. Yebam. 64b).[42] At no point do the rabbis explicitly blame wives for the deaths of their husbands, but it is implied. The Talmud mentions a woman named Homa as being married three times (Rehaba of Pumbadita, Isaac son of Rabba bar Hannah, and Abbaye) and widowed three times (b. Yebam. 64b; b. Ketub. 65a). In a description akin to a Hollywood romantic comedy, the latter Talmudic text describes how the (unnamed) wife of Rava, the judge overseeing Homa's court case (for, like Babatha's situation, the family of her late third husband refuses to honor their financial obligations so Homa goes to court), chases Homa out of town, shouting, "You have killed three, but you will not kill my husband." Rava, who is sexually attracted to Homa, is not blamed, only Homa is.

In contrast to the above narratives, in Tobit Sarah explicitly is not responsible for killing her grooms. Asmodeus, the demon, is. Sarah's slave accuses her of killing her husbands, but the narrative makes it clear that this accusation does not reflect what happened. When she prays, Sarah does not mention Asmodeus, but that need not mean she is unaware of him. Perhaps mentioning a demon in a prayer was inappropriate. Tobias, even before he meets Sarah, is aware that a demon has killed each of her seven grooms the first night of their marriage (6:14-15). If Tobias knows about the problem and has heard "people saying that it was a demon that killed them" (6:14), how can we assume that Sarah does not know about Asmodeus?

Interpreted in this manner, our text can be understood as resisting the idea of the wife as the husband killer and that the deaths of husbands are the fault of wives.[43] The deaths of Sarah's husbands are *not* her fault: the demon Asmodeus snuffed out their lives (3:8; 6:14-18; 8:3). Like the Gospel text telling about the Samaritan woman (John 4), whom Jesus correctly divines has been married to five husbands without ascribing sin or shame to the woman, Sarah does not indicate by her actions or in her prayer that she understands herself to be guilty of killing her husbands. Likewise, when Sadducees relate to Jesus the story of the seven brothers who practice levirate marriage—the same woman marries each

42. Frank Zimmerman, *The Book of Tobit* (New York: Harper and Brothers, 1958), 62. Isaac Sassoon, *The Status of Women in Jewish Tradition* (Cambridge: Cambridge University Press, 2011), 124 discusses "the Qatlanit Law."

43. I am grateful to Amy-Jill Levine for this suggestion.

brother sequentially—with the goal of pointing out the ridiculousness of the belief in resurrection (Mark 12:20-22; Matt 22:25-26; Luke 20:29-30), they make no condemnation of the woman.[44] These narratives resist the concept of the "killer wife."

Asmodeus the Demon

The etymology of the name Asmodeus, Sarah's demon, is not certain. It comes from either the Zoroastrian Avestan *Aesma Daeva*, "the demon of wrath," or the Hebrew *Ashmedai*, from שמד, *shemad*, "to destroy, exterminate."[45] Joseph Fitzmyer proposes that the Hebrew is not the original but a folk etymology "concocted to keep the tradition closer to home."[46] In the earliest Zoroastrian scriptures, the Gathic texts, which date to about the tenth to ninth century BCE, to go the evil way is to follow Aeshma; later Pahlavi texts (dated from c. 226–651 CE) depict Aeshma as a counterpart to Ahriman (Angra Mainyu), the god of evil.[47] Asmodeus appears again in the Testament of Solomon, a Jewish text dated from the first to the third century CE that describes his role as a disrupter of the newly married in details that are "clearly drawn" from Tobit.[48] The Talmud presents an Asmodeus who is king of the demons (b. Pes. 110a; 112b) but who can also be benevolent; for example, he helps King Solomon learn an important lesson about what is truly valuable in life (b. Git. 68 a-b). In the Kabbalah, incantations sometimes incorporate the name of Asmodeus.[49] Asmodeus the demon, therefore, had a long and storied existence in multiple texts.

44. *Contra* Ilan, "Babatha the Killer-Wife," 268.

45. M. Hutter, "Asmodeus," in *Dictionary of Deities and Demons in the Bible*, ed. Karel van der Toorn, Bob Becking, and Pieter W. van der Horst, 2nd ed. (Leiden: Brill, 1999), 106.

46. Joseph A. Fitzmyer, *Tobit* (Berlin: de Gruyter, 2003), 151; Beate Ego, "The Banishment of the Demon in Tobit: Textual Variants as a Result of Enculturation," in Brenner-Idan and Efthimiadis-Keith, *Tobit and Judith*, 69, n. 9. Cf. Toni Craven, "Wives," in *Women in Scripture: A Dictionary of Named and Unnamed Women in the Hebrew Bible, the Apocryphal/Deuterocanonical Books, and the New Testament*, ed. Carol Meyers, Toni Craven, and Ross S. Kraemer (Grand Rapids: Eerdmans, 2000), 359, who favors "the destroyer" and sees parallels with the destroying angel of 2 Sam 24:16; Wis 18:25; Rev 9:11.

47. Hutter, "Asmodeus," 106; Fitzmyer, *Tobit*, 150.

48. F. C. Conybeare, "The Testament of Solomon," *JQR* 11 (1898): 20, n. 2.

49. J. Roth, "Asmodeus (Ashmedai)," in *Encyclopaedia Judaica*, ed. Fred Skolnik, 2nd ed. (Detroit: Thomson Gale, 2007), 2:593.

Sarah: Death, Exile, and Hope in God's Mercy

Although Tobit and Sarah are the two faces of death in the book of Tobit, it is easier to imagine Tobit's association with death. In his prayer of despair, he asks God to release him into his eternal abode. He prefers dust and death to the experience of being alive listening to the reproaches of others (3:6). He views his blindness as tantamount to death. In his initial encounter with Raphael disguised as a kinsman, he laments that he cannot see the light of heaven and lives as if he were walking among the dead.

The suggestion of death with regard to the character of Sarah is not as obvious. Indeed, Sarah also prays for death, having lost all hope after listening to the ruthless reproaches of one of the maidservants. In the end, however, she remains open to God's plan, allows God freedom and closes her prayer instead with a plea for divine mercy and favor (3:15). Nowhere in the narrative does Sarah utter another word or engage in dialogue other than to say "Amen" with Tobias at the end of his prayer on their wedding night (8:8). Although other characters address Sarah, such as her father (10:12) and her father-in-law Tobit (11:17), the narrative records no dialogical response from Sarah. Unlike Tobit, who compared his blindness to death, Sarah does not provide any hints of her experience of death.

Biblically, death is not necessarily the cessation of biological functions or physical nonexistence. Rather, death is a debilitating and severe form of illness; to die is to be in a weakened, broken, and disordered state of life. Death is anything that limits life from achieving the full potential that God has intended. For Tobit, death is blindness and poverty. For Sarah, it is the loss of seven husbands and all the possibilities that attend to that loss. Their losses participate in a loss *writ large*, the loss of their homeland.

The story endows Sarah with beauty, innocence, and trustworthiness (3:14-15; 6:12). Despite these positive traits, however, Sarah remains without a husband. The irrational longing of the jealous demon Asmodeus to bind himself to Sarah leaves Sarah childless and seven times a widow. The absence of a husband spells deathly doom for Sarah. She loses the possibility to bear children not due to infertility, as is the case with her ancestress namesake and matriarch Sarah and the other barren women in the Scriptures, but because all eligible husbands are dead. It is not something that she has or does but something beyond her that places her on the path of death.

Worse, the loss of seven husbands tarnishes Sarah's honorable reputation and standing before a community of suitable bachelors and practically makes her unmarriageable. In fact, those who might be worthy are afraid to come close to her, as Tobias confesses to Raphael when the angel informs him that he will marry Sarah (6:15). Sarah's loss of her honorable reputation places her on the verge of social death; her situation has become a sentence of death. Like Tobit, Sarah is alive but destroyed. Like Tobit, Sarah is virtually dead.

The stories of Sarah and Tobit run parallel in that both recount events that make lives weak. Before the throne of God, their prayerful expressions of sorrow enjoy equal hearing. Their fates carry the same weight. God responds and reorders both their situations so that life for both characters may prevail in the end. In this way, Sarah's role in the story is as important as Tobit's. It is not Tobit alone who represents the collective. Rather, both Tobit and Sarah create for the narrative a complete portrait of lives that have crumbled and lives defined by losses. In other words, they both represent the burdens of exilic life. After all, to be in exile is to decompose, disintegrate, and die as a people. Their losses and misfortunes together show how life away from the land forbids the full life that God intends for God's people from unfolding.

Francis M. Macatangay

Sarah Contemplates Suicide and Prays (3:10-15)

In 3:6, Sarah goes to the upstairs floor of her father's house to commit suicide. She is in anguish, "grieved in spirit" (ἐλυπήθη ἐν τῇ ψυχῇ), and weeping. But she does not carry out her plan to hang herself (ἀπάγξασθαι). Unlike Tobit, who thinks primarily about himself, Sarah fears how her suicide would affect her father.[50] Not only will her father grieve her loss; others in the community will blame him for her death: he had but one child to protect, and he failed to keep her alive.

Honor and Shame

As an obedient daughter, Sarah understands that her behavior will affect her father's honor—that is, the respect in which he is held by his peers. Sarah's death would affect Raguel's social position, for fathers were judged on how well their children and wives behaved. Sarah grants

50. Fitzmyer, *Tobit*, 148, says that "she realizes that that would only produce criticism of her parents, especially of her aged father," but nowhere does Sarah mention her mother.

Tob 3:10-15

[10]On that day she was grieved in spirit and wept. When she had gone up to her father's upper room, she intended to hang herself. But she thought it over and said, "Never shall they reproach my father, saying to him, 'You had only one beloved daughter but she hanged herself because of her distress.' And I shall bring my father in his old age down in sorrow to Hades. It is better for me not to hang myself, but to pray the Lord that I may die and not listen to these reproaches anymore." [11]At that same time, with hands outstretched toward the window, she prayed and said,

"Blessed are you, merciful God!
Blessed is your name for
ever;
let all your works praise you
forever.
[12]And now, Lord, I turn my face to
you,
and raise my eyes toward you.

[13]Command that I be released
from the earth
and not listen to such
reproaches any more.
[14]You know, O Master, that I am
innocent
of any defilement with a man,
[15]and that I have not disgraced
my name
or the name of my father in the
land of my exile.
I am my father's only child;
he has no other child to be
his heir;
and he has no close relative or
other kindred
for whom I should keep myself
as wife.
Already seven husbands of mine
have died.
Why should I still live?
But if it is not pleasing to you,
O Lord, to take my life,
hear me in my disgrace."

that Raguel would be sorrowful were she to kill herself, but he also would be reproached by his peers. In Euripides's *The Suppliants*, when Evadne kills herself by throwing herself on her dead husband's funeral pyre, her father Iphis is heartbroken, as "nothing is there more sweet unto an aged father than a daughter; our sons are made of sterner stuff, but less winning are their caresses."[51] His response is to starve himself to death, but it is rare for the death of a daughter to prompt suicide by parents.[52]

51. "Euripides," in *The Complete Greek Drama*, ed. Whitney J. Oates and Eugene O'Neill Jr., vol. 1: *The Suppliants*, trans. E. P. Coleridge (New York: Random House, 1938).

52. Anton J. L. van Hooff, *From Autothanasia to Suicide: Self-Killing in Classical Antiquity* (London: Routledge, 1990), 104.

Sarah's means of death, had she done it, would have been through hanging. The story of Sarah's changing her mind and *not* hanging herself can be understood as resistance to the Greek trope of female suicide. Hanging was, as Eva Cantarella observes, "the privileged instrument of female death" in the Greek and Roman world.[53] Despite Homer's characterization of the hanging of female slaves lacking in loyalty as an "unclean death" in *The Odyssey* (22.489), in Greek mythology women frequently died in this manner.[54] Describing Evadne's suicide, Philostratus states that she "determined to die for love of him, not by drawing a knife against her throat nor by hanging herself from a noose, modes of death often chosen by women in honour of their husbands" (*Imag.* 2.30.2).[55] Sophocles's heroine, Antigone, escapes being buried alive by hanging herself (*Ant.* 1204), and Epicaste, Oedipus's mother, hangs herself when she discovers that she'd married her own son (*Od.* 11.269).[56] Erigone, the daughter of Icarius, hanged herself out of grief over the death of her father (*Apd.* 3.14.7). Romans also were aware of the "link between woman and the noose."[57] In his *Peri Parthenion*, Hippocrates explains that young virgins are prone to suicide by hanging due to a cumulation of blood near the heart and the diaphragm; the cure was to get married: "Whenever girls suffer from these effects I recommend them to live with men as soon as possible" (*Hipp.* 8:464–71).[58] The cure-all to problematic young women? Marriage.

Cantarella observes that, in hanging, "women are detached from the ground, separated from the earth"—often referred to as "mother earth"—from which women (such as Pandora) were made.[59] In the second creation story in Genesis, only the man is created from the "dust of the earth" (Gen 2:7); the woman is created out of the man's "rib" (2:21-22). Neither the Tanakh nor the New Testament give examples of women who commit suicide by hanging. Perhaps the issue is that women were thought

53. Eva Cantarella, "Dangling Virgins: Myth, Ritual and the Place of Women in Ancient Greece," *Poetics Today* 6 (1985): 91–101. I'm grateful to Amy-Jill Levine for this reference.

54. Van Hooff, *From Autothanasia to Suicide*, 65.

55. Philostratus, *Imagines*, trans. Arthur Fairbanks (London: William Heinemann, 1931), 257.

56. Cantarella, "Dangling Virgins," 92.

57. Cantarella, "Dangling Virgins," 95.

58. Cantarella, "Dangling Virgins," 97, notes that "the disease disappears upon marriage," according to Hippocrates.

59. Hesiod, *Op.* 61; Cantarella, "Dangling Virgins," 98–99.

to derive power from the earth. The Jerusalem Talmud (y. Hag. 2:2, 77d) describes Simeon b. Shetah, a sage of the second to first century BCE, as killing eighty witches in Ashkelon by hanging, "since their witchcraft was rendered inoperable if their feet are not touching the ground."

Presumably Sarah's mother, Edna, likewise would be despondent upon the suicide of a daughter, and the relationship between Sarah and her mother seems very close. Yet in her prayer, Sarah expresses concern only for her father and his reputation. When it comes to matters of public honor, how her behavior affected her mother was less important.

Sarah, taking a customary pose for prayer, stretches her hands out (e.g., Ezra 9:5; 1 Kgs 8:22, 38). In contrast to Ezra, who states, "O my God, I am too ashamed and mortified to lift my face to you" (Ezra 9:6), Sarah turns her face and raises her eyes (τοὺς ὀφθαλμούς μου ἀνέβλεψα) toward God (3:12). In so doing, Sarah shows that she is not ashamed, nor is she taking a humble stance. She knows she has done nothing wrong: she is "innocent" (v. 14); she has "not disgraced" her name nor that of her father (v. 15).

Sarah's first concern is about sullying her *own* name; this concern challenges gender ideology behind the identification of daughters and wives through male relatives.[60] In so doing, Sarah joins the ranks of numerous women within Jewish literature who have their own agency and stick up for themselves (such as Hannah in 1 Sam 1:15-16; Judith in Jdt 13:15-16; Esther in [Greek] Esth 2:20-22; 14:11-15; Susanna, verses 42-43). This reference to her own name reflects Sarah's autonomy and agency, expressed also in her comment that her father has "no close relative or other kindred for whom I should keep myself as wife" (Tob 3:15). Like Tobit's prayer (3:6), Sarah's prayer also uses the imperative (e.g., ἐπίταξον "command," 3:6); she orders God "that [she] be released from the earth"—hence the concern for hanging—so that she need "not listen to reproaches any more" (3:13), referring to those of her slave. Both prayers reflect the pain that words can inflict, and they express Tobit's and Sarah's desperation for release.

In verse 14, Sarah states that she is καθαρά—literally, "pure,"—of all ἀκαθαρσίας, "uncleanness," with a man. This language reflects the importance of female sexual purity, which is also present in Judith and Susanna. Piety and attractiveness are linked together for the women of

60. Most women in literary sources are identified by their relationships to men, usually their husbands, for example, "Pheroras's wife" (in Josephus's *Ant.* 17:42, 62-76) and Joanna, one of Jesus's patrons, as "the wife of Herod's steward Chuza" (Luke 8:3).

the Hellenistic-Jewish narratives (Jdt 8:7-8; Sus 2, 3; Esth 2:7, 20 [LXX]; and Tob 6:12). In contrast to Tobit, Sarah acknowledges that God might have a different plan (3:15) so does not assume that her desires are necessarily aligned with the divine.

Suicide in the Ancient World and Now

Ancient Greeks and Romans generally did not view suicide negatively. Plato's *Phaedo* describes how Socrates, condemned to death, explained to his puzzled followers that since a central goal of philosophers "is to practice for dying and death," it would be odd were they to resist death "when what they have wanted and practiced for a long time comes upon them" (64a). However, Socrates also argued that humans were, essentially, the "possessions," of the gods, and thus suicide was not something to be done without first receiving a sign from the gods (62bc). Stoic philosophers argued that suicide was an appropriate response "when it was called for by obligations owed to one's country or friends, when the physical conditions of life were so inhospitable that one could no longer practice virtue, or when one was going to be forced to perform actions so base or contrary to one's character that life was no longer worth the price."[61] The Stoic philosopher Seneca imagines God as stating:

> Above all, I have taken care that no one should hold you captive against your will: the way of escape lies open before you: if you do not choose to fight, you may fly. For this reason, of all those matters which I have deemed essential for you, I have made nothing easier for you than to die. I have set man's life as it were on a mountainside: it soon slips down. Do but watch, and you will see how short and how ready a path leads to freedom. (*On Providence* 6.7-8)[62]

Suicide becomes how humans can rebuff fortune and obtain freedom. Death, for Seneca, was freedom; he viewed the body as a prison so at death the soul "renews its life in heaven" (*Ep.* 65.16).[63]

---

61. Englert Walter, "Seneca and the Stoic View of Suicide," *The Society for Ancient Greek Philosophy Newsletter* 184 (1990): 19.

62. Seneca the Younger, *Minor Dialogs Together with the Dialog "On Clemency,"* trans. Aubrey Stewart, Bohn's Classical Library Edition (London: George Bell and Sons, 1900), 213.

63. Seneca the Younger, *Letters from a Stoic—Epistulae Morales ad Lucilium,* trans. Richard Mott Gummere, vol. 1, LCL (London: Heinemann, 1917–1925), 455.

The Tanakh does not forbid suicide. It describes six suicides—of Abimelech (Judg 9:54); of Samson (Judg 16:30); of Saul and his arms-bearer (1 Sam 31:4-5); of Ahithophel (2 Sam 17:23); and of Zimri (1 Kgs 16:18); five are carried out in order to avoid being killed by an enemy, and the sixth (Saul's arms-bearer) takes place out of loyalty. The text condemns none of these cases. But though no explicit command forbidding suicide is given, the sovereignty of God over life and death is repeatedly emphasized: "I kill and I make alive" (Deut 32:39); "The LORD kills and brings to life" (1 Sam 2:6).

Suicides are depicted in Jewish-Hellenistic literature, and they fit the Stoic models. Second Maccabees (7:1-42) and 4 Maccabees (1:8, 10; 8:3-4, 20; 10:2; 12:6-7; 13:19; 14:11–18:24) recount the story of the seven brothers tortured and killed by Antiochus Epiphanes (168–164 BCE). Whereas 2 Maccabees announces the death of the mother without details, "Last of all, the mother died, after her sons" (7:41), 4 Maccabees explains that she commits suicide by throwing herself into the flames "so that no one might touch her body" (17:1) and describes her as courageous, noble, and holy minded (17:2-5); she is "the spokeswoman for the supremacy of the Jewish religion and family values."[64]

In John 8:22, "the Jews" understand Jesus's words, "I am going away, and you will search for me, but you will die in your sin. Where I am going, you cannot come" (John 8:21) to be a reference to suicide: "Is he going to kill himself?" they ask. The evangelist makes it clear that the Jews are mistaken; when in John 10:18 Jesus states, "No one takes it from me, but I lay it down of my own accord. I have power to lay it down, and I have power to take it up again," he is not speaking of killing himself but of his controlling his fate. In the New Testament, the only clear case of suicide is that of Judas, whom Matthew 27:5 describes as hanging himself out of regret; Judas appears here as a new Ahithophel, David's betrayer. Acts 1:16-20 gives a contrasting—and nonsuicidal—account of Judas's death.

In early Christianity, certain church fathers condemned suicide, with St. Augustine likely the first to provide a justification for the prohibition.[65] He viewed it as an infringement of the commandment "Thou

---

64. Toni Craven, "Martyred Mother with Seven Sons," in Meyers, Craven, and Kraemer, *Women in Scripture*, 405.

65. D. Amundsen, "Suicide and Early Christian Values," in *Suicide and Euthanasia: Historical and Contemporary Themes*, ed. Baruch A. Brody (Boston: Kluwer Academic, 1989), 83.

shall not kill" (Exod 20:13) and suggested that the commandment "is to be taken as forbidding self-destruction, especially as it does not add 'thy neighbor,' as it does when it forbids false witness, 'Thou shalt not bear false witness against thy neighbor'" (*City of God* 1.20).[66] St. Thomas Aquinas in the thirteenth century built on Augustine's argument by adding that suicide is morally wrong because it transgresses three types of responsibilities: one's responsibility to God, to others, and to oneself (*Summa Theologica* I-IL, q. 64, art. 5).[67]

Judaism's perspective on suicide is based on the understanding that the body belongs to God, since God created and owns everything (e.g., Exod 19:5: Deut 10:14; Ps 24:1). God, as creator and owner, specifies obligations and proscriptions meant to protect life and health, including the teaching that individuals do not have the right even to wound their own bodies, let alone to take their own life. In b. Baba Qamma 91b, for example, the sages interpret Genesis 9:5 ("For your own lifeblood I will surely require a reckoning: from every animal I will require it and from human beings, each one for the blood of another, I will require a reckoning for human life") to be a prohibition of self-harm. The rabbinic view is nuanced by the argument that if a person is being forced to commit adultery, murder, or idolatry, or die, one must accept death (Sanh. 74a). Consequently, allowing oneself to be killed for the sake of God (referred to as *Kiddush haShem*, "the sanctification of God's name") or in defense of Judaism is permitted, but otherwise suicide is not. Later Jewish legal codes, such as those of the twelfth century written by Maimonides or those of the sixteenth century by Joseph Karo in the *Shulchan Aruch*, discriminate between suicide while of sound mind and suicide while of unsound mind (e.g., experiencing mental illness).[68] The latter occurrences are not condemned. Although Orthodox Jews have traditionally denied a full funeral service and regular burial rites to suicide victims, growing awareness in many Orthodox communities of mental illness has led to the offering of full funerary rites. Conservative, Reform, and

---

66. Robin E. Gearing and Dana Alonzo, "Religion and Suicide: New Findings," *Journal of Religion and Health* 57 (2018): 2478–99.

67. Thomas Aquinas, *Summa Theologica*, trans. Fathers of the English Dominican Province, vol. 4 (Westminster, MD: Christian Classics, 1981), 167.

68. Steven H. Resnicoff, "Jewish Law Perspectives on Suicide and Physician-Assisted Dying," *Journal of Law and Religion* 13 (1998): 289–349.

Reconstructionist Jews traditionally treat victims of suicide no differently from any other deceased persons.

Some present-day Christian perspectives on suicide cohere with the historical teaching that suicide is a sin comparable to other sins resulting in the taking of life, such as murder and abortion.[69] According to the Catechism of the Catholic Church, however, "Grave psychological disturbances, anguish, or grave fear of hardship, suffering, or torture can diminish the responsibility of the one committing suicide," (#2282) and this, as with the Jewish perspective, softens the understanding of suicide as a sin.[70] Historically, those who committed suicide were not allowed burial in Catholic cemeteries, but—again, similar to Jewish practice—the Catholic Church now allows a funeral Mass and burial in a Catholic cemetery for those who take their own lives.[71] More often than not, during funeral services, prayers are offered seeking God's forgiveness for the deceased.

Instances of suicide must be viewed with compassion, not judgment. Individuals who end their lives do so because they are suffering, and they want to end their pain. Often they have tried multiple means of ameliorating their situations, such as through therapy or medications, without positive results. It is not that they wish to die—it is that they simply want the anguish to cease.

Sarah wants to end her own suffering, but she is concerned about how achieving that would affect her father. Beverly Bow notes that Tobit's prayer (3:2-6, 11-15) is "larger in scope than Sarah's. Sarah is concerned with how her marital situation affects her own father . . . and Tobit speaks of his ancestors, presents himself as paradigmatic for all (the men of) Israel" and that "a man's religious interests and obligations are more far-reaching than a woman's."[72] Perhaps Sarah's world is smaller, but it is also less self-centered than that of Tobit.

69. P. J. Wogaman, *Ethical Perspectives for the Community* (London: Westminster John Knox, 1990).

70. Saint Joseph's University, "What Is the Catholic Church's Position on Suicide and Physician-Assisted Suicide?," March 4, 2016, https://sites.sju.edu/icb/catholic-churchs-position-suicide-physician-assisted-suicide-declaration-euthanasia/. See *Catechism of the Catholic Church* 2280–83, https://www.usccb.org/sites/default/files/flipbooks/catechism/.

71. W. Phipps, "Christian Perspectives on Suicide," *ChrCent* (1985): 970–72.

72. Beverly Bow, "Sarah 2," in Meyers, Craven, and Kraemer, *Women in Scripture*, 153.

Sarah, from a Widow's Perspective

The dilemma of the young widow Sarah reflects past and current circumstances for widows globally, but Sarah's loss was compounded by the death of seven husbands. This left her shrouded in suspicion regarding the unusual circumstances of their demise. She was held suspect as possibly being evil herself. We read that word of her seven losses spread to Tobias who lived a significant distance from her in an age when news did not spread as easily. The notoriety of losing seven husbands would have been overwhelming.

If her husband died unnaturally, a widow might not feel the same level of support from the community and extended family. Losing one's husband to physical injury or illness evokes sympathy and compassion. Losing one's husband at the hand of an entirely other facet of evil would have been inexplicable to the community. Sarah's ties to her supports might have unraveled thread by thread as each husband met the same fate. Only her maid/slave accused her to her face (3:7-10).

Sarah converses with God, pleading her innocence and cleanness of her hands. In 3:19 she examines herself and her previous husbands, wondering if she or they were unworthy. I suspect many widows who lost (and lose) their husbands due to unnatural causes have examined themselves relentlessly for any blame in the demise of their husband.

In 3:21, 22 Sarah shows faith in God's mercy, and that God does not delight in her being lost. She had faith even though it was vastly challenged.

Sarah lost her chance to consummate her vows, thus removing her opportunity to conceive.

To be a widow is to be bereft of one of the most valued partnerships in one's life. To be a widow without community support due to the exceptional circumstances of a husband's death can single out the widow through shame. To be that same widow and not have children, when children were—and are—considered to be a blessing of the Lord, can crush the most resolute and resulted in Sarah's suicidal ideations.

Sarah's having to depend on her father and mother to house and feed her when she was expected to marry and bear children who would in turn support her may have left her feeling as a burden to others. I didn't experience that when I became a widow, as I had a full-time job, but I suspect that my father felt the burden of worry about his daughter being alone and raising three young children to adulthood.

I've not felt the same compulsion to remarry that Sarah did, but if I were living in her time and culture, I likely would have made a concerted effort to remarry. In comparing Sarah's obligation to attempt remarriage repeatedly, I consider myself privileged to have been raised in a culture that didn't place such pressure on me. I have choices. Sarah believed she had few choices to navigate out of the murky waters of her circumstances.

Despair can lead to hopelessness, and reproach—or the perception of reproach—to shame. Sarah began to view her future as nonexistent and contemplated her own death.

In 3:15 she begged to be loosed from reproach or be dead.

Believing that I am the seed of Abraham through faith (Gal 3:7-9, 29) changed my perception of widowhood (albeit years after the death of my husband) and caused me to trust that "the LORD [would] provide" (Gen 22:14), regardless of the possibility that others might have suspected my being disadvantaged or lacking in some esteemed quality due to losing my husband by suicide.

Elisabeth Cunningham

Answers to Two Prayers (3:16-17)

These verses tell Tobit's audience that all will work out for Tobit and Sarah. Raphael, the angel whose name in Hebrew means exactly what he does, "God heals," will facilitate the cure for Tobit's blindness and enable Sarah to marry successfully. By "loosening the wicked demon from her" (3:17; my translation), Raphael frees Sarah from Asmodeus. The Greek λῦσαι, "loosening," is likely translated from the Aramaic פטר, "dismiss, discharge,"—a term used in Babylonian divorce certificates as well as in magical formulations, such as those found in incantation bowls, when residents sought to "divorce" demons from their households.[73] The implication here is that Asmodeus is acting as Sarah's husband. Given the tight grasp Asmodeus has on Sarah, it is no wonder that he destroys the men who seek to marry her. In order for his hold on her to be broken, he must be divorced from Sarah.[74] Divorce, mentioned several times in the Bible (particularly in Deut 24:1-4), was usually initiated by men, though contracts among the Jewish Elephantine papyri (dating to the

73. Also noted by Ego, "Banishment of the Demon," 70.
74. Fitzmyer, *Tobit*, 161; Paul E. Dion, "Raphaël l'exorciste," *Bib* 57 (1976): 407–8; John G. Gager, *Curse Tablets and Binding Spells from the Ancient World* (New York: Oxford University Press, 1992), 229–31.

Tob 3:16-17

[16]At that very moment, the prayers of both of them were heard in the glorious presence of God. [17]So Raphael was sent to heal both of them: Tobit, by removing the white films from his eyes, so that he might see God's light with his eyes; and Sarah daughter of Raguel, by giving her in marriage to Tobias son of Tobit, and by setting her free from the wicked demon Asmodeus. For Tobias was entitled to have her before all others who had desired to marry her. At the same time that Tobit returned from the courtyard into his house, Sarah daughter of Raguel came down from her upper room.

fifth century BCE) show that women could also initiate proceedings.[75] The Gospel of Mark (10:12) and writings of Paul (1 Cor 7:10-11) assume that women can divorce their husbands as well. Asmodeus does not initiate the divorce; the "loosening" is begun by Tobias through the ritual Raphael teaches him, and then Raphael completes it.

Sarah had been married, but she did not have sexual relations with any of her husbands, thus she is still a virgin; each of her husbands died, so she is a widow—yet she does not fit the usual descriptions of virgin, wife, or widow. Not fitting into any of these traditional female roles (by fitting into all of them at once) makes her identity anomalous. Anomalous individuals can be dangerous since they cannot easily be socially located. By marrying Sarah, consummating their relationship, and fathering her children, Tobias will bring her back into the normative roles of (not-virginal) wife and mother.

75. Bernadette Brooten, "Konnten Frauen im alten Judentum die Scheidung betreiben? Überlegungen zu Mk 10, 11-12 und 1 Kor 7, 10-11," *EvT* 42 (1982): 65–80.

Tobit 4

Living a Good Life

Chapter 4 begins with Tobit's preparing for what he thinks is his imminent death. He instructs Tobias on how to live righteously, and he also reveals that there is a family friend who has a stash of silver waiting to be retrieved. Matters of feminist interest include the promise of prosperity, maternal mortality, questions of why Tobit withheld knowledge of the silver from Anna, why he finds it necessary to ask Tobias to bury him properly and not neglect Anna, the way Tobit commands the giving of alms, and the function of what is sometimes called the "golden rule."

Tobit, Thinking He Is about to Die, Remembers He Has Money (4:1-2)

I wonder why Tobit only now remembers this stash that could help his financially struggling family. George Nickelsburg, asking the same question, suggests, "God jogged Tobit's memory."[1] But the question then becomes: why didn't God jog his memory earlier? Why, when Tobit could no longer work, did he not mention these funds? Is Tobit trying to hide

---

1. George W. E. Nickelsburg, "Tobit," in *Harper's Bible Commentary*, ed. James L. Mays (New York: Harper and Row, 1988), 796.

⁴:¹That same day Tobit remembered the money that he had left in trust with Gabael at Rages in Media, ²and he said to himself, "Now I have asked for death. Why do I not call my son Tobias and explain to him about the money before I die?"

these funds from his wife and son? Or, to be more charitable, Tobit may have been unprepared to send Tobias on the quest to retrieve them earlier.

Perhaps Tobit did not recall that he'd left silver with Gabael until he faced his own death. Or could it be that storing these funds with his cousin was the equivalent of hiding money under the mattress, as we sometimes hear people who are distrustful about banks do, and so maybe Tobit was embarrassed to admit to this?

Carey Moore, finding that "Tobit's thoughts turn, first, to his son's material well-being (v. 1) and then, quite quickly, to Tobiah's spiritual well-being (vv. 3-19),"[2] concludes that "it is characteristic of Tobit, despite his abject misery, to be much concerned for his family." I think not. Tobit has to this point *not* demonstrated concern for his family: this is the first time that he does. Now we see that the family at one point had money—this is a story of riches to rags, back to riches. This gives insight into the reasons behind Tobit's whiny despair: he was used to having his needs met, and he was used to helping others by giving charity from his bounty. He is frustrated by this novel situation: now *he* is in need.

Tobit had prayed for death; he now thinks that he will die. His assumption that God will do what he asked—that is, take his life—is evidence of his arrogance. The contrast between Tobit and Sarah highlights this hubris: both pray for death, but Sarah leaves the decision to God (3:15: "But if it is not pleasing to you, O Lord, to take my life, hear me in my disgrace"). Sarah admits that God might see things differently from how she does. Tobit fails to consider that God might have a different perspective from himself; for Tobit, there is only one view, his, and his view is the same as God's. He wants to do right by his family, but he cannot, and he takes out his frustrations on them and on God. Tobit is a man of faith who, in a muddling way, tries to make sense of his situation by speaking of God's "exacting penalty" for his sins (3:5).

2. Carey A. Moore, *Tobit: A New Translation with Introduction and Commentary* (New Haven: Yale University Press, 1996), 163.

Facing death can cause us to take stock of our possessions; in particular, individuals facing physical decline express concerns about who will get what. They desire to be remembered and bequeathing a favorite dish or piece of jewelry is one way they stay alive in the memories of those left behind. They may also desire to help loved ones in need. I know of one elderly woman in Jerusalem who lived at home until she was hospitalized during the last few days of her life. For seven or eight years, Natasha, a Russian-Jewish immigrant, who had moved to Israel in her forties, lived with her in her apartment, cooked the meals and helped with showers, took her for walks to the park, and otherwise served as both caregiver and companion. Natasha was, except for the elderly woman and a few friends (mostly fellow Russian immigrants like her), on her own. In contrast to Tobit, who at least experienced the hardship of exile with the company and support of his family, Natasha left the rest of her family—parents, siblings, and extended relatives—behind in Russia. Unlike Tobit, she was not exiled: she chose to immigrate to Israel because life for Jews in Russia was oppressive, and she sought a better life for herself. She had the courage to uproot herself and come to live in a new and very different country and culture. But she too experienced displacement. She had to learn a new language (Modern Hebrew), and to find her way in Israel on her own. Her making a living by being the live-in help for the elderly was not easy—it was hard work, for little pay. Natasha would never have been able to purchase an apartment in Jerusalem. Her elderly charge—a woman who had outlived most of her family and friends and who knew what it was to be alone—generously decided that she would leave her apartment to Natasha upon her death. One lone woman helping another. Tobit could count on Anna, Tobias, and other relatives such as Raguel and Gabael to help him, though he is hesitant to ask for their help.

Rages, which corresponds to the city of Rai in modern-day Iran, was an important city in the kingdom of Media.[3] It is mentioned also in Judith, where it is called "Ragau" (1:5, 15). Today, twenty thousand Jews live in Iran, and there are more than a dozen synagogues in the capital, Tehran. The population of Jews fell dramatically after Iran's 1979 revolution; prior to that, there were eighty to one hundred thousand Jews living in the country. Still, Iran's current Jewish community is the largest in a Middle Eastern Muslim country (with Turkey's being a close second).[4]

---

3. Moore, *Tobit*, 163.

4. Larry Cohler-Esses, "How Iran's Jews Survive in Mullahs' World," *Forward*, August 18, 2015, https://forward.com/news/319269/irans-jews-win-secure-place-in -mullahs-world-with-strings-attached/.

Jews live in Iran as "protected second-class citizens" who cannot hold high-level government jobs and, while there are Jewish schools to which they may send their children, the principals of these institutions must be Muslim. "[U]nder Sharia . . . if a Muslim kills a Jew, there will be blood money payment. But if a Jew kills a Muslim, the penalty is execution."[5] Tobit's narrative, like that of Esther, who rose to be queen of Persia, is fictional, but both stories attest to the reality of a Jewish presence in Iran of great longevity.

Tobit Instructs His Son (4:3-4)

Despite intending to tell Tobias about the money, Tobit first counsels him on several different topics: care of parents, followed by a concern for righteous living. Perhaps he is reflecting the teachings he learned from his grandmother, Deborah (1:8). Perhaps he is emphasizing burial, the activity by which he showed his righteousness. Tobit instructs his son about how he, the veritable master of burial, wishes himself to be buried. Respect for and care of parents is a fundamental expectation of Judeo-Christian piety, expressed in the fifth commandment: "Honor your father and your mother" (Exod 20:12//Deut 5:16). Expressing respect includes caring for parents when they are ill and, when they die, providing them a proper burial, just as Ishmael and Isaac together bury their father Abraham (Gen 25:9). Such concern for parents is likewise expressed in the New Testament, when a potential disciple asks Jesus for permission to "go and bury my father" (Matt 8:21//Luke 9:59). Jesus's harsh answer, "Let the dead bury their own dead" (Matt 8:22//Luke 9:60), conveys the primacy of discipleship.

Given what has transpired so far in the narrative, Tobit's request strikes me as odd. Tobias knew about his father's efforts in ensuring that fellow Israelites were properly buried, efforts important enough to risk punishment. Tobias understood that he needed to interrupt his search for a poor person to invite for dinner (2:3) in order to tell his father about the dead Israelite in the marketplace—so that Tobit could bury the body. Tobit's request suggests to me that either he lacked trust in his son or he was so obsessed with burial that he could not help but make this request. In either case, he strikes me as being annoying—even insulting—to Tobias. And yet, parents might repeat concerns of personal import, even when they know the child is well aware of these concerns. Being kind toward the

5. Cohler-Esses, "How Iran's Jews Survive."

³Then he called his son Tobias, and when he came to him he said, "My son, when I die, give me a proper burial. Honor your mother and do not abandon her all the days of her life. Do whatever pleases her, and do not grieve her in anything. ⁴Remember her, my son, because she faced many dangers for you while you were in her womb. And when she dies, bury her beside me in the same grave.

dying, those whose memories are failing, those who want to ensure that their concerns are remembered and heeded, is a sign of honor and respect.

The fifth commandment mentions both parents, while Tobit tells Tobias to "Honor your mother" (4:3). Honoring the father in this situation would mean providing him a proper burial, taking care of his mother, and living a good life so that Tobit's memory would be for a blessing. Tobit counsels Tobias not to neglect Anna as she ages. We could conclude that he assumes that Tobias *would* neglect his mother, but this would be an ungenerous reading. Tobias has done nothing to indicate a lack of concern (granted, to this point in the narrative, Tobias has not done much). Emphasis need not indicate doubt. It can, and probably does here, emphasize concern. When a grandmother tells her daughter, "Remember to give the baby her blanket," the grandmother is not calling into question her daughter's maternal ability. Tobit's advice accords not only with the fifth commandment but also with Proverbs 23:22 ("Do not despise your mother when she is old") and Proverbs 30:17 ("The eye that mocks a father and scorns to obey a mother will be pecked out by the ravens of the valley and eaten by the vultures").

The elderly, and especially elderly widows, could be vulnerable. As an only child, Tobias would have the responsibility to care for his mother before and after she is widowed. Anna is presently capable of being in the workforce, but there may come a time when she is no longer physically or mentally capable of maintaining a job. My mother-in-law, in her eighties, says, "Aging is not for sissies." One of the often-overlooked challenges of aging in North America (and elsewhere) for widows and widowers is that seniors' communities tend to be geared toward couples. This can exacerbate the sense of loneliness experienced by an individual who has lost a partner.

Tobit evinces sensitivity to Anna's potential needs. But in counselling Tobias not to bring his mother sorrow, there is also irony, for Tobit has already caused Anna sorrow by falsely accusing her of stealing. He will cause her sorrow again by sending Tobias to retrieve the silver. The irony continues. When Anna tells Tobit her wish for Tobias to remain at home (5:18-21), Tobit dismisses her request.

Tobit focuses on Anna's maternal role in terms of both her old age and her pregnancy. He does not mention labor pains (as in, e.g., Isa 13:8 and Jer 13:21); nor does he mention women's dying in childbirth, as happened to Rachel (Gen 35:16-19) and the unnamed wife of Phineas (1 Sam 4:19-21). Instead, he tells Tobias that "she faced many dangers for you while you were in her womb" (Tob 4:4).

Ross S. Kraemer, exploring epigraphic and papyrological evidence of diaspora Jews in late antiquity—a few centuries later than Tobit—notes that Jewish women, like their Greek and Roman sisters, jeopardized their lives every time they gave birth, although determining actual maternal mortality rates is impossible.[6] A poignant epitaph, dating to about 150 BCE from Leontopolis, Egypt, reads:

> This is the grave of Arsinoe, wayfarer. Stand by and weep for her, unfortunate in all things, whose lot was hard and terrible. For I was bereaved of my mother when I was a little girl, and when the flower of my youth made me ready for a bridegroom, my father married me to Phabeis, and Fate brought me to the end of my life in bearing my firstborn child.[7]

When a mother died during or soon after childbirth, the family secured wet nurses (frequently slaves or manumitted slaves) to provide milk and sometimes to help raise the child. A papyrus, dated to 13 BCE, records a contractual agreement hiring Theodote, apparently a Jew, for eighteen months of wages for nursing a child named Tyche.[8] The papyrus follows the typical pattern of wet nurse contracts.[9] According to Kraemer, "literary sources and burial inscriptions alike suggest that ties between wet nurses and their charges were often strong."[10]

---

6. Ross S. Kraemer, "Jewish Women in the Diaspora World of Late Antiquity," in *Jewish Women in Historical Perspective*, ed. Judith R. Baskin (Detroit: Wayne State University Press, 1991), 59–60.

7. *CPJ/CIJ* 1510; *JIGRE* 33 in Ross Shepard Kraemer, ed., *Women's Religions in the Greco-Roman World: A Sourcebook* (Oxford: Oxford University Press, 2004), 122.

8. *CPJ* 146; *BGU* 1106 in Kraemer, *Women's Religions in the Greco-Roman World*, 125.

9. Kraemer, *Women's Religions in the Greco-Roman World*, 125.

10. Ross S. Kraemer, "Nurse Caring for Her Children," in *Women in Scripture: A Dictionary of Named and Unnamed Women in the Hebrew Bible, the Apocryphal/Deutero-canonical Books, and the New Testament*, ed. Carol Meyers, Toni Craven, and Ross S. Kraemer (Grand Rapids, MI: Eerdmans, 2000), 485.

Between the years 2000 and 2017, the maternal mortality ratio (the number of maternal deaths per 100,000 live births) decreased by approximately 38 percent worldwide. But the World Health Organization (WHO) asserts that far too many women still die from childbirth-related issues. In 2017, every day 810 women died from what the WHO says are avoidable issues linked to pregnancy and childbirth.[11] Well over 90 percent of all deaths occur in low- and lower-middle-income countries, with girls between the ages of ten and fourteen facing the greatest risk of mortality.

The maternal mortality rate in the United States more than doubled between 1990 and 2013 from approximately twelve to twenty-eight deaths per 100,000 births, higher than in other developed countries.[12] The Centers for Disease Control and Prevention (CDC) notes substantial racial disparities in pregnancy-related mortality: black women were 3.3 times more likely than white women to suffer a pregnancy-related death; Native American and Alaska Native women were 2.5 times more likely to die than white women.[13] Multiple reasons for this disparity include the increasing risk to women who lack secure housing as well as access to transportation and health facilities.[14] The dangers now are not as high as in Tobit's time, but too many women still die in pregnancy and childbirth in our day.

Tobit's focus is on the dangers Anna faced during pregnancy rather than at childbirth. Did he notice the fatigue, the headaches, the swelling, the nausea, the food cravings, and so this is what he remembers as challenges she experienced during pregnancy? Did he consider them dangers because of how they affected Anna or how they impinged on his life? (E.g., Did he have to care for her more than usual? Was she not able to tend to tasks typically her responsibility, so he had to do them?) I wonder what Anna would say if she could be asked what *she* considered the most arduous aspects of pregnancy and childbirth.

11. World Health Organization, "Maternal Mortality, September 19, 2019, https://www.who.int/en/news-room/fact-sheets/detail/maternal-mortality.

12. Priya Agrawal, "Maternal Mortality and Morbidity in the United States of America," *Bulletin of the World Health Organization* 93 (2015): 135.

13. E. E. Petersen, N. L. Davis, D. Goodman, et al., "Vital Signs: Pregnancy-Related Deaths, United States, 2011–2015, and Strategies for Prevention, 13 States, 2013–2017," *Morbidity and Mortality Weekly Report* 68 (2019): 423–29.

14. Petersen et al., "Vital Signs," 423–29.

Finally, Tobit tells his son to bury Anna "beside me." Spousal burial notices date back, in the Bible, to Genesis 25:9-10, where Ishmael and Isaac bury "Abraham . . . with his wife Sarah," in the cave Abraham purchased. Tobit assumes that Anna would agree with this plan, but the text gives no notice that he consulted with her. He ignores the possibility that, after his death, Anna might remarry or relocate. That Judith, a widow, had a number of suitors (Jdt 16:22) makes this a possibility.

Tobit Counsels Tobias on How to Live Well (4:5-11)

Tobit commands his son to live in accordance with Torah, and he promises that "those who act in accordance with truth will prosper in all their activities" (4:6). The next verse repeats the connection between righteous action and reward by stating that if Tobias helps the poor, then God will help him. Speaking of storing a good treasure, he suggests that good deeds add to a heavenly bank account, which, by implication, determines heavenly reward. Finally, he insists that almsgiving—the best "good deed"—delivers from death and darkness. It is an "excellent offering" and therefore comparable to placing a sacrifice on the altar of the Jerusalem temple.

On the lips of Tobit, these instructions are ironic: Tobit followed the moral act of burying exposed corpses, and his (apparent) "reward" is blindness. Yet the irony is limited, for the end of the book reveals earthly rewards: healing, marriage, pregnancy and childbirth, long life.

There is a selfishness to Tobit's message. Acts of kindness, compassion, and righteousness become self-serving, the means to personal success rather than actions valued in and of themselves. This way of thinking also offers a pretense of control in an uncontrollable world: if we perform certain actions, God will reward us. Such thinking continues to be popular in sectors of Protestant thought today. Called "prosperity theology" or the "prosperity gospel," it originated in church congregations and revivals as an offshoot of Pentecostalism in post–World War II United States. Through radio and television, by the late 1970s it was firmly entrenched as a national movement.[15] According to the prosperity gospel, deliverance from sin through Christ brings one health (underpinned by such verses as Tob 4:6-7, as well as Exod 15:26; Ps 103:2-5; 1 Pet 2:24; Jas 5:14-16) and wealth (2 Cor 8:9). Since the prosperity gospel

---

15. Kate Bowler, *Blessed: A History of the American Prosperity Gospel* (Oxford: Oxford University Press, 2013), 4.

[5]"Revere the Lord all your days, my son, and refuse to sin or to transgress his commandments. Live uprightly all the days of your life, and do not walk in the ways of wrongdoing; [6]for those who act in accordance with truth will prosper in all their activities. To all those who practice righteousness [7]give alms from your possessions, and do not let your eye begrudge the gift when you make it. Do not turn your face away from anyone who is poor, and the face of God will not be turned away from you. [8]If you have many possessions, make your gift from them in proportion; if few, do not be afraid to give according to the little you have. [9]So you will be laying up a good treasure for yourself against the day of necessity. [10]For almsgiving delivers from death and keeps you from going into the Darkness. [11]Indeed, almsgiving, for all who practice it, is an excellent offering in the presence of the Most High.

perceives wealth as coming from God, mass accumulation of wealth is a sign of living a sanctified life. One American woman, interviewed for *The Daily Show* in July 2016, asserted that then presidential candidate Donald Trump "represents the godly people of America." When pressed by the interviewer as to whether she thought that Trump "has always acted like a good Christian," the woman responded, "Absolutely. How can you build that kind of empire if you're not praying to God for good things every day?"

Pastors associated with the prosperity gospel include Joel Osteen, author of the self-help bestseller *Become a Better You*, who leads the Lakewood Church, a megachurch in Houston, Texas, that averages fifty-two thousand attendees per week; Creflo Dollar, pastor of Atlanta's fifteen-thousand-member World Overcomers Church, who encourages "his mostly black church members to increase their wealth by increasing their faith"; and Joyce Meyer, who travels across the United States with her "message of abundance and hope heard largely by audiences of white middle-aged women."[16] As Kate Bowler writes, the prosperity gospel "tries to solve the riddle of human suffering. It is an explanation for the problem of evil. It provides an answer to the question: Why me?"[17] It remains a force today, with millions of followers and millions of dollars associated with it.

16. Bowler, *Blessed*, 3.
17. Kate Bowler, "Death, the Prosperity Gospel and Me," *New York Times* (February 13, 2016).

Almsgiving is a predominant theme in Tobit. The giving of alms—caring for the poor—is also an important praxis of Jewish piety in the Tanakh (e.g., Deut 15:10-11; Lev 19:9, 10; Ps 112:9; Prov 14:21, 31; Isa 58:6-8). The Tanakh, however, does not promise *individuals* rewards, nor does it threaten them with punishment. Instead, it addresses the entire nation, and Israel's behavior as a people is its focus. For example, the punishments and rewards listed in Deuteronomy 11:1-32 are addressed to a plural "you," emphasizing communal, not individual, responsibility for being loyal to the covenant. Jews do not observe the laws of the Torah in order to receive material rewards; rather, we do so out of love of God and loyalty to the covenant (Deut 6). The characterization of Judaism as legalistic, and as a tradition in which the individual must work to earn God's favor by performing good deeds, is an unfortunate and harmful mischaracterization. Early Reformation theologians promulgated this misunderstanding of Jewish tradition; Martin Luther (1483–1546), for example, perceived the Roman Catholic Church to be a "works-righteousness" religion, and he projected this view onto Judaism as well. Luther then used his stereotypes of Roman Catholicism and Judaism as "religions of works" as a foil against which to cast Protestant Christianity, a "religion of faith."[18] Luther's understanding of Judaism was inaccurate, just as his characterization of the Catholicism of his day was.

According to Tobit, succeeding in life for Jews, particularly in the diaspora, is by behaving righteously in accordance with Torah. Providing for Israel's poor promoted communal ties and helped to solidify identity. Tobit's comments about righteousness can be seen in this context of belonging and security: if you help others in need, they will reciprocate. Carey Moore suggests, "This *quid pro quo*, or measure-for-measure emphasis, is consistent with the deuteronomistic theology of the book."[19] But as noted above, Deuteronomy is talking about national behavior more than individual performance. Deuteronomy is framed by multiple texts that deny this *quid pro quo* version of theodicy. Indeed, Deuteronomy denies the *quid pro quo* version of theodicy by placing under God's special care the widow, the orphan, and the stranger, society's most vulnerable. They are poor, but in the Deuteronomist's view, it is not because they have sinned.

---

18. Scott H. Hendrix, *Luther: Visionary Reformer* (New Haven: Yale University Press, 2015), 274–77.

19. Moore, *Tobit*, 166.

Tobit advises Tobias to attend to the poor and give generously in proportion to whatever wealth he has attained (4:7-8). Proportional giving is found in other Jewish-Hellenistic literature (T. Iss. 3:6-8; 4:2-6), in the New Testament (Mark 12:41-44//Luke 21:1-4; 2 Cor 8:12), and in rabbinic writings (b. Git. 7a). The reference in Tobit 4:9 to regular almsgiving as a means of "laying up a good treasure for [oneself] against the day of necessity" is one of the earliest Jewish texts to suggest that the financial help provided the poor was transferred to a heavenly "bank account," in the sense that "the hand of the poor man who begged for alms became a replacement for the altar."[20] Similarly, the book of Ben Sira likewise compares almsgiving to an offering (Sir 35:1-4): "The one who keeps the law makes many offerings; one who heeds the commandments makes an offering of well-being. The one who returns a kindness offers choice flour, and the one who gives alms sacrifices a thank offering."

Almsgiving evolves into one of most important ways for Jews to express love of God and commitment to the covenant, and it becomes a crucial compensation for not being able to give directly to the temple.[21] Sirach 40:17 states, "[K]indness is like a garden of blessings, and almsgiving endures forever." Jesus warns his disciples not to be distracted by accumulating possessions "on earth" but instead instructs them to "store up for [them]selves treasures in heaven, where neither moth nor rust consumes and where thieves do not break in and steal. For where your treasure is, there your heart will be also" (Matt 6:19-21; Luke 12:33-34). Earthly possessions can be ruined or stolen; we cannot safeguard them completely from such, and they cannot protect us from harm, either. The basic message is that life is more than stuff, and those who recognize that will be the richer for it.

Gary A. Anderson points out that Tobit's statement in 4:10, "almsgiving delivers from death," interweaves Proverbs 10:2 and 11:4 into a "unique formulation."[22] Like Daniel, who advises King Nebuchadnezzar to give alms in order to pay down his heavenly debt and clear the sins he has amassed (Dan 4:27), Tobit, thinking he is about to die, communicates what he counts as essential counsel to a son he loves and hopes will live a pious, long life.

Verse 11 calls almsgiving "an excellent offering [δῶρον, 'gift'] in the presence of the Most High." Anderson notes, "To call almsgiving a gift

---

20. Gary A. Anderson, *Sin: A History* (New Haven: Yale University Press, 2010), 12.
21. Anderson, *Sin*, 148.
22. Anderson, *Sin*, 146.

in the sight of God calls to mind an offering or sacrifice that one might bring to the temple," and the Greek word (δῶρον) used in verse 11 is usually used to translate the Hebrew word קרבן (*korban*),[23] a gift, or donation made on the altar in the Jerusalem temple, in the presence of God (for example, Lev 1:2). Tobit "is suggesting that placing coins in the hand of a beggar is like putting a sacrifice on the altar—for both the hand and the altar provide direct access to God."[24] Anderson furthermore points out that given the narrative's earlier description of Tobit's dedication in bringing sacrifices to the temple (1:5–9), the message conveyed is that in the diaspora, the performing of "charitable acts" (1:3, 16) replaces sacrifices for the temple in Israel (1:5-9).[25]

Beverly Bow and George Nickelsburg remark, "The performance of charitable deeds is the responsibility only of the male characters. . . . The women in this story thus have no possessions from which they can give alms."[26] They overstate. Anna earned her own income; while she uses the funds to support her family, nothing prevented her from sharing the little she had. Sarah too has access to wealth, and the biblical tradition does depict women as both giving and receiving economic relief. As noted earlier, the "woman of strength" is actively involved in charity: "She opens her hand to the poor, and reaches out her hands to the needy" (Prov 31:20), and in Mark 12:41-44 and Luke 21:1-4, Jesus praises the generosity of the widow who donated "her whole life" to the temple. Epigraphic data also attest that women were among the most important donors supporting the construction of synagogues, particularly in Asia Minor.[27] Bow and Nickelsburg see the book of Tobit as restricting the concern for money, and so charity, to men. In this case, however, absence of evidence is not evidence of absence. Had Tobit a daughter, he might have given the same speech.

The sign of a compassionate society is that it cares for its members who are in need. Life does not provide an even playing field: some people are

---

23. Anderson, *Sin*, 148.

24. Anderson, *Sin*, 148.

25. Anderson, *Sin*, 148.

26. Bow and Nickelsburg, "Patriarchy with a Twist," 131–32.

27. Bernadette J. Brooten, *Women Leaders in the Synagogue: Inscriptional Evidence and Background Issues* (Chico, CA: Scholars Press, 1982), 157–65; Tal Ilan, "Women in Jewish Life and Law," in *The Cambridge History of Judaism*, vol. 4: *Judaism: The Late Roman-Rabbinic Period*, ed. Steven T. Katz (Cambridge: Cambridge University Press, 2006), 637; Kraemer, *Women's Religions in the Greco-Roman World*, # 661 from Phocaea, Asia Minor CIJ 738; and from Apamea, Syria # 661, 163 and # 68, 165.

born into poverty and for reasons beyond their control cannot improve their financial situation. Tobit's focus on almsgiving is one of the most appealing aspects of this document; I especially appreciate the wisdom of giving what one can from what one has. *Everyone*, not just the wealthy, can contribute.

Tobit's Instructions on Endogamy (4:12-13)

From caring about those in need in one's community, Tobit pivots to the *maintaining* of community by warning Tobias against "taking" (λαμβάνω, 4:12) a wife who is a "foreign woman" (ἀλλοτρία)—that is, not from his own tribe. The language of women being "taken" in marriage can suggest that men are the actors and women are the acted-upon. But some people still use the "giving the bride away" language today, and it does not necessarily imply that the woman has no choice. Perhaps in Tobit's day the "taking" of the bride refers to the moving from one household to another—typically (though not exclusively) the woman moved to the husband's home (patrilocality). Tobit substantiates his entreaty to endogamy with examples from Israel's patriarchs and by suggesting that endogamy led to their being "blessed in their children" and in their inheritance of land (4:12). Devorah Dimant observes, "The desirable marriage within the family is with one's cousin, preferably a paternal one, aimed at preserving the family purity and property."[28]

I view Tobit's counsel to his son to marry a woman from his own people to be part of the desire to retain his community and culture. Such a desire is understandable, especially in a situation in which an individual or group is uprooted from its native soil. Immigrants typically must balance maintaining what is familiar (foods, mother-tongue, customs) with adapting to a new culture and sometimes a new language. I appreciate traveling to Toronto, Canada's largest and most diverse city, and visiting Little Italy, Greektown, Little Portugal, Chinatown, or Little India and experiencing festivals, eating at restaurants, or just walking around. Such diversity adds to the city's intellectual and artistic richness. Ethnic groups ought to have the right to maintain their cultural identities. Indigenous peoples in Canada were denied this right when their children were removed from their homes and forced to attend residential schools

---

28. Devorah Dimant, "Aramaic Tobit at Qumran," *Ancient Jew Review*, April 17, 2017, https://www.ancientjewreview.com/read/2017/3/22/aramaic-tobit-at-qumran.

Tob 4:12-13

¹²"Beware, my son, of every kind of fornication. First of all, marry a woman from among the descendants of your ancestors; do not marry a foreign woman, who is not of your father's tribe; for we are the descendants of the prophets. Remember, my son, that Noah, Abraham, Isaac, and Jacob, our ancestors of old, all took wives from among their kindred. They were blessed in their children, and their posterity will inherit the land. ¹³So now, my son, love your kindred, and in your heart do not disdain your kindred, the sons and daughters of your people, by refusing to take a wife for yourself from among them. For in pride there is ruin and great confusion. And in idleness there is loss and dire poverty, because idleness is the mother of famine.

where they were cut off from their families and ancestral languages and cultures.²⁹ The fear of seeing one's cultural group disappear is palpable. Marrying endogamously can counter this fear, and sharing ethnic and cultural commonalities can make for a successful marriage. But there are plenty of marriages between people of different ethnic backgrounds too. If the individuals involved are open and curious, there can be opportunities to teach one another about each other's cultures and expand their community circles.

Tobit next reiterates his warning that Tobias not "disdain your kindred . . . by refusing to take a wife for yourself from among them" (4:13). Although Tobit glosses "kindred" with "the sons and daughters of your people" (the text mentions "daughters"; they are not the result of an inclusive-language translation), nowhere is there mention of Israelite women's marrying, or wanting to marry, non-Israelite men. As Nickelsburg suggests: "In an alien culture it can be tempting for a member of the minority to marry into the majority to prove oneself better than one's compatriots."³⁰

Finally, stringing together bromides, Tobit connects pride to ruin and confusion, ties idleness to poverty, and classifies "idleness" as the "mother of famine" (4:13). The use of "mother" rather than "father" in this metaphor matters. Female danger comes in many forms: through foreign wives and even through famine. It is up to the reader whether or

29. John S. Milloy, *A National Crime: The Canadian Government and the Residential School System 1879–1986* (Winnipeg: University of Manitoba Press, 1999).
30. Nickelsburg, "Tobit," 796.

not to connect this negative reference to motherhood to earlier comments about Anna. Previously, Tobit noted that Anna "faced many dangers" while Tobias was "in her womb." There the mother is the one in danger. Now the child, famine, creates the danger. Images of mothers, like images of foreign wives, can be both positive and negative; they are, however, rarely if ever neutral.

Tobit Counsels Further Ethical Behavior (4:14-19)

In 4:14-19, Tobit encourages Tobias to exercise good business practices, self-discipline, and piety. His counsel on paying "at once" builds on—and betters—Deuteronomy 24:15, "You shall pay them their wages daily before sunset, because they are poor and their livelihood depends on them," and Leviticus 19:13, "You shall not keep for yourself the wages of a laborer until morning."

This is a long and tedious list of instructions—it is a speech from someone who thinks he is going to die—made by a father to his beloved son. We don't know where Anna was while Tobit spoke. Was she within earshot? Was she working on her weaving? Was she frustrated by Tobit's overly dramatic mood and thus keeping her distance?

Verse 15 introduces the negative version of the "golden rule," typically called the "silver rule": "And what you hate, do not do to anyone." This was a widespread teaching in the ancient world, found in the fifth-century BCE *Analects of Confucius* 5.2 and Herodotus's *The Histories* 3.142.3, as well as in several Jewish sources. The Letter of Aristeas 207 (second century BCE) contains advice for the king: "Insofar as you do not wish evils to come upon you, but to partake of every blessing, (it would be wisdom) if you put this into practice with your subjects." The story of Ahikar, with which the author of Tobit is familiar, offers, "Now it is your turn to treat me as I treated you. Do not kill me but take me to your house until the times change." In the Gospels (Matt 7:12; cf. Luke 6:31), Jesus says, "In everything do to others as you would have them do to you; for this is the law and the prophets." Hillel, a slightly older contemporary of Jesus, responds to a gentile's request, "Teach me the Torah while I stand on one foot," by advising, "That which is hateful to you do not do to another; that is the entire Torah, and the rest is its interpretation. Go study" (b. Sabb. 31a).

Christians at times misunderstand the Jewish version to be restricted, since in Tobit and from Hillel the formulation is "negative" (Do *not* do), while they regard Jesus as proactive ("Do"). Hence Jesus's formulation

Tob 4:14-19

[14]"Do not keep over until the next day the wages of those who work for you, but pay them at once. If you serve God you will receive payment. Watch yourself, my son, in everything you do, and discipline yourself in all your conduct. [15]And what you hate, do not do to anyone. Do not drink wine to excess or let drunkenness go with you on your way. [16]Give some of your food to the hungry, and some of your clothing to the naked. Give all your surplus as alms, and do not let your eye begrudge your giving of alms. [17]Place your bread on the grave of the righteous, but give none to sinners. [18]Seek advice from every wise person and do not despise any useful counsel. [19]At all times bless the Lord God, and ask him that your ways may be made straight and that all your paths and plans may prosper. For none of the nations has understanding, but the Lord himself will give them good counsel; but if he chooses otherwise, he casts down to deepest Hades. So now, my child, remember these commandments, and do not let them be erased from your heart.

is the "Golden Rule" while the negative version is the (ostensibly) less valued "Silver Rule." Jesus invokes the Law and the Prophets, and Hillel invokes the entire Jewish tradition. Both formulations are, without this broader context, open to abuse. The negative "do not do" could lead to a lack of proactive engagement. On the other hand, the proactive "do" can lead to abuses where the followers of Jesus impose their own values onto peoples of other religions and other cultures in a way that disrespects choice and cultural difference. All summaries of ethical practice need nuance.

Tobit now turns to personal behavior by doubly warning Tobias against consuming alcohol to excess (4:15), though he is not advocating abstinence. Proverbs 23:29-35 provides a vivid description of the detrimental effects of overly imbibing, and Leviticus 10:9 prohibits priests from consuming alcohol before performing duties at the temple. Genesis 9:20-27 describes how Noah becomes drunk on wine, with detrimental results, and Genesis 19:30-38 depicts Lot's daughters using wine to get their father drunk in order to conceive children with him; incest, then, is the result of drunkenness. The rabbis, like Tobit, do not condemn drinking but do advise against inebriation (b. 'Erub. 64a–65b). New Testament writings also warn against inebriation: "Do not get drunk with wine, for that is debauchery" (Eph 5:18). Wine was a regular part of the diet in the ancient Mediterranean and, if consumed in moderation, was considered beneficial for digestion (1 Tim 5:23).

The exhortations then return to the all-important topic of almsgiving. Recognition that "there will never cease to be some in need on the earth" is at the heart of the commandment to "Open your hand to the poor and needy neighbor in your land" (Deut 15:11). Providing financial support to the poor, an important practice in Judaism, is reflected linguistically: the Hebrew words for "righteousness" and "almsgiving" derive from the same root: "the one who gives support to others (Hebrew: *tzadik*) is righteous (*tzedakah*)."[31] According to Tobit 12:8b, "almsgiving with righteousness" even surpasses prayer with fasting.

Tobit does not instruct his son to engage in total divestment; there is nothing here of "[s]ell all you have and give to the poor" (Luke 18:22). Instead, Tobit limits the amount of generosity: "[g]ive some of your food . . . some of your clothing" but "give all your surplus" (4:16). Jesus and Tobit envision different circumstances. For Jesus, one is to hate one's natal family and join the new family gathered in his name (Luke 14:26: "Whoever comes to me and does not hate father and mother, wife and children, brothers and sisters, yes, and even life itself, cannot be my disciple"). His earliest followers may well also have been celibate. In a case where an individual has no familial responsibilities, total poverty is an option. Tobit, however, has a family, and he anticipates that his son will as well. Total divestment would put Tobias's future wife and children in danger.

Twelfth-century Jewish philosopher Maimonides addresses the complicated dimensions of providing charity, among them the attitude of the giver and the dignity of the receiver. He established a ladder of charitable giving (צדקה, "righteousness") in which double-blind gifts (neither the giver nor the receiver knows who the other is) are ranked high on the ladder, and the gifts in which both the donor and the recipient are known to one another as well as others are near the bottom, interposed with other rungs based on the donor's attitude and impetus and the beneficiary's benefit over a sustained period. The ladder, from most to least charitable, is as follows:

1. A donation that enables the beneficiary to escape the need for charity altogether (e.g., giving a gift or interest-free loan to start a business).

2. A double-blind donation (e.g., secretly leaving a gift in a courtyard where a poor person can privately retrieve it without the giver revealing themselves).

---

31. Amy-Jill Levine, *Sermon on the Mount: A Beginner's Guide to the Kingdom of Heaven* (Nashville: Abingdon, 2020), 56.

3. An anonymous donation to a known beneficiary (e.g., leaving a gift on their doorstep).

4. A revealed donation to an unknown beneficiary (e.g., the donor walks and drops money behind them for beneficiaries to pick up unseen).

5. A public donation that is given spontaneously (e.g., giving money in person).

6. A public donation that is solicited (e.g., granting a request for money).

7. A willing but inadequate donation.

8. A grudging donation, motivated by pity or guilt.[32]

Maimonides's ladder is based on two considerations: (1) giving charity is to be done for its own sake rather than to receive praise or some sort of compensation, and (2) the beneficiary ought not to feel a sense of shame.[33]

Tobit's comment that Tobias should "place your bread on the grave of the righteous" (4:17) alludes to the practice of caring for ancestors by offering food at their graves. This was practiced widely in the ancient Near East, as reflected in literary evidence (e.g., the Ugaritic *Aqhat Epic*) and confirmed by archaeology.[34] Grave goods have been found, including food receptacles, jugs, and libation tubes, in preexilic remains in Israel.[35] Deuteronomy 26:14 prescribes that a farmer intending to give a tenth of his produce (the annual tithe) at the Jerusalem temple was not to offer "any of it to the dead." The point of the verse is not to condemn the practice of feeding the dead but to convey how, had the farmer's tithe first been offered at a tomb, the impurity linked with death would make his tithe unacceptable for donation at the temple.[36] Today, offerings for the dead continue in the form of flowers at the gravesite, small stones on the tombstone (in the Jewish tradition), and donations to a cause or charity about which the deceased cared.

---

32. Cited in Julian De Freitas, Peter DeScioli, Kyle A. Thomas, and Steven Pinker, "Maimonides' Ladder: States of Mutual Knowledge and the Perception of Charitability," *Journal of Experimental Psychology: General* 148 (2019): 159.

33. De Freitas et al., "Maimonides' Ladder," 159.

34. Bernard M. Levinson, "Deuteronomy," in *The Jewish Study Bible*, ed. Adele Berlin and Marc Zvi Brettler, 2nd ed. (Oxford: Oxford University Press, 2014), 404.

35. Jon Davies, *Death, Burial and Rebirth in the Religions of Antiquity* (New York: Routledge, 1999), 64–66.

36. Levinson, "Deuteronomy," 404.

TRANSLATION MATTERS

The Greek version of Tobit 4:17, rendered in the NRSV, "Place your bread on the grave of the righteous," presents the translator with challenges. The meaning of the first three words (ἔκχεον τοὺς ἄρτους) is puzzling since the verb (ἐκχέω) usually means "to pour" and the object (ἄρτους) is "bread." "Pour out your bread on the grave" sounds odd; one would have expected the verb to be matched with a liquid, such as wine or oil. Other (non-Greek) versions of the verse show that translators found this phrase problematic: the Vetus Latina reads, *funde vinum tuum et panem tuum*, "Pour your wine and your bread"; and Jerome, the translator of the Vulgate, eliminates the awkward "pouring" and has *panem tuum et vinum*, "your bread and wine."[37] Moore translates the verse as "pour out your wine on the graves of the righteous," noting the parallel in the Book of Ahikar,[38] which reads: "My son, pour out your wine on the graves of the righteous and do not drink it with evil men"[39] Ben Sira pokes fun at the practice in 30:18: "Good things poured out upon a mouth that is closed are like offerings of food placed upon a grave." Jubilees 22:17 likewise derides it:

> They offer their sacrifices to the dead
> And they worship evil spirits,
> And they eat over the graves,
> And all their works are vanity and nothingness.

Commentators who think Tobit is recommending offering sacrifices to the dead alter the translation, as, for example, the 1970 New American Bible's rendering of 4:17: "Be lavish with your bread and wine at the burial of the virtuous,"[40] with the footnote: "Tobit counsels his son either to give alms in honor of the dead, or, more probably, to give the 'bread of consolation' to the family of the deceased, cf. Jeremiah 16:7; Ezekiel 24:17." These translators suggest that the food is being offered not *to* the dead but rather to the *mourners* of the dead. But this is not accurate. Tobit's (and Ahikar's) reference is to the provision of food for the dead, not as a sacrifice, but to care for the dead, as was the widespread custom noted above.

Tobias's age is not given in the text, but throughout this "last testament" Tobit refers to him as a παιδίον, "child." The NRSV translates "my son" throughout the chapter (4:2, 3, 4, 5, 12, 13, 14, 20, and 21), except in

37. Robert J. Littman, *Tobit: The Book of Tobit in Codex Sinaiticus* (Leiden: Brill, 2008), 94.

38. Moore, *Tobit*, 162, 173.

39. F. C. Conybeare, J. R. Harris, and A. S. Lewis, *The Story of Ahiqar*, 2nd ed. (Cambridge: Cambridge University Press, 1913), 41 (of the Syriac texts).

40. The 2011 New American Bible Revised Edition has altered the translation to "Pour out your wine and your bread on the grave of the righteous, but do not share them with sinners," but maintained the same footnote as is found in the NAB of 1970.

[20]"And now, my son, let me explain to you that I left ten talents of silver in trust with Gabael son of Gabrias, at Rages in Media. [21]Do not be afraid, my son, because we have become poor. You have great wealth if you fear God and flee from every sin and do what is good in the sight of the Lord your God."

verse 19, where the literal "my child" is used (it is odd that it is used only here: the translation's frequent use of "son" rather than "child" adds to the androcentrism of the text). Tobias is probably in his teens or early twenties, not yet married—but about to be—and not an experienced traveler (so Tobit does not want him to travel alone).

Verses 7-18 are missing from the Septuagint but appear in the Old Latin, the Vulgate, and G1, and fragments of these verses are also found among the Dead Sea Scrolls.[41] Francis M. Macatangay persuasively argues that scribal error explains the missing verses, and so they are not later additions to the original text: "[I]t is likely that the copyist got confused and his eyes mistakenly jumped from one verse to another, since εὐοδωθήσονται is in Tob 4:6 and the same verb εὐοδωθῶσιν is in Tob 4:19."[42] It is unlikely that later editors freely added or subtracted from moral teachings such as these.[43]

Tobit Finally Tells Tobias about the Silver (4:20-21)

Anna might have been working prior to her family's dire financial situation, but the crisis makes her income the sole means of sustaining the family. Neither then nor now does Tobit tell his wife about the money left with Gabael. And even here, Tobit at no point explicitly tells his son to retrieve it; as Joseph Fitzmyer notes, "He at most implies that Tobias should go get the money."[44] Tobias, nonetheless, gets the message.

41. Moore, *Tobit*, 165.

42. Francis M. Macatangay, *The Wisdom Instructions in the Book of Tobit* (Berlin: de Gruyter, 2011), 51.

43. Macatangay, *Wisdom Instructions*, 52.

44. Fitzmyer, *Tobit*, 179. The Vulgate adds this imperative by having Tobit state to Tobias, "so inquire, then, how you may go to him, get from him the fore mentioned sum of money, and restore to him his handwritten note."

Tobit 5–6

How to Hire an Angel

These two chapters introduce the angel Raphael, Tobias's journey to retrieve the silver (a journey that leads him to his future wife), and the provision for how Sarah's trouble with the demon Asmodeus will end. These chapters also generate several issues worthy of feminist analysis, including trust and vulnerability, as well as the power dynamics between Tobit and Tobias, Tobias and "Azariah," Tobit and Azariah, and Tobit and Anna.

Tobias Prepares for His Journey to Retrieve Tobit's Silver (5:1-3)

Verse 1 uses the word "father" twice (πατρί; πάτερ) to convey Tobias's sense of nervous impatience for this long speech to end so that he can ask what is *really* on Tobit's mind: "How can I obtain the money?" (v. 2). Tobias states that he "will do everything" that Tobit asked of him, reminiscent of numerous biblical responses: "Everything that the Lord has spoken we will do!" state the elders of Israel when Moses presents the commandments to them (Exod 19:8; 24:3, 7); "All that you have commanded us we will do, and wherever you send us we will go!" say the Israelites in affirming Joshua as Moses's successor (Josh 1:16); Ruth tells Naomi, "All that you tell me I will do," regarding how to approach Boaz (Ruth 3:5). Tobias's sincerity may well have been genuine, but I detect a bit of "Yes, yes, father, I'll do it" in order to encourage Tobit to stop waxing on.

Tob 5:1-3

5:1Then Tobias answered his father Tobit, "I will do everything that you have commanded me, father; 2but how can I obtain the money from him, since he does not know me and I do not know him? What evidence am I to give him so that he will recognize and trust me, and give me the money? Also, I do not know the roads to Media, or how to get there." 3Then Tobit answered his son Tobias, "He gave me his bond and I gave him my bond. I divided his in two; we each took one part, and I put one with the money. And now twenty years have passed since I left this money in trust. So now, my son, find yourself a trustworthy man to go with you, and we will pay him wages until you return. But get back the money from Gabael."

Tobias does have questions (like Moses in Exod 3–4). He's never done what he is now being asked to do: voyage to a strange land to meet a man he does not know in order to retrieve valuables. Tobias asks his father how he can convince Gabael to trust him: what σημεῖον, "sign" (or "evidence"), can he give so that his identity as Tobit's son can be known? Tobit explains that he and Gabael exchanged a "bond" (χειρόγρᾶφον), literally a handwritten note, to protect Gabael from being charged with theft of the silver and to ensure that Tobit would be able to prove ownership when he wished to retrieve it. Tobit will give Tobias his half of the bond, and with this, Gabael will trust him to take the ten talents of silver to Nineveh. A talent was a monetary unit of between fifty-seven and seventy-nine pounds (twenty-six to thirty-six kilograms); Tobit's deposit, therefore, was a substantial amount—around 680 pounds (310 kilograms) of silver. He either deeply trusted Gabael to leave such treasure with him or had no choice.

Tobit evinces further trust in Gabael by sending an even more precious possession to him: his only child. If we define trust as "accepted vulnerability to another's possible but not expected ill will (or lack of good will),"[1] Tobit trusted Gabael to a significant degree. He also trusted his son to retrieve the money. Yet Ahikar's story is in the background as a warning that sometimes trusting family members is a mistake.

Tobit seeks to diminish the risk involved in this journey by having someone accompany his son, so he instructs Tobias to find a "trustworthy" (πιστόν) man as a companion. He is concerned for Tobias's

---

1. Annette Baier, "Trust and Antitrust," *Ethics* 96 (1986): 235.

well-being, but he may also worry that Tobias is not mature enough to complete the task. The term πιστόν conveys Tobit's desire for Tobias to have someone "reliable" to get him to Media and back, with the money, but it also conveys the meaning of "faithful," in the sense of being devoted to God. Given that the travel companion will be an angel with impeccable credentials when it comes to his relationship with God, the use of πιστόν adds both humor and irony to the scene.

Tobit tasks Tobias to find a companion, but it will be Tobit who runs the selection process. Tobias strikes me as a beloved son, a bit mollycoddled by his parents and straining to stretch his wings—though a bit nervous about it too.

Tobias Encounters Raphael in Disguise (5:4-8)

Tobias must find a travelling companion for the journey to Media. The companion will be the angel Raphael, but the characters in the story are ignorant of his identity. Angels feature frequently in biblical stories and are not always named (Gen 18:1-15; Jdg 6:11-24; 13). The identity of divine beings—angels as well as gods—is an element with which writers of ancient texts play. Jesus's identity is hidden from his two disciples on the road to Emmaus in Luke 24:13-35 (cf. Mark 16:12-13). The Greek god Zeus takes on multiple identities: he transforms into an eagle (Virgil, *Aen.* 5.252), a white bull (Ovid, *Metam.* 2.862), and a swan (Apollodorus, *The Library* 3.10.7); in Homer's *Odyssey* the goddess Athena transforms herself into Mentor, an old family friend of Odysseus (22.210), a little girl (7.20), and a young man (13.251).

Dennis MacDonald argues that Tobit's author used Homer's *Odyssey* as a source for his narration.[2] There are many striking parallels: for example, Odysseus and Tobit were conscientious about sacrificing to their respective deities, but both endure suffering (*Od.* 1.65-67; Tob 1:4, 6-7a); Tobias and Telemachus (Odysseus's son) leave home on journeys for the benefit of their fathers, accompanied by heavenly messengers in disguise (*Od.* 1.82-89; Tob 3:16-17); both sons are asked to stay longer away from home and are promised great wealth (*Od.* 4.587-91; Tob 8:20-21); Penelope and Anna both are anguished mothers left behind to worry about their

---

2. Dennis R. MacDonald, "Tobit and the *Odyssey*," in *Mimesis and Intertextuality in Antiquity and Christianity*, ed. Dennis R. MacDonald (Harrisburg: Trinity Press International, 2001), 1–40. The idea was first explored by Carl Fries, "Das Buch Tobit Und Die Telemachie," *ZWT* 53 (1911): 54–87.

⁴So Tobias went out to look for a man to go with him to Media, someone who was acquainted with the way. He went out and found the angel Raphael standing in front of him; but he did not perceive that he was an angel of God. ⁵Tobias said to him, "Where do you come from, young man?" "From your kindred, the Israelites," he replied, "and I have come here to work." Then Tobias said to him, "Do you know the way to go to Media?" ⁶"Yes," he replied, "I have been there many times; I am acquainted with it and know all the roads. I have often traveled to Media, and stayed with our kinsman Gabael who lives in Rages of Media. It is a journey of two days from Ecbatana to Rages; for it lies in a mountainous area, while Ecbatana is in the middle of the plain." ⁷Then Tobias said to him, "Wait for me, young man, until I go in and tell my father; for I do need you to travel with me, and I will pay you your wages." ⁸He replied, "All right, I will wait; but do not take too long."

absent sons (*Od.* 4:703-705; Tob 10:4) but welcome them home with tears, and both associate their sons' return with their own deaths (*Od.* 17.36, 38-42; Tob 11:9).³ It is probable that the author of Tobit read Homer's work, but I am not convinced that Tobit's author used the *Odyssey* as the blueprint for his story.

Irony and humor abound as Tobias and Tobit question the "young man" (νεανίσκε), named Azariah (עזריה in Hebrew is "Yahweh has helped," an apropos title, given Azariah's role in the story). Tobias, desperate to sound older than he is or than he feels, uses an address that matches himself better than Azariah: "young man" (νεανίσκε). He then asks about the "young man's" home and his travel experience along the prospective route. Azariah's response identifies Tobias as a "fellow" Israelite immediately—insight that derives from his divine abilities rather than Tobias's wearing clothing distinguishing him in any way as an Israelite. Azariah says that he has come to "work hard [ἐργατεύεσθαι]," and indeed he has: he does the work of God in this tale. But given that Tobias is not described as engaging in work, the remark can be interpreted as pointed. The reference to having stayed with Gabael in Media—precisely the place that Tobias needs to get to—is a stroke of divine "luck." Pleased with the "young man's" answers, Tobias asks him to wait "until I go in and tell my father" (v. 7). Moore suggests this detail "diminishes Tobias's

3. MacDonald, "Tobit and the *Odyssey*."

stature *vis-à-vis* 'Azariah' by emphasizing the boy's dependence on his father."[4] Tobias presumably is dependent on Tobit to pay the companion's wages—perhaps out of the silver attained? At the same time, Tobias's deference enhances Tobit's honor: an obedient son reflected well on a father. Such deference might also reflect Tobias's youth.

The status differential between Azariah and Tobias becomes complicated by Azariah's response: "All right, I will wait; but do not take too long."[5] This "young man" is not to be treated as an inferior.

Several geographical errors mark this section of the narrative. The distance between Rages and Ecbatana is approximately two hundred miles, so travel between the cities would require many more than two days. Ecbatana is located not on a plain but is 2,500 feet above sea level. Different versions (G1 and the Vulgate) of Tobit correct these inaccuracies by deleting mention of the cities altogether. Amy-Jill Levine and Geoffrey Miller persuasively suggest that the author deliberately made such mistakes and thereby showed the "disjunction between the real and the recounted"—and that for those living in the diaspora, as Levine suggests, "things are not as they should be."[6] Such errors would be readily apparent to readers of the day and so would signal that they were reading a fictional tale.

Tobit Interviews Azariah (5:9-10)

The irony of the angel in disguise undergirds Tobias's announcement to his father that he has found the "man" (ἄνθρωπος) and Tobit's asking his son to direct the "man" in to see him. Taking over the interviewing process, Tobit plans to ask about Azariah's family and tribe as well as to determine his faithfulness to God and reliability. Implied in his statement is that family and tribe can determine these qualities—though Tobit has already noted that he alone among the Israelites was faithful. He thus implicitly admits that he had overstated.

---

4. Carey A. Moore, *Tobit: A New Translation with Introduction and Commentary* (New Haven: Yale University Press, 1996), 184.

5. Also Moore, *Tobit*, 185.

6. Amy-Jill Levine, "Redrawing the Boundaries: A New Look at 'Diaspora as Metaphor: Bodies and Boundaries in the Book of Tobit,'" in *A Feminist Companion to Tobit and Judith*, ed. Athalya Brenner-Idan and Helen Efthimiadis-Keith, FCB 2.20 (London: Continuum, 2015), 6. Geoffrey D. Miller, "Raphael the Liar: Angelic Deceit and Testing in the Book of Tobit," *CBQ* 72 (2012): 505 n. 46.

⁹So Tobias went in to tell his father Tobit and said to him, "I have just found a man who is one of our own Israelite kindred!" He replied, "Call the man in, my son, so that I may learn about his family and to what tribe he belongs, and whether he is trustworthy enough to go with you."

¹⁰Then Tobias went out and called him, and said, "Young man, my father is calling for you." So he went in to him, and Tobit greeted him first. He replied, "Joyous greetings to you!" But Tobit retorted, "What joy is left for me any more? I am a man without eyesight; I cannot see the light of heaven, but I lie in darkness like the dead who no longer see the light. Although still alive, I am among the dead. I hear people but I cannot see them." But the young man said, "Take courage; the time is near for God to heal you; take courage." Then Tobit said to him, "My son Tobias wishes to go to Media. Can you accompany him and guide him? I will pay your wages, brother." He answered, "I can go with him and I know all the roads, for I have often gone to Media and have crossed all its plains, and I am familiar with its mountains and all of its roads."

In response to Azariah's "Joyous greetings," Tobit returns to self-pity. When he asks (v. 10), "What joy is left for me any more?" he ignores his son, his wife, and the possibility of regaining his silver. But the author winks at the readers when Tobit states, "I cannot see the light of heaven" (v. 10). That light, in the form of an angel, is standing right before him. It will take Tobit and Tobias some time before they recognize him. When Tobit states that he can hear people but not see them, he reminds us that a limitation in one of our senses often results in an enhancement of another: there is potential, in this situation, for Tobit to hear and listen in ways that he could not before. Maybe he will pay more attention to the tone of the words he hears; maybe he will be able to understand what is *not* being said.

Tobit prayed for death, and now he counts himself among the dead (v. 10). His exaggeration can be seen as humorous, or annoying, or even offensive—as if being blind is meant to be understood as the same as being dead.[7] Although he sees himself as dead, he is also planning his secure future by ensuring that his son will travel safely to Media. When Raphael replies, "Take courage; the time is near for God to heal you; take courage" (v. 10), we readers already know that Tobit will be healed.

---

7. See the earlier discussion of blindness and disability studies (pp. 38–39, 40–44).

Tobit says that he will pay Azariah's wages, but in verse 7, Tobias claimed that responsibility. The angel is not the only one who is disguising himself. Tobit pretends that Tobias is in charge of this hire, but he undermines his son when he speaks with Azariah. Is Tobias present for this conversation? If so, how mortifying for him to hear his father pour out his complaints to a new and unfamiliar person, and then to see his father make statements infantilizing him, a young man about to head out on his first adventure independent of his family. Tobit refers in verse 10 to Azariah as "brother" (ἄδελφε), raising him to his (Tobit's) status level, as an equal, leaving Tobias out and further undercutting his power. In so doing Tobit deals with Tobias in ways that women sometimes are treated: their agency, for example, in the workplace, can be undermined by not being fully included as equals to the power holders.

Tobit Is Persuaded That "Azariah" Is Trustworthy (5:11-14)

Tobit contradicts his earlier statement that he alone was loyal when "all" other members of his family "deserted the house of David and Jerusalem" (1:4). We now learn that Hananiah and Nathan accompanied him on his pilgrimages to Jerusalem. Tobit increasingly appears as a buffoon. He seems driven to his excesses—touting his righteousness, overstating, complaining—by a core insecurity. He is not malevolent. He's an underdog: we support him *because* of his flaws and his good heart, while at the same time he's annoying.

Tobit calls Azariah his brother in 5:10, *before* he has any information about Azariah's family and tribe. In the next seven verses (11-17) Tobit refers to him as brother another six times—he is trying to establish a connection. It is sincere—he wants to create a bond, since his son's safety is at stake, but it is forced and an example of Tobit trying too hard. Even the angel is annoyed: "Why do you need to know my tribe?" he asks. Tobit then changes the question from tribe to immediate family and name, "Whose son you are and what your name is" (5:12). This rephrasing allows the angel to focus on himself rather than the tribe: he begins with the stage name, "Azariah"—which should be a hint to Tobit that he can "help" his son. He then identifies his great father as Hananiah (חנניה), a name meaning "God has had mercy."

Tobit's telling Azariah "Do not feel bitter toward me" (5:14) concerning his probing indicates a tension between the two. Given Tobit's earlier statements about disloyalty to king and temple, his querying about tribe and family could indicate that he was testing the loyalty of his

¹¹Then Tobit said to him, "Brother, of what family are you and from what tribe? Tell me, brother." ¹²He replied, "Why do you need to know my tribe?" But Tobit said, "I want to be sure, brother, whose son you are and what your name is." ¹³He replied, "I am Azariah, the son of the great Hananiah, one of your relatives." ¹⁴Then Tobit said to him, "Welcome! God save you, brother. Do not feel bitter toward me, brother, because I wanted to be sure about your ancestry. It turns out that you are a kinsman, and of good and noble lineage. For I knew Hananiah and Nathan, the two sons of Shemeliah, and they used to go with me to Jerusalem and worshiped with me there, and were not led astray. Your kindred are good people; you come of good stock. Hearty welcome!"

interlocutor's family. Women's loyalties to their natal family, their husbands, their children, are always tested: their loyalty to themselves is tested too. Juggling the needs of various family members is challenging, and sometimes choosing to prioritize one member over others is interpreted as disloyalty. Tobit says he knew Hananiah and Nathan, the two sons of Shemeliah, so he recognizes the angel's identity by reference to other family members. This recognition might answer Tobias's question (v. 2) about how Gabael will recognize him when he goes to get the silver: Tobias might need to provide names of family members to show to Gabael that he is Tobit's son.

Tobit seems up until now unaware of this additional son of Hananiah, and he expresses no surprise about the discovery. Maybe Tobit has lost contact with his family. Such loss of contact can happen when people are dispersed—one loses touch with births, deaths, and other family news. In a patrilocal society such as Tobit's, a newlywed couple lives with or very near the man's parents, and the woman, if she wished to maintain contact with her distant family members, would need to put effort into doing so. Tobit had moved away from his family and perhaps did not take up the responsibility of maintaining contact with them.

When Azariah tells his name and that of his father, Tobit responds by praising his people as being "of good and noble lineage" (ἐκ γενεᾶς καλῆς καὶ ἀγαθῆς), as "good people" (ἄνθρωποι ἀγαθοί) of "good roots" (ῥίζης ἀγαθῆς), and so he highlights associations of the term "good" (Hebrew טוב, *tov*) with his family. His response suggests that we can tell a lot about children if we know their parents: because Tobit knew Hananiah to be a good person, his son Azariah would be of the same character. Such assumptions can work in either positive or negative ways for children. Children whose parents are respected and trusted have a measure of goodwill that might open doors, then it is up to the children to establish their own reputations. But children of parents with poor reputations have obstacles to overcome in order to establish trust. Neither result is fair: individuals ought to be judged on their own merits rather than on to whom they are related. Parents also are judged by how their children behave—mothers are particularly blamed, unfairly, if the child has problems. For Azariah in this scenario, and for Tobias when he travels to Media, this assumption works in their favor.

The Arrangement between Tobit and Azariah (5:15-17a)

Tobit's paying the angel wages and then offering an incentive could be taken as amusing: angels don't need payroll. The offer also highlights Tobit's ongoing concern for money, which is understandable given the trauma of exile and his experience of having money and valuables and then losing them. Raphael's promise that they would "leave in good health and *return to you* in good health" hints at the restoration of Tobit's own health. There is humor, too, in the notion that Tobit is proud to have struck an agreement—a verbal contract—with a counterpart that he considered more or less his equal. One of the book's most entertaining lines is Tobit's benediction invoking an angel to "accompany you both for your safety" (5:17), which is precisely what is happening. The line echoes Genesis 24:40: Abraham said that an angel from God would accompany his servant and would "make your way successful. You shall get a wife for my son from my kindred, from my father's house." Tobias's journey is also to procure a proper wife, but he does not know this yet.

Anna Laments Tobias's Departure (5:17b–6:1a)

Tobias kissed (ἐφίλησεν) not only his mother but also his father; this practice is mentioned throughout the Tanakh as occurring between parents and children, between men (e.g., Gen 27:26-27; 29:13; 33:4; 2 Sam 20:9), and in the New Testament too as a formal greeting (e.g., Rom 16:16; 1 Cor 16: 20; 1 Thess 5:26). Kissing the cheeks of a friend when saying hello or goodbye is commonplace in various parts of the globe. In more conservative countries, kissing is done *only* between same-sex individuals: the intent is to avoid sexual connotations, and the assumption is that the majority of people are heterosexual.

Tob 5:15–6:1a

[15]Then he added, "I will pay you a drachma a day as wages, as well as expenses for yourself and my son. So go with my son, [16]and I will add something to your wages." Raphael answered, "I will go with him; so do not fear. We shall leave in good health and return to you in good health, because the way is safe." [17]So Tobit said to him, "Blessings be upon you, brother."

Then he called his son and said to him, "Son, prepare supplies for the journey and set out with your brother. May God in heaven bring you safely there and return you in good health to me; and may his angel, my son, accompany you both for your safety."

Before he went out to start his journey, he kissed his father and mother. Tobit then said to him, "Have a safe journey."

[18]But his mother began to weep, and said to Tobit, "Why is it that you have sent my child away? Is he not the

As in chapter 2, Anna's robust personality is again on display—this time with tears. She takes issue with Tobit's sending away "my child" (5:18) and later "our child" (5:19). Her fears were warranted: the journey was risky enough to necessitate a traveling companion; her anger is warranted as well.

Anna challenges Tobit's decision to send Tobias to Media. In verse 18 she asks why he is sending their son away, as if she does not know the purpose of the travel. But verse 19 shows that she does—she is trying to forestall the inevitable by posing such a question. Tobit does not answer her question, and she moves on to her next tactic: to point out how dependent she and Tobit are on Tobias, since he is the "staff of our hand" (ῥάβδος τῆς χειρὸς). Isaiah 51:18 refers to Jerusalem as a woman who has "no one to take her by the hand among all the children she has brought up,"[8] and b. Yebamot 65b refers to a case in which a woman seeks a divorce from a husband who could not father children, and the statement in the text supporting the woman's request is put as follows: "Does this woman not require a staff for her hand and a hoe for her burial? In other words, the woman said that she wanted children so that they could care for her in her old age and bury her when she would die." Tobias is like

8. In ancient Canaan, it was a son's filial duty "to take his hand when he is drunk, to bear him up when he is full of wine," as is stated in the fourteenth-century BCE Aqhat epic from Ugarit (Ras Shamra in modern Syria), 1.27-34 (Dennis Pardee, "The Aqhatu Legend," in *The Context of Scripture*, vol. 1: *Canonical Compositions from the Biblical World*, ed. W. W. Hallo [Leiden: Brill, 1997], 348).

staff of our hand as he goes in and out before us? [19]Do not heap money upon money, but let it be a ransom for our child. [20]For the life that is given to us by the Lord is enough for us." [21]Tobit said to her, "Do not worry; our child will leave in good health and return to us in good health. Your eyes will see him on the day when he returns to you in good health. Say no more! Do not fear for them, my sister. [22]For a good angel will accompany him; his journey will be successful, and he will come back in good health." [6:1]So she stopped weeping.

a cane that provides stability and security for herself and Tobit, and he provides the moral support on which they can depend.[9] We have not seen Tobias "go in and out" (other than when, at his father's request, he went to find a poor person to invite for the Shavuot meal) so the dependence on him seems to be for the future. Anna would prefer Tobias alive and well in her life rather than the money Tobit is sending him to get. Her suggestion to use it as a ransom (v. 19) seems to suggest that Gabael should keep the money and send Tobias safely home. Retrieving the money is not worth their son's life. Her fears get expressed as anger.

Tobit assures Anna that their son will be safe. He specifies that "[y]our eyes will see him" (οἱ ὀφθαλμοί σου ὄψονται) on the day that he returns (v. 21), reminding her that *she*, at least, can see their son. He tells her not to fear and calls her "sister" (ἀδελφή), emphasizing the blood relationship between them: she can trust her husband's judgment.

For Anna, the safety of her son is what is truly important. But she does not realize her son will be protected by an angel. We readers—who know that this journey will lead to positive outcomes—recognize that it is good that Tobit prevails. Anna comes across like an overly protective mother, a depiction that is not fair, since she does not know what we readers know, and her concerns are legitimate.

Tobit comforts Anna and calms her fears: his words are efficacious, for Anna's crying ceases (6:1). Earlier it was Raphael, Tobit's superior, telling Tobit not to fear (5:16). "Do not worry," he tells her, and then, more irony: "A good angel will accompany them." Tobit unknowingly states exactly what the reader already knows is happening.

---

9. Daniel A. Bertrand, "'Un bâton de vieillesse', à propos de Tobit 5, 23 et 10, 4 (Vulgate)," *RHPR* 71 (1991): 33.

Chapter 6

In chapter 6 we see the interaction of Tobias with a dog and a fish and his contemplation of marriage with Sarah. Among the issues we consider are gossip, the perception of Sarah as a "damsel in distress," a cure for demon possession, and the idea of a marriage made in heaven.

Tobias and Azariah Encounter an Unusual Fish (6:1b-6a)

There is something endearing about the dog. His presence is mentioned without fanfare, as an aside, yet the author locates the dog at the beginning of Tobias's journey to Media (6:2) and at the end (11:4). Tobit offers one of the few positive references to dogs in Second Temple period Jewish texts; references in the Tanakh are overwhelmingly negative.[10] Today dogs are recognized as excellent pets for their unconditional love, emotional support, devoted companionship, and ability to deter home break-ins. Having to take a dog for daily walks is good exercise for their human owners, and it provides the potential connection to other dog owners. An Australian study shows that dog ownership can reduce loneliness and contribute to positive mental health.[11] Other studies suggest that the companionship and physical activity that comes with owning a dog can reduce cardiovascular health risks.[12] My husband and I know first-hand the benefits of canine companionship. Marley, our yellow Labrador Retriever, came into our lives as a wildly energetic ten month old after his first owners had to give him up when they were called back into military service. Marley has seen us through thick and thin, and we cannot imagine our life and home without him. He turned fifteen this year and, while he is in remarkably good health, signs of age are beginning to manifest themselves. When Marley stumbles, on occasion my

---

10. Joshua Schwartz, "Good Dog–Bad Dog: Jews and Their Dogs in Ancient Jewish Society," in *A Jew's Best Friend? The Image of the Dog throughout Jewish History*, ed. Phillip Ackerman-Lieberman and Rakefet Zalashik (Eastbourne: Sussex Academic Press, 2013), 54. Schwartz suggests *Tobit* "rides the saddlepoint between the negative Biblical period and the more positive Second Temple, Mishnaic and Talmudic periods" (54).

11. L. Powell, K. M. Edwards, P. McGreevy, et al., "Companion Dog Acquisition and Mental Well-Being: A Community-Based Three-Arm Controlled Study," *BMC Public Health* 19 (2019): 1428.

12. M. Mubanga, L. Byberg, C. Nowak, "Dog Ownership and the Risk of Cardiovascular Disease and Death—A Nationwide Cohort Study," *Scientific Report* 7 (2017): 15821.

Tob 6:1b-6a

¹ᵇThe young man went out and the angel went with him; ²and the dog came out with him and went along with them. So they both journeyed along, and when the first night overtook them they camped by the Tigris river.

³Then the young man went down to wash his feet in the Tigris river. Suddenly a large fish leapt up from the water and tried to swallow the young man's foot, and he cried out. ⁴But the angel said to the young man, "Catch hold of the fish and hang on to it!" So the young man grasped the fish and drew it up on the land. ⁵Then the angel said to him, "Cut open the fish and take out its gall, heart, and liver. Keep them with you, but throw away the intestines. For its gall, heart, and liver are useful as medicine." ⁶So after cutting open the fish the young man gathered together the gall, heart, and liver; then he roasted and ate some of the fish, and kept some to be salted.

husband's and my eyes meet. We each know what the other is thinking: how will we manage without him?

That the dog "came out" (ἐξῆλθεν) with Tobias suggests that they both exited from one area—the courtyard? the house?—into another (onto the road?). There is a sense of comradery conveyed in the spare description of the two coming out together to begin the journey. Homer depicts a similar companionship existing between Odysseus and his dog Argos when Argos—old, neglected, and full of ticks (17.298-99)—still "lifted his head and pricked up his ears" when his long-absent master returned home (17.288-89): this loyal dog recognized his master when other people in the court did not. Sometimes animals are more sensitive companions than humans.

The Tanakh identifies dogs as protectors of property and flocks (e.g., Isa 56:10; Job 30:1). Tobias, accompanied by an angel *and* a dog, is well safeguarded. Out of all of the animals appearing in the story (the birds that cause Tobit's blindness; the goat that prompts Tobit to accuse Anna of stealing; the fish that attacks Tobias), the dog is the one that has the most benign impact. Calling someone "dog" was an ancient insult (in Homer's *Iliad* 1.158-68, Achilles calls Agamemnon a dog; the Cynics' philosophical school derives its name from the word for "dog" [κυνικός] because of the members' rejection of conventional behaviors). Jesus's two references to dogs have been incorrectly understood as evidence that Jews generally used the term "dog" to mean "gentiles." In Matthew 7:6, Jesus advises his followers not to "give what is holy to dogs" or "throw pearls before swine, or they will trample them under foot and turn and maul you." Not giving something of value to either a dog or a pig is sensible advice, but it has nothing to do with a gentile mission. The second reference to dogs is in Matthew when Jesus refers to a Canaanite woman who wishes for Jesus to exorcize the demon from her daughter as a dog. Again, "dog" is an all-purpose epithet rather than an ethnic- or gender-specific one. Jesus indeed insults the woman, and her response is a clever one, as she uses it to her advantage: "Yes, Lord, yet even the dogs eat the crumbs that fall from their masters' table" (Matt 15:27).

Had the birds whose droppings caused Tobit's blindness not been bizarre enough, now nature attacks again in the form of a large ravenous fish that tries to "swallow" Tobias's "foot." The fish foreshadows the demon who attacks Sarah's husbands in that both fish and demon "seek to muddy human/non-human borders."[13] Tobit's author, furthermore, is playing with the story of Jonah, in which a huge fish swallows Jonah, and he stays in its belly for three days and three nights (Jonah 1:17). Jonah didn't have the advantage of the companionship of an angel and so the fish successfully eats him, but for Tobias, Azariah tells him what to do: "Catch hold of the fish and hang on to it!" and all is well. Indeed, rather than ending up in the belly of the fish, Tobias will employ the fish's internal organs to rid his future wife of her demon, and *he* makes a meal of the fish.

The Tanakh frequently uses euphemisms for male genitalia; the most common is רגל, "foot," or רגלים, "feet" (Deut 28:57; Ezek 16:25; Isa 7:20; Ruth 3:4; Prov 19:2).[14] If we apply this euphemism to 6:3, the fish is attacking Tobias's penis. Foreshadowing Asmodeus, he is attempting to prevent conception. Tobias's "crying out," then, acquires a more visceral meaning. Tobias reasserts his masculinity by following the angel's advice: he catches and guts the fish. Instead of the fish eating him, Tobias consumes part of the fish and preserves the rest. Raphael does not eat any of the fish; more on the eating habits of angels later (12:19).

This part of the narrative begins Tobias's transition from a "child/son" to "adult/man." In 6:2 and earlier (4:4, 5, 13, 14, 19, 20, 21; 5:3, 9, 17, 18, 21) Tobias is παιδίον, a term indicating "young boy" or "youth." In 6:3, 4, 7, and 11, παιδαρίω, the diminutive of παῖς ("child"), refers to Tobias. Helen Efthimiadis-Keith suggests that the use of this word places em-

---

13. Levine, "Redrawing the Boundaries," 20.

14. Sharon R. Keller, "Aspects of Nudity in the Old Testament," *Notes in the History of Art* 12 (1993): 34.

phasis on Tobias's "youth and naiveté."[15] He is young, but I'm not sure "naïve" fits his situation—who, young or old, would be prepared for such a fish? But Tobias *is* in the position of student: he must learn from the angel how to handle what unfolds. Raphael serves as his tutor and guide not only in directions, but also in medicine and exorcism. After the marriage ceremony, Tobias is referred to as a νεανίσκον, "young man" (8:1), indicating that his transformation is complete.

Gall (ἡ χολή) was used in antiquity for the treatment of eye disorders. Heinrich Gross refers to gall as a "natural remedy" and notes that modern medicine still sometimes "uses chemically caustic agents" to cure certain ailments.[16] Hebrew words translated in the Septuagint as χολή include לענה, "wormwood" (for example, Deut 29:17; Amos 5:7); ראש, "venom" or "bitter and poisonous herb" (Deut 29:17), and מררה, "gall" or "bile" (Job 16:13) or "venom" (Job 20:14). Sirach 38:4 endorses the use of natural remedies, "The Lord created medicines out of the earth, and the sensible will not despise them." The employment of a natural substance usually considered negative (i.e., poisonous) for the body to prompt healing is one basis of homeopathy. Homeopathic medicine applies the principle of "like cures like" so that a small amount of a substance that causes similar symptoms to an illness can be used to activate the body's immune system and so protect it if the illness is contracted.[17] For example, red onion is used in homeopathic medicine for allergies because it causes a healthy person's eyes to water, and "treatments for other ailments are made from poison ivy, white arsenic, crushed whole bees."[18] Over the centuries women were most deeply associated with this type of healing. Women were herbalists and experts in botany; they incorporated herbs and roots in cooking, and they used plants for healing, for anaesthetics, and as sedatives for childbearing. This knowledge likely was transmitted from elder to younger women at home in families and kin groups. With the passage of time, this type of traditional healing did not stop but was largely sidelined by the professionalization of the discipline of medicine, dominated by men, particularly in the nineteenth century.[19]

15. Helen Efthimiadis-Keith, "The Significance of Food, Eating, Death and Burial in the Book of Tobit," *JSem* 22 (2013): 567.

16. Heinrich Gross, *Tobit, Judit* (Würtzburg: Echter-Verlag, 1987), 42, my translation.

17. https://www.webmd.com/balance/what-is-homeopathy.

18. https://www.webmd.com/balance/what-is-homeopathy.

19. L. Whaley, *Women and the Practice of Medical Care in Early Modern Europe, 1400–1800* (New York: Palgrave MacMillan, 2011). In ancient texts in which women are

Using the Fish Heart and Liver (6:6b-9)

Tobias does not yet understand why he will need to burn the fish's heart and liver to heal "a man or woman afflicted by a demon or evil spirt," but we readers do. We also know that the gall will cure Tobit's blindness. Assyro-Babylonian medical texts suggest that to rid eyes of a filmy white membrane "an eel gallbladder is laid in salt, then mixed with grilled pomegranate and other . . . ingredients to make an ointment."[20] Bile was considered effective in treating contagious bacterial infections of the eye. First-century CE Roman encyclopaedist Celsus recommended that "goat's bile . . . is suitable enough for the treatment of trachoma."[21]

Azariah explains that the cure of burning the fish heart applies to "a man or woman" (ἀνθρώπου ἢ γυναικός, v. 8). This gender inclusivity—found in the original text rather than imposed by modern translators—reflects awareness that demon-harassment, and so the cure, is not gender specific. The assumption that medical treatments work in the same way for women as they do for men is still frequently made, however, often to the detriment of women's health and well-being. Women's and men's immune systems are not the same, nor are their hormones, and thus diseases and chemicals in medicines impact each differently. Women having heart attacks have often been misdiagnosed because research focuses on the symptoms men experience.[22] Women exposed to ionizing radiation during childhood fall ill with cancer at a rate ten times higher than predicted by the United States Nuclear Regulatory Commission because

---

described as having used "magic" (i.e., their knowledge of botany) "to poison the food of enemies probably reflects the degree of vulnerability males felt about having to eat food made by (mostly) female cooks, and their sense of powerlessness over women in the kitchen" (Michele Murray, "The Magical Female in Graeco-Roman Rabbinic Literature," *Religion & Theology: A Journal of Contemporary Religious Discourse* 14 [2007]: 300).

20. F. Köcher, *Die babylonisch-assyrische Medizin in Texten und Untersuchungen* (Berlin: de Gruyter,1963), 23:9 quoted in Annie Attia, "Disease and Healing in the Book of Tobit and in Mesopotamian Medicine," in *Mesopotamian Medicine and Magic: Studies in Honor of Markham J. Geller*, ed. Strahil V. Panayotov and Luděk Vacín (Leiden: Brill, 2018), 55.

21. A. Cornelius Celsus, *On Medicine*, vol. 2: *Books 5–6*, LCL 304, trans. W. G. Spencer (Cambridge, MA: Harvard University Press, 1938), 6.28. Trachoma is a bacterial infection affecting the eyes.

22. Caroline Criado Perez, *Invisible Women: Exposing Data Bias in a World Designed for Men* (New York: Abrams, 2019), 217–19.

Tob 6:6b-9

The two continued on their way together until they were near Media. [7]Then the young man questioned the angel and said to him, "Brother Azariah, what medicinal value is there in the fish's heart and liver, and in the gall?" [8]He replied, "As for the fish's heart and liver, you must burn them to make a smoke in the presence of a man or woman afflicted by a demon or evil spirit, and every affliction will flee away and never remain with that person any longer. [9]And as for the gall, anoint a person's eyes where white films have appeared on them; blow upon them, upon the white films, and the eyes will be healed."

the predictor models were based on "Reference Man," a twenty-five- to thirty-year-old, five-foot-six male weighing 154 pounds.[23]

In 6:9, the verbs are "to anoint" (ἐγχρῖσαι, appears in both G1 and G2) and "to blow" (ἐμφυσῆσαι, missing in G1). Maria Chrysovergi observes that "in ancient literature, both in magico-medical and true medical treatises, the verb 'to anoint' always occurs in remedies."[24] The verb also is associated with the Hebrew word משיח, in English "Messiah," meaning "anointed one." In the Tanakh the term never refers to a divine being but rather to fully human kings who have a special relationship with God (such as Saul in 1 Sam 24:6, and Cyrus—a non-Israelite—in Isa 45:1). The word came to refer to a divine savior and was used by Christians to designate Jesus, called in Greek χριστός, *Christos*, "anointed one." Using the word "anointing" to heal eyes, therefore, brings with it associations to kings and to the divine.

Azaria Tells Tobias about Sarah (6:10-15)

We do not know what else the angel and the young man discussed on the road, but when they near Ecbatana, they speak about marriage. Raphael now addresses his companion with kinship language, "Brother Tobias" (v. 11), highlighting the familial relationship asserted in 5:13 and elevating Tobias's status: an angel calls him brother. Tobias reciprocates in verse 14 with "Brother Azariah." It would seem that his triumph over the fish has instilled new self-confidence. The ostensible blood connection

23. Perez, *Invisible Women*, 116.
24. Maria Chrysovergi, "Attitudes towards the Use of Medicine in Jewish Literature from the Third and Second Centuries BCE" (PhD diss., Durham University, 2011), 148.

Tob 6:10-15

[10]When he entered Media and already was approaching Ecbatana, [11]Raphael said to the young man, "Brother Tobias." "Here I am," he answered. Then Raphael said to him, "We must stay this night in the home of Raguel. He is your relative, and he has a daughter named Sarah. [12]He has no male heir and no daughter except Sarah only, and you, as next of kin to her, have before all other men a hereditary claim on her. Also it is right for you to inherit her father's possessions. Moreover, the girl is sensible, brave, and very beautiful, and her father is a good man." [13]He continued, "You have every right to take her in marriage. So listen to me, brother; tonight I will speak to her father about the girl, so that we may take her to be your bride. When we return from Rages we will celebrate her marriage. For I know that Raguel can by no means keep her from you or promise her to another man without incurring the penalty of death

between Azariah and Tobit's family means that Raguel too is kin, and that opens the possibility that the angel might be a fitting groom for Sarah. This is not the case, readers know, because (good) angels do not have sexual relations. Whether Azariah's groom potential occurred to Tobias cannot be determined.

In describing Sarah's bride qualifications—an only daughter, next-of-kin, sensible, brave, beautiful, daughter of a "good man," Tobias's "right" to marry her—the angel plays matchmaker. Like Abraham's servant, who tells Rebekah's parents of how God has blessed Isaac with wealth (Gen 24:35), Raphael points out the prospective bride's attributes. Sarah is "wise" (φρόνιμον), "brave" (ἀνδρεῖον), and "very beautiful" (καλὸν λίαν). Referring to her as a girl (τὸ κοράσιον) he points out her youth, despite her seven husbands. He foregrounds her wisdom (or "sensibility," as the NRSV puts it) and bravery—because they are more important than her beauty, given her situation. Sarah's wisdom has already been demonstrated by her weighing the decision to hang herself and opting not to do so.[25] Her bravery (ἀνδρεῖον) is shown in her capacity to cope with the deaths of seven grooms—presumably beside her in the marital bed. Sarah is a survivor of trauma.

Because of what he's heard about Sarah, Tobias needs to be convinced that she is a good match. Raphael mentions her personal attributes only

---

25. José Lucas Brum Teixeira, *Poetics and Narrative Function of Tobit 6* (Berlin: de Gruyter, 2019), 211.

according to the decree of the book of Moses. Indeed he knows that you, rather than any other man, are entitled to marry his daughter. So now listen to me, brother, and tonight we shall speak concerning the girl and arrange her engagement to you. And when we return from Rages we will take her and bring her back with us to your house."

[14]Then Tobias said in answer to Raphael, "Brother Azariah, I have heard that she already has been married to seven husbands and that they died in the bridal chamber. On the night when they went in to her, they would die. I have heard people saying that it was a demon that killed them. [15]It does not harm her, but it kills anyone who desires to approach her. So now, since I am the only son my father has, I am afraid that I may die and bring my father's and mother's life down to their grave, grieving for me—and they have no other son to bury them."

after noting that she is her father's sole heir. Israelite inheritance laws were patrilineal except in families with only daughters, as long as those daughters married within their father's tribe (Num 27:1-11; 36:1-11). Because Tobias is "next of kin," she is his. The angel suggests neither that Sarah be asked about the match, nor that Tobias present himself to her to see if *she* is interested. Instead, he states that should her father, Raguel, not agree to the marriage, he will face "the penalty of death according to the law of Moses" (v. 13). This might be a reference to Numbers 36:6-8, where fear about losing land to another tribe if daughters marry outside of their father's tribe is expressed, or perhaps the angel is simply exaggerating in order to be persuasive. Raphael suggests that Raguel "knows" what Tobias is entitled to with regard to his daughter—but if this is the case, why did Raguel not send for Tobias? The angel is doing what he can to convince Tobias to marry Sarah. Raphael even offers to speak to Sarah's father, stepping into Tobit's role as Tobias's father, and follows that offer with declarations of how "we" will arrange the marriage and "we" will take her back "with us." The intensity of his commitment borders on the pushy and overbearing.

Tobias knows the story of Sarah's multiple marriages and the fates of the husbands. He has "heard people saying" (ἄκουσόν μου, ἄδελφε, καὶ λαλήσομεν)—through gossip—what has happened to Sarah. Gossip is often associated with women: 1 Timothy 5:13-14 warns young widows not to be "gossips [φλύαροι]," and 1 Timothy 3:11 states that women are not to be "slanderers [διαβόλους]." The Roman satirist Juvenal (50–130 CE), writes to his friend Postumus, who plans to marry, about the vices of women, gossip being one of them. According to Juvenal, a woman "knows what is going on all over the world . . . [and] she tells to everyone she meets at every street corner" (*Sat.* 6:398-412).[26] Rabbinic texts also link gossip to women; b. Qidd. 49c states: "Ten measures of gossip [שיחה] came down into the world, nine were taken by women (and one by the rest of the world)."[27] Gossip can be viewed as an "alternative rhetorical mode relied upon by women who have been historically restricted from public spheres of conversation."[28]

Tobias is scared about marrying her because of the pain his death would cause his parents; here he matches Sarah's concern for her father in 3:10. He is an only son, and if he dies, it will kill his parents—and then they would have no one to bury them (v. 15). The prospect of Tobit and Anna not having a proper burial is deeply ironic given Tobit's focus on ensuring fellow Israelites receive this dignified treatment. The irony will increase when Tobias's future father-in-law spends the wedding night digging a grave for Tobias.

Tobias knows that it is not Sarah but a demon who is killing the men (v. 14). The gossip does not blame Sarah. Since Tobit can be understood as resisting the idea of the "killer wife" motif and that the deaths of husbands are the fault of wives (3:8; 6:14-18; 8:3), "the people" who exonerated Sarah and inculpated the demon Asmodeus likely were *women*—women who were protecting Sarah. Tobias heard *their* stories about how Sarah's husbands died.

"Azariah" Instructs Tobias (6:16-18)

Raphael offers a convincing argument. He begins with Tobit's commandment concerning endogamy; he turns to his own (supernatural) knowledge; he provides instruction for exorcizing the demon; and he ends with the injunction that the couple, before going to bed (i.e., consummating the marriage), pray. Finally, he tells Tobias that the match

26. *Juvenal and Persius*, trans. G. G. Ramsay (London: William Heinemann, 1918).

27. The word rendered "gossip," שיחה, is understood as "low talk, whisper," in Marcus Jastrow, *A Dictionary of the Targumim, the Talmud Babli and Yerushalmi, and the Midrashic Literature with an Index of Scriptural Quotations*, vol. 2 (New York: G. P. Putnam's Sons, 1903); also Miriam B. Peskowitz, *Spinning Fantasies: Rabbis, Gender, and History* (Berkeley: University of California Press, 1997), 131–53.

28. Cynthia D. McPeters, "Invitational Rhetoric and Gossip: A Feminist Rhetorical Reading of Agatha Christie's Jane Marple" (MA thesis, Appalachian State University, 2017), 4.

[16]But Raphael said to him, "Do you not remember your father's orders when he commanded you to take a wife from your father's house? Now listen to me, brother, and say no more about this demon. Take her. I know that this very night she will be given to you in marriage. [17]When you enter the bridal chamber, take some of the fish's liver and heart, and put them on the embers of the incense. An odor will be given off; [18]the demon will smell it and flee, and will never be seen near her anymore. Now when you are about to go to bed with her, both of you must first stand up and pray, imploring the Lord of heaven that mercy and safety may be granted to you. Do not be afraid, for she was set apart for you before the world was made. You will save her, and she will go with you. I presume that you will have children by her, and they will be as brothers to you. Now say no more!" When Tobias heard the words of Raphael and learned that she was his kinswoman, related through his father's lineage, he loved her very much, and his heart was drawn to her.

with the family member was made in heaven. These points soothe Tobias's nerves and induce his love for Sarah.

Because "Sarah" means "princess" in Hebrew, when Raphael tells Tobias, "You will save her" (v. 18), we find elements of the stereotype—well-known from Grimm's fairy tales and Disney movies—of the damsel in distress awaiting the prince who will rescue her, usually through marriage.[29] Yet Tobias cannot rescue Sarah on his own. He requires supernatural help, and so the idea of the "male savior" is thus itself called into question. Through marriage with Sarah, moreover, Tobias himself is rescued from financial concerns—and so is his family. The stereotype of the princess being saved by her prince is undermined.

The angel ends his instruction, or pep talk, with the notice that Sarah was "set apart for you before the world was made." Beverly Bow and George Nickelsburg note, "The angel does not say to Tobias: '*You* are destined for *her*.' The recipient of divine favor is the groom, not the bride. Even heaven here regards Sarah as a commodity."[30] It is true that

---

29. Cassandra Stover, "Damsels and Heroines: The Conundrum of the Post-Feminist Disney Princess," *LUX: A Journal of Transdisciplinary Writing and Research from Claremont Graduate University* 2 (2013), art. 29, http://scholarship.claremont.edu/lux/vol2/iss1/29.

30. Beverly Bow and George W. E. Nickelsburg, "Patriarchy with a Twist: Men and Women in Tobit," in *A Feminist Companion to Tobit and Judith*, ed. Athalya Brenner-Idan

the perspective provided is that of Tobias, not Sarah. But Sarah is not present when the angel speaks to Tobias, so it is logical he is the focus. Sarah is distinguished by being set apart; this enhances rather than lowers her status. Similar to how God had "appointed" or "assigned" (הכיח) Rebekah for Isaac (Gen 24:44, also 14), Sarah too was divinely chosen. The rabbis shared the understanding that a specific bride was destined for a specific groom; a discussion addressing the fear of a potential groom that another man might marry his beloved suggests that it is pointless for a man to pray that God grant him a particular woman for a wife because "[i]f she is fit for you, and it has been decreed that she will be your wife, she will not go away from you" (b. Mo'ed Qat. 18b). The Yiddish term *bashert* in the eighteenth century came to refer to one's divinely appointed partner, and it is still a concept used by Jews today.[31]

The experience Tobias shared with Azariah and the attacking fish taught Tobias to trust his traveling companion, so when he hears Azariah's comments and recognizes that Sarah is a relative, his fear vanishes and his attitude toward Sarah changes. He "loved her very much" (6:18).

The angel's concluding promise to Tobias is that the children he and Sarah would produce "will be as brothers to you" (v. 18), echoing the bond of brotherhood Raphael and Tobias have with each other (e.g., 6:11, 14) and that the angel thinks of Tobias as his son. The assumption is that the couple will produce sons. Though Tobias does not come across as a brave warrior, the quotation from Psalm 127:4-5 reflects the high value fathers place upon sons: "Like arrows in the hand of a warrior are the sons of one's youth. Happy is the man who has a quiver full of them. He shall not be put to shame when he speaks with his enemies in the gate." "Quiverfull Christians" are members of a conservative Christian theological movement that rejects the use of birth control and espouses that couples should leave the number of children they have "in God's hands," as it is God who opens and closes the womb. Nancy Campbell, an advocate of Quiverfull ideology, suggests that the womb is a "weapon against Satan" since the children produced are considered members of an army of God.[32]

---

and Helen Efthimiadis-Keith, FCB 2.20 (London: Bloomsbury, 2014), 135, emphasis added.

31. Alexander Harkavy, *Yiddish-English-Hebrew Dictionary* (New York: Hebrew Publishing Company, 1928), 112.

32. http://aboverubies.org/index.php/2013-11-12-17-55-51/english-language /motherhood/321-motherhood-protect-your-womb.

TRANSLATION MATTERS

Tobit 6:18 in the NRSV reads, "When Tobias heard the words of Raphael and learned that she was his kinswoman, related through his father's lineage, he loved her very much, and his heart was drawn to her." G1 6:18 uses the verb φιλέω (ἐφίλησεν αὐτήν); in G2 the verb is ἀγαπάω (λίαν ἠγάπησεν αὐτήν). Only in G2 is "very" (λίαν) found. The First Letter of John 4:11 is the only biblical passage where a similar expression to Tobit 6:18 appears: "Beloved, since God *loved us so much*, we also ought to love one another." The Tobit Aramaic fragment 4Q197 4 ii 19-4 iii 1 found at Qumran reads: [33]רחמה ולבה <דבק> בה [לחד]א ש[כדי ש]מע טוביה מלי רפא[ל די היא ל] ה אחא ומן / [בית זרע אבוהי the verb רחם is used to communicate Tobias's love for his prospective bride; it conveys "to love" or "to have mercy."[34] The same verb is used to express the love that Sarah's father, Tobias, and the demon have for her.[35] The verb is used in describing the love of someone with higher status for someone with lower status, e.g., a mother for a child (Isa 49:15), a father for his child (Ps 103:13), God for his people (Exod 33:19).[36] The use of this verb for expressions of affection from the two men *and* the demon for Sarah implies the superior status of the males (including Asmodeus) compared to Sarah. The noun based on the root רחם means "womb" or "uterus" (see, e.g., Gen 20:18; 29:31; 30:22; 49:25; Num 12:12; Jer 20:18; Hos 9:14).

33. Joseph Fitzmyer, *Tobit* (Berlin: de Gruyter, 2003), 221.

34. L. Koehler, W. Baumgartner, and J. J. Stamm, *The Hebrew and Aramaic Lexicon of the Old Testament*, vol. 3 (Leiden: Brill, 1996), 1216–17.

35. Moore, *Tobit*, 209.

36. רחם, *TWOT*, 825.

Tobit 7–9

Ridding Your Life of a Demon in One Simple Step

Several crucial actions occur in chapters 7, 8, and 9: Tobias and the angel Raphael disguised as Azariah arrive at the house of Edna and Raguel, Sarah's parents; Sarah and Tobias marry; Tobias exorcises the demon Asmodeus and retrieves Tobit's silver from Gabael. We shall pay particular attention to the following details from a feministic perspective: depictions of crying, which was gendered in Mediterranean antiquity as it is in many cultures today; slaughtering animals for food and other eating practices; marriage; inheritance; the attention to Edna and Sarah's mother-daughter relationship, one of the few such depictions in ancient literature; the relation among magic, medicine, and miracle, for despite magical aspects of the fumigation ritual performed to exorcise the demon, there is no accusation of magic in the text, and, further, the fact the ritual was performed by men contributes to its presentation as legitimate; appeals to the creation story; the role of only children; women's domestic work; the rubric of chosenness; Tobias's concerns for his father and father-in-law but not his mother; the retrieval of Tobit's silver in light of Anna's worries; and, finally, how Tobias is shown to be, at last, a fully mature man.

Edna, Raguel, and Sarah Welcome Tobias and "Azariah" (7:1-9a)

Raguel and Edna invite Tobias and Azariah with openness and warmth—with hospitality. The Hebrew word עֶדְנָה, "Edna," meaning

131

Tob 7:1-9a

[7]Now when they entered Ecbatana, Tobias said to him, "Brother Azariah, take me straight to our brother Raguel." So he took him to Raguel's house, where they found him sitting beside the courtyard door. They greeted him first, and he replied, "Joyous greetings, brothers; welcome and good health!" Then he brought them into his house. [2]He said to his wife Edna, "How much the young man resembles my kinsman Tobit!" [3]Then Edna questioned them, saying, "Where are you from, brothers?" They answered, "We belong to the descendants of Naphtali who are exiles in Nineveh." [4]She said to them, "Do you know our kinsman Tobit?" And they replied, "Yes, we know him." Then she asked them, "Is he in good health?" [5]They replied, "He is alive and in good health." And Tobias added, "He is my father!" [6]At that Raguel jumped up and kissed him and wept. [7]He also spoke to him as follows, "Blessings on you, my child, son of a good and noble father! O most miserable of calamities that such an upright and beneficent man has become blind!" He then embraced his kinsman Tobias and wept. [8]His wife Edna also wept for him, and their daughter Sarah likewise wept. [9]Then Raguel slaughtered a ram from the flock and received them very warmly.

"delight, enjoyment, pleasure," occurs only in Genesis 18:12, when God informs Sarah and Abraham that they will have a son. Sarah states, "After I have grown old, and my husband is old, shall I have pleasure?"—she is likely referring not to the birth of the child but to his conception and therefore to her own sexual pleasure.[1] For these two senior citizens, the text expresses what could be considered a charming delight in this reawakening of sexual activity. Perhaps Tobit's Sarah will have some pleasure of her own, after seven dead grooms, but the narrative does not directly move to that concern.

Raguel and his family were Israelites living in the diaspora, strangers in a strange land, and they are generous with the two travelers, whom they may not have identified as fellow Israelites immediately. How they would have recognized them as such is difficult to know. Perhaps through the wearing of *tzitzim* (Hebrew for "fringes"; Jewish men—and possibly women—were instructed [e.g., Num 15:38; Deut 22:12] to wear fringes on their garments to remind them of the command-

---

1. Amy-Jill Levine, "Redrawing the Boundaries: A New Look at 'Diaspora as Metaphor: Bodies and Boundaries in the Book of Tobit,'" in *A Feminist Companion to Tobit and Judith*, ed. Athalya Brenner-Idan and Helen Efthimiadis-Keith, FCB 2.20 (London: Continuum, 2015), 15.

ments. According to Matthew 9:20, Jesus was wearing them when the woman suffering from hemorrhages touched "the fringe of his cloak" and also in 14:36). The men otherwise would have worn χιτών, "tunics," that were the typical apparel of men living in the eastern Mediterranean basin.[2] Perhaps Tobias and Azariah used a greeting (not in the text) with which Raguel was familiar, or maybe their accent revealed their identity as Israelites. The Gospels provide evidence for regional accents: people identify Peter as a Galilean after they hear him speak (Mark 14:70; Luke 22:59; Matt 26:73).[3]

Because of Israel's awareness of being foreigners in Egypt, the Torah frames care for strangers as an obligation.[4] It repeatedly warns against taking advantage of a stranger: for example, "You shall not wrong a stranger or oppress him, for you were strangers in the land of Egypt" (Exod 22:20; 23:9). Care for a stranger is to be manifest in practical terms through the provision of "food and clothing" (Lev 19:33-34; Deut 10:18-19), which no doubt meant that women were involved in providing this care.

The story of Abraham's hospitality to his three visitors in Genesis 18:1-8 is a helpful intertext for Tobit 7–9. Abraham greets his guests with respect, provides water so that the three could bathe their feet, gives them bread so that they could "refresh" themselves, asks Sarah to make cakes, and gives a "tender and choice" calf for a meal. Though Abraham speaks modestly about the provisions he serves his visitors (i.e., "a little water" in v. 4, "a morsel of bread" in v. 5), he and Sarah invest significant effort to please his guests.

Both Tobit and Genesis 18 feature women called "Sarah" who are (to this point) childless and visits of divine beings whose real identity

2. Victor H. Matthews, "Cloth, Clothes," in *New Interpreter's Dictionary of the Bible*, vol. 1, ed. Katharine Doob Sakenfeld (Nashville: Abingdon, 2006), 693, notes, "As Israel and Judah were drawn into the cultural sphere of foreign empires, the wealthy and government officials tended to adopt foreign clothing styles."

3. Gary A. Rendsburg, "Shibboleth," in *Encyclopedia of Hebrew Language and Linguistics*, vol. 3, ed. Geoffrey Khan (Leiden: Koninklijke Brill, 2013), 556–57, notes that regional dialects existed in ancient Hebrew as well: Judges 12:4-6 tells the story about how, during a war between the Gileadites and the Ephraimites, the Gileadites identified who was an Ephraimite by their pronunciation of the word שבלת, *shibbolet*, as סבלת, *sibbolet*. The meaning of the word *shibbolet* (or *sibbolet*) is not certain: it might refer to the current of the river (Ps 69:3) or to sheaves of grain (Gen 41:5-7). This story in Judges is the origin of the English word "shibboleth."

4. Jeffrey H. Tigay, "Exodus," in *The Jewish Study Bible*, ed. Adele Berlin and Marc Z. Brettler, 2nd ed. (New York: Oxford University Press, 2014), 148.

is concealed. Just as the three strangers give Abraham the unexpected but happy news of Sarah's impending pregnancy (Gen 18:10-14), so the two strangers offer Raguel and Edna, and Sarah as well, the good news that she will finally be wed (for longer than a night; Tob 8:14). The dark humor in each reinforces the comparison of the two vignettes: in Genesis 18:12, Sarah overhears the prediction and laughs at the suggestion of becoming pregnant, and she alludes to her own sexual desire (Gen 18:12); Raguel tells Tobias to "eat and drink, and be merry tonight" (7:10) yet that very evening, just in case, prepares a grave for Tobias (8:9-10). In Genesis, the attention shifts from Abraham to Sarah; in Tobit, the focus goes from Sarah to Tobias.

Like Abraham, Raguel offers his visitors a warm greeting, calling them brothers (ἀδελφοί) and welcoming them "in good health" (καὶ καλῶς ἤλθατε ὑγιαίνοντες, v. 1). Recognizing the importance of good health, the typical first question in a letter or when meeting someone in person was about the state of their health (the letter to Aristobulus prefixed to the introduction of 2 Maccabees, begins with "Greetings and good health" [χαίρειν καὶ ὑγιαίνειν; 1:10]). Raguel then brings them home to what he specifically calls "*his* house" (τὸν οἶκον αὐτοῦ; v.1), as if he is intent on making an impression on his guests.

When Tobias and Azariah arrive, Edna is inside the house. It is she, and not Raguel, who asks the crucial questions. Raguel focuses on external appearances by noting that Tobias, the "young man" (νεανίσκος), resembles Tobit—the perfect son as an image of his father, with no female admixture. Edna, on the other hand, asks about her visitors' point of origin ("Where are you from?"), whether they know Tobit, and whether he is in good health (καὶ εἶπεν αὐτοῖς Ὑγιαίνει). It is not unusual for there to be a question about the health of an individual who is not present, though given what transpired in Tobit's life such questions take on added significance. Perhaps Edna and Raguel found it strange that Tobit did not join Tobias.

Edna takes the initiative to engage with the two visitors; she is seeking to make connections. This vignette makes me think about what happens when one is introduced to someone who went to the same school or is from the same religious, ethnic, racial, or national group. My Hong Kong–born friend, who has lived in Canada for over forty years, says that many members of her community consider it important to establish ties with other people from Hong Kong because they do not feel a deep connection with North American culture. Discovering connections with other members of one's "tribe" brings comfort, especially for people belonging to minority communities. Members of my family speak of the "game" of "Jewish geography" in reference to this same impulse to make connections by finding out if fellow Jews have friends or acquaintances in common. Edna's questioning of Tobias and Azariah might be the ancient equivalent of "Jewish geography." At the same time, she may be less trusting than her husband.

Edna asks Tobias and Azariah where they are from. They respond not with a primarily geographic answer but one concerning lineage: "We belong to the descendants of Naphtali who are exiles in Nineveh." Their answer shifts the focus from "where" to "whom": they provide their tribal name, which suggests that they understand that Edna and Raguel already know their Israelite identity. They identify themselves as exiles in Nineveh, implying a sense of alienation from their current home and a connection with their former one. They also, as my Hong Kong friend observed, wished to make a connection with members of their same community.

Edna finally asks Tobias, "Do you know our kinsman Tobit?" (7:3), and so discovers the family connection. The family link is through Tobit, probably on Raguel's side, since he says to Edna that Tobias (7:2) reminds him of *my* kinsman Tobit (τῷ ἀδελφῷ μου). Edna refers to Tobit as *our* kinsman (τὸν ἀδελφὸν ἡμῶν) in 7:4. We do not learn anything about the natal family of either Edna or Anna from the book of Tobit. Edna seems to have felt fully absorbed into Tobit's family. Once she marries Tobias, perhaps Sarah too will lose her connection to her own parents. Through marriage we gain relatives: I never had brothers growing up but my husband's two brothers now belong to my family.

Edna asks, "Is he [Tobit] in good health?" (7:4), and Tobias responds in the affirmative. If we understand "good health" to mean no ailments at all, then many people might not be able to claim that they possess good health. If it means that we are not at death's door or that we are doing well enough, then many more answer in the affirmative. Perhaps Tobias still perceives his father to be in good health in the areas that count for him: strength of mind, resolve, the ability to move around. One can be blind, deaf, unable to walk, and in a variety of other bodily states classified as "disabled" and still be in very good health, mentally and physically.

Given that Raguel is cognizant of Tobit's condition (7:7) without Tobias's telling him, it is likely Edna also knows about the blindness. Her question, then, may be understood to imply, "other than blindness . . ." so we might see her as concerned about his spiritual or psychological state.

Raguel laments the calamity that has befallen the "upright and benefi-cent" Tobit (7:7) and so touches on one of the book's central themes, that of theodicy. Yet Raguel first finds the joyous news: that Tobias has such a "good and noble father." "Good and noble" are not mutually exclusive to "blind" or "suffering misfortune." One's physical situation is not necessarily indicative of one's character. When Raguel mentions Tobit's blindness, Edna—and Sarah, who suddenly appears—join him in grieving (7:8).

The scene to this point has been marked by weeping. Raguel weeps when Tobias announces that Tobit is his father (7:6); he weeps again after expressing his concerns for Tobit's blindness (7:7); in 7:8, Edna and Sarah also weep. The focus on blindness and weeping—both related to eyes—lends a problematic humor to the text, as we can picture the entire family wiping their eyes over concern for Tobit's blindness.

Michael Trimble notes in Greek antiquity, both men and women weep: "Crying as an emotional response, especially to sadness and bereavement, is portrayed in the earliest of Western literature, and there are many descriptions of it in Homer's *Iliad* and *Odyssey*. Great heroes weep."[5] In Virgil's epic *Aeneid*, Aeneas weeps when he sees Juno's temple and the images of war scenes because they remind him of what—and whom—he has lost (1.464-65). While crying was acceptable for men, especially if the crying were related to a comrade's death in battle, unrestrained crying —indeed, unrestrained action in general—was not.[6] Emotive crying by a man risked his being associated with women. For example, crying during Demodocus's playing of the lyre, "Odysseus, clutching his flaring sea-blue cape in both powerful hands, drew it over his head and buried his handsome face, ashamed his hosts might see him shedding tears" (*Od.* 8.99-103).[7] A later verse finds Homer suggesting that Odysseus is behaving like a woman: "Great Odysseus melted into tears, running down from his eyes to wet his cheeks . . . as a woman weeps, her arms flung round her darling husband, a man who fell in battle" (*Od.* 8.586-89).[8] Thus, even in antiquity, crying was gendered; there were socially accepted ways and times for men and women to cry.

Gendered sentiments still hold in our day: "Boys don't cry" remains the behavioral norm in some families, since the prevailing view is that babies and women cry (the association of the two has its own set of problems, since it infantilizes women); men do not. In patriarchal contexts, telling a man he is acting like a woman is a deep insult. Telling a man he is acting

---

5. Michael Trimble, *Why Humans Like to Cry: Tragedy, Evolution, and the Brain* (Oxford: Oxford University Press, 2012), 22.

6. Trimble, *Why Humans Like to Cry*, 22.

7. Homer, *The Odyssey*, trans. Robert Fagles (New York: Viking Penguin, 1996), 194.

8. Homer, *The Odyssey*, 208.

like a baby would be comparable. There is increasing understanding that this attitude is not healthy;[9] here Tobit might be a corrective. Over time, I've learned to become more accepting of the times when I have cried in public—for example, sometimes during extremely tense meetings when discussing something I cared deeply about. I still feel uncomfortable when it happens, but that is an improvement over when I was younger: I would get so angry at myself and would feel profoundly embarrassed, especially if I was in a leadership position and cried in front of others—leaders don't cry, I thought! But that is nonsense. I've spent far too much time and energy beating myself up afterward about what I considered to be a weakness. Now, in my fifties, I understand crying to be a natural expression of emotion: it is human, it is honest, and it shows you care. I've come to recognize that when friends or colleagues cry in public, I don't think less of them. I try to treat myself with that same understanding.

Raguel and Edna's hospitality culminates in a lavish meal, including a butchered ram (7:9). For Tobit, and the culture in which it is embedded, killing animals for food was normative. Such slaughter can reinforce the view not only of humans as superior to the rest of creation but also of creation as a commodity to do with as we choose.

Feminists Carol Adams and Lori Gruen draw parallels between the ways women are treated in patriarchal societies with the ways animals are treated: as possessions of humans, without respect.[10] They argue that vegetarianism should be considered a central feminist ethical obligation, since it is consistent with the rejection of dominating relationships in the form of the powerful (humans, men, whites) controlling the subordinate (animals, women, people of color).[11] Fred Rogers, the highly regarded former host of the children's television series *Mr. Rogers' Neighborhood*, was a lifelong vegetarian known for justifying his dietary choices: "I don't want to eat anything that has a mother."[12] For many

9. Christia S. Brown, "Boys Who Cry Might Have It All Figured Out," *Psychology Today*, November 20, 2012; https://www.psychologytoday.com/ca/blog/beyond-pink-and-blue/201211/boys-who-cry-might-have-it-all-figured-out.

10. Irina Aristarkhova, "Thou Shall Not Harm All Living Beings: Feminism, Jainism, and Animals," *Hypatia* 27 (2012): 643.

11. Carol J. Adams, *The Sexual Politics of Meat: A Feminist-Vegetarian Critical Theory* (New York: Continuum, 1990); Lori Gruen, "Empathy and Vegetarian Commitments," in *The Feminist Care Tradition in Animal Ethics*, ed. Josephine Donovan and Carol J. Adams (New York: Columbia University Press, 2007).

12. Michael Long, "What Would Mister Rogers Eat? Thanksgiving in the Neighborhood," *HuffPost*, January 21, 2015; https://www.huffpost.com/entry/what-would-mister-rogers-eat_b_6193910.

people today, treating animals nonviolently and embracing a vegetarian diet is increasingly feasible, although a recent Gallup poll reveals that fewer than one in ten Americans adheres to a nonmeat diet, and of that number, 5 percent say they are vegetarian (abstain from eating meat) and 3 percent say they are vegan (abstain from eating any animal products).[13] While the number of vegetarians and vegans has not risen significantly over the past few years, sales of plant-based food rose by 8.1 percent in 2017 alone, and sales of plant-based alternatives to dairy products are currently approximately 40 percent of dairy beverage sales. It appears that more and more North Americans are opting to consume less meat. Ethical concerns about animals are among the many reasons that motivate people to make such choices.[14]

But not all killing of animals is violent. For example, Jewish food activists participating in the Adamah Jewish Environmental Leadership Training program at the Isabella Freedman Jewish Retreat Center in Connecticut, which combines Jewish values, organic farming, and sustainable living, make humane treatment of animals—including their deaths—a top priority. Provoked to active engagement by the eco-food movement as well as by the charges of labor violations and allegations of inhumane treatment of animals against Agriprocessors, the company in Postville, Iowa, that runs the largest kosher slaughterhouse in the United States, these activists seek to eat what they grow. As one participant states, "Knowing the animal you are eating, you tend to eat less. You eat slower. Being an omnivore is your choice and being able to do that in a respectful and humane way is valuable."[15]

The diet of peoples living in Mediterranean antiquity was largely plant-based; Pliny the Elder refers to gladiators as *hordearii* ("barley-men") because they ate so much of that grain (*Nat.* 18.14).[16] Daniel, Hananiah, Azariah, and Mishael (Dan 1:12,16) eat only vegetables, apparently in

---

13. R. J. Reinhart, "Snapshot: Few Americans Vegetarian or Vegan," *Gallup*, August 1, 2018; https://news.gallup.com/poll/238328/snapshot-few-americans-vegetarian -vegan.aspx.

14. Additional reasons include health concerns and the impact of agriculture on the environment; Reinhart, "Snapshot: Few Americans Vegetarian or Vegan."

15. Sue Fishkoff, "Death of a Goat: Jewish Food Activists Slaughter Their Own Meat," *Wisconsin Jewish Chronicle*, October 23, 2008; https://www.jewishchronicle .org/2008/10/23/death-of-a-goat-jewish-food-activists-slaughter-their-own-meat/.

16. The full quote is: "Barley is the oldest among human foods, as is proved by the Athenian ceremony recorded by Menander, and by the name given to gladiators, who used to be called 'barley-men.' Also the Greeks prefer it to any other grain for porridge."

order not to transgress Jewish food laws (expressed in Lev 11 and Deut 14) while living at the court of King Nebuchadnezzar.[17] For most people in antiquity, meat was a relatively rare indulgence reserved for special occasions, such as the welcoming of visitors to one's home.

I am reminded of Sarah's goat, gifted to her by her employers (Tob 2:12). My secret hope is that she did not need to kill it and eat it but instead kept it for its wool. I stopped eating red and white meat around the age of twelve. At the time, my sister and I kept our horses in stalls at a friend's farm. On this farm was a bull named George. We got to know George because we'd see him almost every time we went to care for our horses, muck out the stalls, or ride. George often was in one of the outside paddocks and was a friendly being—he would approach the fence when he saw us and it was quite something to be able to pet an animal that was so huge and scary looking. One day we arrived at the barn and George's decapitated head was on the ground by a paddock, and his skin was hanging over the fence. His legs were chopped up and left by the side of the fence as well. It was a horrifying experience. All three of us wept from shock and sadness. My mom, at the time in her thirties, was especially traumatized and said then and there that she would never eat meat again. As I write this, she is in her eighties and has kept her promise. My sister and I stopped as well, but mostly because it was my mom who cooked the meals. Once I left home, I began eating chicken (but not beef) for several years, well into my thirties. It was helpful having chicken as an option if at a restaurant or invited to someone else's house for dinner. But in my early forties, quite suddenly, I stopped being able to eat it. It was as though my body made the decision for me. Only after that did I allow myself to watch films of how chickens are treated in slaughterhouses. I now mostly eat vegetarian food, but I occasionally eat fish, so I suppose I am currently comfortable being a pescatarian.

Tobias and Raguel Strike an Agreement for Tobias to Marry Sarah (7:9b-11)

There are two verbs used in 7:9b: ἐλούσαντο καὶ ἐνίψαντο, "bathing and washing." The first, λούω, refers to the two travelers bathing their entire bodies to get rid of the dust and sweat from their journey. The

---

17. Lawrence M. Wills, "Daniel," in *The Jewish Study Bible*, ed. Adele Berlin and Marc Z. Brettler, 2nd ed. (New York: Oxford University Press, 2014), 1638.

Tob 7:9b-11

When they had bathed and washed themselves and had reclined to dine, Tobias said to Raphael, "Brother Azariah, ask Raguel to give me my kinswoman Sarah." [10]But Raguel overheard it and said to the lad, "Eat and drink, and be merry tonight. For no one except you, brother, has the right to marry my daughter Sarah. Likewise I am not at liberty to give her to any other man than yourself, because you are my nearest relative. But let me explain to you the true situation more fully, my child. [11]I have given her to seven men of our kinsmen, and all died on the night when they went in to her. But now, my child, eat and drink, and the Lord will act on behalf of you both." But Tobias said, "I will neither eat nor drink anything until you settle the things that pertain to me." So Raguel said, "I will do so. She is given to you in accordance with the decree in the book of Moses, and it has been decreed from heaven that she should be given to you. Take your kinswoman; from now on you are her brother and she is your sister. She is given to you from today and forever. May the Lord of heaven, my child, guide and prosper you both this night and grant you mercy and peace."

second verb, νίπτω, means to wash one part of the body: probably their hands.[18] There was no biblical requirement for the washing of hands before consuming food,[19] but that does not preclude its being done prior to eating, especially since, in 7:9a, Raguel slaughters a lamb himself. He would have washed his hands before eating, and it is reasonable to think that his guests joined him. Tobias, now washed and reclining, asks his companion, "Brother Azariah, ask Raguel to give me my kinswoman Sarah" (7:9). Tobias does not make the request himself. Sometimes it

18. "λούω" and "νίπτω" in J. Lust, E. Eynikel and K. Hauspie, *Greek-English Lexicon of the Septuagint*, rev. ed. (Stuttgart: Deutsche Bibelgesellschaft, 2003), 377 and 417, respectively. This is counter to Bernard Couroyer, "Tobie VII, 9: Problème de Critique Textuelle," *RB* 91 (1984): 351–56, who argues that the two-verb construction is a doublet, so is not meant to convey two different types of washing. Unfortunately, 7:9 is not present among the Aramaic or Hebrew texts from Qumran.

19. As noted by Carey Moore, *Tobit: A New Translation with Introduction and Commentary* (New Haven: Yale University Press, 1996), 219. Handwashing comes to be practiced by Jews in the Hellenstic period; Mark 7:3 states that "the Pharisees, and all the Jews, do not eat unless they thoroughly wash their hands, thus observing the tradition of the elders"; the writer is accurate about the Pharisees observing the process (Josephus confirms this in *Ant.* 13.297) but not about all Jews doing so. The Sadducees, for example, did not (Jonathan Klawans, "The Law," in *The Jewish Annotated New Testament*, ed. Amy-Jill Levine and Marc Zvi Brettler, 2nd ed. [Oxford: Oxford University Press, 2017], 655).

is a good strategy to rely on a trusted ally to make the request on our behalf, especially if we are feeling particularly vulnerable or stressed. Functioning *in loco parentis*, Raphael serves as Tobias's surrogate father, the one expected to set the terms of the marriage contract.

Raguel, overhearing this conversation, offers the famous advice, "Eat and drink, and be merry" (7:10). This cheerful invitation to Tobias is reminiscent of the well-known adage expressing fatalistic celebrating in the face of disaster, "Let us eat and drink, for tomorrow we die," found, for example, in Isaiah 22:13. The author probably intended for his readers to fill in the missing part ("for tomorrow we die"), since this sentiment, as noted above, adds dark humor to this scene when it is juxtaposed with Raguel's forthright description in the very next verse of his daughter's grim "true situation" (v. 11). Readers know that, thanks to Raphael, Tobias is already aware of what he faces in marrying Sarah and that this is a match not even threat of death can deter.

Raguel assures Tobias that he has legal rights to Sarah and then relates what has befallen Sarah's seven prior husbands. Promising to explain everything fully, he offers only a single sentence, "I have given her to seven men of our kinsmen, and all died on the night when they went in to her." Discussing what has befallen Tobias's predecessors shows some integrity, although the association of this tragic past with the celebratory meal lends this vignette a darkly humorous veneer at Sarah's expense.[20] And Raguel makes no mention of the demon, so his comments leave open the possibility of Sarah's being to blame for the deaths.

Raguel speaks to Tobias as "my child" (παιδίον) and so he both takes the paternal role and, ironically, casts his future son-in-law not as a man but as one who has not yet achieved manhood. Precluding the possibility that Tobias might have a comment, Raguel rushes on to tell the "child" (same word) that the time has come to eat and drink and to be assured of divine protection. An adult might have raised a few questions, from "What have you done to stop these deaths?" to "How can you be sure tonight will be different from all other nights?" Not Tobias.

Sarah's father, Raguel, determines her next partner: she is like a possession passed from man to man through an agreement that only men make. Raguel refers to his having "given" Sarah (ἔδωκα, v. 11) in marriage but that now he does not have the power to "give" her (δοῦναι)

---

20. Amy-Jill Levine also notes the humor of this in "Tobit," in *The New Oxford Annotated Bible: New Revised Standard Version with the Apocrypha*, ed. Michael D. Coogan, 3rd ed.(Oxford: Oxford University Press, 2001), 22.

to anyone but Tobias. Sarah is the object of this language. Raguel later in verse 11 tells Tobias to "[t]ake [κομίζου] your kinswoman. . . . She is given [δέδοταί] to you from today and forever." Again, the groom, the active agent, "takes" the bride, who is "given" by her father to her husband. Rebekah has a say in whom she marries; in Genesis 24:57-58, her mother and brother consult Rebekah about whether she wishes to leave home with Isaac's servant to marry Isaac. Sarah is not offered such an opportunity. Indeed, Sarah, as "object rather than subject," is inherited by Tobias (7:10).[21] In contrast, Sarah is passed from one man to the next. In our day, rituals still treat brides as if they are objects. They are "given" in marriage, such as when the father of the bride accompanies her down the aisle to where the groom and the officiant stand, and the officiant asks, "Who gives this woman in marriage?" It is the father, or sometimes both parents, who respond, not the bride. Alternative rituals are sometimes chosen. For example, both parents might walk the bride down the aisle, or the groom, too, might be accompanied by his parents, symbolizing how he is "given" to the bride, or the bride walks alone down the aisle, as I did for my wedding, since it was important to me to symbolize that I was a free agent. If my parents were disappointed by this change in the traditional ritual, they didn't mention it to me.

Irene Nowell suggests that Sarah's "chief function is marriage to the appropriate kinsman."[22] But such could also be said of Tobias. His father repeatedly instructs him to marry the right woman—a member of his family—and this is precisely what he does. Indeed, the narrator more frequently associates Tobias with this function than Sarah.

Raguel understands that Tobias wishes to marry his daughter, and he affirms that Tobias is the only one who "has the right" to marry her, since he is his closest living relative (v. 10; the shorter [G1] text of 6:12 suggests that Tobias is the only one left).

Whether this marriage is related to the tradition of the levirate remains an open question. According to Deuteronomy 25:5-10, if a married man died before having a child, it was the *levir*'s ("husband's brother," from the Latin *levir*) duty to marry the widow. The first son born from the union would be counted as the heir of the deceased brother, so that the dead man's name would not be "blotted out of Israel" (Deut 25:6). The biblical law is obligatory on the part of the deceased's brother, so Tobias,

21. Levine, "Redrawing the Boundaries," 12.

22. Irene Nowell, "The Book of Tobit: Narrative Technique and Theology" (PhD diss., The Catholic University of America, 1983), 145.

who is not a brother of the seven dead grooms, is not duty-bound to marry Sarah.[23] Yet in the levirate system presented in the book of Ruth, a book that is very much about exogamy since Ruth the Moabite marries not one but two men from Israel, there are two men, Boaz and a Mr. So-and-So (Hebrew: פלני אלמני), who have a first choice to marry Ruth if they wish.

TRANSLATION MATTERS

Tobit 7:11 in G2 (the longer Greek text, represented by Codex Sinaiticus) reads: "I have given her to seven men of our kinsmen, and all died on the night when they went in toward her." The same verse appears slightly but meaningfully altered in G1 (the shorter Greek text, considered to be a condensed version of G2, found in Vaticanus and Alexandrinus): "I have given my child to seven husbands, and when they came in toward her, they died during the night." The editor of G1 has adjusted the wording of G2 by describing the first seven grooms as being unrelated to Sarah's family, with the implication that they died because their marriages to Sarah were exogamous.[24] The demon Asmodeus thus confirms, in a gruesome way, the importance of marriage within the family.

In the Gospels, some Sadducees tell Jesus the story of a woman who—like Sarah—has had seven husbands, all brothers, die without children (Mark 12:20-22; Matt 22:25-26; Luke 20:29-33). The Sadducees, who do not believe in resurrection and therefore seek to show that it is an unworkable idea, ask Jesus to whom the woman would be married during the resurrection. The similarity of the Gospel story with Sarah's tale might be evidence of the writers' familiarity with our narrative.

Tobias affirms his maturity not by asking questions but by insisting that he and Raguel complete the legal matters related to the marriage. Raguel agrees by giving Sarah to Tobias "in accordance with the decree

23. Cf. George W. E. Nickelsburg, "Tobit," in *The Harper Collins Study Bible: Including Apocryphal Deuterocanonical Books*, rev. ed. (New York: HarperCollins, 2006), 1304. Likewise in Ruth, since he is not a brother of Ruth's dead husband, Boaz is not obligated to marry Ruth (Adele Reinhartz, "Ruth," in *The Jewish Study Bible*, ed. Adele Berlin and Marc Z. Brettler, 2nd ed. [New York: Oxford University Press, 2014], 1579).

24. Tobias Nicklas, "Marriage in the Book of Tobit," in *The Book of Tobit: Text, Tradition, Theology; Papers of the First International Conference on the Deuterocanonical Books, Pápa, Hungary, 20–21 May 2004*, ed. Géza G. Xeravits and József Zsengellér (Leiden: Brill, 2005), 151.

in the book of Moses [βίβλου Μωυσέως]" (7:11); the decree is at Numbers 36:8, which describes how tribes retain their resources: "Every daughter who possesses an inheritance in any tribe of the Israelites shall marry one from the clan of her father's tribe so that all Israelites may continue to possess their ancestral inheritance." The Lord declared that, after the five daughters of Zelophehad made the case before Moses and the entire community (in Num 27:2-11), it would be an injustice were the name of their deceased father to be cut off from his Manassite clan by his daughters not being allotted land. Moses and Eleazar the priest have been giving the land only to those whose names were recorded in a census, and all were males (Num 26:52-56). Moses, after consulting with God, decrees in Numbers 27:5-7 that the daughters—Mahlah, Noah, Hoglah, Milcah, and Tirzah—were correct about the potential injustice to their father's name and that they ought to inherit land. Later, the male members of the tribe of Manasseh point out to Moses that, when the daughters married, their inherited land would pass into their new husband's clan, thereby reducing the lands of the Manassites. The resulting decree of Numbers 36:8 declares that the five daughters of Zelophehad (and any other daughters who inherit land) must marry a man belonging to the clan of their father's tribe. This second law limited daughters' choices of whom to marry and furthermore rendered their land ownership to be temporary—that is, it was theirs until they married, at which point the land would pass into their husband's hands.[25] The idea that a man might join his new wife's clan apparently was not considered within the realm of possibility.[26] Sarah had no brothers, so was in the same position as the daughters of Zelophehad, and, as they eventually did (in Num 36:10-12), was about to marry the "right" man in accordance with Numbers 36:8.

Raguel reiterates how this marriage has been divinely inspired. Despite its being his own daughter's marriage, he speaks of the match from the groom's perspective: "it has been decreed from heaven that *she* should be given to *you*" (7:11; cf. 6:18). Focussing on the divine inspiration for the pairing might have been Raguel's way of quelling any nerves

---

25. Katherine Doob Sakenfeld, "Numbers," in *Women's Bible Commentary*, ed. Carol A. Newsom and Sharon H. Ringe, expanded edition (Louisville: Westminster John Knox, 1998), 55.

26. Also Katherine Doob Sakenfeld, "Daughters of Zelophehad," in *Women in Scripture: A Dictionary of Named and Unnamed Women in the Hebrew Bible, the Apocryphal/ Deuterocanonical Books, and the New Testament*, ed. Carol Meyers, Toni Craven, and Ross S. Kraemer (Grand Rapids: Eerdmans, 2000), 221.

Tobias might have had given Sarah's previous marriages. Maybe Raguel had to convince *himself*, too, that this eighth marriage would be different from the seven others. If God divinely appointed Tobias to marry Sarah, how could such a union go wrong?

A marriage deemed brought about by God, while reassuring, risks unrealistic expectations. The couple might be highly disappointed when they discover that good marriages—even those decreed in heaven—take work. Sarah and Tobias's marriage, presented as divinely ordained, nevertheless faces a demonic challenge. In contrast to most of the existent sources on Jewish marriage in the ancient world, which tend to be, as Michael L. Satlow observes, "highly ideological," by which I understand Satlow to mean that only the good parts are shown, the glimpses Tobit offers into the interactions between the married couples are not.[27] They are complicated and messy: Tobit accuses Anna of stealing, and she defends herself (2:11-14); they argue about sending Tobias on a dangerous journey (5:18–6:1); they worry and quibble with one another about their son's long absence; Tobit attempts to comfort Anna (10:1-7). As Geoffrey David Miller observes, Tobit presents "a realistic portrait of what married life is like: some wives quietly obey their husbands, some couples speak openly with each other, and some even yell at one another."[28]

Like Abraham's servant, to whom Laban offers food after his journey to find a wife for Isaac but who refuses until the match with Rebekah is set (Gen 24:33), Tobias refuses Raguel's offer of food and drink until his union with Sarah is settled (v. 11). Raguel calls Sarah Tobias's "sister" (ἀδελφήν) in 7:11 and adds further, "[F]rom now on you are her brother [ἀδελφὸς] and she is your sister [ἀδελφή]." There is no original hint of incest in the "brother" and "sister" language for husband and wife. As in most cultures, Israel also outlawed incest: Leviticus 18:1-18; 20:11-21 clarifies that a man was not to marry his mother, stepmother, sister, half-sister, granddaughter, aunt, daughter-in-law, or sister-in-law—any of which would "be a disgrace to your own family" (Lev 18:10).[29] The use of sibling terminology expresses affection for a spouse, and is applied

27. Michael L. Satlow, *Jewish Marriage in Antiquity* (Princeton: Princeton University Press, 2001), 93.

28. Geoffrey David Miller, *Marriage in the Book of Tobit* (Berlin: de Gruyter, 2011), 185.

29. Egyptian culture, in contrast, allowed for incestual marriage, at least among Pharaohs, who frequently married their sisters or even daughters; David Lorton, "Legal and Social Institutions of Pharaonic Egypt," in *Civilizations of the Ancient Near East*, ed. J. M. Sasson and J. Baines, vol. 1 (New York: Scribner, 1995), 349.

frequently in Tobit: Raguel calls his wife Edna "sister" in 7:15; Tobias calls Sarah twice his sister on their wedding night in 8:4 and 7; Raguel refers to Sarah as Tobias's sister in 8:21; in 5:21 and 10:6 Tobit calls Anna his sister; and Edna tells Tobias in 10:12 that Sarah now is his sister. In the fourth- or third-century BCE Song of Solomon, which celebrates human love, the male refers to his female lover as "my sister" (4:9, 10, 12; 5:1, 2). Such terms communicated how a marriage makes the couple more deeply bound to one another. Sarah and Tobias were already related, but their marriage brings them even closer, enhancing their emotional ties to one another. The use of such familial terms also highlights a favorite theme of Tobit's author: endogamous marriage.[30]

Tobias and Sarah Are Married (7:12-14)

Sarah is not present for her father's transaction; she appears only later, when she is called. Her father and future husband decide her eighth marriage partner without her presence or knowledge. But such a description does not align with what we see of the relationship between Sarah and her father. Raguel was anxious for Sarah to marry successfully. After digging seven graves for seven men, he looked for all possible ways that this marriage would turn out differently, and he engaged in wishful thinking by interpreting Tobias's unexpected visit to be part of God's plan.[31] Raguel directs Tobias three times (once in v. 11, twice in v. 12) to "take her" and, further, "lead her away in good health to your father" (v.12), almost as if he wanted her out from under his roof. Once she is settled in her own home, and out of his, his life surely will be simpler. Raguel perceives Sarah as his to "give away" but at the same time, he loves his daughter and wants her taken to Tobit in Nineveh safely; the two perspectives are not mutually exclusive. He makes no mention of Anna.

Edna, Sarah's mother, is not involved in the marriage negotiations either, but Raguel calls her and asks her to bring writing material to complete the transaction (7:13). Edna fetches the writing material and Raguel draws up the marriage contract—a *ketubah* (from the Hebrew term for "writing"). Marriage contracts were used throughout the ancient Near East, as attested by many Sumerian, Old Babylonian, Neo-Babylonian,

---

30. Miller, *Marriage in the Book of Tobit*, 78–79.

31. Miller, *Marriage in the Book of Tobit*, 156, points out that perhaps Raguel is like Laban who, after he hears Abraham's servant's story about his meeting with Rebekah, says, "The thing comes from the LORD; we cannot speak to you anything bad or good" (Gen 24:50).

¹²Then Raguel summoned his daughter Sarah. When she came to him he took her by the hand and gave her to Tobias, saying, "Take her to be your wife in accordance with the law and decree written in the book of Moses. Take her and bring her safely to your father. And may the God of heaven prosper your journey with his peace." ¹³Then he called her mother and told her to bring writing material; and he wrote out a copy of a marriage contract, to the effect that he gave her to him as wife according to the decree of the law of Moses. ¹⁴Then they began to eat and drink.

and Neo-Assyrian contracts and by references to them in various law codes, including that of Hammurabi.³² Tobit 7:13 is the earliest extant reference to this document among Jewish sources, although nine papyrus *ketubot* (plural), of which four are almost fully intact, from the fifth century BCE, from the Jewish colony on Elephantine (near Aswan, Egypt) have been preserved.³³ The marriage contract of Mibtahiah, identified as the daughter of Mahseiah, dates to 449 BCE. One line states: "I [c]ame to your house (and asked you) to give me your daughter Mipta(h)iah for wifehood" (נתן לאנתו).³⁴ It lists as the contracting parties her father and the bridegroom, Eshor, who pays a *mohar* (מהר) or "marriage price" of five shekels to Mahseiah, the bride's father. The groom gave the *mohar* as a gift to the father of the bride; it could be paid in labor (as does Jacob in Gen 29:18), in goods or commodities (1 Sam 18:25), or in money and is usually given back to the newly married couple.³⁵ Miptahiah brought to Eshor a dowry (including woolen clothing, a bowl and cups made of

---

32. Miller, *Marriage in the Book of Tobit*, 105 n. 339.

33. Merten Rabenau, *Studien zum Buch Tobit* (Berlin: de Gruyter, 1994), 118. There is no explicit reference to a *ketubah* in the Tanakh, though the fact that Deuteronomy 24:1-3 indicates that a man who wished to divorce his wife wrote her a "certificate of divorce" (כריתות ספר) makes it likely that a legal document binding a couple in marriage also was used but happens not to have been mentioned. Miller, *Marriage in the Book of Tobit*, 106, notes that such a perspective is "reasonable yet speculative." The Jewish Elephantine Papyri show that wives could initiate divorce, perhaps reflecting an ancient Israelite practice that was not otherwise known (see Tal Ilan, "On a Newly Published Divorce Bill from the Judaean Desert," *HTR* 89 [1996]: 195–202).

34. Bezalel Porten et al., *The Elephantine Papyri in English: Three Millennia of Cross-Cultural Continuity and Change*, 2nd rev. ed. (Atlanta: SBL, 2011), 179.

35. Porten et al., *The Elephantine Papyri in English*, 179. Porten notes here that the expression "give for wifehood" was found in Akkadian as well.

bronze, a palm-leaf box, and a papyrus-reed bed) worth 65.5 shekels.[36] The text further states that in the case of divorce, Miptahiah would retain sole ownership of these items, even if she is the one initiating it.[37] The end of the contract bears the name of the scribe, along with the signatures of the witnesses and the principals (the father of the bride, the groom, and the groom's father).[38] T. M. Lemos observes that, "as with Mesopotamian marriage contracts, the primary purpose of the Elephantine contracts is to record the dowry" and that the "chief purpose of the dowry was to prevent the bride from falling into poverty if her husband divorced her. Should the couple divorce, the woman would receive her dowry back in full."[39]

The Torah specifies that husbands were obligated to provide their wives with food, clothing, and sexual satisfaction (Exod 21:10). The protection of a wife's financial rights along with preventing divorced and widowed women from becoming impoverished is reflected in early fifth-century BCE "documents of wifehood" found among the Elephantine papyri. Such contracts were kept by the bride since they were proof that, should the marriage end or the husband die, she was to have her dowry back.[40]

Beverly Bow points out that the shorter Greek text (G1) allows for the possibility that Edna not only brought the writing materials but also signed the *ketubah* because the Greek word for "setting seals" of 7:13 is in the plural form: "Then he called [ἐκάλεσεν] Edna his wife, and taking a scroll, he wrote out a contract, and *they* set their seals to

---

36. Porten et al., *The Elephantine Papyri in English*, 180; T. M. Lemos, *Marriage Gifts and Social Change in Ancient Palestine: 1200 BCE to 200 CE* (Cambridge: Cambridge University Press, 2010), xx.

37. "Tomorrow o[r] (the) next day, should Miptahiah stand up in assembly and say: 'I hated Esh[or] my husband,' silver of hatred is on her head. She shall place upon the balance-scale and weigh out to Esh[or] silver, 6[+1] (= 7) shekels, 2 q(uarters), and all that she brought in in her hand she shall take out, from straw to string, and go away wherever she desires, without suit or without process" (lines 22–26; B. Porten and A. Yardeni, *Textbook of Aramaic Documents from Ancient Egypt: Newly Copied, Edited and Translated into Hebrew and English*, vol. 2, *Contracts* (Jerusalem: The Hebrew University, 1989), 33, cited in Lemos, *Marriage Gifts and Social Change*, 65). Among the personal archives of Dead Sea documents belonging to refugees of the Bar Kochba Revolt are two divorce bills, one written by a wife to her husband; see Tal Ilan, "On a Newly Published Divorce Bill," 195–202.

38. Lemos, *Marriage Gifts and Social Change*, 109.

39. Lemos, *Marriage Gifts and Social Change*, 110.

40. Lemos, *Marriage Gifts and Social Change*, 110.

it [ἐσφραγίσαντο]," with "they" being Raguel, Edna, and Tobias.[41] There are no extant examples, however, of women's signatures on such documents. All of the scribes and witnesses reflected in the contracts from Elephantine are male, as are the others from the ancient Near East.[42] The subsequent verse (14), in both Greek versions, is similar:

G2: "After that they began to eat and drink."

G1: "And they began to eat."

This implies that all (Sarah, Tobias, Edna, and Raguel) were present.

Verse 15, in both versions, states: "Then Raguel called Edna his wife." Bow suggests that this indicates that Edna was absent from the meal, but the use of "called" (ἐκάλεσεν) can be used to get someone's attention (such as in Tob 5:10). The implication (in both G1 and G2) is that Edna brought the scroll and then stayed for the meal, but this does not mean she signed the contract. Contra Bow, the text's statement that "they set their seals to it" probably refers to Raguel and Tobias.

A Private Moment between Edna and Sarah (7:15-16)

Calling Edna "sister" as an expression of affection, Raguel asks her to prepare the room for the couple. Perhaps he asked her rather than one of his slaves because it was a more personal touch for his daughter, on this high-stress evening, and because he knew that Edna wanted to do this. It gave this mother and daughter the opportunity to be alone. One could imagine the slave being asked to prepare the room on Sarah's first wedding night, but as the grooms began dying, with each subsequent wedding Edna took over the task, including walking her daughter into the room and trying to assuage her dread of another failed wedding night.

This palpably sad moment between mother and daughter is one of the few mother-daughter exchanges in ancient literature. In the Tanakh, the only story of a mother and daughter (-in-law) is the book of Ruth. When Naomi's husband and sons die in Moab, she decides to return to Bethlehem. Her two Moabite daughters-in-law, Orpah and Ruth, seek to accompany her, but she instructs them: " 'Go back each of you to your mother's house. May the LORD deal kindly with you, as you have dealt

41. Emphasis added. Bow makes this suggestion in "Edna," in Meyers, Craven, and Kraemer, *Women in Scripture*, 72.

42. Miller, *Marriage in the Book of Tobit*, 109.

¹⁵Raguel called his wife Edna and said to her, "Sister, get the other room ready, and take her there." ¹⁶So she went and made the bed in the room as he had told her, and brought Sarah there. She wept for her daughter. Then, wiping away the tears, she said to her, "Take courage, my daughter; the Lord of heaven grant you joy in place of your sorrow. Take courage, my daughter." Then she went out.

with the dead and with me. The Lᴏʀᴅ grant that you may find security, each of you in the house of your husband.' Then she kissed them, and they wept aloud" (Ruth 1:8-9). As with Edna and Sarah, so we see in the book of Ruth genuine, reciprocal affection between Naomi and her daughters-in-law.

The Greek "Homeric Hymn to Demeter" and Ovid's "Calliope tells of the rape of Proserpine," from *The Metamorphoses*, describe the inextricable bond between Demeter and Persephone, a mother and daughter.⁴³ Demeter's role as mother is the main emphasis, but the myth also communicates the depth of Demeter and Persephone's connection and how their experiences "both reciprocate and replicate each other."⁴⁴

The myth of Demeter and Persephone associates the theme of death with the mother-daughter relationship: Demeter is the goddess of the harvest who, when her beloved, beautiful daughter is taken by Hades, the god of the underworld, down to his realm, wanders the world seeking her daughter.⁴⁵ Her grief manifests in self-destructive behavior; she refuses food and drink and stops bathing until, in a moment of anger toward another woman, she is shaken from her depression and begins to direct her anger outward, through the control she had over the fertility of the earth and not allowing anything to grow. In this way, she persuades her husband, Zeus, to rescue Persephone. But Hades thwarts her return by placing pomegranate seeds in her mouth and so binds her to the underworld. Persephone will spend two-thirds (or, in another version, half) of the year with Demeter—and the earth bears fruit—and the other time with Hades—and the earth loses its fertility.

Just as Demeter's emotional state is affected by her daughter's life, so Edna too is distressed for her daughter. She weeps for Sarah but also

43. Ellen Handler Spitz, "Mothers and Daughters: Ancient and Modern Myths," *The Journal of Aesthetics and Art Criticism* 48 (1990): 411–20.

44. Spitz, "Mothers and Daughters," 411.

45. Spitz, "Mothers and Daughters," 412.

for herself. Edna does not know why seven bridegrooms have died, but she knows that Sarah has suffered profoundly. And now her daughter faces another wedding night. Edna wipes away Sarah's tears and finds words of comfort for her. Twice Edna tells her to "take courage" (θάρσει). Her words anticipate Raphael's encouragement of Tobias prior to his encounter with Asmodeus (6:18).

Edna knew that Sarah, upon marriage, would live with her husband's family, as she herself, and her mother before her, had done. Edna is thus caught in a trap faced by many parents: the regret over the departure of the child to become a member of a new family coupled with the joy that the child is (happily) married. Edna might have felt a sense of reprieve when the seven bridegrooms died, for now Sarah would remain home. My mother admits to having conflicted feelings any time I left home, be it to university, living overseas, or marriage. She was excited for me and wanted to see me succeed and be happy, but at the same time she lamented the geographical distance separating us. I too was filled with contradictory emotions: nervousness about moving outside of my comfort zone, excitement about the opportunity to undertake a new adventure, sadness about saying goodbye, and guilt for making my mother cry. Such separations are difficult—perhaps more for the mother than for the daughter.

Edna understood that Sarah's identity—like her own—was shaped by marriage, so she provides the needed emotional support. As Beverly Bow and George Nickelsburg observe, Edna's relationship to Sarah is "depicted only in emotional terms," as is that of Anna with Tobias.[46] The narrative depicts neither mother as giving instruction, whether practical or religious, to her child, but absence of evidence is not evidence of absence. After all, the text does indicate Deborah provided religious instruction to Tobit (1:8).

Tobias Drives Asmodeus from Sarah's Bedroom (8:1-3)

"They" of verse 8 refers to Raguel, Tobit, and Azariah (Raphael), since Edna and Sarah are already in the bedroom. There is no indication when Asmodeus enters, and he may have been there the whole time. Readers know that the couple will be safe; Tobias only needed to follow Raphael's

---

46. Beverly Bow and George W. E. Nickelsburg, "Patriarchy with a Twist: Men and Women in Tobit," in *A Feminist Companion to Tobit and Judith*, ed. Athalya Brenner-Idan and Helen Efthimiadis-Keith, FCB 2.20 (London: Bloomsbury, 2015), 60.

Tob 8:1-3

8:1When they had finished eating and drinking they wanted to retire; so they took the young man and brought him into the bedroom. 2Then Tobias remembered the words of Raphael, and he took the fish's liver and heart out of the bag where he had them and put them on the embers of the incense. 3The odor of the fish so repelled the demon that he fled to the remotest parts of Egypt. But Raphael followed him, and at once bound him there hand and foot.

instructions, which he does: "he took the fish's liver and heart out of the bag where he had them and put them on the embers of the incense" (8:2).

Fumigation—exposing a person, place, or thing to the smoke of smoldering materials—was a well-known ancient ritual used as a therapeutic treatment for ailments including epilepsy, fever, a "wandering womb," and the expulsion of demons.[47] The "wandering womb" disease was widely held by ancient Greeks to be an ailment in which the womb travelled without obstruction throughout a woman's body, seeking moisture and causing suffering depending on where it attached itself (for example, the heart, liver, brain, bladder, rectum).[48] The illness has been referred to as "hysteria," a term that stemmed from the Greek word for womb (ὑστέρα, *hystera*), though it is not a term used by ancient physicians themselves.[49] Fifth-century BCE Greek physician Hippocrates advises the following treatment: "You should fumigate [the female patient] under her nose, burning some wool and adding to the fire some asphalt, castoreum, sulfur and pitch. Rub her groin and the interior of her thighs with

47. Christopher A. Faraone, "Magical and Medical Approaches to the Wandering Womb in the Ancient Greek World," *ClAnt* 30 (2011), 2. Annie Attia, "Disease and Healing in the Book of Tobit and in Mesopotamian Medicine," in *Mesopotamian Medicine and Magic: Studies in Honor of Markham J. Geller*, ed. Strahil V. Panayotov and Ludek Vacin (Leiden: Brill, 2018), 57–58.

48. *Mul.* 2. 123, 124, 127, 137 (viii. 266. ii, 20, 272. 9, 310. 6-7 cited in Lesley Dean-Jones, *Women's Bodies in Classical Greek Science* [Oxford: Clarendon, 1994], 71).

49. Dean-Jones, *Women's Bodies in Classical Greek Science*, 70 n. 89. Dean-Jones notes how the idea of a "mobile womb" could "function in Classical Greek culture to the benefit of both men and women, ratifying the social expectations of male and female sexual conduct while allowing a forum in which women could justifiably demand that their sexual desires be fulfilled without usurping the male social role of erotic initiative" (76) since sexual intercourse was considered one of the cures to the wandering womb disease.

a very sweet-smelling unguent."[50] To prevent the womb from becoming mobile in the first place, Hippocratic doctors recommend marriage as soon as possible after menstruation begins, frequent intercourse, and bearing as many children as possible: all of these behaviors will keep the womb heavy, and immobile, with moisture.[51] The logic of the cure follows: "acrid smells in the nose force the wandering womb down and away from the upper body, while sweet unguents below entice the womb back to its proper place in the lower abdomen."[52] A similar internal logic is found in Tobit 8:2-3: the putrid smell of fish guts causes Asmodeus to run far, far away from Sarah's bedroom.

Christopher Faraone suggests that the fumigation act in Tobit might reflect an "actual ritual," since it is similar to directions found in later Greek magical handbooks (these are collections of spells, incantations, formulae, and rituals written on papyrus and dating from the second century BCE to the fifth century CE) and because it appears as well in the first- to third-century CE document Testament of Solomon.[53] Set during Solomon's building of the Jerusalem temple, the Testament of Solomon describes how Solomon discovers that a demon called Ornias has been harassing one of the construction workers. Solomon prays for help and receives it from the archangel Michael in the form of a ring through which he can trap demons. Solomon then imprisons and interrogates various demons: he finds out their activities and how to undermine their power. The demon Asmodeus, who is brought to him already bound, explains that his purpose "is to plot against the newly wedded, so that they may not know one another," and recounts that the angel Raphael thwarted his power by fumigating a fish's liver and gall and causing him to flee (T. Sol. 24). Gideon Bohak refers to Tobias's fumigation of Asmodeus as an "exorcism."[54] Although Asmodeus may not inhabit Sarah's body, the demon certainly "possesses" her.[55]

---

50. Hippocrates's *Diseases of Women* 1.221, cited in Faraone, "Magical and Medical Approaches," 5.

51. Hippocrates's *Diseases of Women* 1.221.

52. Faraone, "Magical and Medical Approaches," 5.

53. Faraone, "Magical and Medical Approaches," 15.

54. Gideon Bohak, *Ancient Jewish Magic: A History* (Cambridge: Cambridge University Press, 2008), 89–90.

55. Bohak, *Ancient Jewish Magic*, 88. Faraone disagrees: "There is no hint in the text of Tobit that Tobias speaks to Asmodeus or places him under oath and the demon is never said to inhabit Sarah's body" ("Magical and Medical Approaches," 15 n. 73).

Scholars are divided as to whether the fumigation ritual ought to be defined as falling within the ancient practices of magic or medicine.[56] Fumigation with a fish heart and liver are not attested in ancient Mesopotamian medical texts, though fish oil, lion and goat hair, and other organic materials are.[57] We could interpret Tobias's heating of the fish's liver and heart as aligning with the ancient magical practice of "an act of performative persuasion through analogy" or "persuasive analogy," in which an act attempts to have a target take on the characteristics performed in the act.[58] Artemidorus, a second-century CE professional diviner, wrote the Greek treatise *Oneirocritica* (*On the Interpretation of Dreams*), which, in 1.44, describes how to interpret a heart and liver that appear in dreams: "The heart signifies a wife if the observer is a man, but a husband if the observer is a woman on account of it having complete sway over the body . . . [a]nd the liver a child and life and anxieties."[59] Amy-Jill Levine draws attention to the fact that the liver and gall were associated with reproduction, and the fumigation was related to the idea that "heat generates sperm."[60]

The Greeks understood men's bodies to be "naturally" dry and hot, while females were moist and cool—and it was thought that "dryness" was the preferred condition. The sixth-century BCE Greek philosopher Heraclitus opines that "the dry soul is the wisest and best" (Heraclitus,

---

56. Attia, "Disease and Healing in the Book of Tobit," 43. George W.E. Nickelsburg states: "Raphael instructs Tobiah to wrestle the beast to the ground and cut out its heart and liver. These will provide the necessary magical equipment to drive off the demon and heal Tobit (6:1-8)" (*Jewish Literature between the Bible and the Mishnah*, 2nd ed. [Minneapolis: Fortress, 2005], 31); Eileen Schuller refers to the fumigation of the fish's liver and heart and the fleeing of Asmodeus to Egypt as a "magical rite" ("Tobit" in *Women's Bible Commentary*, ed. Carol A. Newsom and Sharon H. Ringe, 3rd ed. [Louisville: Westminster John Knox, 2012], 381).

57. Attia, "Disease and Healing in the Book of Tobit," 58.

58. H. S. Versnel, "The Poetics of the Magical Charm: An Essay in the Power of Words," in *Magic and Ritual in the Ancient World*, ed. P. Mirecki and M. Meyer (Leiden: Brill, 2002), 123.

59. Amy-Jill Levine, "Diaspora as Metaphor: Bodies and Boundaries in the Book of Tobit," in *Jews and Judaism: Essays in Honor of, and in Dialogue with, A. Thomas Kraabel*, ed. J. A. Overman and R. S. MacLennan (Atlanta: Scholars Press, 1992), 116; Daniel E. Harris-McCoy, *Artemidorus' Oneirocritica: Text, Translation, & Commentary* (Oxford: Oxford University Press, 2012), 97.

60. Levine, "Diaspora as Metaphor," 116; Levine points to Aristotle, *Generation of Animals* 717b24 and 717a5, and notes that "the emission of semen in men is due 'to the penis being heated by its movement;' further the final concoction or 'maturation' of semen occurs through the heating of copulation."

On Nature 74).[61] Faraone observes that "ancient Greek animal-herders thought that one must artificially heat up and dry out the females of the herd in order to encourage them to mate" and that this practice might be behind the magical spells whose goal is to heat up the female through the burning of "herbs or ousia (bits of hair, fingernails, or garment threads used to target the victim)."[62] The first-century BCE Roman poet Vergil notes that horse breeders would not give mares water and food, thinking that this made them "thirsty for seed" (*Georg.* 2.130), and the third-century CE Roman author Aelian (Claudius Aelianus) advises the rubbing of salt and sodium carbonate on the genitals of female goats and horses in order to ready them for mating (*Nat. an.* 9.48).[63] Another possible purpose for the fumigation ritual in Tobit was to prepare Sarah for mating—and getting pregnant.

Despite the possible connections with behaviors associated with magical practice—a practice typically condemned—Raphael's instructions to Tobias are not presented as prohibited, wrong, or unusual. On the contrary, it is precisely the burning of the fish's organs and the binding of the demon that lead to positive outcomes.

Raphael's binding of Asmodeus also has associations with magical rituals. The term "to bind" is used in curse tablets found throughout the Roman Empire; figures on such tablets show the target of the curse with arms and legs bound together.[64] The binding of a being—whether a demon or a human being—signified the efficacy of the curse. "Binding" language and imagery appear on many of the over seventy earthenware magic bowls from Sassanid Empire Babylon (fourth to sixth century CE) bearing incantations and protective spells written in Babylonian Jewish Aramaic.[65] Several bowls are illustrated on the inside bottom with bound figurines. Inscriptions refer explicitly to the binding of the spirits; for example, Bowl 8 reads: "Bound are the demons, sealed are the devs [demons], bound are the idol spirits, sealed are the liliths, male and female,

61. George T. W. Patrick and Ingram Bywater, *Heraclitus of Ephesus* (Chicago: Argonaut, 1969), 102.

62. Christopher A. Faraone, *Ancient Greek Love Magic* (Cambridge, MA: Harvard University Press, 1999), 164.

63. Aelian, *On the Characteristics of Animals*, trans. A. F. Scholfield (London: William Heinemann, 1959), 267.

64. John G. Gager, *Curse Tablets and Binding Spells from the Ancient World* (New York: Oxford University Press, 1992). Fritz Graf, "Die Religion der Romer: Eine Einfuhrung; Magic in the Roman World: Pagans, Jews, and Christians," *JR* 83 (2003): 496–99.

65. Joseph Naveh and Shaul Shaked, *Amulets and Magic Bowls: Aramaic Incantations of Late Antiquity* (Jerusalem: Magnes, 1985).

bound is the evil eye."[66] In the "Book of the Watchers" of 1 Enoch, written around the same time as Tobit, God instructs the archangel Raphael to bind the fallen angel Azazel "and cast him into the darkness" (10:6).[67]

Additional details found in Tobit 8:1-3 suggest magical practice. According to 8:3, Asmodeus flees to Egypt, a place linked with magic in antiquity. Robert K. Ritner notes that "magical techniques" were associated with "all Egyptian 'religious' practices from the earliest periods through the Coptic era (from the third to seventh centuries CE), influencing as well the Greco-Egyptian magical papyri."[68] The Talmud also notes the connection between Egypt and magic: "Of the ten measures of witchcraft that came to the world, nine were given to Egypt" (b. Qidd. 49b). Linking Egypt with magical practice was an attempt to undercut that nation's power and status, and the association was made by those who considered Egyptian practices to be "other" and threatening.

Ancient literature frequently associates women with magic. Those accused of magic were perceived to be socially subversive, but the accused might have had a very different view of their practices.[69] The first-century BCE sage Hillel asserts: "The more flesh the more worms; the more possessions the more care; the more women the more witchcrafts" (m. 'Abot 2:7). The Babylonian Talmud offers the opinion that "the daughters of Israel freely indulged in witchcraft" (b. 'Erub. 64b). Exodus 22:18 states, "You shall not permit a female sorcerer to live"; the Hebrew word for "witch" or "sorcerer," מכשפה, is in the feminine form. When women were deemed threatening, labeling them as witches or practitioners of magic was an effective means of undermining their social power.[70]

There is no accusation in Tobit, however, that Tobias or Raphael practice magic. The means by which Asmodeus is disposed are presented as legitimate actions because of the identity of the practitioners. Gender matters: two males perform the rites. And it is the angel Raphael who gives instructions for how to conduct the ritual.

---

66. Naveh and Shaked, *Amulets and Magic Bowls*, 73–75.

67. George W. E. Nickelsburg and James C. VanderKam, *1 Enoch: A New Translation* (Minneapolis: Fortress, 2004), 28.

68. Robert Kriech Ritner, *The Mechanics of Ancient Egyptian Magical Practice* (Chicago: University of Chicago, 2008), 2. Ritner notes, "The Western dichotomy of 'religion vs. magic' is thus inappropriate for describing Egyptian practice."

69. Michele Murray, "The Magical Female in Graeco-Roman Rabbinic Literature," *Religion & Theology: A Journal of Contemporary Religious Discourse* 14 (2007): 289.

70. Murray, "The Magical Female," 284–309.

Tobias and Sarah Pray Together, and Then Sleep (8:4-9a)

Frank Zimmerman, Carey Moore, and Joseph Fitzmyer are among commentators who find verse 4 out of place: why would Raguel and Edna stay in the room so long?[71] Zimmerman suggests moving it between verses 1 and 2 to show Sarah's parents leaving prior to the ritual and suggests that the misplacement of the verse is either the result of "a later storyteller's delicacy or shyness" about Tobias and Sarah's being in bed together or because of a scribal error, since the word "bedroom is found in verses 1 and 4."[72] No textual evidence supports Zimmermann's argument. Nor do I see a problem with the present setting of verse 4. There is no reason why Sarah's parents would not have watched the burning of the fish organs. Perhaps these modern commentators are uncomfortable with a bedroom scene.

TRANSLATION MATTERS

In the Vulgate's translation of 6:14-15, Raphael advises Tobias to defer the consummation of his marriage with Sarah until after they have spent three days in prayer. Jerome's translation of 8:4-7 reads, "Then Tobiah exhorted the virgin and said to her, 'Sarah, get up; let us pray to God today, tomorrow, and the next day, because for three nights we are joined to God. When the third night is over, we shall be united in wedlock. For we are indeed children of saints, and we cannot be joined together as pagans are who know not God.'" Chastity, a theme found throughout Jewish Hellenistic literature, is reflected also in 8:7, where Tobias insists that he is acting from sincerity rather than lust.[73] But no other ancient version of the book, independent of the Vulgate, contains the detail of a three-day delay. The Vulgate offers, in the words of commentator Carey A. Moore, "a pious addition by the celibate Jerome."[74] In his translation of Judith, Jerome likewise accentuates Judith's chastity (Jdt 15:11; 16:26) and devotion to prayer.[75]

---

71. Fitzmyer, *Tobit*, notes that the sequence "is a bit puzzling" (240), while for Moore, *Tobit*, verse 4 "seems logically out of place" (237).

72. Frank Zimmermann, *The Book of Tobit* (New York: Harper and Brothers, 1958), 91–92.

73. Lawrence Wills, *The Jewish Novel in the Ancient World* (Ithaca: Cornell University Press, 1995); Levine, "Tobit," 23.

74. Moore, *Tobit*, 244.

75. Vincent T. M. Skemp, "Learning by Example: *Exempla* in Jerome's Translations and Revisions of Biblical Books," *VC* 65 (2011): 267–72.

Tob 8:4-9a

4When the parents had gone out and shut the door of the room, Tobias got out of bed and said to Sarah, "Sister, get up, and let us pray and implore our Lord that he grant us mercy and safety." 5So she got up, and they began to pray and implore that they might be kept safe. Tobias began by saying,

"Blessed are you, O God of our ancestors,
and blessed is your name in all generations forever.
Let the heavens and the whole creation bless you forever.
6You made Adam, and for him you made his wife Eve
as a helper and support.

From the two of them the human race has sprung.
You said, "It is not good that the man should be alone;
let us make a helper for him like himself."
7I now am taking this kinswoman of mine,
not because of lust,
but with sincerity.
Grant that she and I may find mercy
and that we may grow old together."
8And they both said, "Amen, Amen." 9Then they went to sleep for the night.

Neither Raguel nor Edna knows if the ritual was efficacious; however, there is no indication that they are aware of the existence of Asmodeus in the first place. Given the association of heat, as well as the heart and the liver, with reproduction, plus the fact that Raphael does not tell Tobias to explain the ritual,[76] the parents could have understood that his action, while unusual, was appropriate given the circumstances.

Tobias's prayer (8:5) draws a parallel between his marriage and that of Adam and Eve; this reference and 1 Timothy 2:13 are the only two biblical references to the primordial couple outside of Genesis. The prayer implies that God was just as involved in the bringing together of Sarah with Tobias as he was in the creation of Eve for Adam; it confirms Raphael's statement that Sarah "was set apart [μεμερισμένη] for you before the world was made" (6:18). The word μεμερισμένη is a passive participle that is a "theological passive," indicating that God is the subject of the action of "setting apart" or "allotting." This sentiment is also found in 7:11 when Raguel says to Tobias, "it has been decreed from heaven that she should be given to you [ἐκ τοῦ οὐρανοῦ κέκριταί σοι δοθῆναι]." God isn't mentioned explicitly in this statement (though "heaven" [οὐρανοῦ]

---

76. Raphael's only other instructions to Tobias are to pray with Sarah in "imploring the Lord of heaven that mercy and safety may be granted to you" (6:18).

is), but κέκριταί (decreed) is another theological passive, indicating that God ruled on Tobias and Sarah being together.

Our narrator draws from the second of the two different Genesis accounts of the creation of human beings, and the choice reflects his understanding of gender relations. Genesis 1:26-27 describes how man and woman are created simultaneously "in the image of God," hence they are equals. In the second account, Genesis 2:7, 18, 21-24, the man is created first out of the earth, and the woman is then created out of his "side" (צלע, NRSV: "rib"). The Hebrew describing their relationship in Genesis 2:18, 20, עזר כנגדו, literally means "an equal helper," which does not convey a status differential.[77] Yet the second story is used in later texts to justify men's superiority and control over women. For example, in the New Testament, 1 Timothy 2:13-14 uses it to underpin the argument that women ought to keep silent and not take on church leadership roles, and 1 Corinthians 11:8-10 employs it to justify women's having "a symbol of authority" on their heads. Genesis Rabbah 18:2 midrash (rabbinic interpretation of biblical texts), written between 300 and 500 CE, present Rabbi Yehoshua of Sikhnin, in the name of Rabbi Levi, describing how God contemplated which part of the man's body would be used to create the woman, and after considering other parts and their potential negative repercussions (e.g., not from the head, "that she not be swell-headed"; not from the eye, "that she not be painting her eyes with red [to entice men]"; "not from the hand, that she not be touching [things that are not hers and steal them]," etc.) decides on the man's side because "even when he stands naked, that part [i.e., the rib] is covered," in the hopes that women would be modest.[78] According to the rabbis, however, the woman ends up manifesting all of the negative traits that God was trying to avoid (she is not humble, not modest, not honest, etc.). As Anne Lapidus Lerner points out, "This midrash presents an essentialist, misogynistic catalogue of women . . . [and] God is depicted as seeing woman prone to unacceptable behavior."[79]

---

77. Carol Meyers, "Eve," in *Women in Scripture: A Dictionary of Named and Unnamed Women in the Hebrew Bible, the Apocryphal/Deuterocanonical Books, and the New Testament*, ed. Carol Meyers, Toni Craven, and Ross S. Kraemer (Grand Rapids, MI: Eerdmans, 2000), 80-81.

78. See discussion in Judith Romney Wegner, "The Image and Status of Women in Classical Rabbinic Judaism," in *Jewish Women in Historical Perspective*, ed. Judith R. Baskin (Detroit: Wayne State University Press, 1991), 79.

79. Anne Lapidus Lerner, *Eternally Eve: Images of Eve in the Hebrew Bible, Midrash, and Modern Jewish Poetry* (Waltham, MA: Brandeis University Press, 2007), 45.

In Tobit 8:6, the narrator adds to the quotation from Genesis 2:18, "I will make him a helper," the word "support" (στήριγμα), thereby reinforcing the unequal relationship. As Alice Ogden Bellis notes, this small but significant addition "indicates his understanding of gender relations" and corresponds with Tobias's saying in 8:7: "I now am taking this kinswoman of mine, not because of lust, but with sincerity."[80] Tobias's prayer, supposedly offered by *both* Tobias and Sarah (8:4-5), and to which both answer "Amen, Amen," does not state that "we take one another" but provides Tobias's perspective alone.

Self-control and chastity are themes in other Jewish-Hellenistic writings. For example, the Testament of Joseph presents Joseph as epitomizing chaste, disciplined behavior in response to the enticing charms of "the Egyptian woman" (3:1, 6, etc.), and Rachel, in the Testament of Issachar, displays self-restraint when it comes to sexual pleasure ("She despised intercourse with a man and chose continency" [2:1]).[81] The Greek version of Esther, a translation of the Hebrew text of Esther for Greek-speaking Jews of the second or first century BCE, has the beautiful and righteous Esther say to God, "You have knowledge of all things, and you know that I hate the splendor of the wicked and abhor the bed of the uncircumcised and of any alien" (14:15). Susanna, like Esther, is also beautiful and pious—she is educated by her parents "according to the law of Moses" (1:3)—and, falsely accused of adultery by two elders, proclaims her innocence. "The Lord heard her cry" (1:44) and saves her through "a young man named Daniel"; the two elders are put to death. In the widow Judith, as with Susanna and Esther, the qualities of piety and beauty combine (Jdt 8:7-8), and chastity too, for "[m]any desired to marry her, but she gave herself to no man all the days of her life after her husband Manasseh died" (16:22). One way to understand the emphasis on self-discipline practiced by Jewish characters—men and women—is that it shows personal control within a diasporic setting.

---

80. Alice Ogden Bellis, "Eve in the Apocryphal/Deuterocanonical Books," in *Women in Scripture: A Dictionary of Named and Unnamed Women in the Hebrew Bible, the Apocryphal/Deuterocanonical Books, and the New Testament*, ed. Carol Meyers, Toni Craven, and Ross S. Kraemer (Grand Rapids: Eerdmans, 2000), 82.

81. Richard I. Pervo, "The Testament of Joseph and Greek Romance," in *Studies on the Testament of Joseph*, ed. George W. E. Nickelsburg (Missoula: Scholars Press, 1975), 15–28; Marinus de Jonge, "Rachel's Virtuous Behavior in the *Testament of Issachar*," in *Greeks, Romans, and Christians: Essays in Honor of Abraham J. Malherbe*, ed. David L. Balch, Everett Ferguson, and Wayne A. Meeks (Minneapolis: Fortress, 1990), 340.

Sarah's double "Amens" in chorus with Tobias (8:8) are the only words that she speaks, other than her prayer in chapter 3. Irene Nowell argues that Sarah "must not be regarded simply as a pawn in the action," given that "her existence is crucial for the action of the story."[82] Indeed, Sarah is hardly docile: she beats her slaves, she prays for help—even using the imperative with God—and she has the resilience to endure the deaths of seven husbands and to stand in marriage to an eighth groom. She might not know the demonic cause of her misery, but Sarah is a survivor. And she has the fortitude to hope, along with Tobias, not only that he too will be a survivor, and still be alive in the morning, but that they may "grow old together" (8:7).

Raguel Secretly Digs a Grave for Tobias (8:9b-18)

Sarah's father discreetly, and, for readers, humorously, prepares a grave for what he expects will be the next dead groom. The digging is a communal activity: Raguel calls on his household slaves (τοὺς οἰκέτας) to do this manual labor; he is present, probably supervising rather than lifting a shovel himself. Our narrator, consistent with so many other texts, overlooks these enslaved persons and gives no attention to what they might be thinking and whether they know why the men are dying.

Raguel's motivation for digging the grave is that he does not wish to "become an object of ridicule and derision" (8:10) if yet another son-in-law dies. Raguel's wealth would have garnered him power, but he is nonetheless worried about losing it. All of these dead sons-in-law could damage his reputation. So he accompanies his slaves to see for himself that they do a good job.

Having honor in one's community meant that one was perceived by others with esteem. Anthropologists refer to ancient Mediterranean society as "agonistic," from the Greek words ἀγωνιστής (contestant, rival) and ἀγών (contest, struggle).[83] Honor and shame were fundamental cultural values within ancient Mediterranean culture for both men and women. The notion that women embodied shame, in the form of passivity, rather than honor and that women were concerned—and of concern—only with regard to the honor of men has been firmly

---

82. Nowell, "The Book of Tobit," 147, cited in Moore, *Tobit*, 239.

83. Rick F. Talbott, *Jesus, Paul, and Power: Rhetoric, Ritual, and Metaphor in Ancient Mediterranean Christianity* (Eugene, OR: Cascade Books, 2010), 104.

But Raguel arose and called his slaves to him, and they went and dug a grave, [10]for he said, "It is possible that he will die and we will become an object of ridicule and derision." [11]When they had finished digging the grave, Raguel went into his house and called his wife, [12]saying, "Send one of the slaves and have her go in to see if he is alive. But if he is dead, let us bury him without anyone knowing it." [13]So they sent the slave, lit a lamp, and opened the door; and she went in and found them sound asleep together. [14]Then the slave came out and informed them that he was alive and that nothing was wrong. [15]So they blessed the God of heaven, and Raguel said,

"Blessed are you, O God, with
every pure blessing;
let all your chosen ones bless
you.
Let them bless you forever.
[16]Blessed are you because you
have made me glad.
It has not turned out as I
expected,
but you have dealt with us
according to your great
mercy.
[17]Blessed are you because you
had compassion
on two only children.
Be merciful to them, O Master,
and keep them safe;
bring their lives to fulfillment
in happiness and mercy."
[18]Then he ordered his slaves to fill in the grave before daybreak.

disproved.[84] Women could earn honor: Plutarch tells of Pieria, a woman who successfully negotiated on her peoples' behalf with a rival city, and how "both cities repute and honor Pieria" (*Mulier. virt.* 254B), and another woman, Polycrite, was "confronted by citizens who came to meet her, welcoming her with joy and garlands and giving expression to their admiration for her" (*Mulier. virt.* 254E).[85] As already noted, Judith acquired more honor through her bravery than her husband possessed in his lifetime.

In contrast to Tobit's burial of dead Israelite bodies, Raguel digs a grave before he has a corpse.[86] There is further irony in the grave being prepared for Tobias, an only child concerned about burying his own parents (6:15). There is macabre humor also in the idea that Raguel believes that

84. For example, Unni Wikan ("Shame and Honour: A Contestable Pair," *Man* 19 [1984]: 635–52) argues against the notion that honor is fundamentally a male quality; F. Gerald Downing, "'Honor' among Exegetes," *CBQ* 61 (1999): 53–73.

85. Quotes from Zeba Crook, "Honor, Shame, and Social Status Revisited," *JBL* 128 (2009): 605.

86. Levine, "Tobit," 23.

he has successfully hidden the deaths of Sarah's seven previous grooms and that, when a slave is sent in, if she finds an eighth one, he should be buried "without anyone knowing it" (v. 12). The slaves knew about the deaths, as did Sarah and Edna. The fact that young men were entering Raguel's house but not exiting it surely would have been noticed by the neighbors. Sarah's slaves have already shamed her for the deaths (3:7-9), and Tobias (in Nineveh!) had "heard that she already has been married to seven husbands and that they died in the bridal chamber" (6:14), so the "secret" that Raguel has been trying to contain is no secret at all. None of this would be helpful for finding a partner for Sarah—her reputation was at risk here too.

Tobias survives the first night of his married life thanks to Raphael's remedy. Asmodeus, the demon, is banished, but Raguel and Edna know nothing of this. The slave reports that all is well, "So *they* [i.e., Raguel and Edna] blessed the God of heaven" (v. 15). The rest of the prayer is Raguel's alone. He thanks God for his mercy: first for himself ("you have made me glad"), and then for the couple, "two only children" (δύο μονογενεῖς; v. 17). Fitzmyer points out how having only one child was "a mark of special favor," reflected in the deep sadness expressed in the Tanakh when that child's life is either threatened or taken (e.g., Gen 22's story of Abraham and Isaac; the story of Jephthah's daughter in Judg 11:34-40; Zech 12:10).[87]

Raguel's comment in 8:15, "let all your chosen ones [οἱ ἐκλεκτοί σου] bless you," refers to fellow Israelites, God's chosen people (e.g., Deut 7:6; 1 Chr 16:13; Ps 105:6, 43). The idea of being a "chosen people" was not unique to the Israelites; other ancient peoples thought themselves to have national deities as well (e.g., the nineth-century BCE Mesha inscription in 3b-4 states that a sanctuary was built for Kemosh, the national god of Moab, in the capital city of Karchoh).[88] Christians make the same claim (1 Pet 2:9). Being "chosen" by a deity meant having a distinct relationship with that deity and also meant having a special identity. Such a relationship motivated interest in endogamy, since one would want to develop families with fellow members. The idea of election is beneficial for group cohesion and identity, since all members of the group share the responsibility for serving the deity that has chosen them.

87. Joseph A. Fitzmyer, *Tobit* (Berlin: de Gruyter, 2003), 250.

88. K. A. D. Smelik, "The Inscription of King Mesha (2.23)," in *The Context of Scripture*, vol. 2: *Monumental Inscriptions from the Biblical World*, ed. William W. Hallo (Leiden: Brill, 2002), 137.

Early the next morning, Raguel orders his slaves to fill in the grave "before daybreak" (8:18). Rather than hiding the death of another groom, he seeks to hide his morbid calculation. Raguel seems more worried about what his neighbors will think about him than the emotional state of his wife or his daughter.

Preparations for the Wedding (8:19-21)

Finally, something positive happens in this family, and the celebration is to last fourteen days, double the usual time of a wedding celebration (Gen 29:27; Judg 14:12; Tob 11:18). Raguel insists that Tobias stay "eating and drinking with *me*" (8:20, emphasis added), not *us*.[89] Naomi Jacobs suggests that because Edna is not described as eating of the wedding feast of her own daughter, her secondary role is reinforced.[90] But this is not necessarily the case. The author might not note the women's presence at the table. Or, maybe—and this is my preference—Edna is with other women instead, celebrating the occasion together and sharing their own wedding party, just as Queen Vashti throws the women their own drinking party (Greek Esther 1:9).

When Raguel asks Edna to bake "many" loaves of bread (8:19), we hear the echoes of Abraham asking Sarah to make the three loaves of bread for the three strangers to their tent in Mamre (Gen 18:6). A scriptural connection (with Israelite matriarch Sarah) elevates Edna's seemingly simple act. Edna is the caretaker of her family, supporter of her husband and daughter, preparer of Sarah's marital bedroom, baker of bread for the wedding celebration. Because the family was wealthy, Edna would have been assisted by slaves. Perhaps Edna found preparing food for a celebration of her only child's wedding particularly meaningful and bittersweet.

Cooking and baking, as well as the slaughter of animals (which Raguel does in 7:9) in a Hellenistic Jewish family involved the observance of dietary laws (*kashrut*). These laws, found in Leviticus 11 and Deuteronomy 14:2-21, stipulate which foods are acceptable for consumption, which are to be avoided, and how to cook the acceptable foods. Tobit identifies himself as the *only* one among his tribe to follow *kashrut* laws

89. Naomi S. S. Jacobs, "Seen and Heard, but Hardly Eating: Female Consumption in the Book of Tobit," in Brenner-Idan and Efthimiadis-Keith, *A Feminist Companion to Tobit and Judith*, 90.

90. Jacobs, "Seen and Heard, but Hardly Eating," 96–97.

¹⁹After this he asked his wife to bake many loaves of bread; and he went out to the herd and brought two steers and four rams and ordered them to be slaughtered. So they began to make preparations. ²⁰Then he called for Tobias and swore on oath to him in these words: "You shall not leave here for fourteen days, but shall stay here eating and drinking with me; and you shall cheer up my daughter, who has been depressed. ²¹Take at once half of what I own and return in safety to your father; the other half will be yours when my wife and I die. Take courage, my child. I am your father and Edna is your mother, and we belong to you as well as to your wife now and forever. Take courage, my child."

(1:10-11)—though it is difficult to understand how he could do so without Anna and Tobias eating the same food as he and with Anna being central to food preparation. Tobit's eating in accordance with laws of *kashrut* is meant to demonstrate his righteousness, although it is likely that most other Jews observed these laws as well; dietary concerns are a major means of preserving ethnic identity. Jacobs interprets the lack of mention of whether either Anna or Tobias observed the food laws to signify that their behavior—and their righteousness—does not matter.[91] This strikes me as an overstatement. The text does not state that Raguel, Edna, and Sarah followed *kashrut* laws, but a typical Israelite family would have done so, since it would surely matter if they did not.

Raguel specifies that his daughter needs cheering up because she "has been depressed"—or "in distress, great pain, grieved, afflicted" (κατωδυνωμένην, 8:20). We see this term, which is always associated with ψυχή ("soul, life"), in Judges 18:25; 1 Samuel 1:10, 22:2; 30:6; and 2 Kings 4:27. There are at least eight reasons why Sarah's soul is grieved: her seven dead grooms, and the fact that she is about to leave home. To this point, only Edna appears cognizant of how everything that has transpired in her life has affected Sarah. Now we realize that Raguel too sees his daughter and her pain.

In the same way that Edna twice tells Sarah to "take courage" (θάρσει), so Raguel says the same thing, also two times, to Tobias. Perhaps Tobias

---

91. Jacobs, "Seen and Heard, but Hardly Eating," 87: "[F]or Tobit, the official narrator, it simply does not matter whether or not Hannah and Tobiah are eating Gentile food." But there is no indication that this is what they did, and absence of evidence is not evidence of absence. It makes more sense to presume that they followed kosher laws than that they did not.

is becoming the son Raguel never had. The invitation to eat and drink "with me" (v. 20) suggests that Raguel wished to bond with Tobias.

Raguel offers to Tobias "half of what I own" (v. 21)—for him to take immediately—suggesting that Raguel and Edna are wealthy enough to live on half of their riches. At such a goodbye the emotions run high, and Raguel's statement that he and Edna are now as much Tobias's parents as they are Sarah's is a confirmation of the tight family relationship (the same is said of Anna and Tobit for Sarah in 10:12).

There is a disconnect between these expressions of close family connections and Tobias's lack of thought for his own parents who might be worrying about him; after all, he has delayed his departure for home by two weeks. If Tobias was too distracted, Raguel and Edna, who feel deep love for their daughter, could have been sensitive enough to send word to Anna and Tobit that their son is alive and well. Maybe they were trying to replace Anna and Tobit. Or they were so overwhelmed (and relieved) by the success—finally—of Sarah's eighth marriage that they were absorbed only by this. No attention is paid to Raphael during the wedding celebration—his presence does not matter anymore.

Tobit from a Postcolonial Cameroonian Perspective

Aspects of the Jewish culture and society presented by the author of Tobit are similar to what I experienced as a young boy growing up in Cameroon. My life experience has therefore been instrumental in shaping my understanding of the roles played by the various protagonists in this sacred text.

Postcolonial Cameroon was a patriarchal society and conformity was the order of the day. Conforming to the "masculine stereotype" was essential for Cameroonian males. Doing chores such as cleaning the home or helping out in the kitchen were regarded as demasculinizing.

The process of conforming created a void in the community that was taken up by women. Their tender and loving kindness nurtured bonds of respect and understanding. As the children matured the bond became stronger, nudging men further to edge of the family unit. Women became confidants of their children, and this empowered them. The irony in all of this is that although the society of my childhood was patriarchal, the matriarchs welded potent soft power.

Like men in postcolonial Cameroon, Tobit is about keeping up appearances. He was driven by the desire to appear righteous and maintaining a "pious status" in public was a duty to which he devoted his life. So he made bold claims; audiences and circumstances defined what he said, and he was prone to ineptitude.

Early in the text, Tobit's righteousness is put to the test by a series of unfortunate events; he lost his sight and the ability to provide for his family. His sorrows were compounded by his wife's being voted "employee of the year." He implodes under the weight of his wife's success and accuses her of theft. Unfortunately, this was not his only flaw; he also had a large ego.

Without much thought or consideration, he commissions his son Tobias to travel to Rages on a dangerous and unnecessary mission. Deception, secrecy, and dishonesty are traits common to the men in the story, and they use the façade of "masculine superiority" to hide or disguise their inherent deficiencies.

The sapiential character of this book is predicated on contributions made by women. Although society considered them inferior, they had the strength of character and presence of mind to question, interrogate, or challenge their spouses. Anna does not take the accusation of theft lightly; she retorted by questioning the very essence of Tobit's spirituality, "Where are your acts of charity? Where are your righteous deeds? These things are known about you" (2:14b). She questioned her husband's recklessness regarding their son's mission to Rages. She exposed its vainness, insinuating that it was driven by his selfish desire to finance his funeral arrangements and not to provide for his family.

This sacred text might have been written in an era when the society was androcentric, one that belittled the value and contribution of women—but reading between the lines it becomes apparent that the women were more influential than the men gave them credit for. Women were saviors of men and were faithful to the tenets of Judaism (5:20): "[T]he life that is given to us by the Lord is enough for us."

Gabriel Kwenga

Tobias Directs Azariah to Retrieve the Silver (9:1-6a)

Tobias, all grown up, now orders Azariah, whom he addresses as an equal "brother" and not, as he first did, as "young man" (5:4, 7, 10), to retrieve Tobit's silver. In directing Azariah to take camels and servants, Tobias is already claiming Raguel's property. He seems to want to make a show of wealth to Gabael by sending so many slaves and camels—perhaps he feared that Gabael would not give him the silver, so felt the need to impress him.

Tob 9:1-6a

9:1Then Tobias called Raphael and said to him, 2"Brother Azariah, take four servants and two camels with you and travel to Rages. Go to the home of Gabael, give him the bond, get the money, and then bring him with you to the wedding celebration. 4For you know that my father must be counting the days, and if I delay even one day I will upset him very much. 3You are witness to the oath Raguel has sworn, and I cannot violate his oath." 5So Raphael with the four servants and two camels went to Rages in Media and stayed with Gabael. Raphael gave him the bond and informed him that Tobit's son Tobias had married and was inviting him to the wedding celebration. So Gabael got up and counted out to him the money bags, with their seals intact; then they loaded them on the camels. 6In the morning they both got up early and went to the wedding celebration.

Tobias finally thinks of his father and how he "must be counting the days" (9:4). In stating this to Azariah, Tobias justifies why he cannot go himself to collect the money, as this would delay his return home further. He makes no reference to his mother, Anna, whom readers know is also worried about her son's well-being (5:18-20; as well as in 10:4-7). Tobias knew that Azariah had met and interacted with Tobit, so mentioning only his father was logical, but maybe he feared that telling Azariah that he wanted to return home to his mother would make him seem juvenile. The irony of the fourteen-day celebration is revealed: the longer the feast lasts, the longer Tobit (and Anna) remain worried about their only child. The next chapter exposes this anxiety (10:1-3).

Raphael, rather than Tobias, fulfills the original purpose of the journey: the retrieval of Tobit's silver from Gabael. Moore notes that "commentators rightly complain" about the part of Tobit describing the retrieval of silver as seeming ancillary, since "now married to an heiress, Tobiah no longer needed the money."[92] The scene reminds me of 5:19-20, where Anna challenges Tobit's decision to send Tobias away. Her central argument was that the silver was not the most important thing. Anna's perspective ultimately triumphs: retrieving Tobit's silver *wasn't* the most important thing. The angel Raphael arranges the more important purpose: marriage to Sarah.

92. Moore, *Tobit*, 248–49.

When they came into Raguel's house they found Tobias reclining at table. He sprang up and greeted Gabael, who wept and blessed him with the words, "Good and noble son of a father good and noble, upright and generous! May the Lord grant the blessing of heaven to you and your wife, and to your wife's father and mother. Blessed be God, for I see in Tobias the very image of my cousin Tobit."

Azariah Brings Gabael Back to the Wedding Celebration, and Gabael Meets Tobias (9:6b)

Gabael's blessing parallels the blessing that Raguel pronounced when Tobias and Raphael first appeared on his and Edna's doorstep in 7:7: "Blessings on you, my child, son of a good and noble father." Gabael remarks on how much Tobias looks like Tobit, just as Raguel stated to Edna (7:2). In contrast to Raguel, though, Gabael does not call Tobias a child; he refers to him as his father's son. Tobias is now a married man and a full adult who resembles his father in looks as well as (some aspects only, hopefully) in character (9:6b). Gabael, taking on a paternal role, blesses the newlyweds, making explicit mention of "your wife, and to your wife's father and mother." The only woman in Tobias's immediate family whom Gabael does not bless is Anna. Perhaps Gabael has not met her, or maybe his focus is on his own family's natal rather than marital relations.

Tobit 10

The Good Mother

C hapter 10 returns to the Tobiad home. We have not heard about life in the home of Anna and Tobit for almost five chapters, and what we find is not good. In contrast to the festive activities in Ecbatana, grief and despair mark Tobit and Anna's home as they wait for and worry about their absent son from whom they have not heard one word. The chapter prompts remarks from a feminist perspective on worry, a mother's anguish on losing a child, bereavement, parental expectations, goodbyes, how the means of addressing someone matters, when women are not invited to an important meeting, and the absence of women in modern spheres of life.

Tobit and Anna Worry about How Long Tobias Has Been Away (10:1-7a)

Tobit worries about why Tobias is not returning within the anticipated time frame. Joseph Fitzmyer suggests that he "is concerned not so much about the life and well-being of Tobiah as he is about the lack of success in the journey that his son has undertaken and in securing the money that he had left in Rages."[1] Fitzmyer overly stresses Tobit's

---

1. Joseph A. Fitzmyer, *Tobit* (Berlin: de Gruyter, 2003), 261.

10:1Now, day by day, Tobit kept counting how many days Tobias would need for going and for returning. And when the days had passed and his son did not appear, 2he said, "Is it possible that he has been detained? Or that Gabael has died, and there is no one to give him the money?" 3And he began to worry. 4His wife Anna said, "My child has perished and is no longer among the living." And she began to weep and mourn for her son, saying, 5"Woe is me, my child, the light of my eyes, that I let you make the journey." 6But Tobit kept saying to her, "Be quiet and stop worrying, my dear; he is all right. Probably something unexpected has happened there. The man who went with him is trustworthy and is one of our own kin. Do not grieve for him, my dear; he will soon be here." 7She answered him, "Be quiet yourself! Stop trying to deceive me! My child has perished." She would rush out every day and watch the road her son had taken, and would heed no one. When the sun had set she would go in and mourn and weep all night long, getting no sleep at all.

economic concerns and thereby unwittingly plays into the anti-Semitic stereotype stemming from the Middle Ages, when the church banned Jews from owning land and from earning a living through most trades except as money-lenders, that depicts Jews as avaricious. Tobit muses about whether Gabael was not able to give his son the money in the context of trying to understand why Tobias has not yet arrived home. This worried father cannot countenance the possibility that the delay is due to the injury or death of his son, so he looks for other reasons for his delay.

Anna is worried about Tobias too. But unlike her husband, she is convinced that Tobias has met a catastrophic end. Anna weeps, mourns, and loses sleep. Yet every day she hurries to the road to look for her son. In the chaotic diaspora, family members could go missing or have to hide themselves away or flee, as did Tobit (Tob 1:19).

The anguish of the grieving mother is poignantly expressed in Suse Lowenstein's sculptural work *Dark Elegy*. Lowenstein's son was murdered in the 1988 bombing of Pan Am Flight 103 by two Libyan nationals, and initially she made a sculpture of herself, "not only at that moment of hearing the heart-breaking news, but also in varying positions of grief, rage and hopelessness."[2] When other women who had lost loved ones in this act of terrorism learned about Lowenstein's project, they asked to

2. http://www.darkelegy103.com/about.html.

be depicted as well. Today seventy-five sculptures of grieving mothers and widows, in larger-than-life-size pieces, are part of the work.[3]

As Ekaterina E. Kozlova notes, "Examples of emptied, anguished, and protesting motherhood can be found in every historical period marked by socio-political upheaval."[4] It was the love of mothers for their missing children that fueled the *Asociación Madres de Plaza de Mayo* (Mothers of the Plaza de Mayo). Beginning in the 1970s, Argentinian mothers who had at least one child "disappeared" by the military government defied the government's law against mass assembly by gathering every Thursday to hold a vigil in front of the presidential palace at the Plaza de Mayo in Buenos Aires. They sought information about their children abducted by governmental agents during the Dirty War (1976–1983); the mothers asserted that at least thirty thousand individuals became "Desaparecidos" or "the disappeared," and the movement was instrumental in calling both local and world attention to these human rights abuses.[5] The mothers initially hoped for the return of their children to them alive, but that did not happen. Over the years, though, the mothers' actions yielded results: some of the children illegally adopted by other families were traced, and, in certain cases, connections between birth parents and their children have taken place. Additionally, human rights regulations not in existence before the movement were introduced.[6]

Anna's sad ritual conveys both the mother's love for her child and the suffering she endures when the child's fate is unknown. Anna fears that her son is dead. She also knows that until blindness befell him, Tobit continued to defy governmental regulations by burying the dead. He had been hunted down to be put to death for this in the past (Tob 1:19; 2:8). Anna might even have feared that the authorities targeted her son this time.

There are moving examples of maternal grieving in the Tanakh. Abraham casts Hagar out into the desert with her only son, Ishmael, with minimal water and food. When their water runs out, Hagar places the dying Ishmael under a bush so that she does not have to see him die (Gen

---

3. http://www.darkelegy103.com/about.html.

4. Ekaterina E. Kozlova, *Maternal Grief in the Hebrew Bible* (Oxford: Oxford University Press, 2017), 2.

5. Marguerite Guzman Bouvard, *Revolutionizing Motherhood: The Mothers of the Plaza de Mayo* (Wilmington: Scholarly Resources Inc., 1994).

6. Alejandro Rebossio, "Argentina's Other Stolen Babies," *El Pais*, May 12, 2015; https://english.elpais.com/elpais/2015/05/12/inenglish/1431437758_857439.html.

21:15); she sits a short distance away, "burst into tears," and mourns for her son (21:16). Sitting on the ground and weeping, as Kozlova notes, were characteristic Israelite mourning behaviors.[7] Egyptian women expressed mourning in similar ways; a wall painting inside the tomb of Ramose, a government official in the ancient Egyptian city of Thebes during its Eighteenth Dynasty (c. fourteenth century BCE), depicts groups of women with tear-stained faces, wearing white robes and their hair loose, kneeling on the ground, with their hands reaching up to place dust on their heads as they weep for Ramose.[8]

Israelite men expressed their grief emotionally—and publicly—as well. When Jacob thinks that his beloved son Joseph is dead, he becomes distraught and "tore his garments, put sackcloth on his loins, and mourned for his son many days" (Gen 37:34). When his other children tried to console him, he rejected their attempts, saying that he would "go down to Sheol . . . mourning" (37:35) and join his son there, in the underworld. Jacob is so heartbroken he prefers to die from grief than live without his son. When Jacob himself later dies, Joseph in turn "[throws] himself on his father's face and wept over him and kissed him" (50:1), and a state procession ensued from Jacob's Egyptian place of death to his burial place in Canaan. The crowd, including Jacob's sons, observes a seven-day mourning period, public enough for the local Canaanites to notice (Gen 50:10-11). Talmudic writers understood the stipulation of seven days of mourning to be the scriptural foundation for the grieving ritual of *shivah*: the seven days of the most intensive mourning practiced by Jews who have lost close family members (y. Mo'ed Qaṭ. 3.5), though in contrast to what is described in Genesis 50:10, *shivah* takes place after, not before, burial.

Tobit is not of the disposition to imagine worst-case scenarios to explain why Tobias has not yet arrived home. Instead of jumping to dire conclusions as does Anna, he looks for a reasonable explanation for the delay. Anna, on the other hand, is torn between believing her son will not return and feeling compelled to watch for him. This turmoil creates self-blame: "Woe is me, my child, the light of my eyes, that I let you make the journey." She wonders why she let him go and so signals that she had the ability to keep him home. In 5:18-22, Anna had expressed her resistance to Tobias's going away to retrieve the funds, but Tobit made the decision. Anna perhaps recognizes that she could have fought harder not to let him go. Her walking to the place where she last saw her son

---

7. Kozlova, *Maternal Grief in the Hebrew Bible*, 72–74.

8. John Davies, *Death, Burial and Rebirth in the Religions of Antiquity* (London: Routledge, 1999), 36.

was a physical means of working out this inner turmoil, of gaining some control—doing *something*—when she felt utterly powerless to help her son. Walking every day to the road might have served another purpose: making Tobit feel guilty. He did not need to see her in order to know what she was doing.

In language reminiscent of the stereotypical overprotective and over-bearing Jewish mother, Anna now claims Tobias for herself alone.[9] In verses 4, 5, and 7, she refers to Tobias as "my child," not "our child." She sidelines Tobit because in her view only she is behaving appropriately, since only she is grieving Tobias. Anna's grief isolates her from Tobit as she presents herself as if she were a single mother of her only child. Even her reference to Tobias as the "light of her eyes" (10:5) excluded the blind Tobit. Psychologists who study parental grieving after the death of a child would refer to Anna's dismissal of Tobit as a "loss-oriented" coping strategy in which "feelings and actions are centered around the relation between the parent and the child," and the partner (if there is one) is neither part of the focus nor involved.[10]

Whereas Anna's feelings are transparent, Tobit—who is also worried (10:1-3)—tries to hide his anxiety, or avoid it, by attempting to comfort Anna.[11] Modern psychologists would approve of Tobit's action: helping others may relieve the stress of our own concerns.[12] Suppressing emotions, however, can have such negative consequences as raising stress levels (by increasing blood pressure) and impeding the ability to develop authentic rapport with others.[13] Tobit, alternatively, might be trying to avoid his own anxious feelings by focusing on those of Anna. Research on the use of coping behaviors when experiencing stressful life events

9. Martha A. Ravits, "The Jewish Mother: Comedy and Controversy in American Popular Culture," *Multi-Ethnic Literature of the United States* 25 (2000): 4–5.

10. Leoniek Wijngaards-de Meij, Margaret Stroebe, Henk Schut, Wolfgang Stroebe, Jan van den Bout, Peter G. M. van der Heijden, and Iris Dijkstra, "Parents Grieving the Loss of Their Child: Interdependence in Coping," *British Journal of Clinical Psychology* 47 (2008): 39.

11. Noted by Amy-Jill Levine, "Tobit," in *The New Oxford Annotated Bible: New Revised Standard Version with Apocrypha*, ed. Michael D. Coogan, 3rd ed. (Oxford: Oxford University Press, 2001), 24.

12. Christy Matta, *The Stress Response: How Dialectical Behavior Therapy Can Free You from Needless Anxiety, Worry, Anger and Other Symptoms of Stress* (Oakland, CA: New Harbinger Publications, 2012), 85.

13. Emily A. Butler, Boris Egloff, Frank Wilhelm, Nancy C. Smith, Elizabeth A. Erickson, and James J. Gross, "The Social Consequences of Expressive Suppression," *Emotion* 3 (2003): 48–67.

reveals that women use a higher number of coping strategies than men. Within the context of bereavement, studies show that women tend to confront their emotions more than men, whereas men reported dealing with bereavement by using avoidant coping strategies more exclusively.[14] By turning his focus on Anna, and trying to comfort her, Tobit may be avoiding his own feelings of anxiety.

Tobit attempts to reassure his wife with words echoing 5:21, when Anna had tried to convince him that retrieving the silver was not worth risking their son's life. Earlier, Tobit assured his wife, "Do not worry; our child will leave in good health and return to us in good health. Your eyes will see him on the day when he returns to you in good health. Say no more! Do not fear for them, my sister [ἀδελφή in G1; the word for 'sister' does not appear in Sinaiticus (G2)]." Now he tells her, "Be quiet and stop worrying, sister [ἀδελφή, 'sister,' in the Sinaiticus version; ἀδελφή does not appear in the G1; 'sister' is translated as 'my dear' in the NRSV]; he is all right. Probably something unexpected [περισπασμός, 'distracting'] has happened there. The man who went with him is trustworthy and is one of our own kin. Do not grieve for him, my dear; he will soon be here." Tobit points out that Tobias is not alone on his journey as a comforting fact, but Anna does not mention the companion. For Anna, in her grief and in her worry about her son going on a risky journey, unless she is with him, from her perspective, Tobias is alone.

Whereas Anna acquiesced to Tobit's exhortation earlier, now she refuses to obey his requests. She neither becomes quiet nor stops worrying. Perhaps Anna senses that Tobit is trying to comfort her because her behavior is exacerbating his own worry.[15] Even were his focus on Anna, to help her feel less distraught, that he was worried too should have been apparent to his wife.

Anna once more speaks her mind: "Be quiet yourself!" (v. 7), she tells her husband. Further, she accuses him of lying about Tobias's being safe and soon arriving home, just like he, earlier, accused her of stealing the goat. She asks the loquacious Tobit to stop talking. Nerves are frayed, and Anna cannot keep listening to her husband's chatter.

---

14. Wijngaards-de Meij et al., "Parents Grieving the Loss of Their Child," 27.

15. Something that Beverly Bow also suggests, "Anna 1," in *Women in Scripture: A Dictionary of Named and Unnamed Women in the Hebrew Bible, the Apocryphal/Deuterocanonical Books, and the New Testament*, ed. Carol Meyers, Toni Craven, and Ross S. Kraemer (Grand Rapids: Eerdmans, 2000), 50.

TRANSLATION MATTERS

Tobit 10:7b in MS Sinaiticus (G2) reads, "She would rush out every day and watch the road her son had taken, and would heed no one." The VL, or Old Latin, reads, "and she would eat nothing," and G1 offers, "for days she would eat no food, and during the nights she did not cease lamenting her son Tobiah." It is difficult to understand which is original: what would Anna not do, eat or listen? Joseph Fitzmyer opts for G1 and VL's version, suggesting that "more than likely the reading of MS S has been altered."[16] Carey Moore proposes that "the Old Latin (along with G1) has probably preserved a reading lost by G2,"[17] and Naomi Jacobs notes, "Although not found in Sinaiticus, this reading [i.e., 'and she would eat nothing'] is amply attested in three independent versions: in the Greek text types G1 and G3 as well as among Old Latin manuscripts."[18] I agree that "and she would eat nothing" is likely the original text.

Jacobs correctly suggests that "Tobit wishes to recall the biblical Hannah, Samuel's mother, who has trouble eating due to being childless" (1 Sam 1:7-8). She contrasts Anna's not eating with the dietary practices of the male characters: Tobit avoids eating gentile food; he delays his Shavuot dinner in order to await the guest he sent his son to find and then delays it again to bury the corpse Tobias finds instead; Tobias refuses to eat until he can marry Sarah; Raphael affirms that he has not consumed food or drink. Jacobs argues that Anna's avoidance of food "is neither about being pious nor about doing the right thing; it is purely personal and may even suggest a lack of faith."[19] I agree with Jacobs that Anna's lack of eating is "purely personal" but find the suggestion that she might lack faith harsh. Anna is suffering. Tobias is late in returning home, and she is sick about it: she cannot sleep, and she has lost her appetite. These are very human reactions. Anna, "whose fasting is the only reference to female consumption in Tobit, is also the female character with the greatest degree of agency."[20] According to Jacobs, since one's relationship to food is related to one's agency, then choosing *not* to eat is as much as Anna is allotted. As Jacobs points out, however, Anna is not a woman without agency. She goes to work, and she goes out to the road to wait for Tobias—she does not sit idly. Like Hannah in 1 Samuel 1:7, she is not eating because she is miserable (v. 11) and deeply troubled (v. 15). As she sits and waits at the road for Tobit, she is probably—again like Hannah—pouring out her soul to the Lord (v. 15).

16. Fitzmyer, *Tobit*, 265.

17. Carey A. Moore, *Tobit: A New Translation with Introduction and Commentary* (New Haven: Yale University Press, 1996), 254.

18. Naomi S. S. Jacobs, "Seen and Heard, but Hardly Eating: Female Consumption in the Book of Tobit," in *A Feminist Companion to Tobit and Judith*, ed. Athalya Brenner-Idan and Helen Efthimiadis-Keith, FCB 2.20 (London: Bloomsbury, 2015), 92. G3 preserves the text of only Tob 6:9–12:22 and is considered related to G2 in a secondary way; for example, Robert Hanhart includes variants from G3 in the apparatus of G2 (see R. Hanhart, *Text und Textgeschichte des Buches Tobit* [Göttingen: Vandenhoeck & Ruprecht, 1984]).

19. Jacobs, "Seen and Heard, but Hardly Eating," 94.

20. Jacobs, "Seen and Heard, but Hardly Eating," 97.

In an alignment with patriarchal stereotypes about males, Tobit appears more in control of his emotions. Tobit reminds Anna—and himself, perhaps—that their son's guide, Azariah, is "trustworthy." Readers know just how much this is the case. But Anna might not be as trusting of relatives as Tobit to care for her son the way she thought they ought to or, more particularly, the way she did. Maybe she feared that other relatives would not mind having a son—and inheritor of familial property—out of the way.

Tobias is very much alive; his marriage to Sarah has delayed his return. Readers know that Tobit, and not Anna, is right, and this elevates Tobit's status and diminishes Anna's, even though they might have empathized with her. But at the same time, Anna's actions show that she still has hope that Tobias will return. And she should not be faulted for not knowing something that she could not know. Women could show more emotion than men; Anna, then, in expressing more angst about Tobias, was conforming to gender expectations. So too was Tobit, as he comforted his wife.

Tobias Convinces Raguel That He and Sarah Must Go Back to Nineveh (10:7b-10)

The familial concern is not one-sided. Tobias loves his parents, and he knows that the length of his absence will injuriously affect them. The earlier Hebrew fragment 4QTob[e] has Tobias worrying in verse 7 about how he has left *them* behind, that is, both his father and his mother, as opposed to G2, which mentions the father only.[21] The change in the later manuscript suggests an attempt to restrict Anna's presence in Tobias's life: he is too much of a mama's boy, and Tobias might feel pressure from Raguel wanting to have him as his son. Tobias, in saying that he wishes to be sent back to "my father" (πρὸς τὸν πατέρα μου) calls Raguel "father" but reminds him not too subtly that he has his own father, whom he would now like to see. Here we see Raguel's longing for a son. It is not that he doesn't care for his daughter Sarah—he does—but the statement that the fourteen days of wedding celebrations were part of what he had "sworn to do for his daughter" (ὤμοσεν Ραγουηλ ποιῆσαι τῇ θυγατρὶ) gives a sense that the festivities were obligatory on his part. When Raguel begs Tobias, "Stay, my child, stay with me" (μεῖνον παιδίον μεῖνον μετ᾿ ἐμοῦ),

---

21. Fitzmyer, 4Q200; frg. 4; 1.6; 5-6.

Tob 10:7b-10

Now when the fourteen days of the wedding celebration had ended that Raguel had sworn to observe for his daughter, Tobias came to him and said, "Send me back, for I know that my father and mother do not believe that they will see me again. So I beg of you, father, to let me go so that I may return to my own father. I have already explained to you how I left him." [8]But Raguel said to Tobias, "Stay, my child, stay with me; I will send messengers to your father Tobit and they will inform him about you." [9]But he said, "No! I beg you to send me back to my father." [10]So Raguel promptly gave Tobias his wife Sarah, as well as half of all his property: male and female slaves, oxen and sheep, donkeys and camels, clothing, money, and household goods.

he reverts to using παιδίον, "young boy" or "youth," more commonly used in the earlier parts of the narrative to refer to Tobias (4:4, 5, 13, 14, 19, 20, 21; 5:3, 9, 17, 18, 21; 6:2). After the marriage ceremony, the narrator refers to Tobias as a νεανίσκον, "young man" (8:1).

Like the concubine's father in Judges 19, who might sense that once his daughter and the Levite leave his house in Bethlehem he'll never see his daughter again, Raguel is generous but his hospitality borders on the excessive. It is time for the couple to leave, but he does not want them to. He offers to send messengers to Raguel's parents—something he did not offer earlier. Tobias is adamant about going home to his own father. Raguel relents, and he expresses his disappointment and hurt at his new-found son's not wanting to stay longer in giving to Tobias "promptly" all that he needs to leave: if he'll not stay, Raguel's reaction is as if he states, "Well then, fine! Here you go!" Fathers in this book sometimes act like passive-aggressive whiners.

In fulfillment of Raphael's words in 6:12, Tobias returns not only with a new wife but with her abundant inheritance. Like the narrator of Genesis 12:16, who itemizes the slaves, male and female, along with the nonhuman possessions given to Abram by Pharaoh (when he thought Sarah was his sister and not his wife), Tobit's narrator lists Tobias's new belongings, human, animal, and inanimate, together (v. 10).

Departures such as these often meant that family members would not see a daughter very frequently thereafter, if at all. As far as we know, Rebekah does not see her family again. Nor, as far as we know, does Sarah.

As I write this I am thinking of my grandmother, Lois Murray, my father's mother, who was born and raised on Prince Edward Island in Eastern Canada. After her marriage—at sixteen—she and my grandfather left for Manitoba, a province in the Canadian prairies, to farm. I recall being about thirteen or fourteen years old and speaking with my grandmother about her life. I remember exactly where we were seated when she told me in a matter-of-fact way that she never saw her parents again after her marriage. This information astonished me and stayed with me, probably because when she married she wasn't much older than I was at the time, and I couldn't imagine not seeing my family again. I didn't think to ask her how she felt when she said goodbye to her parents. I wish I could ask her now, but she died many years ago. Did the whole family gather to send her and her husband off? Did everyone say what they felt was important? Did her parents give her and her new husband parting advice? Did they recognize that they would never again see them, or did they push that thought away so that the farewells were less devastating? Or maybe they truly expected to see one another again? I will never have answers to these questions.

Edna and Raguel Say Goodbye to Tobias and Sarah (10:11-13)

Raguel embraces Tobias before he hugs his daughter. Raguel has spent an intensive time bonding with Tobias, the surviving groom and the son for whom he has longed. He will miss him as if he were his own child, hence the use of παιδίον ("child," v. 11). He will miss his daughter too, as he loves her.

On Raguel's mind is his legacy: twice in verse 12 he identifies Sarah as his daughter, and with Tobias, Sarah has the chance to bear children. Raguel's family will continue through the couple's progeny—and he expresses hope that he will meet his grandchildren—an indication that the families hoped to meet again one day. He hands off Sarah to her husband, along with her dowry equaling half of her father's riches. She brings even more wealth to Tobias's family in the promise of the rest of Raguel's possessions when he and Edna die. Thanks to Sarah, the couple will be able to provide for Tobit and Anna and their future children. While Sarah will have some command over the money, it is Tobias who will have control.

For the first time in the narrative, Raguel speaks directly to his daughter (v. 12). In contrast to his warm parting wishes to his son-in-law for a safe journey, prosperity, and children, his final words to Sarah amount to sterile instructions about appropriate behavior. Citing the fifth commandment, to honor parents (Exod 20:12) and treat them with respect and obedience, Raguel broadens the commandment to include parents-in-law.

¹¹Then he saw them safely off; he embraced Tobias and said, "Farewell, my child; have a safe journey. The Lord of heaven prosper you and your wife Sarah, and may I see children of yours before I die." ¹²Then he kissed his daughter Sarah and said to her, "My daughter, honor your father-in-law and your mother-in-law, since from now on they are as much your parents as those who gave you birth. Go in peace, daughter, and may I hear a good report about you as long as I live." Then he bade them farewell and let them go. Then Edna said to Tobias, "My child and dear brother, the Lord of heaven bring you back safely, and may I live long enough to see children of you and of my daughter Sarah before I die. In the sight of the Lord I entrust my daughter to you; do nothing to grieve her all the days of your life. Go in peace, my child. From now on I am your mother and Sarah is your beloved wife. May we all prosper together all the days of our lives." Then she kissed them both and saw them safely off. ¹³Tobias parted from Raguel with happiness and joy, praising the Lord of heaven and earth, King over all, because he had made his journey a success. Finally, he blessed Raguel and his wife Edna, and said, "I have been commanded by the Lord to honor you all the days of my life."

His hopes for a good report about Sarah suggest a warning that she is to bring honor rather than shame to her family. The hope evokes Sarah's own concern, expressed just prior to her prayer (3:10), that her actions not adversely affect her father. Behind these concerns is the cultural view that measured a woman's actions according to how she affected the males in her family. But this point also holds for men. Sons can bring shame on a family too: Eli's sons were "scoundrels" (1 Sam 2:12), and he reprimands them for the "evil reports" spread about them by people (1 Sam 2:23). Nephews can, as well, just like Nadin did in the *Story of Ahikar*.

Just as Raguel instructed Sarah, Edna instructs Tobias. As elsewhere in the narrative, Edna's attention is on Sarah's well-being. She counsels Tobit not to cause Sarah distress—an allusion to the fact that she has experienced so much suffering already. Edna refers to Tobias as ἄδελφε, "brother" (GI, v. 13), and τέκνον καὶ ἄδελφε, "child and brother" (G2, v. 13). Her reference to Tobias as "brother" shows that she elevates him to her level. Neither Raguel's (nor Tobit's) manner of addressing Sarah elevates her.

Edna has a distinctive and nuanced voice. She is obedient—her husband tells her to act, and she complies. On the one hand, she engages in stereotypical activities of wives, such as baking bread and preparing rooms. On the other hand, she asks important questions and makes statements demonstrating her sensitivity to Sarah's welfare. Raguel sees Sarah's suffering, but it is Edna who is Sarah's champion. Edna and Anna in their roles as wives and mothers are different one from the other—just as all wives and mothers are. But both share a deep love for their children.

The narrator tells us that Tobias is happy to leave—he will soon see his parents. He will set their worry to rest when they see that he is still alive, and they will rejoice when they observe all that he is bringing with him: a new wife and many riches. The narrator does not mention Sarah. She is leaving her parents and her home, all that she has known, and she will not see them again for a while, if ever. A young woman setting out on such a journey, traveling with her brand new husband to an unfamiliar household, must have been full of many emotions: excitement about what she would see and discover in her new life, nervousness or fear about whether she would like her role as wife, poignancy about saying goodbye to her family and the home she knew so well.

Tobit 11

Sarah Arrives at Her New Home

Chapter 11 sees the newlyweds arrive in Nineveh, where Tobias will heal his father's blindness. Feminist issues revolve around Raphael's treatment of Tobias; his interaction with the men and avoidance of the women in the narrative; and how Sarah leaves behind her immediate family but is now part of a newly created one.

Raphael and Tobias Meet Tobit and Anna (11:1-6)

"Kaserin" (Κασεριν), otherwise unknown, is another sign to readers of the fictional nature of this story; the shorter and later Greek (G1) text removes it and has only: "they drew near to Nineveh," perhaps seeking to make the text sound more accurate.

The text gives no indication that Tobias had forgotten Tobit's blindness, yet Raphael finds it necessary to remind Tobias of "how we left your father" (11:2). Perhaps this is the narrator's way of reminding the reader. Or the angel doubts that Tobias, experiencing the excitement of a new marriage and the challenges of a return trip, can retain any focus on his father's condition. And the point about how they left Tobit might remind Tobias that his mother, Anna, did not agree to the trip. The implication is that Tobias is somewhat immature.

The suggestion that they "run ahead and prepare the house" (11:3) intimates Raphael's sense that the house needed his and Tobias's attention

Tob 11:1-6

[11:1]When they came near to Kaserin, which is opposite Nineveh, Raphael said, [2]"You are aware of how we left your father. [3]Let us run ahead of your wife and prepare the house while they are still on the way." [4]As they went on together Raphael said to him, "Have the gall ready." And the dog went along behind them.

[5]Meanwhile, Anna sat looking intently down the road by which her son would come. [6]When she caught sight of him coming, she said to his father, "Look, your son is coming, and the man who went with him!"

(to clean it and perhaps organize food and drink) to prepare it for welcoming the returning party. If they prepared the house, Tobit could turn his full mind to greeting his new daughter-in-law. By running ahead, Raphael ensures that Tobit's healing and Sarah's arrival each have their own space, so that they need not share the spotlight. Raphael expresses no concern about Anna, as there is less urgency about her state, yet, given her emotional state, Raphael appears rather uncaring.

Raphael's suggestion of "running ahead" furthermore reduces the amount of time he spends with Sarah and the other female members (such as slaves) of the traveling party.[1] The author of Tobit never has Raphael speak directly with women in the narrative. This detail suggests familiarity with 1 Enoch's Book of the Watchers, an early Jewish interpretation and expansion of Genesis 6:1-4. It recounts how the בני-האלהים (lit. "sons of God") were angels (the "Watchers") who mated with human women, causing the birth of giants (Nephilim or "fallen ones").[2] Porous boundaries between the divine and human women lead to negative consequences. Asmodeus, Sarah's banished demon, and Raphael, Tobias's guardian angel, represent opposing approaches to human-supernatural relations: Asmodeus behaves as if there were no boundaries, whereas Raphael avoids speaking with women. Asmodeus is in Sarah's bedroom, and Raphael can't get far enough away from her. There is some humor here at the expense of the heavenly realm.

1. Amy-Jill Levine, "Diaspora as Metaphor: Bodies and Boundaries in the Book of Tobit," in *Jews and Judaism: Essays in Honor of, and in Dialogue with, A. Thomas Kraabel*, ed. J. A Overman and R. S. MacLennan (Atlanta: Scholars Press, 1992), 112.

2. Myriam T. Brand, "Evil and Sin," in *The Jewish Annotated Apocrypha*, ed. Jonathan Klawans and Lawrence M. Wills (Oxford: Oxford University Press, 2020), 646.

At last, Anna's ritual of staring at the road yields results: she catches the first glimpse of her son's return. Tobias is like the prodigal son of the Gospel of Luke: he is thought to be dead but is discovered to be "alive again" (Luke 15:24, 32). But in the prodigal son parable, it is the father, not the mother, who waits, and the son squanders his inheritance on prostitutes (Luke 15:30), whereas Tobias returns with a wife whose inheritance brings his family wealth.[3] Tobit's female-centric details are lost in Luke's later text. Despite the contrasts, however, both stories highlight parental love for their children, no matter if they make disappointing decisions or if they cause worry by taking risky journeys and don't send word about delays. Seeing them safely at home after a time away is a joyful moment.

Anna is bursting with love when she sees her son, whom she feared dead. The dog, last mentioned when Tobias and Raphael set off for their journey, comes back as well. As Heinrich Gross suggests, "That the dog is running after them means that the two travel companions return home in the same condition as they left in 5:17,"[4] putting to rest the worry that the journey would alter Tobias in a negative way. Traveling can indeed change us. Putting ourselves in new, unfamiliar settings stretches us and leads to discoveries that might modify our perspectives on the world, as well as our personal goals. My ventures abroad have deeply impacted my life, as I've already noted. Family and friends at home might struggle, consequently, with how the returning traveler has changed.

In contrast to Anna's earlier identification of Tobias as "her" son (10:4-7), upon seeing him again she is full of joy and conciliation, and so she tells Tobit, "Look, *your* son has come back" (11:6). She refers to Azariah (Raphael) as "the man," showing again that she, like Tobit, is ignorant of his true identity. She does not describe to Tobit the caravan full of possessions, the slaves, or the new bride.

Tobias Greets His Parents and Cures His Father's Blindness (11:7-13a)

With Raphael's declaration that Tobit's blindness will be cured, the narrator forces attention back on Tobit. The future passive "will be opened" (ἀνεῳχθήσονται), as Joseph Fitzmyer states, "has to be understood as the

---

3. My thanks to Lauren L. Murphy, editor for Liturgical Press, for helping me improve these observations.
4. Heinrich Gross, *Tobit, Judit* (Würzburg: Echter Verlag, 1987), 42, my translation. See earlier commentary on the dog in Tobit 6:2.

Tob 11:7-13a

7Raphael said to Tobias, before he had approached his father, "I know that his eyes will be opened. 8Smear the gall of the fish on his eyes; the medicine will make the white films shrink and peel off from his eyes, and your father will regain his sight and see the light." 9 Then Anna ran up to her son and threw her arms around him, saying, "Now that I have seen you, my child, I am ready to die." And she wept. 10Then Tobit got up and came stumbling out through the courtyard door. Tobias went up to him, 11with the gall of the fish in his hand, and holding him firmly, he blew into his eyes, saying, "Take courage, father." With this he applied the medicine on his eyes, 12and it made them smart. 13Next, with both his hands he peeled off the white films from the corners of his eyes.

theological passive"—Tobit's eyes will be opened by God.[5] Read in isolation, though, there is no need to attribute the opening of Tobit's eyes to the divine (v. 7), since verse 8 states that it is the effectiveness of the medicine that cures Tobit's blindness.

But the narrative context supports Fitzmyer's reading: the next section (13b-15) has Tobit praising God for his ability to see again. Yet if the divine receives credit for the curing of Tobit's eyes—for making the medicine or magic work (see pp. 151–56)—so too should the divine be blamed for causing Tobit to become blind. I am reminded of people in the aftermath of disasters who attribute their survival to "God looking out for them" without, perhaps, being aware of or caring about the implications of either what such a statement means for the persons who did not survive (i.e., that God was not looking out for them) or the inconsistent attribution to God of their survival but not the causing of the disaster.

Living without the view of a higher power in control is challenging. If God is not in control, then events are simply random. There is no reason why one person lives and another dies. If there is no greater power ordering our world, then humans can do what we can to control our lives but, beyond the limits of that, things just happen. One of the reasons why religious faith can be so comforting is that it counters the idea that all is random, since "everything happens for a reason" (as those who have such faith say). Yet justifying suffering or death as divine will can be unnerving too, as such a perspective seems to presuppose a deity who is callous and cruel. Intellectually I struggle to believe in a higher

5. Joseph Fitzmyer, *Tobit* (Berlin: de Gruyter, 2003), 276.

power, but I recognize, and have experienced, the emotional comfort of trusting that a deity exists who has ultimate control over everything.

Verse 7 implies that opening Tobit's eyes both restores vision and indicates enlightenment.[6] There are many examples of this in the Tanakh. For example, in Genesis 3:5 the serpent explains that by eating the fruit of the tree in the middle of the garden "your eyes will be opened, and you will be like God, knowing good and evil"; in 3:7, "the eyes of both were opened, and they knew that they were naked"; and in 21:19, God opens Hagar's eyes and she sees the well so that she and her son Ishmael may drink and live. The association of "seeing eyes" with spiritual and intellectual insight implies that the opposite, physical blindness, indicates spiritual obtuseness. Out of respect to people who are blind, the usage of blindness in this way ought to stop.

Tobit from a Blind Person's Perspective

Tobit scholar Michael Kiel recognizes that when Tobit becomes blind, he prays, thinking that his blindness is from God as retribution for sin. Later, though, Kiel notices Tobit's thoughts have changed, and the storyline no longer points to God acting in a retributive manner that focuses on sin and punishment.[7] But, if it is not through a retribution system, readers may be left wondering where God is active in Tobit. As a blind person, I have found God active in this text in many ways.

First, God acts through others. In 8:2-3 and 11:11-13, Tobias brings healing to his wife and father. Along with that, the healing comes through the fish, often referred to as medicine (6:5). Here, God acting through Tobit exemplifies the importance of community and collective care to God's action. By using the fish as medicine to heal, God can also be found acting through the medical community. That is important because when speaking about healing and disability, faith and medicine are often put in opposition. These point to the communal nature of God's action regarding disability.

Second, God acts as a listener and promise keeper. Often disabled people feel strongly about whether or not they want healing, and so it is important

6. Or, as Jacobs suggests, will receive "a sudden new awareness (Gen 3:5)" ("Tobit," in Klawans and Wills, *The Jewish Annotated Apocrypha*, 170).

7. Michael Kiel, *The "Whole Truth": Rethinking Retribution in the Book of Tobit* (London: T&T Clark, 2012).

that in chapter 3 Tobit prays for healing, in 5:10 Rafael notes that the healing is coming, and then in 11:7-8 Rafael says healing is happening and uses the very same words that Tobit uses to describe his own condition. This is honoring and listening to how Tobit articulates his own experience of disability and keeping a promise of healing that was asked for. God honoring a disabled person's desires and language here is deeply redemptive, especially when the Church often does not.

God also acts as giver of mercy (also translated "pity," 11:17). Many disabled people today are tired of receiving pity or even mercy from others. If the world were accessible to us, we would not need mercy or pity but instead could receive something much fuller from our communities in the form of inclusion, justice, and love. I wonder, if society were fully accessible to Tobit as a blind man, then what could God have given him that would extend even beyond physical healing just to be included back in his culture? While God is acting in this particular time and culture, the story of Tobit makes it clear that God's honoring of disabled people may start with mercy and physical healing but definitely will not end there.

Finally, God acts in the present in all moments. In 12:12-14, Rafael shares that God was not only present in the healing but also in the moment when Tobit became blind. God being with us in the fullness of our disability experience is so redemptive, especially when healing alone is often glorified as God's work. In the book of Tobit, God shows up present, listening, and willing to give goodness to a disabled person in all moments of disabled life.

Tatum Tricarico

Raphael repeats his instructions from 6:9. His reminder to Tobias that his father is blind and repeating how to apply the medication indicates his lack of trust in the young man, his concern that he is a preoccupied new husband, or a desire to bring attention back to himself. The angel tells Tobias to "plaster up"[8] his father's eyes with the fish gall to eliminate the white film causing the blindness. According to Raphael, if all went as expected, Tobit would gain the ability to "see the light" (v. 8). The comment may be self-referential: with his sight restored, Tobit would be able to see Raphael, a divine being who, because of his connection with God, is associated with light (see Tob 3:17, "God's light"). It also nods

8. J. Lust, E. Eynikel, K. Hauspie, *Greek-English Lexicon of the Septuagint*, rev. ed. (Stuttgart: Deutsche Bibelgesellschaft, 2003), 196.

to Anna since Tobias is the light of Anna's eyes (10:5). Being able to "see the light" is associated with redemption (Job 33:28).

The beginning of chapter 11 bears echoes of Genesis 46:28, when Jacob meets his beloved son Joseph, whom he'd not seen for a long time, "falls upon his neck" (ויפל על צואריו) and states: "I can die now, having seen for myself that you are still alive" (46:30). Like the patriarch, Anna runs to her son and falls on his neck (ἐπέπεσεν ἐπὶ τὸν τράχηλον).[9] She tells Tobias, "I have seen [εἶδόν] you," something that Tobit at the time cannot do. She furthermore, like Jacob, declares that she is now able to face death: "I am ready to die," she declares (v. 9). It is a statement that conveys how much Tobias's return means to her and is not meant to be taken literally. There are echoes as well of Simeon, described in Luke 2:27 as a "righteous and devout" man whom the Holy Spirit told "would not see death before he had seen the Lord's Messiah." When Simeon holds Jesus in the temple, he "praised God" and says, "Master, now you are dismissing your servant in peace" (2:28-29); in other words, now he can die since he's seen Jesus. The Latin for "now you are dismissing" is "Nunc dimittis," the traditional title of the hymn of praise, called the "Song of Simeon," recited in evening worship services in Roman Catholic, Anglican, and Lutheran churches, as well as in the Eastern Orthodox Vespers.[10]

Such intertextual comparisons highlight how the reactions of people to Tobias's return are similar to other biblical vignettes: Anna and Tobias's reunion is patterned after that of Jacob and Joseph, elevating the scene, and there are echoes of the Tobit text in later tales of the prodigal son and Simeon in the temple. Such comparisons also underscore a significant difference: in contrast to the other stories where loving fathers have the starring role, in Tobit, a woman—a loving mother—is at the center of the story.

Tobit "came stumbling out through the courtyard door." The Greek literally states, "was stumbling with regards to his feet" (προσέκοπτεν τοῖς ποσίν). The narrator incorporates a stereotype about the blind by equating Tobit's blindness with helplessness: he is depicted here as moving unsteadily, but blind people are not necessarily more likely than sighted people to stumble.

In accordance with Raphael's instructions, Tobias "peeled off" (ἀπελέπισεν, v. 13) the white films; the scene will be repeated in Acts 9:18, in relation to Saul—the future apostle Paul—who had become

9. This is also found in Genesis 33:4 and 45:14, among other incidences.

10. *Britannica*, "Nunc Dimittis," 1998, https://www.britannica.com/topic/Nunc-Dimittis.

blind after an encounter with a "light from heaven" (v. 3) and has a conversation with Jesus (v. 4-6). God directs Ananias to place his hands on Saul, "and something like scales [ὡς λεπίδες] fell" from Saul's eyes, "and his sight was restored" (Acts 9:18). Readers of Acts, knowing this scene from Tobit, would remember how the restoration of Tobit's sight brought him joy because he could see his son Tobias again and could learn about the success of his journey. They would see the parallel in Acts, how Saul's sight being restored meant that he saw—and recognized the identity of—a son as well: not his own, but Jesus, "the Son of God" (9:20). This intertextual comparison for readers of Acts would intensify the significance of the identity and impact of the "son" that Saul (soon to be "Paul") sees, whom he thereafter begins to "proclaim . . . in the synagogues" (9:20).

In the shorter Greek version (G1), the gall applied to Tobit's eyes made them sting (συνεδήχθησαν), prompting him to rub them (διέτριψε, v. 12). In this way, "the white films scaled off from the corners of his eyes" (v. 13), and Tobit takes a more active part in the restoration of his sight.[11] But since G2 is the earlier reading, Tobit's agency is a later addition, perhaps to make it clear who peeled the scales from his eyes.

Tobias tells Tobit, "Take courage [θάρσει], father" (11:11); these are the same words of comfort Edna spoke to Sarah on the eve of her marriage (7:17) and Raguel says to Tobias before he and Sarah left Ecbatana (8:21). Here the wishing of courage is directed from a child to his father. It is sometimes difficult for children to see their parents as vulnerable or suffering. Children may feel guilty for not being able to protect the very people who protected them growing up, and this shift in care is also difficult for parents. Tobias's wishing his father courage is different in G2 and G1: G1 makes it seem as if Tobias warns his father about the upcoming discomfort, and in contrast to G2 the text explicitly states that the medication stung Tobit's eyes. It furthermore ascribes purpose to the pain—that it is what causes Tobit to rub his eyes and remove the scales. The later reading (G1) is clearer, therefore, about the way the gall worked.

Tobit is cured in the same courtyard (verse 10) where he was blinded (2:9). That Tobit is healed where he originally lost his sight sends the message that no place is "bad" and no place is "good."

---

11. Carey A. Moore, *Tobit: A New Translation with Introduction and Commentary* (New Haven: Yale University Press, 1996), 263, notes this as well.

Tobit's Sight Is Restored and He Praises God (11:13b-15)

Tobit directs praise to God (vv. 14-15) and speaks of how God both afflicted him and then showed mercy toward him (v. 15). This same combination reappears in chapter 13 with regard to God's dealings with Israel. Tobit is not repenting for personal sin here; like his prayer in chapter 3, he is using traditional language of affliction and mercy that, as Amy-Jill Levine notes, "are conventional terms for divine punishment and reconciliation upon the community's repentance."[12] Verse 14 states that Tobit wept (ἔκλαυσεν), the same verb as when he prayed for death (3:1), indicating that he has again been brought to the brink. Tobit says, "I see you, my son, the light of my eyes" (11:14); this is the first time Tobit refers to Tobias as "the light of my eyes," just as Anna earlier has (10:5). Raphael's prediction in verse 8 that Tobit will "see the light," therefore, comes partially true—he sees his son in a new light, as an accomplished young man who facilitates his healing—and soon he will recognize Raphael for who he truly is. In Matthew 5:14, Jesus says to his followers that they are "the light of the world." Today we recognize that the light enters our eyes and is transformed into electrical signals that our brain decodes, but in antiquity, it was thought that the eye propelled light outward.[13] Tobit's vision is cleared to the point of now being able to project light onto his beloved son, whom he thought he had lost. We appreciate people more if we think we have lost them: we take them less for granted afterward.

Tobit's blessing of the "holy angels" (v. 14) is ironic, since he does so without realizing that the angel Raphael stands before him. In contrast with the secrecy of his burials, he is "rejoicing and praising God" in public, at the "top of his voice" (v. 15) for all not only to see his transformation but to hear it as well.

Tobias then lists his accomplishments from the journey for his father. He mentions the retrieval of the money before telling about his marriage to Sarah. In terms of importance and what matters most, he ought to have mentioned Sarah first. But getting the money from Gabael was the purpose of the trip, so it is logical that he begins with the topic about

---

12. Amy-Jill Levine, "Tobit," in *The New Oxford Annotated Bible: New Revised Standard Version with Apocrypha*, ed. Michael D. Coogan, 3rd ed. (Oxford: Oxford University Press, 2001), 26.

13. Amy-Jill Levine, *Sermon on the Mount: A Beginner's Guide to the Kingdom of Heaven* (Nashville: Abingdon, 2020), 99.

Tob 11:13b-15

Then Tobit saw his son and threw his arms around him, ¹⁴and he wept and said to him, "I see you, my son, the light of my eyes!" Then he said,

"Blessed be God,
and blessed be his great
name,
and blessed be all his holy
angels.
May his holy name be blessed
throughout all the ages.

¹⁵Though he afflicted me,
he has had mercy upon me.
Now I see my son Tobias!"

So Tobit went in rejoicing and praising God at the top of his voice. Tobias reported to his father that his journey had been successful, that he had brought the money, that he had married Raguel's daughter Sarah, and that she was, indeed, on her way there, very near to the gate of Nineveh.

which his father is expecting him to report. Tobit immediately sets out to the gate of Nineveh to meet his daughter-in-law.

Tobit Greets Sarah, and the Wedding Is Celebrated in Nineveh for Seven Days (11:16-18)

In chapter 11 Tobit goes from stumbling (in v. 10) to one who nimbly goes from inside to outside his house. His depiction in verses 16 and 17 publicly demonstrating his healed vision before an amazed crowd and his attribution of the cure to God's action are elements one sees in Jesus's miraculous healings.[14] For example, "Great crowds came to him, bringing with them the lame, the maimed, the blind, the mute, and many others. They put them at his feet, and he cured them, so that the crowd was amazed [θαυμάσαι] when they saw the mute speaking, the maimed whole, the lame walking, and the blind seeing. And they praised the God of Israel" (Matt 15:30-31). There are differences too: in the Gospels the cured are not named, whereas we have Tobit's name; in the Gospels the focus is on Jesus (the healer), but in Tobit the focus is on the healed Tobit. In the Gospels the miracles are associated with faith, either the need for it so that the miracle can happen (e.g., Matt 9:27-31) or the increase of it among those who have observed the miracle (e.g., Luke 7:11-17). In Tobit, the onlookers are "the people of Nineveh" (v. 16), which probably

14. George W. E. Nickelsburg, "Tobit," in *The Harper Collins Study Bible: Including Apocryphal Deuterocanonical Books*, rev. ed. (New York: HarperCollins, 2006), 1307.

¹⁶Then Tobit, rejoicing and praising God, went out to meet his daughter-in-law at the gate of Nineveh. When the people of Nineveh saw him coming, walking along in full vigor and with no one leading him, they were amazed. ¹⁷Before them all, Tobit acknowledged that God had been merciful to him and had restored his sight. When Tobit met Sarah the wife of his son Tobias, he blessed her saying, "Come in, my daughter, and welcome. Blessed be your God who has brought you to us, my daughter. Blessed be your father and your mother, blessed be my son Tobias, and blessed be you, my daughter. Come in now to your home, and welcome, with blessing and joy. Come in, my daughter." So on that day there was rejoicing among all the Jews who were in Nineveh. ¹⁸Ahikar and his nephew Nadab were also present to share Tobit's joy. With merriment they celebrated Tobias's wedding feast for seven days, and many gifts were given to him.

refers to gentiles as well as Jews (Israelites), but there is no mention of their faith increasing because of what they saw. It is, specifically, "Jews who were in Nineveh" (v. 17) who rejoiced at the events of the day—no mention of increased faith.

Tobit's life aligns with and enacts typical component parts of an individual lament from the Psalms: he invokes the name of God and expresses trust in God's judgment (3:1-5); he communicates his complaint in which he describes his misery and his desire to die (3:6); and he appeals for divine intervention (3:6) and declares his praise of God for delivery from his distress (11:14-17).

Tobit's walking "in full vigor, and with no one leading him," contrasts with the earlier depiction of him as blind and stumbling (v. 10). Fitzmyer suggests that Tobit "now understands how the affliction of blindness has led only to his benefit and to that of his family."[15] This comment justifies, in retrospect, why bad things happen to a good person but is a simplistic theology. It's easy for Tobit, now healed, to praise God. Had he not been healed, he would still be in despair. The people of Nineveh see the difference in him, and Tobit publicly gives credit to God. But credit ought to go to Tobias and Raphael for bringing the materials of his healing to him. Anna should be given credit too for putting up with Tobit during his despair.

15. Fitzmyer, *Tobit*, 281.

Tobit welcomes the daughter-in-law whom he counseled his son to marry—"a woman from among the descendants of your ancestors" (4:12). His greeting is ebullient; four times he calls Sarah θύγατερ (daughter). Whereas Edna referred to Tobias as her "brother" (10:12), Tobit refers to Sarah as his daughter; she remains in a subordinate, but nevertheless loved, position.[16] Tobit values his family, but gendered hierarchy prevails.

Another celebration of the marriage ensues—seven days this time. Like the mention of the dog at the start and end of Tobias's journey, reference to Ahikar and his nephew Nadab provide another frame: their last appearance was in 1:21-22. Tobit's reference to these relatives brings the focus again on family, Tobit's priority. His nephew Ahikar had supported him for two years (2:10). Now he and Nadab (Nadin, according to the fifth-century *Story of Ahikar*) come to celebrate during a joyous time in Tobit's life. The intertext with the *Story of Ahikar* raises a warning that not all familial relations are trustworthy or good. No females are mentioned as guests at the wedding feast.

The term "Jews" (Ιουδαίοι), used only here, in verse 17, is anachronistic given the narrative's eighth-century BCE setting. "Jew" derives initially from the Hebrew name of the Southern Kingdom of Judah or, in Hebrew, "Yehudah" (יהודה). Elsewhere, Tobit speaks of "Israelites" or "sons/ descendants of Israel" (1:8; 5:9; 13:3; 14:7), which aligns better with the document's setting. By using a postexilic term to refer to these people as "Jews," the writer signals a connection between the time during which the Tobit story is set and the present.

---

16. Beverly Bow and George W. E. Nickelsburg, "Patriarchy with a Twist: Men and Women in Tobit," in *A Feminist Companion to Tobit and Judith*, ed. Athalya Brenner-Idan and Helen Efthimiadis-Keith, FCB 2.20 (London: Bloomsbury, 2015), 141; Levine, "Diaspora as Metaphor," 110.

Tobit 12

An Angel Is Revealed (to the Men)

Chapter 12 draws many major events to a conclusion. Tobit and Tobias credit different entities for the positive occurrences in their lives, and Tobit pays Azariah for his work for Tobias. Then the writer reveals, at long last, Azariah's identity as the angel Raphael—to Tobit and Tobias, and not to any of the female characters—so the narrative catches up with what readers have known since 3:16-17. This knowledge floors Tobit and Tobias (literally). This revelation is meaningful for the characters of the narrative, as they begin to understand the whys and hows of the incidents that have taken place in their lives.

Tobit and Tobias Pay Azariah (12:1-5)

In contradiction with his own advice, "Do not keep over until the next day the wages of those who work for you, but pay them at once" (4:14), Tobit prompts Tobias to pay Azariah for his assistance only after the seven days of the wedding celebration have passed rather than immediately upon his return with Tobias. Perhaps Tobit and Tobias consider Azariah so like a member of family that they did not contemplate paying him and seeing him off rather than having him stay and participate in

Tob 12:1-5

12:1When the wedding celebration was ended, Tobit called his son Tobias and said to him, "My child, see to paying the wages of the man who went with you, and give him a bonus as well." ²He replied, "Father, how much shall I pay him? It would do no harm to give him half of the possessions brought back with me. ³For he has led me back to you safely, he cured my wife, he brought the money back with me, and he healed you. How much extra shall I give him as a bonus?" ⁴Tobit said, "He deserves, my child, to receive half of all that he brought back." ⁵So Tobias called him and said, "Take for your wages half of all that you brought back, and farewell."

the wedding activities. Whereas Tobias now possesses substantial riches and is aware of Azariah's help in attaining them, he is not responsible for the payment. In 5:15-16, Tobit told Azariah, "I will pay you a drachma a day as wages, as well as expenses for yourself and my son." Perhaps Tobias has not given Tobit direct access to the riches and so the father must rely on his son to pay Azariah. During the exchange, Tobit uses "child" (τέκνον) as a term of endearment to address Tobias: children are always "children" to their parents.

Tobias asks his father how much he should pay; he would have known the contracted amount, but he could not know what sort of bonus his father expected to give. Tobias then proposes a staggering "half the possessions" with which he has returned. The literal translation of verse 2 is "It would do me no harm to give him half of the possessions" (οὐ βλάπτομαι διδούς)—neither Tobias nor Tobit needs to worry about financial loss.

Giving "half of the possessions" is a common offer in fairy tales; in the *Tale of the Grateful Dead*, the guide is granted half of what the hero obtains.[1] This motif is also found in biblical stories: three times, King Ahasuerus offers Esther "even to half the kingdom" (Esth 5:3, 6; 7:2), and in Mark 6:23, as a reward for a dance he enjoyed, King Herod offers "even half of my kingdom." The expression conveys a ridiculously large gift.[2] In Tobit this generous offer is made to a character who is, in fact, an angel who does not need the money.

---

1. Joseph A. Fitzmyer, *Tobit* (Berlin: de Gruyter, 2003), 289.
2. Adele Berlin, "Esther," in *The Jewish Study Bible*, ed. Adele Berlin and Marc Z. Brettler, 2nd ed. (New York: Oxford University Press, 2014), 1627.

Tobias lists the services the angel performed: "he has led me back to you safely, he cured my wife, he brought the money back with me, and he healed you" (12:3). The list is not chronological. Tobias knows that family is first for his father, so the safety of his son, his son's successful marriage, and the retrieval of the money are in descending order of priority.

Only after Tobias expresses the reasons for his suggestion of half of his possessions and so answers his own question does Tobit concur. Tobias attributes his safe journey, the curing of his wife, and the healing of Tobit to Azariah, though he skips over how Azariah protected him from the fish (6:3-4). Perhaps the latter was too traumatic an experience to mention or too embarrassing. Tobias takes no credit for the successes of his journey; nor does he credit God. This contrasts with how Tobit attributes his healing to God alone, despite his seeing human involvement (as noted, Tobias brings the gall for his eyes). Tobit sees himself as hard done by, and his reaction and response is more dramatic; being older, he has seen more suffering and has developed more of an ego and entitlement: God cares about his life and even intervenes in it.

Tobias tells Tobit that Azariah "cured" his wife and "healed" you; though the translation uses two different words in English, the Greek word is the same: ἐθεράπευσεν, a verb that means "to heal, to take care of (one's health)"[3] and is the etymological basis for English "therapy" and "therapeutic." This is the same verb used in the Gospels to describe Jesus's healing of the sick and the possessed, for example, "Then they brought to him a demoniac who was blind and mute; and he cured him, so that the one who had been mute could speak and see" (Matt 12:22). Sarah's demonic attack is categorized as a physical disease in the text, no different from blindness. Like other Second Temple texts, in Tobit physical ailments in human beings caused by demons are "cured" through therapeutic ritual. The second-century BCE book of Jubilees explains that Noah is taught "all the medicines for their [the demons'] diseases . . . so that he could cure them with plants of the earth" (10.12); the implication is that "the demons who are active on earth cause disease, a problem that the healing knowledge given to Noah is intended to remedy."[4] Tobit and Anna would not know at this point precisely from what the angel cured Sarah—that would be a story for Tobias to tell his parents when there was more time.

---

3. "θεραπεύω," in J. Lust, E. Eynikel, K. Hauspie, *Greek-English Lexicon of the Septuagint*, rev. ed. (Stuttgart: Deutsche Bibelgesellschaft, 2003), 273.

4. Matthew Goff, "Jubilees," in *The Jewish Annotated Apocrypha*, ed. Jonathan Klawans and Lawrence M. Wills (Oxford: Oxford University Press: 2020), 28.

Tobit and Tobias Learn about Raphael (12:6-15)

From 3:16 until now, the narrative has unfolded with two points of view: one from the perspective of the characters, and another from the perspective of the readers or hearers. As Francis M. Macatangay states, "Raphael becomes the contact point for the two parallel realities in the world of the story."[5] In chapter 12, the two points of view converge when Raphael reveals himself.

Instead of taking his payment and leaving, Azariah calls a meeting. Raphael in verse 6 calls "the two of them," Tobit and Tobias, "privately," but the Greek (κρυπτῶς) literally means "in secret." Joseph Fitzmyer argues that Amy-Jill Levine's suggestion that Raphael was avoiding the women is "as gratuitous as it is eisegetical in light of the following context."[6] By "the following context," he seems to mean Raphael's encouragement to "declare to all people the deeds of God" and to "acknowledge and reveal the works of God" (12:6-7). Rather, the observation that Raphael did not invite Anna and Sarah is based on textual details here and is consistent with the angel's avoiding Sarah earlier. That Raphael immediately after revealing his identity urges disclosure "to all people"—including gentiles—of God's actions makes his secretly telling Tobit and Tobias (and not the female characters) that he is "one of the seven angels who stand ready and enter before the glory of the Lord" even more striking. Raphael, recognizing that God is important, not him, does not follow his own directives to disclose "to all people." Perhaps his concern was that he wished for men, not women, to do the public proclaiming, a theme reflected in 1 Corinthians 14:34 where Paul writes that "women should be silent in the churches. For they are not permitted to speak,"[7] and in 1 Timothy 2:12, "I permit no woman to teach or to have authority over a man."

Among the "good" actions Raphael itemizes is to "conceal the secret of a king, but to acknowledge and reveal the works of God" (v. 7). Tobit has just credited God for the restoration of his eyesight in 11:17, so has

---

5. Francis M. Macatangay, "Apocalypticism and Narration in the Book of Tobit," in *Canonicity, Setting, Wisdom in the Deuterocanonicals: Papers of the Jubilee Meeting of the International Conference on the Deuterocanonical Books*, ed. Géza G. Xeravits, József Zsengellér, and Xavér Szabó (Berlin: de Gruyter, 2014), 214.

6. Fitzmyer, *Tobit*, 291.

7. This despite Paul's frequent acknowledgment of women in leadership positions in Romans 16:1-3, 7, prompting many scholars to view 1 Corinthians 14:33b-36 to be a non-Pauline addition.

⁶Then Raphael called the two of them privately and said to them, "Bless God and acknowledge him in the presence of all the living for the good things he has done for you. Bless and sing praise to his name. With fitting honor declare to all people the deeds of God. Do not be slow to acknowledge him. ⁷It is good to conceal the secret of a king, but to acknowledge and reveal the works of God, and with fitting honor to acknowledge him. Do good, and evil will not overtake you. ⁸Prayer with fasting is good, but better than both is almsgiving with righteousness. A little with righteousness is better than wealth with wrongdoing. It is better to give alms than to lay up gold. ⁹For almsgiving saves from death and purges away every sin. Those who give alms will enjoy a full life, ¹⁰but those who commit sin and do wrong are their own worst enemies.

¹¹"I will now declare the whole truth to you and will conceal nothing from you. Already I have declared it to you when I said, 'It is good to conceal the secret of a king, but to reveal with due honor the works of God.' ¹²So now, when you and Sarah prayed, it was I who brought and read the record of your prayer before the glory of the Lord, and likewise whenever you buried the dead. ¹³And that time when you did not hesitate to get up and leave your dinner to go and bury the dead, ¹⁴I was sent to you to test you. And at the same time God sent me to heal you and Sarah your daughter-in-law. ¹⁵I am Raphael, one of the seven angels who stand ready and enter before the glory of the Lord."

fulfilled the latter. Ironically, given the former of Raphael's instructions, Tobit in chapter 13 addresses God as "King"—and this during a public declaration. But for a human king, secrets must be kept. Tobit would know this, as he held a position at court (1:13-14). No secrets from that time does Tobit disclose.

Leaders do need to have aids that they can trust: assistants, for example, who won't reveal plans that are incomplete. But if those in leadership are engaged in criminal activity, and assistants keep quiet because they fear retaliation, secrecy becomes a betrayal of public trust. Transparency in that situation is the better response. Laws that protect whistleblowers in the United States have been improved over the past two decades.[8]

Raphael's saying to Tobit and Tobias, "Do good and evil will not overtake you," comes across as facile, particularly given his audience. Tobit,

---

8. https://whistleblowersofamerica.org/2019/04/01/what-is-whistleblower-retaliation/.

Anna, and Sarah didn't do anything to deserve the painful experiences that they and, consequently, their families went through. Evil did overtake them, despite their doing good. The statement implies that if bad things happen, the person has done something bad to warrant it. Raphael's statement is unhelpful and leads to victim blaming. A feminist approach means resisting a biblical text that is harmful; taking issue with such passages facilitates positive engagement; the text can be used to teach sensitivity and compassion for those whom the words hurt and alienate. By pointing out the differences among the contexts in which the texts were written versus now, biblical texts remain relevant and inspire positive change.

Verse 8a states that "prayer with fasting is good." Prayer and fasting are frequently described as being done together in biblical history, and there are several fast days during the Jewish calendar year. The most significant of these communal fasts is Yom Kippur, the Day of Atonement: the community prays and fasts together from sundown to sundown. Biblical writers believed fasting to be efficacious in influencing God to answer petitions (Lev 16:29-31; Judg 20:26; 2 Sam 12:16). During the Hellenistic period, fasting continued to be observed (1 Macc 3:44-48; Esth 4:1-3,15; Jdt 8:6), though the writer of Tobit does not explicitly describe any of the characters in the story as engaging in fasting.[9]

Jesus valued prayer with fasting and encouraged his followers to do both (Matt 6:16-18). Orthodox Christians fast on Wednesdays (in remembrance of the betrayal of Christ) and on Fridays (in remembrance of his crucifixion and death). Muslims come together to fast and pray during the month of Ramadan. Jews fast on Yom Kippur, the Day of Atonement. For Jews, Christians, and Muslims, communal fasting is meant to assist in the resetting of the human relationship with God and with other people. The hope is to achieve community renewal, repair of individual relationships with God, self-discipline. Fasting teaches "that we can control our stomachs rather than have our stomachs control us."[10]

Such a practice also sensitizes us to the fact that many people lack sufficient food. If we feel the discomfort of hunger pangs ourselves, perhaps we will more readily empathize with those who go hungry and take action to improve their situation. Communal fasting furthermore

---

9. Amy-Jill Levine, "Tobit," in *The New Oxford Annotated Bible: New Revised Standard Version with Apocrypha*, ed. Michael D. Coogan, 3rd ed. (Oxford: Oxford University Press, 2001), 27.

10. Amy-Jill Levine, *Sermon on the Mount: A Beginner's Guide to the Kingdom of Heaven* (Nashville: Abingdon, 2020), 93.

provides the opportunity of discussing fasting in a healthy manner, i.e., only if it will not bring harm to one's health and if one is not struggling with eating disorders, such as anorexia, bulimia, or binge eating.[11] Studies have shown that individuals who perceive themselves to be ineffective and fear loss of self-control might use food as a means of gaining and maintaining control and efficacy.[12] While recent research has revealed that the number of males suffering from eating disorders has previously been underestimated, such disorders predominantly afflict girls and women.[13] Western society places intensive pressure on females to be slim, prompting young women to be very critical of their bodies and to engage in dieting. Recent studies, moreover, have discovered neurobiological foundations behind why females are more susceptible than men to eating disorders.[14]

The stipulation that monetary support was to be given "with righteousness" suggests that such giving could be given *without* righteousness, such as providing help in order to garner praise or giving money with strings attached, as a means of buying support or attempting to manipulate the recipient. The text stipulates that having fewer funds, acquired fairly, is better than "wealth with wrongdoing" and that it "is better to give alms than to lay up gold" (v. 8b). See Tobit 4:10 (pp. 96–99) regarding the idea that almsgiving "delivers from death" and that the practice of giving monetary support to the poor replaces temple sacrifice. The author of Tobit presumes his audience has some wealth, with at least certain members having the capacity to give money to the less fortunate.

Those who "commit sin and do wrong" (12:10) "are their own worst enemies" (literally, they are "enemies of their own life" [G1] or "their own self" [G2]). The verse perhaps refers to individuals who, when they do wrong, make amends (to the degree possible) but find it hard to put their wrong in the past, for example, ruminating about past behavior that hurt family members or friends. Such unhealthy behavior can prevent

---

11. Levine, *Sermon on the Mount*, 93.

12. Franzisca V. Froreich, Lenny R. Vartanian, Jessica R. Grisham, and Stephen W. Touyz, "Dimensions of Control and Their Relation to Disordered Eating Behaviours and Obsessive-Compulsive Symptoms," *Journal of Eating Disorders* 4 (2016): 1–9.

13. Women "have 1.75-3 times as high lifetime prevalence for anorexia, bulimia, or binge-eating disorder as compared to men" (Barbara Spanjers, "Eating Disorder Statistics: Get the Facts Here," Center for Discovery; https://centerfordiscovery.com/blog/get-the-facts-eating-disorder-statistics/).

14. Catherine Preston, H. Henrik Ehrsson, "Illusory Obesity Triggers Body Dissatisfaction Responses in the Insula and Anterior Cingulate Cortex," *Cerebral Cortex* 26 (December 1, 2016): 4450–60.

momentum—we can be our own worst enemy, since this harsh judgement is coming from ourselves, not from an external enemy. Finding a good therapist and engaging in cognitive behavioral therapy can help in breaking this negative pattern.

Raphael tells the two men that he was the one who drew God's attention to both Tobit's and Sarah's prayers—he "brought and read the record" to God. This claim seems to contradict 3:16, which explicitly states that Sarah and Tobit's prayers "at that very moment [ἐν αὐτῷ τῷ καιρῷ] . . . were heard in the glorious presence of God." Other Second Temple Jewish literature mentions that angels conveyed prayers and good deeds to God; for example, 1 Enoch 15:1-2 states that Watchers interceded between God and humans. This suggests that God does not listen to prayers or know about good deeds unless angels convey them: Raphael also says that he's the one who told God about Tobit's burial of the dead. Perhaps Raphael meant to reassure Tobit that God knew his situation. Part of Tobit's prayer in chapter 3 had asked that God "not turn your face away from me" (3:6). Tobit felt alone, and he asked to "be released" from "so much distress" (3:6). I'm not sure how reassuring Raphael's information was for Tobit, however, as it means that God knew about Tobit's situation and *did nothing*. It is a rather damning position for God.

In verse 14 of G2 (omitted in G1) Raphael tells Tobit that he was "sent to test" him. The verb for "test," πειράσαι, is the same verb used in the Septuagint's translation of the "Akedah" (the "binding") and near-sacrifice of Isaac. Genesis 22:1 states that "God tested Abraham [ἐπείραζεν]" by asking him to offer his beloved son Isaac as a burnt offering. The Akedah connection elevates the Tobit narrative. But Genesis 22 is not the only example of God's testing his people. The Torah explains Israel's forty years of wandering the wilderness as God "testing you to know what was in your heart" (Deut 8:2). The Sermon on the Mount's Our Father prayer includes the line, "And do not bring us to the time of trial [πειρασμόν]" (Matt 6:13), and Jesus himself was "tested" or "tempted" by Satan in the wilderness (Mark 1:12-13; Luke 4:1-13).

These examples explain suffering as God's means of "testing" an individual. One commentator states, "The meaning of Tobit's trial is now revealed. It was not a sign of God's disfavor or of Tobit's sin but a trial of love sent to purify and test him."[15] Well-meaning people, trying to encour-

---

15. G. T. Montague, *The Books of Ruth and Tobit: With a Commentary* (New York: Paulist Press, 1973), 42–43, cited in Carey A. Moore, *Tobit: A New Translation with Introduction and Commentary* (New Haven: Yale University Press, 1996), 271.

age someone who is dealing with a painful situation, sometimes say, "You can get through this: God will never give you more than you can handle." I know some people who smile and say thank you to such a comment, but then mutter to themselves: "Then I wish I could handle less!" The idea that God tests us as a sign of divine love seems sadistic. Such thinking was disturbing enough to the writer of the Epistle of James to assert: "No one, when tempted, should say, 'I am being tempted by God'; for God cannot be tempted by evil and he himself tempts no one. But one is tempted by one's own desire, being lured and enticed by it" (1:13-14). Pope Francis, in 2019, supported a new rendering of the Our Father for the *Roman Missal* prepared by the Italian Bishops' Conference that alters the well-known "lead us not into temptation" with "do not let us fall into temptation."[16] This aligns with what the Epistle of James states, and attempts to dispel the idea that God tests humans, but what does one do with all the biblical verses that suggest the opposite? Abraham unknowingly is being tested by God when he is commanded to prepare his own son for sacrifice (Gen 22:1); God allows "the Satan" to test Job, much to Job's sorrow and pain. Our narrative promotes the understanding that God tests humans—as a sign of love. But such is not loving behavior; it is abusive.

When Tobit was suffering, he felt alone and distraught and asked to die. Thanks to Raphael's revelation, Tobit becomes aware that his suffering was not senseless; it was a test, not a random occurrence. Such a disclosure would be complicated to receive. On the one hand, Tobit might have felt relief hearing that God was actively involved in his life and so he was not alone; on the other hand, he now knew—directly from an angel—that the trials that had brought him so much pain were initiated by God. Tobit has every reason to be angry at God.

It would have been nice if Raphael addressed Sarah. She suffered, for who knows how many months or years, as her wedding nights turned into funerals. Raphael tells Tobit and Tobias that God heard her desperate prayer (v. 12) and that he was sent to heal her (v. 14)—two pieces of information that would have reassured her and perhaps rid her of any lingering "disgrace" (3:15). But Raphael does not invite her into his revelation. Raphael acknowledges Tobit's burial of the dead but says nothing about Sarah's piety and how she honored her father by not committing suicide. Nor does the writer address whether her experiences of being widowed seven times were divinely ordained tests. Sarah might have

16. Levine, *Sermon on the Mount*, 87.

asked Raphael why Tobit received an explanation about his suffering, but she did not. She might have asked whether the divine realm quantified human sadness and if Tobit had been considered sadder than she and so "deserved" the revelation. She might also have asked whether her seven dead husbands were being tested, and whether they were privy to that fact.

Tobit and Tobias, when Raphael called his secret meeting with the two of them, ought to have said, "Let us go and get our wives." If Raphael would have said, "No, this is for you only," the two men then could have stated, "There's nothing you could say to us that our wives would not be able to hear: they are our partners, they have suffered too, and they deserve to hear what you wish to say to us." Tobit and Tobias might have functioned as advocates for their wives. They did not. Maybe Raphael would not have understood such an appeal. Tobias sees in Sarah a helper (8:6) and a wife; Anna supports Tobit in multiple ways; Raguel and Edna work in partnership. Of the main characters only the angel is without a life partner. Anna and Sarah could have objected to this private meeting with Azariah as well. Tobias and Sarah had *just* arrived home, and now Tobias is called away from the celebration of his return to go off for a secret chat without them.

Had Anna a chance to speak with Raphael, she might have asked why God's attention was so focused on Tobit's experience, on testing and healing him, and not on her. She would have pointed out how sick with worry she was when Tobias went away—why was an angel not sent to comfort her? She would argue that she was just as worthy of attention. She was the one who cared for Tobit when he lost his sight, and she kept the household together when Tobit was not able to work.

Tobit and Tobias React to Raphael's Revelation (12:16-22)

Like Abram, who "fell on his face" when God proposed the establishment of a covenant with him (Gen 17:3), and Daniel, whose strength drained from him during his visionary experience so that he fell with his "face to the ground" (Dan 10:9), Tobit and Tobias are afraid and prostrate themselves. Raphael, providing the customary response to those undergoing an epiphany, tells them, "Do not be afraid" (v. 17), and encourages them to replace their trepidation with praising God.

Raphael's statement, "when I was with you, I was not acting on my own will, but by the will of God" (12:18), sounds defensive. It might signal the author's discomfort with having an angel of God lie about his

¹⁶The two of them were shaken; they fell face down, for they were afraid. ¹⁷But he said to them, "Do not be afraid; peace be with you. Bless God forevermore. ¹⁸As for me, when I was with you, I was not acting on my own will, but by the will of God. Bless him each and every day; sing his praises. ¹⁹Although you were watching me, I really did not eat or drink anything—but what you saw was a vision. ²⁰So now get up from the ground, and acknowledge God. See, I am ascending to him who sent me. Write down all these things that have happened to you." And he ascended. ²¹Then they stood up, and could see him no more. ²²They kept blessing God and singing his praises, and they acknowledged God for these marvelous deeds of his, when an angel of God had appeared to them.

identity. Or this angel is distinguishing his behavior from other, fallen, angels who *do* follow their own will. He furthermore states that he did not eat or drink (12:19), a long-held understanding (see Judg 6:18; 13:16) that angels do not consume food. At the same time, Raphael's lack of eating maintains boundaries between humans and angels and can be seen as another means of his distancing himself from human women, by not partaking of the fruit of their labor.

Next, he commissions Tobit and Tobias to record what has occurred (γράψατε πάντα ταῦτα τὰ συμβάντα ὑμῖν), another action commonly done after angelic or divine encounters (Exod 17:14; 1 En. 14:4; Rev 1:19). Raphael knows that the two men can write—they wrote out the *ketubah*. Perhaps there is a corollary implication that the women cannot. Then, like Jesus in Acts 1:9, Raphael rises up "to him who sent me," leaving Tobit and Tobias, like Jesus's disciples (Acts 1:10), staring up toward the heavens (10:20-21).

The chapter ends with verse 22 describing how Tobit and Tobias "kept blessing God and singing his praises and they acknowledged God for these marvelous deeds of his, when an angel of God had appeared to them." They are praising God more after Raphael's conversation with them than they did previously. It is much easier to thank God when life is going well—and after one has been visited by an angel. But the ideal is to be grateful at all times, not just in the good times. This is a positive ending for these two men, but other families living in the diaspora did not have angelic help, and they too suffered. Without an encounter with an angel, how was their suffering justified?

Tobit 13–14

Restoration

Just as Tobit was the primary character in the first two chapters, so also in these final two chapters he dominates. In 12:17-18, Raphael instructs Tobit and Tobias: "Bless God forevermore. . . . Bless him each and every day; sing his praises." And this is exactly what they do. Chapter 13 consists of Tobit's hymn of thanksgiving, motivated by God's healing his blindness. The writer identifies Tobit as exemplary of the exiled people of Israel, expressed in his prayer in 3:2-6, and culminating in this hymn. He articulates eschatological expectations for his people and for the city of Jerusalem with the confidence stemming from his recent healing and the influx of riches into his family. Given what God has done for him, Tobit expects God to do all the more for this people and their holy city.

Chapter 14 recounts Tobit's second testament to Tobias (his first was in 4:4-19) and describes Tobit's death and honorable burial. Instead of consisting mostly of ethical teachings, now Tobit focuses on the future for his son and family, for the people of Israel, and for Jerusalem.

Tobit Thanks God (13:1-7)

The narrative depicts Tobit's hymn of praise (13:1–14:1) as if he recited it out of thankfulness for the restoring of his eyesight, with vocabulary redolent of that of Psalms 92–118. Typical of most psalms, there is little in

Tob 13:1-7

13:1Then Tobit said:
"Blessed be God who lives forever,
  because his kingdom lasts
    throughout all ages.
2For he afflicts, and he shows
    mercy;
  he leads down to Hades in the
    lowest regions of the
    earth,
  and he brings up from the
    great abyss,
  and there is nothing that can
    escape his hand.
3Acknowledge him before the
    nations, O children of
    Israel;

for he has scattered you
    among them.
4He has shown you his
    greatness even there.
Exalt him in the presence of every
    living being,
  because he is our Lord and he
    is our God;
  he is our Father and he is God
    for ever.
5He will afflict you for your
    iniquities,
  but he will again show mercy
    on all of you.
He will gather you from all the
    nations

it that refers to Tobit's personal situation; it is probably a composite work "comprising two or more separate compositions which have been welded together, edited and framed as a unified song of praise."[1] It emphasizes the narrative's theme that Jews living in the diaspora continue to hope in and praise God. Verse 2 contains the first of three references to God's punishing and then having mercy on his people (13:2 and 13:5) and on the city of Jerusalem (13:9), an emphasis seen in Tobit's earlier doxology (11:14-15) with the pairing of the words "afflicted" and "mercy." In chapter 11, the terms refer to Tobit's blindness and then healing. Here in chapter 13 Tobit speaks to fellow Israelites and to the city of Jerusalem.[2] The repetition of the Deuteronomistic view that sin prompts punishment—a concern that is communal, not individual—and repentance leads to redemption repeats the idea that God inflicts suffering on humans because they sin. But we've already seen that Tobit is not a trustworthy narrator. For a character who has just experienced a personal

1. Ruth Henderson, "A Scriptural Model for the Song of Tobit (Tobit 13:1-18)," *JSP* 17 (2017): 58.

2. Carey A. Moore, *Tobit: A New Translation with Introduction and Commentary* (New Haven: Yale University Press, 1996), 277: "The Deuteronomic formula of 'punishment then pardon' frequently refers to God's treatment of Israel as a nation."

among whom you have been
scattered.
⁶If you turn to him with all your
heart and with all your
soul,
to do what is true before him,
then he will turn to you
and will no longer hide his face
from you.
So now see what he has done for
you;
acknowledge him at the top of
your voice.
Bless the Lord of righteousness,

and exalt the King of the ages.
In the land of my exile I
acknowledge him,
and show his power and
majesty to a nation of
sinners:
'Turn back, you sinners, and do
what is right before him;
perhaps he may look with
favor upon you and
show you mercy.'
⁷As for me, I exalt my God,
and my soul rejoices in the
King of heaven."

encounter with an angel, this might not be a troubling message, but for others it is a way of thinking that potentially compounds their pain by blaming them for bringing it on themselves.

Verse 2 confirms God's omnipotence: God sends people to Hades ("in the lowest regions of the earth") and can rescue people from there as well ("and he brings up from the great abyss"). The Hebrew fragment 4Q200 of this verse refers to Sheol (שאול), the dark abode located under the earth where people went after death (Job 10:20-21; Ps 115:17; Num 16:30). The Septuagint typically translates the Hebrew *Sheol* with "Hades," as is done here. Hades was the Greek god of the underworld, but the term usually refers to the netherworld, his domain. In the Tanakh, Sheol is not a place of retribution but rather a type of holding tank for souls of the dead. Those who cared for other people and those who cared only for themselves were sent there. The Tanakh does not contain a well-developed sense of life after death; Jews developed a clearer perspective of the afterlife under Persian, Greek, and then Roman influence. The mid-second-century BCE book of Daniel states, "Many of those who sleep in the dust of the earth shall awake, some to everlasting life, and some to shame and everlasting contempt" (12:2). This is the first clear statement referring to a resurrection, final judgment, and afterlife (see also Ezek 37; Hos 6:2; Isa 26:19), which becomes a part of Jewish, Christian, and Muslim tradition.

The second part of Tobit 13:2, "and he brings up from the great abyss," is not referring to resurrection but to the power of God to rescue from Sheol; Hannah's prayer in 1 Samuel 2:6 reflects a similar sentiment: "The LORD kills and brings to life; he brings down to Sheol and raises up." As Jon Levenson points out, some of those in Sheol are not dead but rather are so ill, weak, or defeated they are there, among the dead.[3] The author of Psalm 88, for example, is not yet dead but mortally ill and is already in Sheol ("I am counted among those who go down to the Pit"; v. 4). God had the power to intervene and rescue people from the abode of the dead: for example, Psalm 40:2, "He drew me up from the desolate pit, out of the miry bog, and set my feet upon a rock, making my steps secure." Tobit is divinely rescued from his suffering —from Sheol—and now praises God and encourages others to do so as well (vv. 3 and 4). Acknowledging God is more difficult, however, for those who are not as lucky as Tobit and are not rescued from their pain.

Verses 3-4a declare that God has "scattered you"—that is, Israel— among "the nations" and that "He has shown you his greatness even there." Readers living in exile are to persevere, despite their challenging circumstances. From Tobit's perspective, all will be well because—even if it seems unlikely—God is in control of their lives. With the benefit of hindsight, Tobit now can see, just as readers always could, what God has done for him (v. 6). Tobit's response is to publicly praise God, as Raphael instructed. But how does this work for those people who cannot see what God has done in their lives? It is difficult, for example, to see how Sarah's seven dead husbands would be able to share in Tobit's enthusiasm.

Tobit's hymn uses male imagery to describe God's relationship with Israel. God is "our father" (13:4), with connotations of a disciplinarian who seeks to teach his children righteousness through chastisement (13:2) and, when his children turn to him in repentance, mercy (13:6). It is a patriarchal image found elsewhere in the Tanakh: God is the all-powerful head of the family, with Israelites as his children (cf. Deut 32:6; Isa 63:16; 2 Sam 7:14; 1 Chr 22:9-10) and in rabbinic literature too; for example, Jews are to behave as "sons of the Lord your God" (b. Qidd. 36a). We see the image of God as Father continued in Christian Scripture: Jesus calls God "Abba" ("Father" in Aramaic[4]) in Mark 14:36, and

---

3. Jon D. Levenson, *Resurrection and the Restoration of Israel: The Ultimate Victory of the God of Life* (New Haven: Yale University Press, 2008), 45.

4. In modern Hebrew, *abba* can correctly be translated as "daddy," but in Jesus's time, the word meant "father," and it was a term that Jesus as well as other Jews

he teaches his followers to do likewise in the prayer known as the Our Father, or Lord's Prayer, in Matthew 6:9 (cf. Luke 11:2). Moses, in his concluding poem, calls God the father of the Israelites in Deuteronomy 32:6, and Jews address God as "Father" in postbiblical prayers in Sirach 23:1; 51:10. In contemporary prayers, such as the Avinu Malkeinu ("Our father, our king"), recited in Jewish services on Rosh Hashanah and Yom Kippur, as well on the Ten Days of Repentance from Rosh Hashanah through Yom Kippur,[5] calling God "Father" calls to mind the affirmative images of fatherhood: God as benefactor, guardian, compassionate and loving, and, "our" father, uniting all of those participating in the prayer into one family.

But this "father" language also reinforces a patriarchal framework in which fathers had supreme power in a family—not only as parent but as chief provider, teacher, disciplinarian, judge, owner. The association of fathers with the divine both draws on and buttresses the hierarchical gender models of male superiority over females. The dominant depictions of God as male can be alienating for individuals who do not identify as male or for those persons whose experience with their own fathers was harmful or negative. I am fortunate that my own relationship with my father is loving and respectful, but I nonetheless get annoyed and distracted by exclusively male language in prayers. The solution that works for me is to use the Reform Jewish High Holy Days prayer book *Mishkan HaNefesh*, which, for example, includes a version of Avinu Malkeinu that refers to God as both "Loving Father" and "Compassionate Mother."[6] But this version too has its potential problems. Mothers are not always compassionate, just as fathers are not always loving.

Our narrative's more frequent metaphor describes God as king (13:6, 7, 10, 11, 15, 16), as one who possesses ultimate power (13:2, 6) and majesty (13:6). God is called King forty-seven times in the Tanakh[7] and

---

used to address God. See further Mary Rose D'Angelo, "Abba and 'Father': Imperial Theology and the Jesus Traditions," *JBL* 111 (1992): 611–20; James Barr, "'Abbā Isn't 'Daddy,'" *JTS* 39 (1988): 28–47.

5. A beautiful rendition: https://www.youtube.com/watch?v=CkiUOF0bQJc.

6. *Mishkan haNefesh: Machzor for the Days of Awe*, ed. Edwin Goldberg, Janet Marder, Sheldon Marder, and Leon Morris (New York: Central Conference for American Rabbis, 2015), 131.

7. Carol Meyers, "Female Images of God," in *Women in Scripture: A Dictionary of Named and Unnamed Women in the Hebrew Bible, the Apocryphal/Deuterocanonical Books, and the New Testament*, ed. Carol Meyers, Toni Craven, and Ross S. Kraemer (Grand Rapids: Eerdmans, 2000), 526.

frequently, too, in intertestamental literature (Sir 23:1, 4; 51:10; 3 Macc 5:7). God is referred to as King in the New Testament as well (e.g., in Rev 15:3, as "King of kings" in Rev 19:16; 1 Tim 1:17; 6:15; and "kingdom of God" is a frequent expression in the Synoptics, e.g., Mark 1:15; Luke 4:43; 11:20; 16:16, etc.).

Hebrew is a gendered language, with all nouns either male or female. Ancient Greek nouns are grammatically gendered masculine, feminine, and neuter. The Hebrew words for God (El, אל, and Elohim, אלוהים) are masculine. Yet the Tanakh offers several female-identified depictions of God, for example, in Numbers 11:12, Moses ascribes to God the maternal actions of bearing and nursing Israel. The second part of Isaiah (chapters 40–66) describes God in motherly terms with regard to the inability to forget Zion (Jerusalem), for example, in the rhetorical questions: "Can a woman forget her nursing child, or show no compassion for the child of her womb?" (Isa 49:15).[8] Carol Meyers notes that such maternal images "helped people understand the intimate and abiding love, care, and compassion of their God."[9] But this suggests a rigid gender division in which only women can possess maternal characteristics. Men are capable of love, care, and compassion—as are women who are not mothers.

Language accentuating God's power and sovereignty buttresses the confidence of readers who might feel that their lives are every bit as obstacle-ridden as that of Tobit and Sarah. But Tobit highlights divine mercy as well: "he shows mercy" (13:2); "he will again show mercy on all of you" (13:5); "he may look with favor upon you and show you mercy" (13:6); "he . . . will again have mercy on the children of the righteous" (13:9). One of Qumran's Hebrew fragments (4Q200 6:5-7) uses the word מרחם, "shows mercy," in 13:2. The writer of Tobit expresses God's mercy using maternal imagery in the Hebrew version.[10]

Tobit also encourages readers to take action, for example: "Acknowledge him" (13:3) and "Exalt him" (13:4); "acknowledge him" (13:6); "Bless the Lord . . . and exalt the King" (13:6); "see what he has done for you" (13:6); "Go . . . and rejoice" (13:13). Tobit's behavior thus becomes paradigmatic for all Israelites: "I acknowledge him and show his power

8. Meyers, "Female Images of God," 527.

9. Meyers, "Female Images of God," 528.

10. רחם in L. Koehler, W. Baumgartner, and J. J. Stamm, *The Hebrew and Aramaic Lexicon of the Old Testament*, vol. 3, trans. and ed. M. E. J. Richardson (Leiden: Brill, 1996), 1218; Meyers, "Female Images of God," 526, also makes this point, though not specifically about Tobit.

and majesty" (13:6); "I exalt my God" and "my soul rejoices" (13:7); "My soul blesses the Lord" (13:15). In following him, they can anticipate being looked upon "with favor . . . and mercy" (13:6), just as Tobit experienced. These actions are to be taken "before the nations" (13:3) and "in the presence of every living being" (13:4)—echoing Raphael's instructions to Tobit and Tobias to acknowledge God "in the presence of all the living" and to tell of God's deeds "to all people" (12:6; also 13:8). This expresses a universalist inclination that is picked up in the final chapter (14:6-7). But having Tobit be the model for all is problematic: he is a buffoon; he is arrogant and entitled.

In 13:5-6, Tobit urges "the children of Israel," who are "scattered" about, to turn toward God so that he may return to them and show them mercy. Yet his presence is "even there," in the diaspora (13:4). The promise of restoration echoes Deuteronomy 30:1-5:

> When all these things have happened to you, the blessings and the curses that I have set before you, if you call them to mind among all the nations where the LORD your God has driven you, and return to the LORD your God, and you and your children obey him with all your heart and with all your soul, just as I am commanding you today, then the LORD your God will restore your fortunes and have compassion on you, gathering you again from all the peoples among whom the LORD your God has scattered you. Even if you are exiled to the ends of the world, from there the LORD your God will gather you, and from there he will bring you back. The LORD your God will bring you into the land that your ancestors possessed, and you will possess it; he will make you more prosperous and numerous than your ancestors.

The call to "return" to God is a call for repentance. The Hebrew word in Deuteronomy 30:2 is שׁוּב, used in a theological sense to mean "to turn back to God" or "to be devoted to God";[11] the Septuagint uses the verb ἐπιστρέφω, "to return." For Tobit, "If you turn to him with all your heart and with all your soul, to do what is true before him, then he will turn to you and will no longer hide his face from you" (13:6), yet later in the same verse, he states, "Turn back, you sinners, and do what is right before him; *perhaps* he may look with favor upon you and show you mercy." This shift from definitive ("he will turn to you") to possible ("perhaps he may look with favor upon you") echoes Jonah 3:9, in which the king of

---

11. שׁוּב in L. Koehler, W. Baumgartner, and J. J. Stamm, *The Hebrew and Aramaic Lexicon of the Old Testament*, vol. 4, trans. and ed. M. E. J. Richardson (Leiden: Brill, 1999), 1429.

Nineveh states: "Who knows? God may relent and change his mind; he may turn from his fierce anger, so that we do not perish." The uncertainty expressed in both texts reinforces God's power and that humans are not to practice their piety with the goal of manipulating God. Whether anything positive happens is God's decision alone, even if humans do the "right" thing. Israelites living in the diaspora are encouraged to restore their commitment by turning back to God, but God is not a robot, and the ultimate decisions about the unfolding of the divine plans are God's.

The ingathering of the exiles "into the land that your ancestors possessed," described in verse 5, is a common motif in Second Temple Jewish literature and comes to be understood in Jewish tradition as a sign of the messianic age, when the people of Israel will be liberated from dominion by foreign rulers and will return to Jerusalem (14:7; Sir 36:10; Bar 5:1-9). Tobit begins with a focus on Jerusalem (1:4-10), and, in a full-circle sense, 13:8-17 again pinpoint Jerusalem. The yearning for a rebuilt temple infuses Jewish liturgy, exemplified in the Passover Haggadah's final line, which is "next year in Jerusalem" for Jews living outside of the land of Israel, and "next year in Jerusalem, the rebuilt" for those living in it. The status of modern Jerusalem remains one of the most contentious issues in the Israeli-Palestinian conflict. During the 1948 Arab-Israeli War, West Jerusalem was among the areas Israel captured and later annexed, while East Jerusalem, including the Old City, was captured by Jordan. Israel took East Jerusalem during the 1967 Six-Day War and subsequently appropriated it. Although Israelis call Jerusalem Israel's "undivided capital," the international community has rejected the annexation of East Jerusalem as illegal and considers it Palestinian territory held by Israel under military occupation. I support a two-state solution: the state of Israel and the state of Palestine, and in my view East Jerusalem should belong to the Palestinians and West Jerusalem to Israel, with shared governance of the Temple Mount, guarded by United Nations peacekeepers. This means that the Israeli government would need to yield its claim of an "undivided" capital.[12]

Given 3:16-17, the positive outcome of the stories of Tobit and Sarah is secure. What was not known and could only be discovered through com-

---

12. Daniel Miller, "The History of 'Israel' and 'Palestine': Alternative Names, Competing Claims," *The Conversation*, July 6, 2021; https://theconversation.com/the -history-of-israel-and-palestine-alternative-names-competing-claims-163156.

pleting the full tale was how the successful ending would be achieved.[13] Carey Moore suggests that the author was "[m]ore interested in character development than in plot development" and wished readers to focus on the narrative's prayers and exhortations.[14] But the characters change little through the story: Tobit begins as a pompous and self-important man and he ends that way too. Readers would not relate with Tobit—a pretentious man blinded by bird poop who treats his wife badly. Nor would many of them identify with the wealthy but unfortunate Sarah. But as entertainment, this story was riveting. Like the *Real Housewives* reality series about wealthy women living in a particular city (the popularity of which has launched series in eleven different American cities and several other spin-offs), you do not need to relate to characters—or even admire them—to be curious about their lives.

Promises of Justice and a Better Future for Those Who Suffer Now (13:8-17)

The second part of the thanksgiving (13:9-18) anachronistically presupposes the Babylonian exile (586–539 BCE) and destruction of the first temple in 586 BCE by Nebuchadnezzar II. Here we get a sense of an eschatological vision: just as Tobit, Sarah, and their families experienced affliction first, then mercy, so too would "the holy city" (13:9) Jerusalem. "He will gather you from all the nations" is a promise of a return to Israel, to Jerusalem—the "chosen city" (13:11)—where "his tent may be rebuilt" (13:10), and the city will "be built as his house for all ages" (13:16). The divine passive (οἰκοδομηθήσετα) in 13:16 signals that God will rebuild the temple, a theme, as already mentioned, expressed in various Jewish texts, including in Ezra–Nehemiah. The text makes special mention of captives (that they be cheered) and of the distressed (that they be loved) among the people of Jerusalem. Rescuing captives (v. 10), usually through the payment of ransom, is considered a major mitzvah (commandment) in Judaism. Rabbinic texts identify captivity as worse than starvation and death (b. B. Bat. 8b), and returning captive soldiers to their homes is a priority in modern-day Israel, where there is

---

13. Francis M. Macatangay, "Apocalypticism and Narration in the Book of Tobit," in *Canonicity, Setting Wisdom in the Deuterocanonicals: Papers of the Jubilee Meeting of the International Conference on the Deuterocanonical Books*, ed. Géza G. Xeravits, József Zsengellér, and Xavér Szabó (Berlin: de Gruyter, 2014), 208.

14. Moore, *Tobit*, 157.

Tob 13:8-17

8"Let all people speak of his majesty,
and acknowledge him in
Jerusalem.
9O Jerusalem, the holy city,
he afflicted you for the deeds of
your hands,
but will again have mercy on the
children of the righteous.
10Acknowledge the Lord, for he is
good,
and bless the King of the ages,
so that his tent may be rebuilt in
you in joy.
May he cheer all those within you
who are captives,
and love all those within you who
are distressed,
to all generations forever.
11A bright light will shine to all the
ends of the earth;

many nations will come to you
from far away,
the inhabitants of the remotest parts
of the earth to your holy name,
bearing gifts in their hands for the
King of heaven.
Generation after generation will give
joyful praise in you;
the name of the chosen city will
endure forever.
12Cursed are all who speak a harsh
word against you;
cursed are all who conquer you
and pull down your walls,
all who overthrow your towers
and set your homes on fire.
But blessed forever will be all who
revere you.
13Go, then, and rejoice over the
children of the righteous,

almost universal military service.[15] Then, the text states, "the nations"—the non-Jewish neighbors—would make pilgrimage to Jerusalem to worship God. This universalism suggests that these neighbors will remain non-Jews but that they will worship "the King of heaven" (v. 11). This eschatological vision has Jerusalem as the site of universal pilgrimage, a sign of the messianic age (Zech 2:11; 14:16). The expectation is for a transformed, ideal world, one in which the temple is rebuilt, Jerusalem is restored, and happiness reigns.

Not only Israelites are expected to be positively affected by this transformed world, but "the nations" are as well. On the one hand, that seems

15. The amount of ransom to be paid can be controversial, as it usually involves the liberation of Palestinian prisoners. A recent case that became well known was that of soldier Gilad Shalit, who was held by Hamas from 2006 until his release in 2011 as part of a deal that exchanged 1,027 prisoners for him (Barak Ravid, "The Israeli Academic Who Played a Critical Role in the Shalit Deal," *Haaretz*, October 14, 2011; https://www.haaretz.com/1.5191182).

for they will be gathered together
and will praise the Lord of the ages.
[14]Happy are those who love you,
and happy are those who rejoice
in your prosperity.
Happy also are all people who grieve
with you
because of your afflictions;
for they will rejoice with you
and witness all your glory forever.
[15]My soul blesses the Lord, the great
King!
[16]For Jerusalem will be built as his
house for all ages.
How happy I will be if a remnant of my
descendants should survive
to see your glory and
acknowledge the King of
heaven.

The gates of Jerusalem will be built
with sapphire and emerald,
and all your walls with precious
stones.
The towers of Jerusalem will be built
with gold,
and their battlements with pure
gold.
The streets of Jerusalem will be
paved
with ruby and with stones of
Ophir.
[17]The gates of Jerusalem will sing
hymns of joy,
and all her houses will cry,
'Hallelujah!
Blessed be the God of Israel!'
and the blessed will bless the holy
name forever and ever."

generous.[16] But on the other hand, the peoples of these nations are expected to come to Jerusalem, "bearing gifts in their hands for the King of heaven" and are to "give joyful praise" (v. 11) to the divinity that Tobit worships. This eschatological vision strikes me as being like that of some Christians that focuses on converting everyone to Christianity—there is no accepting the "others" or "strangers" in one's midst just as they are; they must change. In such a Christian eschatological scenario, nonbelievers in Jesus as Messiah must become believers, and in the one described in Tobit, non-Jewish peoples must worship the God of the Jews.

This topic touches on complicated contemporary issues pertaining to minority rights within countries and whether it is possible for minority groups to preserve their own cultures, including religious practices, when they differ from those of the majority. In Canada in 1988 the Canadian Multiculturalism Law, whose purpose is to protect and increase

---

16. Moore, *Tobit*, 280–81, writes, "Although Tobit may have confined most of his time and charity to his fellow Israelites, here Tobit's (or better, the author's) compassion and broad-mindedness are clearly evident."

cultural diversity (or multiculturalism) in Canada, was passed.[17] The law is intended to, among other things, "ensure that all individuals receive equal treatment and equal protection under the law, while respecting and valuing their diversity,"[18] correctives desperately needed given the egregious ways Canadian governmental policies had treated Indigenous and First Nations peoples. One example of such treatment is the residential school system, created by the government and administered by churches in order to remove Indigenous children from the influence of their own culture and forcefully assimilate them into the dominant Canadian culture.[19] In 2008, the government of Canada finally made a Statement of Apology to former students of Indian residential schools. And although there is no amount of monetary compensation that can make up for the damage incurred to First Nations communities and individuals, it is crucial that the government make these payments, as it provides accountability that will contribute toward the healing process and rebuilding of trust of Indigenous peoples. Financial and human resources, furthermore, ought to be provided so that the remains of children buried in unmarked graves around residential schools can be identified and either returned to their communities or be honored with memorials in the cemeteries in which they are found, in accordance with the wishes of the relevant Indigenous leadership. Had Tobit's eschatological vision depicted non-Israelite peoples being welcomed to participate in the splendor of the messianic age without having to change, it would have been more equitable.

Like other cities mentioned in the Bible, Jerusalem is personified in 13:9 as female; more, she is "personified as a desolate mother, bereft of her children."[20] Carey Moore notes, "God's treatment of Widow Jerusalem/Zion contains disturbing images of spousal abuse. Jerusalem is punished and abandoned by her 'spouse' YHWH for the sins of their children."[21] This imagery is not unique to Tobit but is found in other literature as well: 1 Maccabees 1:38 states that Jerusalem "became a dwelling of strangers;

---

17. Stephen J. Tierney, ed., *Multiculturalism and the Canadian Constitution* (Vancouver: UBC Press, 2007).

18. Section 3.1 e.

19. John S. Milloy, *A National Crime: The Canadian Government and the Residential School System 1879–1986* (Winnipeg: University of Manitoba Press, 1999).

20. Carey A. Moore, "Jerusalem/Zion as Widow and Mother," in Meyers, Craven, and Kraemer, *Women in Scripture*, 531.

21. Moore, "Jerusalem/Zion as Widow and Mother," 530.

she became strange to her offspring, and her children forsook her," and 2:9 says that "her infants have been killed in her streets, her youths by the swords of the foe," while in Baruch 4:12, Jerusalem addresses her enemies, "Let no one rejoice over me, a widow and bereaved of many; I was left desolate because of the sins of my children." The image of Jerusalem as a wife who "plays the whore" is found in Ezekiel (16:1-63), and elsewhere (Hos 2:2-5; Jer 3:1-13), conveying the worship of other gods, described as sexual immorality. In the book of Revelation, the great whore of Babylon is a notorious image of Rome accompanied by accusations of illicit sex (17:2), drunkenness (17:2, 4), and murder (17:6). Cities were grammatically constructed as feminine in Hebrew and in Greek, so this might have led to the personification of cities as females (either as wives or daughters). In the ancient Near East, "a city is always spoken of as the mother of its inhabitants and so is personified as a female. As a mother, a city will inevitably share the fate of her children, that is, all the joys and sorrows of her population."[22] I find the use of gender to identify cities to be offensive, in particular when the language of rape is used, as in my view it is language that should be reserved for humans. Yes, people can treat cities violently, but surely words other than "rape" can be used to convey this.

Tobit's Final Words (14:1-4)

Our story comes full circle: it began with Tobit's honoring of the dead by digging graves for his fellow Israelites, and the last chapter begins with the burial "with great honor" of Tobit himself.

In chapter 14:1-11a, Tobit gives his second testament (his first was in 4:1-13), but this time he truly is on his death bed. Like the dying Jacob, who gives his son Joseph details regarding his burial and then blesses his grandsons (Gen 47:29; 48:9-20), the dying Tobit summons Tobias and his seven grandsons. This second testimony declares that Tobit, after regaining his eyesight, "lived in prosperity" (13:2) and so confirms what Tobit had insisted on in his first, that "those who act in accordance with truth will prosper in all their activities" (4:6).

Tobit's living to a venerable age of 112 years old and his dying "in peace" (v. 2) seem intended to demonstrate God's favor toward him,

---

22. Carey A. Moore, "Enemy Cities as Female," in Meyers, Craven, and Kraemer, *Women in Scripture*, 521.

¹⁴:¹So ended Tobit's words of praise.

²Tobit died in peace when he was one hundred and twelve years old, and was buried with great honor in Nineveh. He was sixty-two years old when he lost his eyesight, and after regaining it he lived in prosperity, giving alms and continually blessing God and acknowledging God's majesty.

³When he was about to die, he called his son Tobias and the seven sons of Tobias and gave this command: "My son, take your children ⁴and hurry off to Media, for I believe the word of God that Nahum spoke about Nineveh, that all these things will take place and overtake Assyria and Nineveh. Indeed, everything that was spoken by the prophets of Israel, whom God sent, will occur. None of all their words will fail, but all will come true at their appointed times. So it will be safer in Media than in Assyria and Babylon. For I know and believe that whatever God has said will be fulfilled and will come true; not a single word of the prophecies will fail. All of our kindred, inhabitants of the land of Israel, will be scattered and taken as captives from the good land; and the whole land of Israel will be desolate, even Samaria and Jerusalem will be desolate. And the temple of God in it will be burned to the ground, and it will be desolate for a while.

but Tobit is not a reliable narrator. The message that a long life and a peaceful death are divine rewards is problematic. There is no good reason to think that Sarah's seven husbands were being punished when the demon killed them. Tobit's burial "with great honor" (v. 2), while providing a satisfactory response to his jeopardizing his personal safety to ensure that others received respectable burials, makes me think of all the family and friends who wished desperately to hold funerals but could not because of the COVID-19 pandemic; or of the people whose bodies remain in hidden graves, whether in Cambodia, El Salvador, or throughout Nazi-occupied Europe; or among the unmarked graves of Indigenous children at Indian residential schools throughout Canada.²³ The pain caused by these situations would be multiplied by a message conveying that divine judgement had been involved.

Tobit summons only males to his bedside. Perhaps this is because he wished to speak to his descendants only, and neither Anna nor Sarah was part of that group. We are not told if Tobias had any daughters. The mention of seven grandsons (v. 3) means that Edna's hope for grandchil-

23. Ian Austen and Dan Bilefsky, "Hundreds More Unmarked Graves Found at Former Residential Schools in Canada," *New York Times*, June 24, 2021.

dren (10:12) was fulfilled. The number of grandsons corresponds with the number of Sarah's grooms Asmodeus killed; seven times Asmodeus robbed Sarah of the chance to have children. That Sarah ended up having seven sons provides a nice literary balance, but if the author meant to convey that this was recompense for Sarah's earlier losses, I doubt that Sarah would agree. I doubt that Edna would agree either. Children are not the same as husbands. On the literary—or fairy-tale—level, this matter might be considered neatly tied up, but in terms of the personal feelings of a seven-time widow, it is not. Tobit urges his family to move to Media, where it "will be safer" (14:4). Perhaps in their country of origin the family would feel more comfortable, but their safety would not be guaranteed even there, since no place is perfectly secure.

With fervid conviction stemming from his personal experience, Tobit makes his most crucial point: that all will occur "at their appointed times [τοῖς καιροῖς αὐτῶν]" (14:4). The Greek καιροῖς can mean the "appropriate seasons or occasions or times" and is used in Matthew 21:41, "They said to him, 'He will put those wretches to a miserable death and lease the vineyard to other tenants who will give him the produce at the harvest time [ἐν τοῖς καιροῖς].'" The Greek, therefore, allows for the occurrence of events during the natural course of time, as opposed to divine causation. For Tobit, though, all is divinely appointed. He declares that the "word of God that Nahum spoke about Nineveh" (v. 4, reflected in the canonical book of Nahum 1:1–3:4, dating to the middle or late seventh century BCE) would come true and so presents as prophecy events that already had occurred by the writer's time, i.e., the destruction of Nineveh, which took place in 612 BCE (14:4, 15); Nebuchadnezzar's destruction of the Jerusalem temple in 586 BCE and the concomitant exile into Babylonia (v. 4); the people's return to the land of Israel under Cyrus the Great in 538 BCE and the rebuilding of both the temple and Jerusalem (v. 5). Modern readers know that these are not predictions per se, and so, in contrast to the hope that ancient readers might have derived from the text, we cannot build our hope on this false premise.

Tobit is like a fairy tale, where everyone (at the "appointed time") lives happily ever after. Reading a story in which everything works out for the central characters in the end is a satisfying activity sometimes. I have friends who, after a high-stress work week, say that watching a Hallmark movie is exactly what they find relaxing to do on the weekend (I admit that sometimes I watch them too). Such films are predictable: there's minimal tension and love always wins in the end. But when it comes to building our own futures, it is wiser to understand that life is not a fairy tale, and it consists of a challenging mixture of positive and negative vicissitudes and changes. Bob Dylan's song "The Times They Are A-Changin'" was released in 1964 and addresses a particular time in American politics, but the song's overarching theme of change fits any time period since change is *always* occurring. In times of turmoil and uncertainty, prayer or meditation can help us to center ourselves, as can journaling or reaching out for support from friends, family, or professional therapists.

The Return of Israelites to Jerusalem (14:5-9)

Verse 5 refers to the return of the people exiled from Judah (from this time forward called Jews) from the Babylonian exile and the reconstruction of the Jerusalem temple beginning around 516 BCE. Verse 6 refers to the eschatological expectation that Jerusalem will be the focus of divine power from which the entire world will be ruled. In the apocalyptic vision of Zechariah 14:16, all nations will come to observe the pilgrimage festival of Sukkot (Booths or Tabernacles): "Then all who survive of the nations . . . shall go up [to Jerusalem] year after year to worship the King, the Lord of hosts, and to keep the festival of booths" (Zech 14:16). Sukkot is an autumn harvest pilgrimage festival, during which it is customary to dwell in temporary booths in accordance with Leviticus 23:42-43. Dwelling in the sukkah is to experience protection from the sun (as Jonah did for a time, in 4:5), and the shade provided is understood as a metaphor for God's protection, as is expressed in the Psalmist's appeal to God: "Guard me like the apple of your eye; hide me in the shadow of your wings" (17:8; also 36:8; 57:2). These temporary shelters remind us of those who lack permanent housing and make us think of the effects of climate change on farmers' ability to experience rich harvests and the consequent problems of food shortages that this provokes.

The NRSV translation of ἐπιστρέψουσιν in Tobit 14:6 as "will convert" is misleading in suggesting that gentiles underwent a formal conversion process to Judaism. Although the verb ἐπιστρέφω can mean "to convert," its more frequent translation, which is more suitable in this context, is "to turn back or return," thus "will turn back" or "will return" to God.[24]

---

24. Alexander A. Di Lella, "Tobit," in *A New English Translation of the Septuagint*, ed. Albert Pietersma and Benjamin G. Wright (Oxford: Oxford University Press, 2007), 476, offers, "Then all the nations in the whole world will turn back and truly fear God. And all will abandon their idols, which deceitfully have made them err in their error."

Tob 14:5-9

⁵"But God will again have mercy on them, and God will bring them back into the land of Israel; and they will rebuild the temple of God, but not like the first one until the period when the times of fulfillment shall come. After this they all will return from their exile and will rebuild Jerusalem in splendor; and in it the temple of God will be rebuilt, just as the prophets of Israel have said concerning it. ⁶Then the nations in the whole world will all be converted and worship God in truth. They will all abandon their idols, which deceitfully have led them into their error; ⁷and in righteousness they will praise the eternal God. All the Israelites who are saved in those days and are truly mindful of God will be gathered together; they will go to Jerusalem and live in safety forever in the land of Abraham, and it will be given over to them. Those who sincerely love God will rejoice, but those who commit sin and injustice will vanish from all the earth. ⁸,⁹So now, my children, I command you, serve God faithfully and do what is pleasing in his sight. Your children are also to be commanded to do what is right and to give alms, and to be mindful of God and to bless his name at all times with sincerity and with all their strength. So now, my son, leave Nineveh; do not remain here.

The gentiles will cease to worship idols (they "will abandon" their idols [14:6]); instead, they "will truly fear God" (καὶ φοβηθήσονται τὸν θεὸν ἀληθινῶς), and "they will bless the God of the ages in righteousness" (εὐλογήσουσιν τὸν θεὸν τοῦ αἰῶνος ἐν δικαιοσύνῃ). But they remain gentiles.²⁵ Although there is the expectation that the gentiles will join in the worship of the God of Israel, their ethnic distinctions will be maintained. In this way, Jewish distinctiveness is preserved, and the distinctiveness of the various nations is likewise respected. If the gentiles all converted to Judaism, then Jews would be the only participants in this eschatological vision, and that would diminish its vibrancy and power.

The reference to idols leading the gentiles into error (v. 6) might strike people who use statues or icons as prayer tools—for example, Catholics and Hindus—as insulting. The author might be assuming that all individuals who use icons worship the icons rather than using them as

25. So Amy-Jill Levine, "Redrawing the Boundaries: A New Look at 'Diaspora as Metaphor: Bodies and Boundaries in the Book of Tobit,'" in *A Feminist Companion to Tobit and Judith*, ed. Athalya Brenner-Idan and Helen Efthimiadis-Keith, FCB 2.20 (London: Bloomsbury, 2015), 10.

instruments to focus their attention on the divine. If idolatrous worship is considered that which leads people astray, I can think of modern forms of it, such as making the accumulation of wealth the top priority, or the consumption of material goods, or caring too much about the number of "likes" we get on social media; all of these things distract us and frustrate us because they are never enough. The author of Ecclesiastes put it well, "The lover of money will not be satisfied with money; nor the lover of wealth, with gain. This also is vanity" (5:10). There are ways of worshiping that might lead to "error" (Tob 14:6)—if, for example, worshipers are doing so in order to draw admiring glances from others, or to hurt someone else, or to pretend in order to deceive someone. Jesus warns his disciples about practicing their piety for self-aggrandizing purposes: "Beware of practicing your piety before others in order to be seen by them" (Matt 6:1).

Tobit's and Anna's Deaths (14:10-12)

The urgency of Tobit's instruction to leave Nineveh is then mitigated in 14:10, when Tobit explains that Tobias should first wait until the deaths of his parents. Despite the danger, the family is to remain in Nineveh until both Tobit and Anna die and can be properly buried. Tobit recognizes that Anna will outlive him and so insists that Tobias care for her and bury her beside him (v. 10); this instruction fulfills Tobit's earlier instruction (4:3-4) that Tobias honor his mother. Once that duty is fulfilled, though, Tobit urges Tobias to flee the city immediately out of concern for the wickedness and deceit in the city and the inhabitants' lack of shame (v. 10). In the context of condemning Nineveh's deceit (or, better, "injustice" or "lack of righteousness" since the Greek is ἀδικία) and shamelessness, Tobit refers to Ahikar, who will be betrayed by Nadab (see pp. 31–32). Tobit seems to be judging the city based not on idolatry or murder but on how members of family treat one another. He then brings up ἐλεημοσύνη, the Greek noun used in the Septuagint to translate the Hebrew צדקה, which means both "almsgiving" and "righteousness" (p. 103): almsgiving is a dominant motif in the narrative, and righteousness is precisely what, according to Tobit, the city of Nineveh lacks.

The detail about Tobit's breath recalls the deaths of Abraham (Gen 25:8) and Jacob (Gen 49:33), each of whom "breathed his last." So too does Jesus (Mark 15:37; Luke 23:46; Matt 27:50). Reading and writing about breathing one's last gives me pause. Given the experience of the COVID-19 pandemic, I think of the many people who have had to be ventilated

[10]"On whatever day you bury your mother beside me, do not stay overnight within the confines of the city. For I see that there is much wickedness within it, and that much deceit is practiced within it, while the people are without shame. See, my son, what Nadab did to Ahikar who had reared him. Was he not, while still alive, brought down into the earth? For God repaid him to his face for this shameful treatment. Ahikar came out into the light, but Nadab went into the eternal darkness, because he tried to kill Ahikar. Because he gave alms, Ahikar escaped the fatal trap that Nadab had set for him, but Nadab fell into it himself, and was destroyed. [11]So now, my children, see what almsgiving accomplishes, and what injustice does—it brings death! But now my breath fails me." Then they laid him on his bed, and he died; and he received an honorable funeral. [12]When Tobias's mother died, he buried her beside his father. Then he and his wife and children returned to Media and settled in Ecbatana with Raguel his father-in-law.

in order to help them breathe and survive this illness.[26] It brings home the fact that being able to breathe is essential for our survival.

Tobit uses his final breaths to tell his son and grandsons what to expect in the future, how to protect themselves, and to give final instructions about Anna's burial. Tobit's dead body rests on his bed (v. 11), a sharp contrast with the Israelite corpses discarded in the streets that he would find and bury. Tobit is a father who loves his family though he does not use his final breaths to explicitly say that; he is expressive in his praise of God but not in his love for his family. His love comes across in the worry he has for their futures, and while it might have been annoying to hear him yet again pontificate about the benefits of almsgiving, none of his family members would have been surprised by this.

Anna is not afforded a death-bed speech, but if she were, hers would be very different from that of Tobit. She would not use her dying moments to expound on a theological point; she would have assured her children of her love for them, her pride in them, and she would have asked them to remember her:

26. The virus's central area of attack is the lungs, though as the virus mutates the impact on the lungs varies. See "Covid-19: Does Omicron Cause Less Damage to the Lungs?," *Medical News Daily*; https://www.medicalnewstoday.com/articles/covid-19-does-omicron-cause-less-damage-to-the-lungs#A-shift-in-preference-for-cell-entry-pathway.

Gather close around me, my children. I bless you, my son Tobias, and my daughter Sarah. You have served God faithfully and you have blessed and honored me through these many years of care. You have taught your children well to fear the Lord and I love them as I love you. Now you must bury me next to your father, and you must leave Nineveh. You will be a blessing to Raguel and Edna and will care for them in their final years. Go in peace and remember me.

After Anna's burial, the family returns to Ecbatana, in Media, to live with Raguel (14:12). Tobit and Sarah's return to Ecbatana so that they could care for Raguel and Edna shows a sensitivity to the fact that Sarah was an only child and, like Tobit's parents, they needed her and Tobit's help.

The Death of Edna and Raguel and Tobias (14:13-14)

Tobias fulfills his father's request to honor Sarah's parents, and thus Edna, like Raguel, is still alive, despite not being named. Tobias sees that his father's predictions come true: Nineveh is destroyed, and like the biblical Nahum, he praises God for the defeat of the city and "for all he had done to the people of Nineveh and Assyria" (v. 15). Nineveh, as capital of the Neo-Assyrian Empire, had been the largest and most powerful city in the world, largely due to the Neo-Assyrian subjugation of other peoples and the tribute they were forced to pay. Such imperial conquest meant brutal suffering for the peoples of the conquered lands, including those living in the Northern Kingdom of Israel when it fell to Neo-Assyria in 722 BCE; 2 Kings 17:1-6, 24; 18:13-16 describes how Israelites were carried off and dispersed in diverse places throughout the empire. These were Tobias's people who had suffered at the hands of Neo-Assyria, and his anger toward Nineveh was understandable: he was happy to hear that the people of that city were now suffering themselves.[27]

His vengeful attitude, while explicable, is ugly; it shows lack of compassion and a disregard for the lives lost. Yes, Ninevites were his enemies, but they were human beings. Many Americans who rejoiced when the Second World War ended were taken aback when they saw the human suffering of the Japanese after the bombing of Hiroshima and became activists in the endeavor to eliminate the existence of nuclear weapons among nations of the world. A better reaction on Tobias's part would have been to find the destruction of his enemy humbling, to be filled

27. Nahum 3:19b similarly states about the fall of Nineveh, "All who hear the news about you clap their hands over you. For who has ever escaped your endless cruelty?"

¹³He treated his parents-in-law with great respect in their old age, and buried them in Ecbatana of Media. He inherited both the property of Raguel and that of his father Tobit. ¹⁴He died highly respected at the age of one hundred and seventeen years. ¹⁵Before he died he heard of the destruction of Nineveh, and he saw its prisoners being led into Media, those whom King Cyaxares of Media had taken captive. Tobias praised God for all he had done to the people of Nineveh and Assyria; before he died he rejoiced over Nineveh, and he blessed the Lord God forever and ever. Amen.

with regret for the horrors of war, and to work toward avoiding it. The author's purpose in telling of the fall of Nineveh was to substantiate how Tobit's other predictions also would come to pass. The author furthermore presents in Tobit an alternative ending to Jonah's story—a story about which earlier we have noted echoes in our text (e.g., the big fish attacking Tobias). In Jonah, the Ninevites repent and thereby escape God's punishment—but they live on to invade Israel, the land from which Tobit has been exiled. In Tobit, the Ninevites do not escape, which means that Israel would not have been conquered and there would be no Israelite exile to Neo-Assyria.

Tobias's family, thanks to, among other things, Tobit's advice, is safe. Tobias lives a very long life—five years beyond that of his father—indeed, he is "one of the longest living postdiluvian persons," a sign of divine blessing (Job 42:12, 16; Prov 16:31).[28] But Tobias, it seems, never returned to Jerusalem. His life in Ecbatana would have been full, taking care of his in-laws, tending to the land that he inherited from Raguel, raising his family with Sarah. Perhaps he held a return to Jerusalem as a hope in his heart and in quiet times thought about what it would be like to live there. Or, more likely, living in Jerusalem was a goal he hoped his children would achieve. Tobias lived to a ripe old age and probably was cared for by his children and grandchildren—just as he had done for his elderly parents and in-laws.

When we are born we are dependent on others, and when we get to the end of our lives, if we live to an age in which our bodies and perhaps our minds begin to falter, we are dependent again. There is a poignancy to this full circle: as newborns we are helpless and dependent on our

28. Moore, *Tobit*, 293.

parents for survival; we are vulnerable as elderly persons, and we must rely on others. This is not easy. One of the sad and striking aspects of the COVID-19 pandemic was the exposure of the weaknesses of long-term care facilities. Many were not well equipped with the resources and know-how to protect the elderly from a highly communicable disease and to maintain their dignity when they succumbed to the virus, particularly when family members were barred from being able to visit and help. Tobias, like his father, toward the end of his life would have been reminded of the power of community—in particular, family. He was lucky to have family members who hopefully would lend a hand to keep him safe and happy. Older people who do not have family must rely on others—perhaps on the children of friends and on professional caregivers. The latter ought to be paid more highly for the important work that they do, as that would go a distance toward solving the shortage of staff in long-term care.

The narrative ends with Tobias blessing God. I wish that it would have ended with information about Sarah—about how her life as a mother and wife went and whether she found moments of happiness. Did she, like Tobit, feel blessed by God? Was she able to put her traumatic past behind her and fully embrace and enjoy her life with Tobias and the family they built? I would have liked to know if Sarah and Tobias had daughters. I wonder how she felt when her family moved back to Ecbatana to care for her parents. I suspect she was happy to see her parents more consistently than when she lived in Nineveh. But a return home meant going back to where her first seven husbands had died, and that must have been difficult. If Tobit teaches us anything, it is that life is difficult: even when you are doing your best, bad things happen. Bad things do happen to good people, and not because they deserve it. Not because they sinned. Tobit also reminds us that we have resources with which to grapple with the difficulties. We might not be visited by angels, but we have prayer, family, friends, and believing in something larger than ourselves.

Conclusion

Feminist Commentaries Are Not for the Faint of Heart

If, when I began working on this commentary many years ago, someone would have told me that I would include in this writing details about my own life experiences, I would have laughed out loud. This is an academic writing project: my personal life and my life as a scholar are separate, I would have said. One does not really have to do with the other—certainly not in a commentary on a biblical book.

But that is not true. Not for a feminist commentary. In a feminist commentary, there is room for showing vulnerability as a writer, because we are seeking to make the text humane and see its characters in a fuller human context. A feminist commentary considers the text, sometimes confronts it, questions its assumptions and shows its implications, and in so doing, sometimes draws on the author's personal experiences as a human being and as an observer of the human experience.

We have seen how this approach prompts discussion about numerous topics that resonate in the twenty-first century, from how we deal with life when bad things happen to good people, to our assumptions about disability, to the existence of human trafficking and slavery, to expectations of behavior depending on the gender identity of a person, to being a member of a minority community, to grappling with grief and false accusations, to bearing children (or not), to relationships between mothers and daughters, fathers and sons, humans and the divine, and more.

We have made explicit the influences of other literatures in Tobit through intertexual readings of biblical texts (Genesis, Job, Jonah, Luke, Matthew, Acts, etc.), in particular noting that Tobit's author plays with Jonah's story by providing readers with an alternative ending, one in which the Ninevites do not escape punishment. We've likewise noted traces of nonbiblical texts (the *Story of Ahikar*, *Antigone* by Sophocles, etc.), even suggesting that Tobit in his concern for burying the dead is a "Jewish Antigone," one who is self-important, entitled, but good-hearted as he grapples with understanding God's plan for his life. We have tried to flesh out the lives of Anna, Sarah, and Edna, the central women in Tobit, in all of their complexity—an especially challenging task in a fictional document.

Writing this commentary has taken me on an intellectual and spiritual odessey. I hope readers have enjoyed the journey with me. While it might be a document written in the third century BCE, Tobit can still speak meaningfully to us today.

Works Cited

Abrams, Judith Z. *Judaism and Disability: Portrayals in Ancient Texts from the Tanach through the Bavli*. Washington, DC: Gallaudet University Press, 1998.

Abusch, Tzvi. *Mesopotamian Witchcraft: Toward a History and Understanding of Babylonian Witchcraft Beliefs and Literature*. Leiden: Brill, 2002.

Ackerman, Susan. "The Queen Mother and the Cult in Ancient Israel." *JBL* 112 (1993): 385–401.

Adams, Carol J. *The Sexual Politics of Meat: A Feminist-Vegetarian Critical Theory*. New York: Continuum, 1990.

Aelian. *On the Characteristics of Animals*. Translated by A. F. Scholfield. London: William Heinemann, 1959.

Agrawal, Priya. "Maternal Mortality and Morbidity in the United States of America." *Bulletin of the World Health Organization* 93 (2015): 135.

Aguilar, Grace. *The Women of Israel*. England, 1845; New York: D. Appleton, 1872.

Aharoni, Yohanan, and Miriam Tadmor. "Kedesh (in Upper Galilee)." In *The New Encyclopedia of Archaeological Excavations in the Holy Land*, edited by E. Stern, 855–56. Vol. 3. Jerusalem: Israel Exploration Society, 1993.

Alpert, Rebecca. "Grief and the Rituals Surrounding Death: A Jewish Approach." In *Bereavement and Death Rituals*, edited by Lucy Bregman, 26–40. Vol. 3 in *Religion, Death, and Dying*. Santa Barbara, CA: Praeger Perspectives, 2010.

Aly, Götz. *Why the Germans? Why the Jews? Envy, Race Hatred, and the Prehistory of the Holocaust*. New York: Metropolitan Books, 2014.

Amundsen, D. "Suicide and Early Christian Values." In *Suicide and Euthanasia: Historical and Contemporary Themes*, edited by Baruch A. Brody, 77–153. Boston: Kluwer Academic, 1989.

Anderson, Gary A. *Sin: A History*. New Haven: Yale University Press, 2010.

Anderson, Janice Capel, and Stephen D. Moore, eds. *Mark and Method: New Approaches in Biblical Studies*. 2nd ed. Minneapolis: Fortress, 2008.

Apollodorus. *The Library*. Translated by Sir James George Frazer. 2 vols. London: William Heinemann, 1921.

Aquino, María Pilar, and María José Rosado-Nunes, eds. *Feminist Intercultural Theology: Latina Explorations for a Just World*. Studies in Latino/a Catholicism. Maryknoll, NY: Orbis Books, 2007.

Aquino, María Pilar, Daisy L. Machado, and Jeanette Rodríguez, eds. *A Reader in Latina Feminist Theology*. Austin: University of Texas Press, 2002.

Aristarkhova, Irina. "Thou Shall Not Harm All Living Beings: Feminism, Jainism, and Animals." *Hypatia* 27 (2012): 636–50.

Armstrong, Sally. *Ascent of Women: A New Age Is Dawning for Every Mother's Daughter*. Toronto: Random House Canada, 2013.

Astell, Mary. *Some Reflections upon Marriage*. New York: Source Book Press, 1970. Reprint of the 1730 edition; earliest ed. 1700.

Attia, Annie. "Disease and Healing in the Book of Tobit and in Mesopotamian Medicine." In *Mesopotamian Medicine and Magic: Studies in Honor of Markham J. Geller*, edited by Strahil V. Panayotov and Ludek Vacín, 36–68. Leiden: Brill, 2018.

Atwood, Margaret. *The Handmaid's Tale*. Toronto: McClelland and Stewart, 1985.

Austen, Ian, and Dan Bilefsky. "Hundreds More Unmarked Graves Found at Former Residential School in Canada." *New York Times*. June 24, 2021.

Bach, Alice, ed. *Women in the Hebrew Bible: A Reader*. New York: Routledge, 1999.

Baier, Annette. "Trust and Antitrust." *Ethics* 96 (January 1986): 231–60.

Bal, Mieke. *Lethal Love: Feminist Literary Readings of Biblical Love Stories*. Bloomington: Indiana University Press, 1987.

Barclay, John M. G. *Jews in the Mediterranean Diaspora: From Alexander to Trajan (323 BCE–117 CE)*. Berkeley: University of California Press, 1996.

Barclay, John M. G. "Mirror Reading a Polemical Letter: Galatians as a Test Case." *JSNT* 31 (1987): 73–93.

Barr, James. "'Abbā Isn't 'Daddy.'" *JTS* 39 (1988): 28–47.

Baskin, Judith R. "Women and Post-Biblical Commentary." In *The Torah: A Women's Commentary*, edited by Tamara Cohn Eskenazi and Andrea L. Weiss, xlix–lv. New York: URJ Press and Women of Reform Judaism, The Federation of Temple Sisterhoods, 2008.

Bauckham, Richard. "Hades, Hell." In *ABD*, edited by David Noel Freedman, 3:14–15. New York: Doubleday, 1992.

Baumeister, R. F., K. Dale, and K. L. Sommer. "Freudian Defense Mechanisms and Empirical Findings in Modern Social Psychology: Reaction Formation, Projection, Displacement, Undoing Isolation, Sublimation, and Denial." *Journal of Personality* 66 (1998): 1081–1124.

BBC News. "Flight Attendant Shares Story of Saving Trafficking Victim." February 6, 2017. https://www.bbc.com/news/world-us-canada-38880612.

Bayliss, Miranda. "The Cult of Dead Kin in Assyria and Babylonia." *Iraq* 35 (1973): 115–21.

Beavis, Mary Ann, Irmtraud Fischer, Mercedes Navarro Puerto, and Adriana Valerio, eds. The Bible and Women: An Encyclopaedia of Exegesis and Cultural History. https://www.bibleandwomen.org.

Bellis, Alice Ogden. "Eve in the Apocryphal/Deuterocanonical Books." In *Women in Scripture: A Dictionary of Named and Unnamed Women in the Hebrew Bible, the Apocryphal/Deuterocanonical Books, and the New Testament*, edited by Carol Meyers, Toni Craven, and Ross S. Kraemer, 82–84. Grand Rapids: Eerdmans, 2000.

Berlin, Adele. "Esther." In *The Jewish Study Bible*, edited by Adele Berlin and Marc Zvi Brettler, 1619–34. 2nd ed. Oxford: Oxford University Press, 2014.

Bertrand, Daniel A. " 'Un bâton de vieillesse', à propos de Tobit 5, 23, et 10, 4 (Vulgate)." *RHPR* 71 (1991): 33–37.

Bird, Phyllis A. *Missing Persons and Mistaken Identities: Women and Gender in Ancient Israel*. Minneapolis: Fortress, 1997.

Blumell, Lincoln. "Beware of Bandits! Banditry and Land Travel in the Roman Empire." *Journeys: The International Journal of Travel and Travel Writing* 8 (2007): 1–20.

Bohak, Gideon. *Ancient Jewish Magic: A History*. Cambridge: Cambridge University Press, 2008.

Bohmbach, Karla G. "Names and Naming in the Biblical World." In *Women in Scripture: A Dictionary of Named and Unnamed Women in the Hebrew Bible, The Apocryphal/Deuterocanonical Books, and the New Testament*, edited by Carol Meyers, Toni Craven, and Ross S. Kraemer, 33–39. Grand Rapids: Eerdmans, 2000.

Børresen, Kari Elisabeth, and Adriana Valerio, eds. *The High Middle Ages*. The Bible and Women: An Encyclopaedia of Exegesis and Cultural History. Atlanta: SBL Press, 2015.

Bow, Beverly. "Deborah 3." In *Women in Scripture: A Dictionary of Named and Unnamed Women in the Hebrew Bible, the Apocryphal/Deuterocanonical Books, and the New Testament*, edited by Carol Meyers, Toni Craven, and Ross S. Kraemer, 68. Grand Rapids: Eerdmans, 2000.

Bow, Beverly. "Edna." In *Women in Scripture: A Dictionary of Named and Unnamed Women in the Hebrew Bible, the Apocryphal/Deuterocanonical Books, and the New Testament*, edited by Carol Meyers, Toni Craven, and Ross S. Kraemer, 72. Grand Rapids: Eerdmans, 2000.

Bow, Beverly. "Sarah 2." In *Women in Scripture: A Dictionary of Named and Unnamed Women in the Hebrew Bible, the Apocryphal/Deuterocanonical Books, and the New Testament*, edited by Carol Meyers, Toni Craven, and Ross S. Kraemer, 152–53. Grand Rapids: Eerdmans, 2000.

Bow, Beverly, and George W. E. Nickelsburg. "Patriarchy with a Twist: Men and Women in Tobit." In *"Women Like This": New Perspectives on Jewish Women in the Greco-Roman World*, edited by Amy-Jill Levine, 127–44. Atlanta: Scholars Press, 1991.

Bowler, Kate. *Blessed: A History of the American Prosperity Gospel*. Oxford: Oxford University Press, 2013.

Bowler, Kate. "Death, the Prosperity Gospel and Me." *New York Times*. February 13, 2016.

Brand, Myriam T. "Evil and Sin." In *The Jewish Annotated Apocrypha*, edited by Jonathan Klawans and Lawrence M. Wills, 645–49. Oxford: Oxford University Press, 2020.

Brave Heart, Maria Yellow Horse. "The Historical Trauma Response among Natives and Its Relationship with Substance Abuse: A Lakota Illustration." *Journal of Psychoactive Drugs* 35 (2003): 7–13.

Brave Heart, Maria Yellow Horse, Josephine Chase, Jennifer Elkins, Jennifer Martin, Jennifer S. Nanez, and Jennifer J. Mootz. "Women Finding the Way: American Indian Women Leading Intervention Research in Native Communities." *American Indian and Alaska Native Mental Health Research* 23 (2016): 24–47.

Britannica. "Nunc Dimittis." 1998. https://www.britannica.com/topic/Nunc-Dimittis.

Brooten, Bernadette J. "Konnten Frauen im alten Judentum die Scheidung betreiben? Überlegungen zu Mk 10, 11-12 und 1 Kor 7, 10-11." *EvT* 42 (1982): 65–80.

Brooten, Bernadette J. *Love Between Women: Early Christian Responses to Female Homoeroticism*. Chicago: University of Chicago Press, 1996.

Brooten, Bernadette J. *Women Leaders in the Synagogue: Inscriptional Evidence and Background Issues*. Chico, CA: Scholars Press, 1982.

Broshi, Magen, Esther Eshel, and Joseph A. Fitzmyer. DJD 19. *Qumran Cave 4.XIV. Parabiblical Texts, Part 2*. Oxford: Clarendon, 1995.

Brown, Ashley. *Letters to the Daughter I'll Never Have*. Norman, OK: Mezcalita Press, 2018.

Brown, Ashley. "No, I'm Not Missing out on the 'Ultimate Love' Because I Chose Not to Be a Mom." *HuffPost*. October 28, 2019. https://www.huffpost.com/entry/no-child-ultimate-love_n_5db1c1b4e4b0131fa99b0095.

Brown, Christia S. "Boys Who Cry Might Have It All Figured Out." *Psychology Today*. November 20, 2012. https://www.psychologytoday.com/ca/blog/beyond-pink-and-blue/201211/boys-who-cry-might-have-it-all-figured-out.

Burns, L. H. "Psychiatric Aspects of Infertility and Infertility Treatments." *Psychiatric Clinics of North America* 30 (December 2007): 689–716.

Butler, Emily A., Boris Egloff, Frank Wilhelm, Nancy C. Smith, Elizabeth A. Erickson, and James J. Gross. "The Social Consequences of Expressive Suppression." *Emotion* 3 (April 2003): 48–67.

Cannon, Katie G. "The Emergence of Black Feminist Consciousness." In *Feminist Interpretation of the Bible*, edited by Letty M. Russell, 30–40. Philadelphia: Westminster, 1985.

Cantarella, Eva. "Dangling Virgins: Myth, Ritual and the Place of Women in Ancient Greece." *Poetics Today* 6 (1985): 91–101.

Carter, Warren. *The Gospel of Matthew in Its Roman Imperial Context.* London: T&T Clark, 2005.

Carter, Warren. *The Roman Empire and the New Testament: An Essential Guide.* Nashville: Abingdon, 2006.

Casson, Lionel. *Travel in the Ancient World.* 2nd ed. Baltimore: Johns Hopkins University, 1994.

Castelli, Elizabeth. "*Les Belles Infidèles*/Fidelity or Feminism? The Meanings of Feminist Biblical Translation." In *Searching the Scriptures: A Feminist Introduction*, vol. 1, edited by Elisabeth Schüssler Fiorenza with the assistance of Shelly Matthews, 189–204. New York: Crossroad, 1993.

Celsus, A. Cornelius. *On Medicine.* Vol. 2: *Books 5–6.* LCL 304. Translated by W. G. Spencer. Cambridge, MA: Harvard University Press, 1938.

Chamberlain, Gethin, and Soudhriti Bhabani. "Five Years after the Gang-Rape and Murder of Jyoti Singh, What Has Changed for Women in India?" *The Guardian.* December 3, 2017. https://www.theguardian.com/society/2017/dec/03/five-years-after-gang-murder-jyoti-singh-how-has-delhi-changed.

Chokshi, Nirah. "What Is an Incel? A Term Used by the Toronto Van Attack Suspect, Explained." *New York Times.* April 24, 2018. https://www.nytimes.com/2018/04/24/world/canada/incel-reddit-meaning-rebellion.html?action=click&module=RelatedLinks&pgtype=Article.

Chrysovergi, Maria. "Attitudes towards the Use of Medicine in Jewish Literature from the Third and Second Centuries BCE." PhD diss., Durham University, 2011.

Claassens, L. Juliana, and Carolyn J. Sharp, eds. *Feminist Frameworks and the Bible: Power, Ambiguity, and Intersectionality.* LHBOTS 630. London: Bloomsbury T&T Clark, 2017.

Claassens, L. Juliana, and Irmtraud Fischer, eds. *Prophecy and Gender in the Hebrew Bible.* The Bible and Women: An Encyclopaedia of Exegesis and Cultural History. Atlanta: SBL Press, 2021.

Cohler-Esses, Larry. "How Iran's Jews Survive in Mullahs' World." *Forward.* August 18, 2015. https://forward.com/news/319269/irans-jews-win-secure-place-in-mullahs-world-with-strings-attached/.

Confortini, Catia C. "Galtung, Violence, and Gender: The Case for a Peace Studies/Feminism Alliance." *Peace and Change* 31 (July 2006): 332–67.

Connell, Robert W. *Gender and Power: Society, the Person and Sexual Politics.* Stanford: Stanford University Press, 1987.

Consolino, Franca Ela, and Judith Herrin, eds. *The Early Middle Ages.* The Bible and Women: An Encyclopaedia of Exegesis and Cultural History. Atlanta: SBL Press, 2020.

Conybeare, F. C., J. R. Harris, and A. S. Lewis. *The Story of Ahiqar.* 2nd ed. Cambridge: Cambridge University Press, 1913.

Conybeare, F. C. "The Testament of Solomon." *JQR* 11 (October 1898): 1–45.

Coogan, Michael D. *The Old Testament: A Historical and Literary Introduction to the Hebrew Scriptures.* 3rd ed. Oxford: Oxford University Press, 2014.

Cotton, H. M., and J. C. Greenfield. "Babatha's Property and the Law of Succession in the Babatha Archive." *ZPE* 104 (1994): 211–21.

Couroyer, Bernard. "Tobie VII, 9: Problème de Critique Textuelle." *RB* 91 (1984): 351–56.

Cousineau, T. M., and A. D. Domar. "Psychological Impact of Infertility." *Best Practices and Research: Clinical Obstetrics and Gynaecology* 30 (April 2007): 293–308.

Craven, Toni. "Daughter (and Son)." In *Women in Scripture: A Dictionary of Named and Unnamed Women in the Hebrew Bible, the Apocryphal/Deuterocanonical Books, and the New Testament*, edited by Carol Meyers, Toni Craven, and Ross S. Kraemer, 360. Grand Rapids: Eerdmans, 2000.

Craven, Toni. "Female (and Male) Servants." In *Women in Scripture: A Dictionary of Named and Unnamed Women in the Hebrew Bible, the Apocryphal/Deuterocanonical Books, and the New Testament*, edited by Carol Meyers, Toni Craven, and Ross S. Kraemer, 359. Grand Rapids: Eerdmans, 2000.

Craven, Toni. "Kinship Wife." In *Women in Scripture: A Dictionary of Named and Unnamed Women in the Hebrew Bible, the Apocryphal/Deuterocanonical Books, and the New Testament*, edited by Carol Meyers, Toni Craven, and Ross S. Kraemer, 358. Grand Rapids: Eerdmans, 2000.

Craven, Toni. "Martyred Mother with Seven Sons." In *Women in Scripture: A Dictionary of Named and Unnamed Women in the Hebrew Bible, the Apocryphal/Deuterocanonical Books, and the New Testament*, edited by Carol Meyers, Toni Craven, and Ross S. Kraemer, 403–5. Grand Rapids: Eerdmans, 2000.

Crook, Zeba. "Honor, Shame, and Social Status Revisited." *JBL* 128 (2009): 591–611.

Cyprian. "Mortality." In *Treatises*, translated by Roy J. Deferrari. The Fathers of the Church 36. Washington, DC: The Catholic University of America Press, 1958.

D'Angelo, Mary Rose. "Abba and 'Father': Imperial Theology and the Jesus Traditions." *JBL* 111 (1992): 611–20.

D'Angelo, Mary Rose. "Women Partners in the New Testament." *JFSR* 6 (1990): 65–86.

Daly, Mary. *Beyond God the Father: A Philosophy of Women's Liberation*. Boston: Beacon, 1985.

Davies, John. *Death, Burial and Rebirth in the Religions of Antiquity*. London: Routledge, 1999.

Dean-Jones, Lesley. *Women's Bodies in Classical Greek Science*. Oxford: Clarendon, 1994.

De Freitas, Julian, Peter DeScioli, Kyle A. Thomas, and Steven Pinker. "Maimonides' Ladder: States of Mutual Knowledge and the Perception of Charitability." *Journal of Experimental Psychology: General* 148 (2019): 158–73.

De Jonge, Marinus. "Rachel's Virtuous Behavior in the *Testament of Issachar*." In *Greeks, Romans, and Christians: Essays in Honor of Abraham J. Malherbe*, edited by David L. Balch, Everett Ferguson, and Wayne A. Meeks, 340–52. Minneapolis: Fortress, 1990.

Dennett, Daniel C. *Consciousness Explained*. New York: Little, Brown and Company, 1992.

Denzey, Nicola. Review of Kathleen E. Corley, *Maranatha: Women's Funerary Rituals and Christian Origins*. *CBQ* 74 (2012): 595–96.

Deselaers, Paul. *Das Buch Tobid: Studien zu seiner Entstehung Komposition und Theologie*. Freiburg, Switzerland/Göttingen, Germany: Universitätsverlag-Vandenhoeck & Ruprecht, 1982.

De Wet, Chris L. "The Book of Tobit in Early Christianity: Greek and Latin Interpretations from the 2nd to the 5th century CE." *HTS Teologiese Studies/ Theological Studies* 76 (2020): 1–13.

Di Lella, Alexander A. "Tobit." In *A New English Translation of the Septuagint*, edited by Albert Pietersma and Benjamin G. Wright, 456–77. Oxford: Oxford University Press, 2007.

Dimant, Devorah. "Aramaic Tobit at Qumran." *Ancient Jew Review* (April 17, 2017). https://www.ancientjewreview.com/read/2017/3/22/aramaic-tobit -at-qumran.

Dimant, Devorah. *From Enoch to Tobit: Collected Studies in Ancient Jewish Literature*. Tübingen: Mohr Siebeck, 2017.

Dinkler, Michal Beth. *Literary Theory and the New Testament*. AYBRL. New Haven: Yale University Press, 2019.

Dion, Paul E. "Raphaël l'exorciste." *Bib* 57 (1976): 399–413.

Dorff, Elliot N. "Jewish Perspectives on Death and Dying." In *Perspectives on Dying and Death*, edited by Lucy Bregman, 91–113. Vol. 1 of *Religion, Death, and Dying*. Santa Barbara: Praeger Perspectives, 2010.

Douglas, M. *Purity and Danger*. London: Routledge and Kegan Paul, 1966.

Downing, Gerald F. "'Honor' among Exegetes." *CBQ* 61 (1999): 53–73.

Dube, Musa W., ed. *Postcolonial Feminist Interpretation of the Bible*. St. Louis: Chalice, 2000.

Eagleton, Terry. *Ideology: An Introduction*. London: Verso, 2007.

Eagleton, Terry. *Literary Theory: An Introduction*. 3rd ed. Minneapolis: University of Minnesota Press, 2008.

Efthimiadis-Keith, Helen. "The Significance of Food, Eating, Death and Burial in the Book of Tobit." *JSem* 22 (2013): 553–78.

Ego, Beate. "A Self-Response to 'Textual Variants.'" *A Feminist Companion to Tobit and Judith*, edited by Athalya Brenner and Helen Efthimiadis-Keith, 75–77. FCB 2.20. London: Bloomsbury, 2015.

Ego, Beate. "The Banishment of the Demon in Tobit: Textual Variants as a Result of Enculturation." In *A Feminist Companion to Tobit and Judith*, edited by Athalya Brenner-Idan and Helen Efthimiadis-Keith, 67–74. FCB 2.20. London: Bloomsbury, 2015.

El Kissi, Yousri, Asma Ben Romdhane, Samir Hidar, Souhail Bannour, Khadija Ayoubi Idrissi, Hedi Khairi, and Bechir Ben Hadj Ali. "General Psychopathology, Anxiety, Depression and Self-Esteem in Couples Undergoing Infertility Treatment: A Comparative Study between Men and Women." *European Journal of Obstetrics & Gynecology and Reproductive Biology* 167 (2012): 185–89.

Eskenazi, Tamara Cohn, and Andrea L. Weiss, eds. *The Torah: A Women's Commentary*. New York: URJ Press and Women of Reform Judaism, The Federation of Temple Sisterhoods, 2008.

"Euripides." In *The Complete Greek Drama*, edited by Whitney J. Oates and Eugene O'Neill Jr. Vol. 1: *The Suppliants*, translated by E. P. Coleridge. New York: Random House, 1938.

Exum, J. Cheryl. "Michal." In *Women in Scripture: A Dictionary of Named and Unnamed Women in the Hebrew Bible, the Apocryphal/Deuterocanonical Books, and the New Testament*, edited by Carol Meyers, Toni Craven, and Ross S. Kraemer, 126. Grand Rapids: Eerdmans, 2000.

Exum, J. Cheryl. "Second Thoughts about Secondary Characters: Women in Exodus 1.8–2.10." In *A Feminist Companion to Exodus to Deuteronomy*, edited by Athalya Brenner, 75–97. FCB 6. Sheffield: Sheffield Academic, 1994.

Exum, J. Cheryl, and David J. A. Clines, eds. *The New Literary Criticism and the Hebrew Bible*. Valley Forge, PA: Trinity Press International, 1993.

Fagenblat, Michael. "The Concept of Neighbor in Jewish and Christian Ethics." In *The Jewish Annotated New Testament*, edited by Amy-Jill Levine and Marc Zvi Brettler, 645–50. 2nd ed. Oxford: Oxford University Press, 2017.

Faraone, Christopher A. *Ancient Greek Love Magic*. Cambridge, MA: Harvard University Press, 1999.

Faraone, Christopher A. "Magical and Medical Approaches to the Wandering Womb in the Ancient Greek World." *ClAnt* 30 (2011): 1–32.

Fell, Margaret. *Women's Speaking Justified, Proved and Allowed by the Scriptures*. London, 1667.

Feminist Biblical Interpretation: A Compendium of Critical Commentary on the Books of the Bible and Related Literature. Translated by Lisa E. Dahill, Everett R. Kalin, Nancy Lukens, Linda M. Maloney, Barbara Rumscheidt, Martin Rumscheidt, and Tina Steiner. Edited by Luise Schottroff and Marie-Theres Wacker. Grand Rapids: Eerdmans, 2012.

Fewell, Danna Nolan, and David M. Gunn. *Gender, Power, and Promise: The Subject of the Bible's First Story*. Nashville: Abingdon, 1993.

Fischer, Irmtraud, and Mercedes Navarro Puerto, with Andrea Taschl-Erber, eds. *Torah*. The Bible and Women: An Encyclopaedia of Exegesis and Cultural History. Atlanta: SBL, 2011.

Fischler, Claude. "Food, Self, and Identity." *Social Science Information* 27 (1988): 275–92.

Fishkoff, Sue. "Death of a Goat: Jewish Food Activists Slaughter Their Own Meat." *Wisconsin Jewish Chronicle*. October 23, 2008. https://www.jewishchronicle.org/2008/10/23/death-of-a-goat-jewish-food-activists-slaughter-their-own-meat/.

Fitzmyer, Joseph A. "The Aramaic and Hebrew Fragments of Tobit from Cave 4m." *CBQ* 57 (1995): 655–75.

Fitzmyer, Joseph A. *Tobit*. Berlin: de Gruyter, 2003.

Feuerbach, Ludwig. *Sämmtliche Werke*. Edited by Wilhelm Bolin und Friedrich Jodl. Vol. 10. Stuttgart, 1911.

Freidenreich, David M. *Their Food: Constructing Otherness in Jewish, Christian, and Islamic Law*. Berkeley: University of California Press, 2011.

Friedman, Mordechai A. *Jewish Marriage in Palestine: A Cairo Geniza Study*. 2 vols. Tel Aviv: Tel Aviv University, 1980–1981.

Fries, Carl. "Das Buch Tobit Und Die Telemachie." *ZWT* 53 (1911): 54–87.

Froreich F. V., L. R. Vartanian, J. R. Grisham, S. W. Touyz. "Dimensions of Control and Their Relation to Disordered Eating Behaviours and Obsessive-Compulsive Symptoms." *Journal of Eating Disorders* 4 (2016): 1–9.

Frymer-Kensky, Tikva. "Bilhah." In *Women in Scripture: A Dictionary of Named and Unnamed Women in the Hebrew Bible, the Apocryphal/Deuterocanonical Books, and the New Testament*, edited by Carol Meyers, Toni Craven, and Ross S. Kraemer, 61–62. Grand Rapids: Eerdmans, 2000.

Frymer-Kensky, Tikva. *Reading the Women of the Bible*. New York: Schocken Books, 2002.

Fuller, Michael E. *The Restoration of Israel: Israel's Re-gathering and the Fate of the Nations in Early Jewish Literature and Luke–Acts*. New York: de Gruyter, 2006.

Gager, John G. *Curse Tablets and Binding Spells from the Ancient World*. New York: Oxford University Press, 1992.

Garland-Thomson, Rosemarie. "Feminist Disability Studies." *Signs* 30 (2005): 1557–87.

Gearing, Robin E., and Dana Alonzo. "Religion and Suicide: New Findings." *Journal of Religion and Health* 57 (2018): 2478–99.

Getty-Sullivan, Mary Ann. *Women in the New Testament*. Collegeville, MN: Liturgical Press, 2001.

Ghosh, Nandini. *Impaired Bodies, Gendered Lives*. New Delhi: Primus Books, 2016.

Girma, Haben. *Haben: The Deafblind Woman Who Conquered Harvard Law*. New York: Twelve, 2019.

Glancy, Jennifer A. "The Mistress-Slave Dialectic: Paradoxes of Slavery in Three LXX Narratives." *JSOT* 72 (1996): 71–87.

Goff, Matthew. "Jubilees." In *The Jewish Annotated Apocrypha*, edited by Jonathan Klawans and Lawrence M. Wills, 1–97. Oxford: Oxford University Press, 2020.

Goldberg, Edwin, Janet Marder, Sheldon Marder, and Leon Morris, ed. *Mishkan haNefesh: Machzor for the Days of Awe*. New York: Central Conference for American Rabbis, 2015.

Goldbloom, Sheila Barshay. *Opening Doors*. Montreal: John Aylen Books, 2019.

Gonzalez, Michelle A. "Latina Feminist Theology: Past, Present, and Future." *JFSR* 25 (2009): 150–55.

Good, Deirdre J. "Reading Strategies for Biblical Passages on Same-Sex Relations." *Theology and Sexuality* 7 (1997): 70–82.

Govier, Trudy. "Trust, Distrust and Feminist Theory." *Hypatia* 7 (1992): 16–33.

Grabbe, Lester L. *Judaic Religion in the Second Temple Period: Belief and Practice from the Exile to Yavneh.* London: Routledge, 2000.

Graf, Fritz. "Die Religion der Romer: Eine Einfuhrung; Magic in the Roman World: Pagans, Jews, and Christians." *JR* 83 (2003): 496–99.

Grimké, Sarah. *Letters on the Equality of the Sexes and the Condition of Woman.* Boston: Isaac Knapp, 1838.

Gross, Heinrich. *Tobit; Judit.* Würzburg: Echter-Verlag, 1987.

Gruen, Lori. "Empathy and Vegetarian Commitments." In *The Feminist Care Tradition in Animal Ethics,* edited by Josephine Donovan and Carol J. Adams, 333–43. New York: Columbia University Press, 2007.

Guest, Deryn. *When Deborah Met Jael: Lesbian Feminist Hermeneutics.* London: SCM, 2005.

Guzman-Bouvard, Marguerite. *Revolutionizing Motherhood: The Mothers of the Plaza de Mayo.* Wilmington, DE: Scholarly Resources, 1994.

Habel, Norman C., and Peter Trudinger. *Exploring Ecological Hermeneutics.* SymS 46. Atlanta: SBL, 2008.

Hamington, Maurice. "Toward a Theory of Feminist Hospitality." *Feminist Formations* 22 (2010): 21–38.

Hanhart, R. *Text und Textgeschichte des Buches Tobit.* Göttingen: Vandenhoeck & Ruprecht, 1984.

Harkavy, Alexander. *Yiddish-English-Hebrew Dictionary.* New York: Hebrew Publishing, 1928.

Harris, Colin. "Mother Convicted in Shafia Daughters' Canal Killings Granted 5-Hour Escorted Absence from Prison." CBC News. https://www.cbc.ca/news/canada/montreal/shafia-honour-killings-tooba-yahya-parole-board-1.5396177.

Harris, R. Laird, Gleason L. Archer Jr., Bruce K. Waltke. *TWOT.* Chicago: Moody, 2003.

Harris-McCoy, Daniel E. *Artemidorus' Oneirocritica: Text, Translation, & Commentary.* Oxford: Oxford University Press, 2012.

Hatziminaoglou, Y., and J. Boyazoglu. "The Goat in Ancient Civilisations: From the Fertile Crescent to the Aegean Sea." *Small Ruminant Research* 51 (2004): 123–29.

Hayes, Christine. *Gentile Impurities and Jewish Identities: Intermarriage and Conversion from the Bible to the Talmud.* Oxford: Oxford University Press, 2002.

Hearon, Holly E., and Philip Ruge-Jones, eds. *The Bible in Ancient and Modern Media: Story and Performance.* Eugene, OR: Cascade Books, 2009.

Henderson, Ruth. "A Scriptural Model for the Song of Tobit (Tobit 13:1-18)." *JSP* 17 (2017): 47–79.

Hendrix, Scott H. *Luther: Visionary Reformer.* New Haven: Yale University Press, 2015.

Hens-Piazza, Gina. *The New Historicism.* GBS, Old Testament Series. Minneapolis: Fortress, 2002.

Hernandez, Jill Graper. "Acquainted with Grief: The Atonement and Early Feminist Conceptions of Theodicy." *Philosophia* 43 (2015): 97–111.

Hezser, Catherine. *Jewish Slavery in Antiquity.* Oxford: Oxford University Press, 2005.

Hezser, Catherine. *Jewish Travel in Antiquity.* Tübingen: Mohr Siebeck, 2011.

Homer. *The Odyssey.* Translated by Robert Fagles. New York: Viking Penguin, 1996.

Hornsby, Teresa, and Ken Stone, eds. *Bible Trouble: Queer Readings at the Boundaries of Biblical Scholarship.* Atlanta: SBL, 2011.

Hutter, M. "Asmodeus." In *Dictionary of Deities and Demons in the Bible,* ed. Karel van der Toorn, Bob Becking, Pieter W. van der Horst, 106–8. 2nd ed. Leiden: Brill, 1999.

Ilan, Tal. "Babatha the Killer-Wife: Literature, Folk Religion and Documentary Papyri." In *Law and Narrative in the Bible and in Neighbouring Ancient Cultures,* edited by Klaus-Peter Adam, Friedrich Avemarie, and Nili Wazana, 263–78. FAT 2.54. Tubingen: Mohr Siebeck, 2012.

Ilan, Tal. *Mine and Yours Are Hers.* Leiden: Brill, 1997.

Ilan, Tal. "On a Newly Published Divorce Bill from the Judaean Desert." *HTR* 89 (1996): 195–202.

Ilan, Tal. "Women in Jewish Life and Law." In *The Cambridge History of Judaism,* vol. 4, *Judaism: The Late Roman-Rabbinic Period,* edited by Steven T. Katz, 627–46. Cambridge: Cambridge University Press, 2006.

Ilan, Tal, Lorena Miralles-Maciá, and Ronit Nikolsky, eds. *Rabbinic Literature.* The Bible and Women: An Encyclopaedia of Exegesis and Cultural History. Atlanta: SBL Press, 2022.

International Labour Organization. "Global Estimates of Modern Slavery: Forced Labour and Forced Marriage." 2017. https://www.ilo.org/global/publications/books/WCMS_575479/lang--en/index.htm.

Isasi-Díaz, Ada María. *Mujerista Theology: A Theology for the Twenty-First Century.* Maryknoll, NY: Orbis Books, 1996.

Jacobs, Naomi S. S. "Book of Tobit." In *Eerdmans Dictionary of Early Judaism,* edited by John J. Collins and Daniel C. Harlow, 1314–15. Grand Rapids: Eerdmans, 2010.

Jacobs, Naomi S. S. *Delicious Prose: Reading the Tale of Tobit with Food and Drink; A Commentary.* Leiden: Brill, 2018.

Jacobs, Naomi S. S. "Seen and Heard, but Hardly Eating: Female Consumption in the Book of Tobit." In *A Feminist Companion to Tobit and Judith,* edited by Athalya Brenner-Idan and Helen Efthimiadis-Keith, 78–97. FCB 2.20. London: Bloomsbury, 2015.

Jacobs, Naomi S. S. "Tobit." In *The Jewish Annotated Apocrypha,* edited by Jonathan Klawans and Lawrence M. Wills, 149–75. Oxford: Oxford University Press, 2020.

Jastrow, Marcus. *A Dictionary of the Targumim, the Talmud Babli and Yerushalmi, and the Midrashic Literature with an Index of Scriptural Quotations.* Vol. 2. New York: G. P. Putnam's Sons, 1903.

Jobling, David. *The Sense of Biblical Narrative: Three Structural Analyses in the Old Testament.* JSOTSup 7. Sheffield: University of Sheffield Press, 1978.

Jobling, David, and Tina Pippin, eds. *Semeia 59: Ideological Criticism of Biblical Texts.* Atlanta: Scholars Press, 1992.

Johnson, Elizabeth A. "God." In *Dictionary of Feminist Theologies,* edited by Letty M. Russell and J. Shannon Clarkson, 128–30. Louisville: Westminster John Knox, 1996.

Johnson, Elizabeth A. *She Who Is: The Mystery of God in Feminist Theological Discourse.* New York: Crossroad, 1992.

Junior, Nyasha. *An Introduction to Womanist Biblical Interpretation.* Louisville: Westminster John Knox, 2015.

Kiel, Michael. *The "Whole Truth": Re-Thinking Retribution in the Book of Tobit.* London: T&T Clark, 2012.

Keller, Sharon R. "Aspects of Nudity in the Old Testament." *Notes in the History of Art* 12 (1993): 32–36.

Kelley, Nicole. "Deformity and Disability in Greece and Rome." In *This Abled Body: Rethinking Disabilities in Biblical Studies,* edited by Hector Avalos, Sarah J. Melcher, and Jeremy Schipper, 31–46. Atlanta: SBL, 2007.

Kingston, Anne. "The 2019 Election Revealed That Sexism Is Status Quo." *Maclean's.* November 5, 2019. https://www.macleans.ca/opinion/the-2019 -election-revealed-that-sexism-is-status-quo/.

Kitzberger, Ingrid Rosa, ed. *Autobiographical Biblical Interpretation: Between Text and Self.* Leiden: Deo, 2002.

Klawans, Jonathan. "Notions of Gentile Impurity in Ancient Judaism." *AJSR* 20 (1995): 285–312.

Klawans, Jonathan. "The Law." In *The Jewish Annotated New Testament,* ed. Amy-Jill Levine and Marc Zvi Brettler, 655–58. 2nd ed. Oxford: Oxford University Press, 2017.

Klein, Lillian R. "Hannah." In *Women in Scripture: A Dictionary of Named and Unnamed Women in the Hebrew Bible, the Apocryphal/Deuterocanonical Books, and the New Testament,* edited by Carol Meyers, Toni Craven, and Ross S. Kraemer, 90–91. Grand Rapids: Eerdmans, 2000.

Köcher, F. *Die babylonisch-assyrische Medizin in Texten und Untersuchungen.* Berlin: de Gruyter, 1963.

Koehler, L., W. Baumgartner, and J. J. Stamm. *The Hebrew and Aramaic Lexicon of the Old Testament.* Vol. 3. Leiden: Brill, 2000.

Koehler, L., W. Baumgartner, and J. J. Stamm. *The Hebrew and Aramaic Lexicon of the Old Testament.* Vol. 4. Leiden: Brill, 1999.

Kottsieper, Ingo. "Tradition of Ahiqar." In *The Routledge Encyclopedia of Ancient Mediterranean Religions,* edited by Eric Orlin, 22–23. New York: Routledge, 2016.

Kozlova, Ekaterina E. *Maternal Grief in the Hebrew Bible.* Oxford: Oxford University Press, 2017.

Kraemer, Ross Shepard. "Jewish Family Life in the First Century CE." In *The Jewish Annotated New Testament*, edited by Amy-Jill Levine and Marc Zvi Brettler, 603–7. 2nd ed. Oxford: Oxford University Press, 2017.

Kraemer, Ross Shepard. "Jewish Women in the Diaspora World of Late Antiquity." In *Jewish Women in Historical Perspective*, edited by Judith R. Baskin, 43–67. Detroit: Wayne State University Press, 1991.

Kraemer, Ross Shepard. "Nurse Caring for Her Children." In *Women in Scripture: A Dictionary of Named and Unnamed Women in the Hebrew Bible, the Apocryphal/ Deuterocanonical Books, and the New Testament*, edited by Carol Meyers, Toni Craven, and Ross S. Kraemer, 485. Grand Rapids: Eerdmans, 2000.

Kraemer, Ross Shepard. "Typical and Atypical Jewish Family Dynamics: the Cases of Babatha and Berenice." In *Early Christian Families in Context: An Interdisciplinary Dialogue*, edited by L. Balch and Carolyn Osiek, 130–56. Grand Rapids: Eerdmans, 2003.

Kraemer, Ross Shepard, ed. *Women's Religion in the Greco-Roman World: A Sourcebook*. Oxford: Oxford University Press, 2004.

Kraemer, Ross Shepard, and Mary Rose D'Angelo, eds. *Women and Christian Origins*. New York: Oxford University Press, 1999.

Kuikman, Jacoba. "Women in Judaism." In *Women and Religious Traditions*, edited by Leona M. Anderson and Pamela Dickey Young, 44–76. 3rd ed. Oxford: Oxford University Press, 2015.

Kwon, JiSeong James. "Meaning and Context in Job and Tobit." *JSOT* 43 (2019): 627–43.

LaCugna, Catherine Mowry. *God for Us: The Trinity and Christian Life*. San Francisco: HarperCollins, 1991.

Lander, Shira L. "Gender." In *The Jewish Annotated Apocrypha*, edited by Jonathan Klawans and Lawrence M. Wills, 636–39. Oxford: Oxford University Press, 2020.

Lapidus Lerner, Anne. *Eternally Eve: Images of Eve in the Hebrew Bible, Midrash, and Modern Jewish Poetry*. Waltham, MA: Brandeis University Press, 2007.

Lemos, T. M. *Marriage Gifts and Social Change in Ancient Palestine: 1200 BCE to 200 CE*. Cambridge: Cambridge University Press, 2010.

Lerner, Gerda. "One Thousand Years of Feminist Bible Criticism." Chap. 7 (pp. 138–66) in *Creation of Feminist Consciousness: From the Middle Ages to Eighteen-Seventy*. New York: Oxford University Press, 1993.

Levenson, Jon D. "Genesis." In *The Jewish Study Bible*, edited by Adele Berlin and Marc Zvi Brettler, 7–94. 2nd ed. New York: Oxford University Press, 2014.

Levenson, Jon D. *Resurrection and the Restoration of Israel: The Ultimate Victory of the God of Life*. New Haven: Yale University Press, 2008.

Levine, Amy-Jill. "Diaspora as Metaphor: Bodies and Boundaries in the Book of Tobit." In *Jews and Judaism: Essays in Honor of, and in Dialogue with, A. Thomas Kraabel*, edited by J. A. Overman and R. S. MacLennan, 105–17. Atlanta: Scholars Press, 1992.

Levine, Amy-Jill. "The New Testament and Anti-Judaism." In *The Misunderstood Jew: The Church and the Scandal of the Jewish Jesus*, 87–117. San Francisco: HarperSanFrancisco, 2006.

Levine, Amy-Jill. "Redrawing the Boundaries: A New Look at 'Diaspora as Metaphor: Bodies and Boundaries in the Book of Tobit.' " In *A Feminist Companion to Tobit and Judith*, edited by Athalya Brenner-Idan and Helen Efthimiadis-Keith, 3–22. FCB 2.20. London: Bloomsbury, 2015.

Levine, Amy-Jill. "Sacrifice and Salvation: Otherness and Domestication in the Book of Judith." In *No One Spoke Ill of Her: Essays on Judith*, edited by J. C. VanderKam, 31–46. Atlanta: SBL, 1992.

Levine, Amy-Jill. "Sacrifice and Salvation: Otherness and Domestication in the Book of Judith." In *A Feminist Companion to Esther, Judith and Susanna*, edited by Athalya Brenner, 208–23. FCB 7. London: T&T Clark, 1995.

Levine, Amy-Jill. *Sermon on the Mount: A Beginner's Guide to the Kingdom of Heaven*. Nashville: Abingdon, 2020.

Levine, Amy-Jill. *Short Stories by Jesus: The Enigmatic Parables of a Controversial Rabbi*. New York: HarperOne, 2014.

Levine, Amy-Jill. "Teaching Jews How to Live in the Diaspora." *BRev* 8 (1992): 42–51.

Levine, Amy-Jill. " 'This Widow Keeps Bothering Me' (Luke 18:5)." In *Finding a Woman's Place: Essays in Honor of Carolyn Osiek*, edited by David L. Black and Jason T. Lamoreaux, 124–50. Eugene, OR: Wipf and Stock Publishers, 2011.

Levine, Amy-Jill. "Tobit." In *The New Oxford Annotated Bible*, edited by Michael D. Coogan, 11–31. 3rd ed. Oxford: Oxford University Press, 2001.

Levine, Amy-Jill, ed. *"Women Like This": New Perspectives on Women in the Greco-Roman World*. Atlanta: Scholars Press, 1991.

Levinson, Bernard M. "Deuteronomy." In *The Jewish Study Bible*, edited by Adele Berlin and Marc Zvi Brettler, 339–428. 2nd ed. Oxford: Oxford University Press, 2014.

Lincoln, Bruce. *Discourse and the Construction of Society: Comparative Studies of Myth, Ritual, and Classification*. New York: Oxford University Press, 1989.

Lindemann, Katy. "I'm a Feminist: So Why Does Infertility Make Me Feel Like a Failure?" *The Guardian*. November 2, 2018.

Littman, Robert J. *Tobit: The Book of Tobit in Codex Sinaiticus*. Septuagint Commentary Series. Leiden: Brill, 2008.

Loeser, Cassandra, Vicki Crowley, and Barbara Pini, eds. *Disability and Masculinities: Corporeality, Pedagogy, and the Critique of Otherness*. London: Palgrave Macmillan, 2017.

Long, Michael. "What Would Mister Rogers Eat? Thanksgiving in the Neighborhood." *HuffPost*. January 21, 2015. https://www.huffpost.com/entry/what-would-mister-rogers-eat_b_6193910.

Lorton, David. "Legal and Social Institutions of Pharaonic Egypt." In *Civilizations of the Ancient Near East*, edited by J. M. Sasson and J. Baines, 1:345–62. New York: Scribner, 1995.

Löwisch, Ingeborg. "Miriam Ben Amram, or How to Make Sense of the Absence of Women in the Genealogies of Levi (1 Chronicles 5:27–6:66)." In *The Bible and Feminism*, edited by Yvonne Sherwood, 355–70. Oxford: Oxford University Press, 2017.

Ludwig, Theodore M. "The Zoroastrian Tradition." In *The Sacred Paths: Understanding the Religions of the World*, 317–29. 3rd ed. Upper Saddle River, NJ: Prentice Hall, 2001.

Lust, J. E. Eynikel, and K. Hauspie. *Greek-English Lexicon of the Septuagint*. Rev. ed. Stuttgart: Deutsche Bibelgesellschaft, 2003.

Macatangay, Francis M. "Apocalypticism and Narration in the Book of Tobit." In *Canonicity, Setting, Wisdom in the Deuterocanonicals: Papers of the Jubilee Meeting of the International Conference on the Deuterocanonical Books*, edited by Géza G. Xeravits, József Zsengellér, and Xavér Szabó, 207–20. Berlin: de Gruyter, 2014.

Macatangay, Francis M. *The Wisdom Instructions in the Book of Tobit*. Berlin: de Gruyter, 2011.

MacDonald, Dennis R. "Tobit and the *Odyssey*." In *Mimesis and Intertextuality in Antiquity and Christianity*, edited by Dennis R. MacDonald, 1–40. Harrisburg, PA: Trinity Press International, 2001.

Maier, Christl M., and Nuria Calduch-Benages, eds. *The Writings and Later Wisdom Books*. The Bible and Women: An Encyclopaedia of Exegesis and Cultural History. Atlanta: SBL Press, 2014.

Maier, Cristl M., and Carolyn J. Sharp. *Prophecy and Power: Jeremiah in Feminist and Postcolonial Perspective*. London: Bloomsbury, 2013.

Marchal, Joseph A. "Queer Studies and Critical Masculinity Studies in Feminist Biblical Studies." In *Feminist Biblical Studies in the Twentieth Century: Scholarship and Movement*, edited by Elisabeth Schüssler Fiorenza, 261–80. The Bible and Women: An Encyclopaedia of Exegesis and Cultural History. Atlanta: SBL Press, 2014.

Matta, Christy. *The Stress Response: How Dialectical Behavior Therapy Can Free You from Needless Anxiety, Worry, Anger and Other Symptoms of Stress*. Oakland: New Harbinger Publications, 2012.

Matthews, Victor H. "Cloth, Clothes." In *New Interpreter's Dictionary of the Bible*, edited by Katharine Doob Sakenfeld, 1:691–96. Nashville: Abingdon, 2006.

Mayo Clinic. "Domestic Violence against Women: Recognize Patterns, Seek Help." April 14, 2022. https://www.mayoclinic.org/healthy-lifestyle/adult-health/in-depth/domestic-violence/art-20048397.

McCracken, David. "Narration and Comedy in the Book of Tobit." *JBL* 114 (1995): 401–18.

McFague, Sallie. *Models of God: Theology for an Ecological, Nuclear Age*. Philadelphia: Fortress, 1987.

McKinlay, Judith E. *Reframing Her: Biblical Women in Postcolonial Focus*. Sheffield: Sheffield Phoenix, 2004.

McKnight, Edgar V., and Elizabeth Struthers Malbon, eds. *The New Literary Criticism and the New Testament.* Valley Forge, PA: Trinity Press International, 1994.

McPeters, Cynthia D. "Invitational Rhetoric and Gossip: A Feminist Rhetorical Reading of Agatha Christie's Jane Marple." MA thesis, Appalachian State University, 2017.

McVittie, Chris, Julie Hepworth, and Karen Goodall. "Masculinities and Health: Whose Identities, Whose Constructions?" *The Psychology of Gender and Health,* edited by M. Pilar Sánchez-López and Rosa M. Limiñana-Gras, 119–41. Cambridge, MA: Academic Press, 2017.

Meyers, Carol. "Daughter of the Inhabitants of the Lands as Marriage Partners." In *Women in Scripture: A Dictionary of Named and Unnamed Women in the Hebrew Bible, the Apocryphal/Deuterocanonical Books, and the New Testament,* edited by Carol Meyers, Toni Craven, and Ross S. Kraemer, 200–201. Grand Rapids: Eerdmans, 2000.

Meyers, Carol. *Discovering Eve: Ancient Israelite Women in Context.* New York: Oxford University Press, 1991.

Meyers, Carol. "Eve." In *Women in Scripture: A Dictionary of Named and Unnamed Women in the Hebrew Bible, the Apocryphal/Deuterocanonical Books, and the New Testament,* edited by Carol Meyers, Toni Craven, and Ross S. Kraemer, 79–82. Grand Rapids: Eerdmans, 2000.

Meyers, Carol. "Female Images of God." In *Women in Scripture: A Dictionary of Named and Unnamed Women in the Hebrew Bible, the Apocryphal/Deuterocanonical Books, and the New Testament,* edited by Carol Meyers, Toni Craven, and Ross S. Kraemer, 524–28. Grand Rapids: Eerdmans, 2000.

Meyers, Carol, Toni Craven, and Ross S. Kraemer, eds. *Women in Scripture: A Dictionary of Named and Unnamed Women in the Hebrew Bible, the Apocryphal/ Deuterocanonical Books, and the New Testament.* Boston: Houghton Mifflin, 2000/Grand Rapids: Eerdmans, 2001.

Miller, Athanasius. *Das Buch Tobias übersetzt und erklärt.* Die Heilige Schrift des Alten Testamentes. Vol. 4.3. Bonn, 1940–1941.

Miller, Daniel. "The History of 'Israel' and 'Palestine': Alternative Names, Competing Claims." *The Conversation.* July 6, 2021. https://theconversation.com /the-history-of-israel-and-palestine-alternative-names-competing-claims -163156.

Miller, Geoffrey David. *Marriage in the Book of Tobit.* Berlin: de Gruyter, 2011.

Miller, Geoffrey David. "Raphael the Liar: Angelic Deceit and Testing in the Book of Tobit." *CBQ* 72 (2012): 492–508.

Miller, J. Maxwell, and John H. Hayes. *A History of Ancient Israel and Judah.* 2nd ed. Philadelphia: Westminster John Knox, 2006.

Milloy, John S. *A National Crime: The Canadian Government and the Residential School System 1879–1986.* Winnipeg: University of Manitoba Press, 1999.

Milne, Pamela. "Voicing Embodied Evil: Gynophobic Images of Women in Post-Exilic Biblical and Intertestamental Text." *Feminist Theology* 30 (2002): 61–69.

Mishkan haNefesh: Machzor for the Days of Awe. Edited by Edwin Goldberg, Janet Marder, Sheldon Marder, and Leon Morris. New York: Central Conference for American Rabbis, 2015.

Mischke, Judith. "Merkel: Clothing Criticism Reveals Double Standards." *Politico.* January 23, 2019. https://www.politico.eu/article/german-chancellor -angela-merkel-clothing-criticism-reveals-double-standards/.

Mitchell, Christine. "1 and 2 Chronicles." In *Women's Bible Commentary*, edited by Carol A. Newsom, Sharon H. Ringe, and Jacqueline E. Lapsley, 184–91. 3rd ed. Louisville: Westminster John Knox, 2012.

Moazami, Mahnaz. "A Purging Presence: The Dog in Zoroastrian Tradition." *Anthropology of the Middle East* 11 (2016): 29.

Moore, Carey. "Enemy Cities as Female." In *Women in Scripture: A Dictionary of Named and Unnamed Women in the Hebrew Bible, the Apocryphal/Deuterocanonical Books, and the New Testament*, edited by Carol Meyers, Toni Craven, and Ross S. Kraemer, 521. Grand Rapids: Eerdmans, 2000.

Moore, Carey. "Jerusalem/Zion as Widow and Mother." In *Women in Scripture: A Dictionary of Named and Unnamed Women in the Hebrew Bible, the Apocryphal/Deuterocanonical Books, and the New Testament*, edited by Carol Meyers, Toni Craven, and Ross S. Kraemer, 530–31. Grand Rapids: Eerdmans, 2000.

Moore, Carey. *Tobit: A New Translation with Introduction and Commentary.* New Haven: Yale University Press, 1996.

Moore, Stephen D. *The Bible in Theory: Critical and Postcritical Essays.* Atlanta: SBL, 2010.

Moore, Stephen D. *Poststructuralism and the New Testament: Derrida and Foucault at the Foot of the Cross.* Minneapolis: Fortress, 1994.

Moss, Candida R., and Joel S. Baden. *Reconceiving Infertility: Biblical Perspectives on Procreation and Childlessness.* Princeton: Princeton University Press, 2015.

Mubanga, M., L. Byberg, and C. Nowak. "Dog Ownership and the Risk of Cardiovascular Disease and Death—A Nationwide Cohort Study." *Scientific Report* 7 (2017): 15821.

Munro, Ealasaid. "Feminism: A Fourth Wave?" *Political Insight* (September 2013). https://journals.sagepub.com/doi/pdf/10.1111/2041-9066.12021.

Murray, Michele. "Jewish Traditions." In *World Religions: Western Traditions*, edited by Amir Hussain, Roy C. Amore, and Willard G. Oxtoby, 80–159. 5th ed. Oxford: Oxford University Press, 2019.

Murray, Michele. "The Magical Female in Graeco-Roman Rabbinic Literature." *Religion & Theology: A Journal of Contemporary Religious Discourse* 14 (2007): 284–309.

Murray, Michele. *Playing a Jewish Game: Gentile Christian Judaizing in the First and Second Centuries CE.* Studies in Christianity and Judaism 13. Waterloo, ON: Wilfrid Laurier University Press, 2004.

Navarro Puerto, Mercedes, and Marinella Perroni, eds.; Amy-Jill Levine, English ed. *Gospels: Narrative and History.* The Bible and Women: An Encyclopaedia of Exegesis and Cultural History. Atlanta: SBL Press, 2015.

Naveh, Joseph, and Shaul Shaked. *Amulets and Magic Bowls: Aramaic Incantations of Late Antiquity.* Jerusalem: Magnes, 1985.

Neusner, Jacob. *The Mishnah: A New Translation.* New Haven: Yale University Press, 1988.

Newman, Barbara. *Sister of Wisdom: St. Hildegard's Theology of the Feminine.* Berkeley: University of California Press, 1987.

Nicklas, Tobias. "Marriage in the Book of Tobit." In *The Book of Tobit: Text, Tradition, Theology: Papers of the First International Conference on the Deuteronomical Books, Pápa, Hungary, 20–21 May, 2004,* edited by Géza G. Xeravits and József Zsengellér, 139–54. Supplements to the Journal for the Study of Judaism 98. Leiden: Brill, 2005.

Nicklesburg, George W. E. *Jewish Literature between the Bible and the Mishnah.* 2nd ed. Minneapolis: Fortress, 2005.

Nicklesburg, George W. E. "Tobit." In *Harper's Bible Commentary,* edited by James L. Mays, 791–803. New York: Harper and Row, 1988.

Nicklesburg, George W. E. "Tobit." In *The Harper Collins Study Bible: Including Apocryphal Deuterocanonical Books,* 1293–1312. Rev. ed. New York: HarperCollins Publishers, 2006.

Nickelsburg, George W. E., and James C. VanderKam. *1 Enoch: A New Translation.* Minneapolis: Fortress, 2004.

Niditch, Susan. *"My Brother Esau Is a Hairy Man": Hair and Identity in Ancient Israel.* Oxford: Oxford University Press, 2008.

Nowell, Irene. "The Book of Tobit: Narrative Technique and Theology." PhD diss., The Catholic University of America, 1983.

Nowell, Irene. *Women in the Old Testament.* Collegeville, MN: Liturgical Press, 1997.

Orlinsky, Harry M. "The Canonization of the Bible and the Exclusion of the Apocrypha." In *Essays in Biblical Culture and Bible Translations,* 279–84. New York: Ktav, 1974.

Otzen, Benedikt. *Tobit and Judith.* London: Sheffield Academic, 2002.

Pardee, Dennis. "The Aqhatu Legend." In *The Context of Scripture,* vol. 1, *Canonical Compositions from the Biblical World,* edited by W. W. Hallo. Leiden: Brill, 1997.

Pasley, James. "20 Staggering Facts about Human Trafficking in the US." *Business Insider.* December 13, 2019. https://www.businessinsider.com/human-trafficking-in-the-us-facts-statistics-2019-7.

Patrick, George T. W., and Ingram Bywater. *Heraclitus of Ephesus.* Chicago: Argonaut, 1969.

Penchansky, David. "Deconstruction." In *The Oxford Encyclopedia of Biblical Interpretation,* edited by Steven McKenzie, 196–205. New York: Oxford University Press, 2013.

Perez, Caroline Criado. *Invisible Women: Exposing Data Bias in a World Designed for Men.* New York: Abrams, 2019.

Pervo, Richard I. "The Testament of Joseph and Greek Romance." In *Studies on the Testament of Joseph*, edited by George W. E. Nickelsburg Jr., 15–28. Missoula: Scholars Press, 1975.

Peskowitz, Miriam B. *Spinning Fantasies: Rabbis, Gender, and History*. Berkeley: University of California Press, 1997.

Petersen, E. E., N. L. Davis, D. Goodman, et al., "Vital Signs: Pregnancy-Related Deaths, United States, 2011–2015, and Strategies for Prevention, 13 States, 2013–2017." *Morbidity and Mortality Weekly Report* 68 (2019): 423–29.

Petit, Lucas P., and Daniele Morandi Bonacossi. "Nineveh, the Great City: Symbol of Beauty and Power." In *Nineveh, the Great City: Symbol of Beauty and Power*, edited by Lucas P. Petit and Daniele Morandi Bonacossi, 15–22. Leiden: Sidestone, 2012.

Philostratus. *Imagines*. Translated by Arthur Fairbanks. London: William Heinemann, 1931.

Phipps, W. "Christian Perspectives on Suicide." *ChrCent* 30 (1985): 970–72.

Plaskow, Judith. "Anti-Judaism in Feminist Christian Interpretation." In *Searching the Scriptures: A Feminist Introduction*, vol. 1, edited by Elisabeth Schüssler Fiorenza with the assistance of Shelly Matthews, 117–29. New York: Crossroad, 1993.

Porten, Bezalel, J. Joel Farber, Cary J. Martin, Günther Vittmann, Leslie S. B. MacCoull, and Sarah Clackson. *The Elephantine Papyri in English: Three Millenia of Cross-Cultural Continuity and Change*. 2nd rev. ed. Atlanta: SBL, 2011.

Porter, Catherine. "Toronto Van Attacker Found Guilty in City's Worst Mass Killing." *New York Times*. March 3, 2021. https://www.nytimes.com/2021/03/03/world/canada/toronto-van-alek-minassian.html.

Portier-Young, Anathea. "Alleviation of Suffering in the Book of Tobit: Comedy, Community, and Happy Endings." *CBQ* 63 (2001): 35–54.

Powell, L., K. M. Edwards, P. McGreevy, et al. "Companion Dog Acquisition and Mental Well-Being: A Community-Based Three-Arm Controlled Study." *BMC Public Health* 19 (2019): 1428.

Preston, Catherine, and H. Henrik Ehrsson. "Illusory Obesity Triggers Body Dissatisfaction Responses in the Insula and Anterior Cingulate Cortex." *Cerebral Cortex* 26 (December 2016): 4450–60.

Pui-lan, Kwok. *Postcolonial Imagination and Feminist Theology*. Louisville: Westminster John Knox, 2005.

Rabenau, Merten. *Studien zum Buch Tobit*. Berlin: der Gruyter, 1994.

Rampton, Martha. "Four Waves of Feminism." October 25, 2015. https://www.pacificu.edu/magazine/four-waves-feminism.

Ramsay, G. G., trans. *Juvenal and Persius*. London: William Heinemann, 1918.

Ratcliffe, Rebecca. "Airlines Urged to Train Staff to Help Spot Victims of Trafficking." *The Guardian*. June 12, 2017.

Ravid, Barak. "The Israeli Academic Who Played a Critical Role in the Shalit Deal." *Haaretz*. October 14, 2011.

Ravits, Martha A. "The Jewish Mother: Comedy and Controversy in American Popular Culture." *Multi-Ethnic Literature of the United States* 25 (2000): 3–31.

Rebossio, Alejandro. "Argentina's Other Stolen Babies." *El Pais*. May 12, 2015. https://english.elpais.com/elpais/2015/05/12/inenglish/1431437758_857439.html.

Reinhart, R. J. "Snapshot: Few Americans Vegetarian or Vegan." *Gallup*. August 1, 2018. https://news.gallup.com/poll/238328/snapshot-few-americans-vegetarian-vegan.aspx.

Reinhartz, Adele. "Ruth." In *The Jewish Study Bible*, edited by Adele Berlin and Marc Zvi Brettler, 1573–97. 2nd ed. Oxford: Oxford University Press, 2014.

Rendsburg, Gary A. "Shibboleth." In *Encyclopedia of Hebrew Language and Linguistics*, edited by Geoffrey Khan, 3:556–57. Leiden: Koninklijke Brill, 2013.

Resnicoff, Steven H. "Jewish Law Perspectives on Suicide and Physician-Assisted Dying." *Journal of Law and Religion* 13 (1998): 289–349.

Ress, Mary Judith. *Ecofeminism in Latin America*. Women from the Margins. Maryknoll, NY: Orbis Books, 2006.

Ringe, Sharon H. "When Women Interpret the Bible." In *Women's Bible Commentary*, edited by Carol A. Newsom, Sharon H. Ringe, and Jacqueline E. Lapsley. 3rd ed. Louisville: Westminster John Knox, 2012.

Rippon, Gina. *Gender and Our Brains: How New Neuroscience Explodes the Myths of the Male and Female Minds*. New York: Pantheon, 2019.

Ritner, Robert Kriech. *The Mechanics of Ancient Egyptian Magical Practice*. Chicago: University of Chicago Press, 2008.

Rose, Martha L. *The Staff of Oedipus: Transforming Disability in Ancient Greece*. Ann Arbor: University of Michigan Press, 2003.

Roth, J. "Asmodeus (Ashmedai)." In *Encyclopaedia Judaica*, edited by Fred Skolnik, 2:593–94. 2nd ed. Detroit: Thomson Gale, 2007.

Ruether, Rosemary Radford. *Sexism and God-Talk: Toward a Feminist Theology*. Boston: Beacon, 1993.

Rutledge, David. *Reading Marginally: Feminism, Deconstruction and the Bible*. BibInt 21. Leiden: Brill, 1996.

Saint Joseph's University. "What Is the Catholic Church's Position on Suicide and Physician-Assisted Suicide?" March 4, 2016. https://sites.sju.edu/icb/catholic-churchs-position-suicide-physician-assisted-suicide-declaration-euthanasia/.

Sakenfeld, Katharine Doob. "Daughters of Zelophehad." In *Women in Scripture: A Dictionary of Named and Unnamed Women in the Hebrew Bible, the Apocryphal/Deuterocanonical Books, and the New Testament*, edited by Carol Meyers, Toni Craven, and Ross S. Kraemer, 220–21. Grand Rapids: Eerdmans, 2000.

Sakenfeld, Katharine Doob. *Just Wives? Stories of Power and Survival in the Old Testament and Today*. Louisville: Westminster John Knox, 2003.

Sakenfeld, Katharine Doob. " 'Love' in the Old Testament." In *ABD*, edited by David Noel Freedman, 4:375–81. New York: Doubleday, 1992.

Sakenfeld, Katharine Doob. "Numbers." In *Women's Bible Commentary*, edited by Carol A. Newsom and Sharon H. Ringe, 49–56. Exp. ed. Louisville: Westminster John Knox, 1998.

Sassoon, Isaac. *The Status of Women in Jewish Tradition*. Cambridge: Cambridge University Press, 2011.

Satlow, Michael L. *Jewish Marriage in Antiquity*. Princeton: Princeton University Press, 2001.

Schellenberg, Ryan. "Suspense, Simultaneity, and Divine Providence in the Book of Tobit." *JBL* 130 (2011): 313–27.

Schneiders, Sandra M. *The Revelatory Text: Interpreting the New Testament as Sacred Scripture*. Rev. ed. Collegeville, MN: Liturgical Press, 1999.

Scholz, Susanne, ed. *Feminist Interpretation of the Hebrew Bible in Retrospect*. Recent Research in Biblical Studies 7, 8, 9. Sheffield: Sheffield Phoenix, 2013, 2014, 2016.

Scholz, Susanne. "From the 'Woman's Bible' to the 'Women's Bible,' The History of Feminist Approaches to the Hebrew Bible." In *Introducing the Women's Hebrew Bible*, 12–32. IFT 13. New York: T&T Clark, 2007.

Schottroff, Luise. *Lydia's Impatient Sisters: A Feminist Social History of Early Christianity*. Translated by Barbara and Martin Rumscheidt. Louisville: Westminster John Knox, 1995.

Schuller, Eileen, and Marie-Theres Wacker, eds. *Early Jewish Writings*. The Bible and Women: An Encyclopaedia of Exegesis and Cultural History. Vol. 3.1. Atlanta: SBL Press, 2017.

Schremer, Adiel. *Male and Female He Created Them: Jewish Marriage in the Late Second Temple, Mishnah, and Talmud Periods* [Hebrew]. Jerusalem: Zalman Shazar Center, 2003.

Schuller, Eileen. "Tobit." In *Women's Bible Commentary*, edited by Carol A. Newsom and Sharon H. Ringe, 376–82. 3rd ed. Louisville: Westminster John Knox, 2012.

Schüngel-Straumann, Helen. "Tobit: A Lesson on Marriage and Family in the Diaspora." In *Feminist Biblical Interpretation: A Compendium of Critical Commentary on the Books of the Bible and Related Literature*, edited by Luise Schottroff and Marie-Theres Wacker, 504–14. Grand Rapids: Eerdmans, 2012.

Schur, Lisa, and Douglas Kruse. "Fact Sheet: Elected Officials with Disabilities." 2019. Rutgers. School of Management and Labor Relations. smir .rutgers.edu.

Schüssler Fiorenza, Elisabeth, ed. *Feminist Biblical Studies in the Twentieth Century: Scholarship and Movement*. The Bible and Women: An Encyclopaedia of Exegesis and Cultural History. Vol. 9.1. Atlanta: SBL Press, 2014.

Schüssler Fiorenza, Elisabeth. "Feminist Hermeneutics." In *ABD*, edited by David Noel Freedman, 783–91. Vol. 2. New York: Doubleday, 1992.

Schüssler Fiorenza, Elisabeth. *In Memory of Her: A Feminist Theological Reconstruction of Christian Origins*. New York: Crossroad, 1983/1994.

Schüssler Fiorenza, Elisabeth. *Jesus: Miriam's Child, Sophia's Prophet; Critical Issues in Feminist Christology.* New York: Continuum, 1994.

Schüssler Fiorenza, Elisabeth. *The Power of the Word: Scripture and the Rhetoric of Empire.* Minneapolis: Fortress, 2007.

Schüssler Fiorenza, Elisabeth. *Wisdom Ways: Introducing Feminist Biblical Interpretation.* Maryknoll, NY: Orbis Books, 2001.

Schutte, P. J. W. "When *They, We,* and the Passive Become *I*—Introducing Autobiographical Biblical Criticism." *HTS Teologiese Studies / Theological Studies* 61 (2005): 401–16.

Schwartz, Joshua. "Good Dog–Bad Dog: Jews and Their Dogs in Ancient Jewish Society." In *A Jew's Best Friend? The Image of the Dog Throughout Jewish History,* edited by Philip Ackerman-Lieberman and Rakefet Zalashik, 52–89. Eastbourne: Sussex Academic Press, 2013.

Seeley, Thomas D. *Honeybee Ecology: A Study of Adaptation in Social Life.* Princeton: Princeton University Press, 1985.

Seidman, Naomi. "'A New Garb for the Jewish Soul': The JPS Bible in the Light of the King James." In *The King James Version at 400: Assessing Its Genius as Bible Translation and Its Literary Influence,* edited by D. G. Burke, J. F. Kutsko, and P. H. Towner, 475–99. Atlanta: SBL, 2013.

Seneca the Younger. *Letters from a Stoic—Epistulae Morales ad Lucilium.* Translated by Richard Mott Gummere. Vol. 1. LCL. London: Heinemann, 1917.

Seneca the Younger. *Minor Dialogues together with the Dialog "On Clemency."* Translated by Aubrey Stewart. Bohn's Classical Library Edition. London: George Bell and Sons, 1900.

Sharafi, Mitra. "How the Taboo on Hindu Widow Remarriage Led to Liberal Abortion Norms in Colonial India." Scroll.in. August 10, 2020. https://scroll.in/article/963935/how-the-taboo-on-hindu-widow-remarriage-led-to-liberal-abortion-norms-in-colonial-india.

Shectman, Sarah. "Women in the Priestly Narrative." *Strata: Bulletin of the Anglo-Israel Archaeological Society* 27 (2009): 175–86.

Sherwood, Yvonne. *A Biblical Text and Its Afterlives: The Survival of Jonah in Western Culture.* Cambridge: Cambridge University Press, 2000.

Sherwood, Yvonne. "Introduction." In *The Bible and Feminism: Remapping the Field.* New York: Oxford University Press, 2017.

Shields, Lauren, Lucia Flores Guevara, and Margaux Yost. "Financial Inclusion for Workers: Including a Gender Lens." December 2018. https://www.idhsustainabletrade.com/uploaded/2018/12/Financial-Inclusion-for-Workers-Including-a-Gender-Lens-IDH-HERfinance.pdf.

Skemp, Vincent T. M. "Learning by Example: *Exempla* in Jerome's Translations and Revisions of Biblical Books." *VC* 65 (2011): 257–84. http://www.jstor.org/stable/41291356.

Smelik, K. A. D. "The Inscription of King Mesha (2.23)." In *The Context of Scripture,* vol. 2, *Monumental Inscriptions from the Biblical World,* edited by William W. Hallo, 137–46. Leiden: Brill, 2002.

Smith, Jacqueline S., Marianne LaFrance, Kevin H. Knol, Donald J. Tellinghuisen, and Paul Moes. "Surprising Smiles and Unanticipated Frowns: How Emotions and Status Influence Gender Categorization." *Journal of Nonverbal Behavior* 39 (2015): 115–30.

Sohn-Kronthaler, Michaela, and Ruth Albrecht, eds. *Faith and Feminism in Nineteenth-Century Religious Communities*. The Bible and Women: An Encyclopaedia of Exegesis and Cultural History. Vol. 8.2. Atlanta: SBL Press, 2019.

Sojourner Truth. "Ain't I a Woman?" Modern History Sourcebook. https://sourcebooks.fordham.edu/mod/sojtruth-woman.asp.

Soll, Will. "The Book of Tobit as a Window on the Hellenistic Jewish Family." In *Passion, Vitality, and Foment: The Dynamics of Second Temple Judaism*, edited by Lamontte M. Luke, 242–74. Harrisburg: Trinity Press International, 2001.

Specia, Megan, and Tariro Mzezewa. "Adventurous. Alone. Attacked." *New York Times*. March 25, 2019. https://www.nytimes.com/k2019/03/25/travel/solo-female-travel.html.

Spitz, Ellen Handler. "Mothers and Daughters: Ancient and Modern Myths." *The Journal of Aesthetics and Art Criticism* 48 (1990): 411–20.

Statistics Canada. "Quality of Employment in Canada: Pay Gap, 1998 to 2021." May 30, 2022. https://www150.statcan.gc.ca/n1/pub/14-28-0001/2020001/article/00003-eng.htm.

Steiner, Richard C. "The Headings of the 'Book of the Words of Noah' on a Fragment of the Genesis Apocryphon: New Light on a 'Lost' Work." *DSD* 2 (1995): 66–71.

Stern, Ephraim. "Kedesh, Tel (in Jezreel Valley)." In *The New Encyclopedia of Archaeological Excavations in the Holy Land*, edited by E. Stern, 860. Vol. 3. Jerusalem: Israel Exploration Society, 1993.

Stover, Cassandra. "Damsels and Heroines: The Conundrum of the Post-Feminist Disney Princess." *LUX: A Journal of Transdisciplinary Writing and Research from Claremont Graduate University* 2 (2013). http://scholarship.claremont.edu/lux/vol2/iss1/29.

Strahil, Panayotov V., and Luděk Vacín, eds. *Mesopotamian Medicine and Magic: Studies in Honor of Markham J. Geller*. Leiden: Brill, 2018.

Strong, Justin David. "From Pets to Physicians: Dogs in the Biblical World." *BAR* 45 (2019): 46–50.

Taitz, Emily, Sondra Henry, and Cheryl Tallan, eds. *JPS Guide to Jewish Women 600 B.C.E.–1900 C.E.* Philadelphia: JPS, 2003.

Talbott, Rick F. *Jesus, Paul, and Power: Rhetoric, Ritual, and Metaphor in Ancient Mediterranean Christianity*. Eugene: Cascade Books, 2010.

Taylor, Marion Ann, and Agnes Choi, eds. *Handbook of Women Biblical Interpreters: A Historical and Biographical Guide*. Grand Rapids: Baker Academic, 2012.

Teixeira, José Lucas Brum. *Poetics and Narrative Function of Tobit 6*. Berlin: de Gruyter, 2019.

Thomas. *Summa Theologica*. Translated by Fathers of the English Dominican Province. Vol. 4. Complete English ed. Westminster, MD: Christian Classics, 1981.

Thurston, Bonnie. *Women in the New Testament: Questions and Commentary*. Companions to the New Testament. New York: Crossroad, 1998.

Tiefenbrun, Susan W. "On Civil Disobedience, Jurisprudence, Feminism and the Law in the *Antigones* of Sophocles and Anouilh." *Law & Literature* 11 (1999): 35–51.

Tierney, Stephen J., ed. *Multiculturalism and the Canadian Constitution*. Vancouver: UBC Press, 2007.

Tigay, Jeffrey H. "Exodus." In *The Jewish Study Bible*, edited by Adele Berlin and Marc Zvi Brettler, 95–192. 2nd ed. New York: Oxford University Press, 2014.

Tisdale, Sally. *Advice for Future Corpses—And Those Who Love Them*. New York: Simon & Schuster, 2018.

Tolbert, Mary Ann. "Social, Sociological, and Anthropological Methods." In *Searching the Scriptures: A Feminist Introduction*, vol. 1, edited by Elisabeth Schüssler Fiorenza with the assistance of Shelly Matthews, 255–71. New York: Crossroad, 1993.

Trentin, Lisa. "Exploring Visual Impairment in Ancient Rome." In *Disabilities in Roman Antiquity*, edited by Martha L. Rose, C. F. Goodey, and Christian Laes, 89–114. Boston: Brill, 2013.

Trible, Phyllis. *God and the Rhetoric of Sexuality*. OBT. Philadelphia: Fortress, 1978.

Trible, Phyllis. "Ruth." In *Women in Scripture: A Dictionary of Named and Unnamed Women in the Hebrew Bible, the Apocryphal/Deuterocanonical Books, and the New Testament*, edited by Carol Meyers, Toni Craven, and Ross S. Kraemer, 146–47. Grand Rapids: Eerdmans, 2000.

Trimble, Michael. *Why Humans Like to Cry: Tragedy, Evolution, and the Brain*. Oxford: Oxford University Press, 2012.

Truth and Reconciliation Commission. "Truth and Reconciliation Commission of Canada: Calls to Action." 2015. www.trc.ca.

United Nations Documents. "Declaration on the Elimination of Violence against Women." December 20, 1993. http://www.un-documents.net/a48r104.htm.

Vachon, Mireille. "Des Nouvelles de Raif Badawi." *La Tribune*. June 17, 2020.

VanderKam, James C. "Ahikar/Ahiqar." In *ABD*, edited by David Noel Freedman, 1:113–15. New York: Doubleday, 1992.

Vander Stichele, Caroline, and Todd Penner, eds. *Her Master's Tools? Feminist and Postcolonial Engagements of Historical-Critical Discourse*. Atlanta: SBL, 2005.

Van Henten, Jan Willem. "Judith as Alternative Leader: A Rereading of Judith 7–13." In *A Feminist Companion to Esther, Judith and Susanna*, edited by Athalya Brenner, 224–52. FCB 7. London: T&T Clark, 1995.

Van Hooff, Anton J. L. *From Autothanasia to Suicide: Self-Killing in Classical Antiquity*. London: Routledge, 1990.

Versnel, H. S. "The Poetics of the Magical Charm: An Essay in the Power of Words." In *Magic and Ritual in the Ancient World*, edited by P. Mirecki and M. Meyer, 105–58. Religions in the Graeco-Roman World 141. Leiden: Brill, 2002.

Walker, Alice. *In Search of Our Mothers' Gardens: Womanist Prose.* New York: Harcourt Brace Jovanovich, 1967, 1983.

Walter, Englert. "Seneca and the Stoic View of Suicide." *The Society for Ancient Greek Philosophy Newsletter* 184 (1990): 1–20.

Weems, Renita J. *Just a Sister Away: A Womanist Vision of Women's Relationships in the Bible.* San Diego: Lura Media, 1988.

Wegner, Judith Romney. "The Image and Status of Women in Classical Rabbinic Judaism." In *Jewish Women in Historical Perspective*, edited by Judith R. Baskin, 68–93. Detroit: Wayne State University Press, 1991.

Weintraub, Pam. "Haunted by History: War, Famine and Persecution Inflict Profound Changes on Bodies and Brains; Could These Changes Persist over Generations?" *Aeon.* April 16. 2018. https://aeon.co/essays/how-the -sufferings-of-one-generation-are-passed-on-to-the-next.

Whaley, L. *Women and the Practice of Medical Care in Early Modern Europe, 1400- 1800.* New York: Palgrave MacMillan, 2011.

Wijngaards-de Meij, Leoniek, Margaret Stroebe, Henk Schut, Wolfgang Stroebe, Jan van den Bout, Peter G. M. van der Heijden, and Iris Dijkstra. "Parents Grieving the Loss of Their Child: Interdependence in Coping." *British Journal of Clinical Psychology* 47 (2008): 31–42.

Wikan, Unni. "Shame and Honour: A Contestable Pair." *Man* 19 (1984): 635–52.

Willet, Elizabeth Ann R. "Infant Mortality and Family Religion in the Biblical Period." *DavarLogos* 1 (2002): 27–42.

Wills, Lawrence M. "Daniel." In *The Jewish Study Bible*, edited by Adele Berlin and Marc Zvi Brettler, 1635–59. 2nd ed. New York: Oxford University Press, 2014.

Wills, Lawrence M. *The Jewish Novel in the Ancient World.* Ithaca: Cornell University Press, 1995.

Wilson, Brittany E. "The Blinding of Paul and the Power of God: Masculinity, Sight, and Self-Control in Acts 9." *JBL* 133 (2014): 367–87.

Wogaman, P. J. *Ethical Perspectives for the Community.* London: Westminster John Knox, 1990.

World Health Organization. "Maternal Mortality." September 19, 2019. https:// www.who.int/en/news-room/fact-sheets/detail/maternal-mortality.

Yee, Gale, ed. *Judges and Method: New Approaches in Biblical Studies.* Minneapolis: Fortress, 1995.

Zimmermann, Frank. *The Book of Tobit.* New York: Harper and Brothers, 1958.

Index of Scripture References and Other Ancient Writings

Hebrew Bible
Genesis

1:26-27	159	18:8-9	33	25:8	224
2:7	78, 159	18:10-14	134	25:9	90
2:18	159–60	18:12	132, 134	25:9-10	94
2:20	159	19:3	33	25:19, 20	4
2:21-22	78	19:30-38	102	27:1	39, 43
2:21-24	159	20:18	129	27:26-27	115
3:5	187	21:2-3	71	28:11	12
3:7	187	21:15	173–74	29:13	115
5:1-32	3	21:16	174	29:18	147
6:1-4	184	21:19	187	29:27	164
9:5	82	22	163, 202	29:31	129
9:20-27	102	22:1	35, 202–3	30:3	6
12:16	179	22:7	34, 35	30:4-8	5
16:1-4	62	22:11	35	30:6	5
16:2	61	22:14	85, 128	30:8	5
16:2-4	5n10	24:15	17	30:22	129
16:6	61	24:33	145	33:1-3	6
17:3	204	24:35	124	33:4	115, 189n9
17:16	4	24:40	115	35:8	14
18:1-8	134	24:44	128	35:16-19	92
18:1-15	109	24:50	146n31	35:22	6
18:6	164	24:54	33	35:22-26	4
		24:57-58	142	35:25	5
		24:59	14	36	4

36:2	4
37:2	6
37:34-35	174
38	5
41:5-7	133n3
41:45	17
45:14	189n9
46:8-26	4
46:28, 30	189
47:29	219
48:9-20	219
49:25	129
49:33	224
50:10	174
50:10-11	174

Exodus
1:8	20
3–4	108
15:26	94
17:14	205
19:5	82
19:8	107
20:2, 5-6	66
20:10	66
20:12	90, 180
20:13	82
21:2-11	66
21:10	148
22:4	11
22:18	156
22:20	133
22:21-23	11
23:8	43
23:9	133
24:3, 7	107
33:19	129
34:11-16	17
34:16	13

Leviticus
1:2	98
8	11

10:9	102
11	139, 164
16:29-31	200
18:1-18	145
18:10	145
19:9, 10	96
19:13	101
19:14	39
19:33-34	133
20:11-21	145
23:42-43	222
25:39-41	66
25:43	66

Numbers
11:12	212
12:1	17
12:10	43
12:12	129
15:38	132
16:30	209
18:2	11n23
19:11-22	36
26:52-56	144
27:1-11	125
27:2-11	144
27:5-7	144
36:1-11	125
36:6-8	125
36:8	144
36:10-12	144

Deuteronomy
5:16	90
6	96
7:1	18
7:3	18
7:6	163
8:2	202
10:14	23, 82
10:18-19	133
11:1-32	96
14	139

14:23	9
15:10-11	96
15:11	103
15:12-18	66
15:13-14	66
16:16-17	11
18:1	11
21:22-23	23
22:12	132
23:16-17	66
24:1-4	85
24:17-22	12
25:5-10	142
25:6	142
27:18	39
27:19	11
28:26	23
28:57	120
29:17	121
30:1-5	213
30:2	213
32:6	210–11
32:39	81

Joshua
1:16	107

Judges
2–6	5
4–5	6
4:6	14
5:2-31	14
5:7	14
5:18	6
6:18	205
9:54	81
11:34-40	163
12:4-6	133n3
13:16	205
14	17
14:12	164
16:30	81
18:25	165

19	179	20:9	115	4:16	28
20:26	200	21:10	23	5:3	196
		24:16	74n46	5:6	196
Ruth				7:2	196
1:8-9	150	**1 Kings**			
1:20	3	8:22	79	**Job**	
3	5	8:38	79	1:11	46
3:4	120	11:1-43	17	2:5	46
3:5	107	11:41	1	2:9	46
		12:12-19	7	2:9-10	48
1 Samuel		12:19-20	10	2:10b	56
1:4-5	30	12:28-29	10	2:14	46
1:6	30	14:4	39	3:11-22	28
1:7	30, 177	15	5	5:17	59
1:7-8	177	16:18	81	7:16	28
1:8	30	17	12	7:21	28
1:10	165			9:17-35	28
1:13-17	30	**2 Kings**		10:1-22	28
1:15-16	79	4:27	165	10:18	28
2:6	81, 210	15:29	7	10:20-21	209
2:12	181	17:1-6, 24	226	13:23-24	59
2:23	181	18:13-16	226	16:13	121
3:2	39	19:35-36	28	20:14	121
4:19-21	92			24:21	68
18:25	147	**1 Chronicles**		30:1	119
22:2	165	1–9	3	33:28	189
24:6	123	3:2	17	42:12	227
27:3	12	5:27–6:6	4n7	42:16	227
30:5	12	16:13	163		
30:6	165	22:9-10	211	**Psalms**	
31:4-5	81	26:7	3	17:8	222
				24:1	23, 82
2 Samuel		**Ezra**		36:8	222
2:2	12	9:5	79	40:2	210
3:3	12, 17	9:6	79	57:2	222
3:29	43	9:6-7	57–58	68:5	12
5	9			68:6	11
6	9	**Nehemiah**		69:3	133n3
7:14	210	1:6	58	88:4	210
11–12	5			92–118	207
12:16	200	**Esther**		103:2-5	94
14:5	12	3:8	20	103:13	129
17:23	81	4:1-3, 15	200	105:6	163

105:43	163
112:9	96
113:7, 9	68
115:17	209
127:4-5	128
128:3	68
137	9n22

Proverbs

1:26	15
5:3-5	18
8:19	15
10:2	97
11:4	97
14:21	96
14:31	96
16:31	227
19:2	120
23:22	91
23:29-35	102
30:17	91
31	15
31:10	16
31:10-31	15
31:13	45
31:20	98
31:24	45

Ecclesiastes (Qoheleth)

5:10	224

Song of Solomon

4:9, 10	146
4:12	146
5:1, 2	146

Isaiah

1:17	12
7:20	120
13:8	92
22:13	141
26:19	209

40–66	212
42:18-20	43
45:1	123
49:15	129, 212
51:18	116
56:10	119
58:6-8	96
59:12	57
61:1	65
63:16	210

Jeremiah

3:1-13	219
6:26	71
7:33	23
13:21	92
16:7	105
20:18	129
22:3	11, 65
22:19	23

Ezekiel

4:13	19
16:1-63	219
16:25	120
24:17	105
37	209

Daniel

1:8	19
1:11-16	19
1:12	138
1:16	138
4:27	97
9:4-19	58
10:9	204
12:2	209

Hosea

2:2-5	219
6:2	209
9:3	19
9:14	68, 129

Amos

5:7	121
8:3	36
8:4-6	37n91
8:4-7	36
8:10	36–37, 71

Jonah

1:17	120
3:9	213
4:5	222

Nahum

1:1–3:4	221
3:19b	226n27

Zechariah

2:11	216
12:10	163
14:16	216, 222

Apocryphal/ Deuterocanonical Books

Judith

1:5	89
1:15	89
5:5	32n82
8:1	3
8:2	5
8:3	5n8
8:6	200
8:7-8	80, 160
10:5	20
10:10	67
10:17	67
12:1-2	20
12:15	67
13:3, 9, 10	67
13:15-16	79
14:6-10	32n82
14:10	13

15:11	157
16:22	94, 160
16:23-24	12
16:26	157

Additions to Esther

1:9	164
2:7	80
2:20	80
2:20-22	79
14:11-15	79
14:15	160

Wisdom

18:25	74n46

Sirach

21:1	211
23:1, 4	212
25:22	48
30:18	105
35:1-4	97
36:10	214
38:4	121
40:17	97
51:10	211–12

Baruch

1–3	58
4:12	219
5:1-9	214

Susanna

2	80
3	80
42–43	79
44	160

1 Maccabees

1:38	218
1:62-63	20
3:44-48	200

2 Maccabees

1:10	134
5:27	20
7:1-42	81
7:41	81

3 Maccabees

5:7	212

4 Maccabees

1:8, 10	81
8:3-4	81
8:20	81
10:2	81
12:6-7	81
13:19	81
14:11–18:24	81
17:1	81
17:2-5	81

New Testament

Matthew

1:1-17	5
5:14	191
6:1	224
6:9	211
6:13	202
6:16-18	200
6:19-21	97
7:6	119
7:12	101
8:21, 22	90
9:20-22	38
9:27-31	192
12:22	197
15:14	39
15:27	120
15:30-31	192
20:30	38
21:41	221
22:25-26	74, 143
26:73	133
27:5	81

27:50	224
28:19	5

Mark

1:12-13	202
1:15	212
5:25-34	38
6:23	196
7:3	140n19
10:12	86
10:46	38
12:20-22	74, 143
12:41-44	97, 98
14:36	210
14:70	133
15:37	224
16:12-13	109

Luke

2:27-29	189
2:36-38	29
4:1-13	202
4:43	212
6:31	101
6:39	39
7:11-17	71, 192
8:3	79n60
8:43-48	38
9:59, 60	90
10:25-27	21
10:38	25
11:2	211
11:20	212
12:33-34	97
14:26	103
15:24, 30, 32	185
16:16	212
18:22	103
18:35	38
20:29-30	74
20:29-33	143
21:1-4	97–98
22:59	133

23:46	224
24:13-35	109

John

4	73
8:21-22	81
9:2	42
10:18	81

Acts

1:9-10	205
1:16-20	81
9:3-6	190
9:18	189–90
9:20	190

Romans

16:1-3, 7	198n7
16:16	115

1 Corinthians

7:10-11	86
11:8-10	159
14:33-36	198n7
14:34	198
16:20	115

2 Corinthians

8:9	94
8:12	97

Galatians

3:7-9, 29	85

Ephesians

5:18	102

1 Thessalonians

5:26	115

1 Timothy

1:17	212

2:12	198
2:13	158
2:13-14	159
3:11	125
5:13-14	125
5:23	102
6:15	212

James

1:13-14	203
1:27	13
5:14-16	94

1 Peter

2:9	163
2:24	94

1 John

4:11	129

Revelation

1:19	205
9:11	74n46
15:3	212
17:2, 4, 6	219
19:16	212

Old Testament
Pseudepigrapha

1 Enoch

10:6	156
14:4	205
15:1-2	202

Book of the Watchers

	184

Jubilees

10.12	197

Letter of Aristeas

207	101

Testament of Issachar

3:6-8; 4:2-6	97

Testament of Job

	1–2

Testament of Solomon

	74

Dead Sea Scrolls and
Related Texts

4Q200	xlvi, 209
6:5-7	212
4Q196-99	xlvi
4Q197 4 ii	
19-4 iii	129

Flavius Josephus
Contra Apionem

2.211	25

Mishnah, Talmud, and
Related Literature

b. Baba Qamma

81a	25
91b	82

b. 'Erubim

64a-65b	102

b. 'Erubim

64b	156

b. Giṭṭin

68 a-b	74

b. Ketubbot

65a	73

b. Mo'ed Qaṭan

18b	128

b. Pesaḥim

110a, 112b	74

b. Qiddušin

36a	210
49b	156
49c	126

b. Šabbat

31a	101

b. Sanhedrin

17b	23
74a	82

b. Yebamot

64b	73

b. Yebamot
65b-66a   68
m. 'Abot 2.7 156
m. Baba Meṣiʻa.
1:5   45
m. Berakot
2.7   64
m. Ketubbot
4.12   12
m. Niddah
5.7   45
m. Sukkah
2.1   64
t. Yebamot
8:5, 6   68
y. Moʻed Qaṭan
3.5   174
y. Qiddušin
66d   23
'Abot de Rabbi Nathan
45b   5
Genesis Rabbah
18:2   159
Pesiqta Rabbati
40:3-4   5

**Other Ancient
    Literature**
**Aelian (Claudius
    Aelianus)**
De natura animalium
9.48   155
Ahikar, Story of
        xlvii,
        31–39,
        101, 105,
        108, 181,
        193–94,
        224–25,
        230
Analects of Confucius
5.2   101

Apollodorus
Library
3.6.7   39
3.10.7   109
3.14.7   78
Aqhat Epic
1.27-34   116n8
Aristotle
Generation of Animals
    717a5   154n60
    717b24   154n60
    737a.28 42
Artemidorus
Oneirocritica
    1.44   154
Augustine
City of God
    1.20   82
Celsus, A. Cornelius
On Medicine
    6.28   122n21
Cyprian
Treatise 7, *On the
    Mortality*
    10   47
Dio Chrysostom
Orations
    36.10-11 39
Euripides
The Suppliants
            76
Heraclitus
On Nature 74
Herodotus
Histories
    3.142.3   101
Hesiod
Opera
    61   78
Hippocrates
On Vision
    9.4-5   40

Peri Parthenion
    8.464–71 78
Homer
Iliad
    1.158-68 119
Odyssey
    1.65-67,
    82-89   109
    4.587-91 109
    7.20   109
    8.62-70   39
    8.99-103,
    586-89   136
    13.251   109
    17.288-89,
    298-99   109
    22.210,
    489   78
To Apollo
    170–72   39
**Homeric Hymn to
    Demeter** 150
Juvenal
Satires
    6.398-412 126
Moses Maimonides
    "Ladder"   103–4
Ovid
Metamorphoses
    2.862   109
    5.385-424 150
Pausanius
Description of Greece
    7.5.7   39
Philostratus
Imagines
    2.30.2   78
Plato
Phaedo
    64a, 62bc 80
Pliny the Elder
Natural History
    18.14   138

P.Oxy
  31.2601   40
Pseudo-Philo
  3.14   5
Seneca the Younger
Letters 65.16   80

On Providence
  6.7-8   80
Sophocles
Antigone   39
  1204   78
Oedipus Rex
  11.269   78

Virgil
Aeneid
  1.464-65   136
  5.252   109
Georgics
  2.130ff.   155

Index of Subjects

almsgiving, 31, 94–99, 103, 201,
   224–25
anger, xxxix, 46, 58, 60–63, 67–68,
   116–17, 150, 214, 226; vengeful-
   ness, 226–27
animals, 11, 119–20; dogs, xxxix, 39,
   67, 118–120, 185, 194; slaughter of,
   for food, xxxix, 131, 137–38, 164

childlessness and infertility, xxxix, 30,
   55, 61–62, 68–70, 75; connections
   to slavery and abuse, 61–64
chosenness, 128, 131, 163, 215
civil disobedience, 1, 24, 27–28, 31

death, xxxix, 14, 18, 23, 28–29, 55–61,
   68, 75–78, 84–85, 87–89, 97, 104,
   112, 150, 173, 186, 189, 191, 201,
   207, 209, 219–21, 225–26; burial
   practices, 1, 23–25, 82–83, 90–92,
   126, 162–63, 174, 220, 225; suicide,
   55, 76–85, 203; Greek trope of
   female suicide, 78; treatment of
   corpses, xxxix, 23–26, 31, 35, 94,
   225
demons, 61, 64, 72–75, 85–86, 107,
   126, 129, 131, 141, 143, 155, 163,

184, 220; demon possession, 118,
   120, 122, 153
depictions of God, 211–12; Deuteronomistic: sin demands punishment, 59, 68, 96, 187, 191, 208;
   problematic message that long
   life and peaceful death are divine
   rewards, 220; omnipotence, 209;
   patriarchal imagery supports hierarchical gender models, 3, 27,
   63, 211
diaspora, 15, 17, 92, 96, 98, 111, 132,
   172, 205, 208, 213–14; exilic/
   postexilic context, 8, 47, 57–58, 76,
   194; minority or marginalized status, xxxix, 20–21, 32, 100, 134–35,
   217–18, 229
disability, illness, and healing, xxxix,
   1, 39, 41–43, 187–88, 229; blindness, 37–42, 60–61, 75, 85, 94, 120,
   122, 135–36, 173, 183, 185–90, 193,
   197, 207–8; blindness and weeping, 136; hysteria, 152; "wandering
   womb," 152; means and methods
   of healing, 40, 121–23, 154, 187–88,
   197; anointing, 123; fumigation,
   131, 152–55

disappointment and sorrow, 36, 55,
59, 76–77, 91–92, 167, 179, 203,
219; bereavement, 136, 171, 176;
despair, 3, 53, 75, 85, 88, 171, 193;
farewells, 180; grief, 58, 71, 78,
150, 171–76, 229; mothers' anguish
over children, 109–10, 171–73;
worry, 84, 109, 117, 145, 166, 171,
176, 178, 182, 185, 196, 204, 225

enslavement, slavery, xxxix, 22,
55–57, 61–62, 64–67, 161, 229; connection to infertility, 62
equity and status, 64, 111, 113, 123,
128–29, 156, 159, 166, 178; status
markers, 41; absence of women,
16, 171; means of address, 110,
167, 171, 181, 196, 211; non-invita-
tion, 37, 171, 198, 203
eschatology, 207, 215–18, 222–23;
Jewish distinctiveness and that of
other nations are preserved, 215,
223; universalism, nature of, 213,
215–16; modern question of minority rights, 217–18

family, 2–5, 10–12, 16–18, 29, 36–39,
48, 84, 88–89, 99, 103, 111, 113–14,
124, 126–27, 135, 145–46, 151,
164–67, 179–81, 185, 194, 197, 207,
210–11, 224–25, 227–28; intrafamily relationships, xxxix, 10–11,
99, 143, 149–50, 229–30; behavior
of fathers, 16, 29, 31, 33–34, 38, 42,
46, 60, 108, 113, 142–43, 161, 167,
171–76, 178–79, 192, 196–97, 210–
11, 213, 215, 218, 225, 230; behavior
of mothers, 13–15, 51, 61–62, 78–79,
84, 86, 90–91, 101, 109–10, 117, 131,
142, 146, 168, 172–73, 175, 182–83,
189, 211–12, 218–19, 228–29; displacement, 8, 67, 89; divorce, 68,
85–86, 116, 148; domestic violence

and abuse, xxxix, 55, 61–62, 67,
218; gendered hierarchy, 27, 194;
"killer wife" motif, 126; "marriage
made in heaven," 118, 127–28;
mother-daughter relationships,
xxxix, 144–51; parental expectations, 26, 171; role of only children,
71, 131, 162–63; women transfer-
ring from one family to another, 99
finances and wealth, 21, 44–46, 87–90,
106–9, 115, 117, 168, 171–72, 180,
192–93, 197, 201, 224
food and eating, 19–20, 26, 33–34, 36,
44, 48, 93, 99, 103–5, 133, 138–40,
145, 148, 150, 155, 164–65, 172,
177, 184, 200–201, 205, 222; dietary laws and practices, 8, 18–20,
138–39, 164–65, 177; preparation
of food, 19–20, 33–34, 48, 164–65,
181, 184

gender constructions, relations, and
status: androcentrism, 3, 106, 167;
line of succession, 4; matrilineal
descent, 4; patrilineal descent, 3,
70, 125; power differentials, 20,
26–27, 32–33, 41, 48, 59, 63–64, 67,
107, 113, 141–42, 156, 161, 166, 211
golden rule/silver rule, 87, 101–2
gossip, xxxix, 118, 125–26

honor and shame, xxxix, 23–24, 42,
46, 48, 55, 60–61, 63, 76–80, 84–85,
104, 111, 161–62, 181, 209, 224
hospitality, 33, 131, 133, 137, 179; care
for strangers, 11–12, 132–34, 164,
217

inheritance, 12, 70, 99, 125, 131, 144,
179, 185

Jerusalem, 21, 23, 28–29, 94, 98, 104,
113, 116, 153, 207–8, 212, 214–19,

221–22, 227; desolate mother, 218–19; modern status, 214; personified as female, 116, 212, 218

marriage, xxxix, 4, 29, 49, 61–63, 67, 72–73, 78, 85, 94, 99–100, 118, 121, 123, 125–27, 131, 135, 141–46, 151, 153, 157–58, 161, 166, 168, 178–80, 183, 190–91, 194, 197; contracts (marriage and divorce), 13, 72, 85–86, 141, 146–49; endogamy, 13, 17–18, 99–100, 126, 146, 163; exogamy, 17–18, 143

narrative: characters are static, 215; fairy-tale motifs, 127, 196, 221–22; farcical elements, 38; irony and humor, 2, 20, 28, 37, 56, 60, 91–92, 94, 109–12, 115, 117, 126, 134, 136, 141, 161–62, 166, 168, 184, 191, 199; metalepsis, 36; metaphors, 43, 50, 67, 100, 211, 222; mirror reading, 17; settings, 1, 15, 157, 161, 185, 194; unreliable narrator, 1–2, 8, 51, 208, 220

prosperity, 87, 180, 219; "gospel" of, 94–95

self-control and chastity, 42, 157, 160, 201
stereotypes: blind persons, 39, 41; enslaved persons, 64; gender-based, 22, 42, 69, 113, 178; Jews, 96; minority groups, 32
suffering: intergenerational, 55; of the innocent, xxxix, 59, 79

Tobit as problematic model, 213; character of (arrogant, buffoon, entitled, pompous, self-important), 38, 113, 213, 215, 230; power dynamics (Tobit and Tobias, Tobias and "Azariah," Tobit and Sarah, Tobit and Anna), 107–29; "testing," 202–3
trust and vulnerability, xxxix, 15, 21, 52, 75, 90, 107–8, 113–15, 117, 128, 135, 141

women: as possessions, 137; association with magic, 131, 156; maternal and female role(s), 16, 39, 52, 68, 76, 86, 91–92, 150, 164, 173–74, 182, 189, 212; maternal mortality, 87, 92–93; misogyny, 20, 48, 63, 159; patriarchy, 5, 14, 27, 41, 63–64, 71, 136–37, 166, 178, 210–11; teaching children, 15, 90; violence against, 1, 26–27, 55, 58–60, 67; weeping, 14, 76, 136, 174; widows and widowhood, 8, 11, 12, 40, 45, 68, 72, 84–86, 91, 94, 98, 125, 160, 173, 218–19, 221; wise woman tradition, 15, 124; women's work and "women's work," 39, 44–52, 177

Author

Michele Murray is professor in the department of religion, society, and culture at Bishop's University, in Sherbrooke, Quebec, Canada, where she served as the dean of arts and science, and dean of arts, for a decade. She holds an MA in Second Temple period Jewish history from Hebrew University of Jerusalem, and a PhD in religion, specializing in Christian origins, from the University of Toronto. Her research areas include Jewish-Christian relations in the ancient world, and interaction among Eastern-Mediterranean religions in late antiquity; she is the author of *Playing a Jewish Game: Gentile Christian Judaizing in the First and Second Centuries CE* (Wilfrid Laurier University Press, 2004), and several articles and book chapters.

Volume Editor

Amy-Jill Levine is Rabbi Stanley M. Kessler Distinguished Professor of New Testament and Jewish Studies, Hartford International University for Religion and Peace; University Professor of New Testament and Jewish Studies Emerita, Mary Jane Werthan Professor of Jewish Studies Emerita, Professor of New Testament Studies Emerita, Vanderbilt University. Her recent publications include *The Gospel of Luke* (with Ben Witherington III, the first biblical commentary by a Jew and an Evangelical), *The Jewish Annotated New Testament Second Edition* (co-edited with Marc Brettler), *The Bible With and Without Jesus: How Jews and Christians Read the Same Stories Differently* (with Marc Brettler), *The Pharisees* (co-edited with Joseph Sievers); and in the Beginner's Guide series, *Sermon on the Mount, Light of the World, Entering the Passion of Jesus, The Difficult Words of Jesus, Witness at the Cross,* and *Signs and Wonders.*

Series Editor

Barbara E. Reid, general editor of the Wisdom Commentary series, is a Dominican Sister of Grand Rapids, Michigan. She is the president of Catholic Theological Union and the first woman to hold the position. She has been a member of the CTU faculty since 1988 and also served as vice president and academic dean from 2009 to 2018. She holds a PhD in biblical studies from The Catholic University of America and was also president of the Catholic Biblical Association in 2014–2015. Her most recent publications are *Luke 1–9* and *Luke 10–24* co-authored with Shelly Matthews (WCS 43A, 43B; Liturgical Press, 2021), *Wisdom's Feast: An Invitation to Feminist Interpretation of the Scriptures* (Eerdmans, 2016), and *At the Table of Holy Wisdom. Global Hungers and Feminist Biblical Interpretation. 2021 Madeleva Lecture in Spirituality* (Paulist Press, 2023).